FUNDRAISING LAW
MADE EASY

FUNDRAISING LAW
MADE EASY

Bruce R. Hopkins

WILEY

John Wiley & Sons, Inc.

Library of Congress Cataloging-in-Publication Data:

Hopkins, Bruce R.
   Fundraising law made easy / Bruce R. Hopkins.
      p. cm.
   Includes index.
   ISBN 978-0-470-50378-2 (cloth)
  1.   Fund raising–Law and legislation–United States. 2.   Charitable uses, trusts, and foundations–United States.   I. Title.
   KF1389.5.H655 2009
   344.7303'170681–dc22

                                         2009013314

Printed in the United States of America

10 9 8 7 6 5 4 3 2 1

Contents

Preface   xi

About the Author   xiii

Chapter 1   Introduction to the Law of Fundraising for Charity   1

Definition of *Charitable Fundraising*   2
Concept of Charitable Sales   4
Definition of *Charitable Contribution*   4
Methods of Fundraising   5
Fundraising Expenses   8
Commensurate Test   19
Fundraising Compensation Issues   20
Step Transaction Doctrine   24
Charitable Pledges   29
Public Policy Considerations   30
Summary   32

Chapter 2   Fundraisers' Law Primer   33

Form of Organization   34
Organizational Tests   35
Operational Test   35
Primary Purpose Rule   36
Principles of Fiduciary Responsibility   36
Charitable Purposes and Activities   38
Recognition of Tax Exemption   39
Private Inurement Doctrine   39

Private Benefit Doctrine   44
Intermediate Sanctions   46
Legislative Activities   47
Political Campaign Activities   52
Prohibited Tax Shelter Transactions   54
Personal Benefit Contracts   54
Governance Policies   55
Summary   64

Chapter 3   State Regulation of Charitable Fundraising   65

Fundraising Regulation at State Level   66
Charitable Solicitation Acts   66
Exemptions from Solicitation Acts   76
Powers of Attorneys General   82
Sanctions   83
Unified Registration   83
Fundraising by Means of Internet   84
Summary   89

Chapter 4   Public Charities and Private Foundations   91

Private Foundation Defined   92
Private Operating Foundations   93
Exempt Operating Foundations   94
Conduit Foundations   94
Nonexempt Charitable Trusts   94
Private Foundation Rules   95
Concept of Public Charity   95
Institutions   96
Donative Publicly Supported Organizations   100
Service Provider Publicly Supported Organizations   107
Comparative Analysis of Publicly Supported Charities   110
Supporting Organizations   111
Public Safety Testing Organizations   117
Import of Public–Private Dichotomy   117
Some Statistics   118
Summary   118

Chapter 5   Federal Annual Reporting Requirements   121

Federal Tax Law Reporting Basics   122
Import of Redesigned Form 990   124
Summary of Parts of Redesigned Form 990   124
Annual Return Schedules   128
Federal and State Regulation of Gaming   132

Preparation of Form 990 Schedule M   141
Preparation of Schedule B   148
Preparation of Other Parts of Form 990   150
Summary   151

Chapter 6   **Charitable Giving Rules**   **153**

Basic Concepts   154
Defining *Charitable Gift*   155
Qualified Donees   156
Gifts for the Use of Charity   156
Conditional Gifts   157
Gifts of Property in General   159
Valuation of Property   160
Limitations on Deductibility   160
Deduction Reduction Rules   163
Qualified Appreciated Stock   163
Twice-Basis Deductions   165
Gifts of Vehicles   166
Gifts of Intellectual Property   166
Gifts of Clothing and Household Items   168
Gifts of Taxidermy   168
Partial Interest Gifts   169
Gifts of or Using Insurance   170
Planned Giving   170
Administrative Matters   177
Summary   177

Chapter 7   **Unrelated Business Rules**   **179**

Unrelated Business Law Statutory Framework   180
Affected Tax-Exempt Organizations   181
Conduct of Business   181
Regularly Carried-on Businesses   183
Related or Unrelated?   184
Unrelated Business Taxable Income   185
Excepted Activities   185
Excepted Income   187
Exceptions to Exceptions   188
Exceptions to Exceptions to Exceptions   189
Fundraising and Unrelated Business Rules   189
Donor Recognition Programs   199
Commerciality Doctrine   201
Provision of Services   202
Summary   208

Chapter 8   Other Federal Tax Law Regulation of Fundraising   209

               Gift Substantiation Requirements   210
               Quid Pro Quo Contributions Rules   212
               Disclosure Requirements   214
               Application for Recognition of Exemption   216
               Public Charity Classifications   217
               Appraisal Rules   217
               Recordkeeping Rules   222
               Form 8283   224
               Unique Reporting Rules   225
               Noncharitable Fundraising Rules   231
               Summary   233

Chapter 9   Fundraising and Constitutional Law   235

               Free Speech Basics   236
               Types of Speech   236
               Police Power   237
               Fundraising Free Speech Principles   238
               Supreme Court Opinions   239
               Subsequent Court Opinions   246
               Airport Terminal Solicitations   248
               Door-to-Door Advocacy   249
               Registration Fees   250
               Outer Boundaries of Speech Rights   251
               Fundraising and Fraud   252
               Due Process Rights   253
               Equal Protection Rights   254
               Delegation of Legislative Authority   255
               Treatment of Religious Organizations   256
               Other Constituional Law Issues   257
               Summary   258

Chapter 10   Fundraising and Governance   259

               Governance Philosophy in General   260
               Board Fundraising Responsibilities   260
               Watchdog Agencies and Fundraising   261
               Organization Effectiveness   270
               Board Effectiveness   271
               Law Compliance   272
               Categories of Expenditures   273
               Disclosures to Public   275
               Mission Statements   278

Fundraising Practices   279
IRS and Governance   281
Officer and Employee Tax Liability   287
Perspectives on Nonprofit Governance   288
Summary   290

Chapter 11   Fundraising and IRS Audits   291

Organization of IRS   292
Reasons for IRS Audits   293
IRS Audit Issues   293
Types of IRS Audits   294
Compliance Checks   296
College and University Compliance Check Project   299
Hardening the Target   306
Winning Audit Lottery   308
Coping with Examiners   311
Tours   313
IRS Audit Process   314
Closing Agreements   314
Appeals Process   315
Fast-Track Settlement Program   316
Retroactive Revocations   317
Church Audit Rules   318
Litigation   319
Summary   320

Chapter 12   Perspectives and Commentaries   321

Charitable Fundraising and the Law   322
Fundraisers and Solicitors: The Differences   325
Scope of State Law   326
The Fundraiser's Contract   327
Charity Auctions and Fundraising Law   333
Fundraising Regulation Benefits   339
Fundraising and Private Inurement   341
Fundraising and Fraud   345
Fundraising and Substantiation Rules   347
Some Proposals for Relief   351
Summary   353

Index   355

Preface

This book exists principally because of your author's belief that the federal and state law concerning the regulation of fundraising for charitable purposes is one of the most fascinating aspects of the panoply of nonprofit law, and I wanted to capture it in a nontechnical form. As to the latter motive, I wanted the subject to be in the format of its companions, the books *Nonprofit Law Made Easy*, *Charitable Giving Law Made Easy*, and *Private Foundation Law Made Easy*. In format, style, and length, it parallels its siblings. The hope is that these four books, in tandem, will be of assistance in guiding nonlawyers through the maze of law concerning charitable fundraising, private foundations, other types of nonprofit tax exempt organizations, and charitable giving.

This book also, however, blatantly mimics still another Wiley book (the one that started it all): *Not-for-Profit Accounting Made Easy*. Lawyers and accountants in the nonprofit realm populate overlapping universes, so these four companion volumes about nonprofit law are a natural fit with the book on nonprofit accounting rules.

As was noted in the preface to *Nonprofit Law Made Easy*, I have never had the opportunity to discuss this accounting book with its author, Warren Ruppel. I cannot imagine, nonetheless, that he extracted as much enjoyment from this writing process as I have. After years of writing technical (and long) books about various aspects of nonprofit law, writing the charitable fundraising, private foundation, nonprofit organizations, and charitable giving books with this approach was pure pleasure. The biggest challenges, not surprisingly, were the decisions as to what to include and what to leave out. This book thus reflects my take on what constitutes the fundamentals of the law concerning the charitable solicitation process.

In any event, I had a far easier time of it than Mr. Ruppel did. He had to create his book; I had merely to imitate it. The substance obviously is different but the format is unabashedly copied. Consequently, the four law books are about the same length as his, there are likewise a dozen chapters in each, every chapter of these books opens with an inventory of what is coming and ends with a chapter summary and there are no footnotes. (The lack of footnotes came the closest, to derogating from the pleasure of writing these books.) The four books also share a similar dust jacket. So Mr. Ruppel and Wiley designed the original vessel; I poured my descriptions of the law into it.

Now, back to this matter of what to include and what to exclude. I included in this book the absolute basics, namely:

- A discussion of the law's definition of charitable fundraising (such as it is)

- Fundraising methods and costs

- Relevant nonprofit law in general (as a primer)

- The states' charitable solicitation acts

- The differences between private foundations and public charities

- Federal annual reporting requirements

- Charitable giving rules

- Unrelated business rules

- Other aspects of federal regulation of fundraising

- Constitutional law principles

But, wanting to do more, I worked in two hot nonprofit law topics, specifically, governance and IRS (Internal Revenue Service) audits, and made them as relevant as I could to the law of charitable fundraising.

Nonprofit law continues to be as dynamic as law can get; consequently, trying to capture what appears to be the basics of elements of this law at any point in time can be tricky business. Congress, the Treasury Department, the IRS, the courts, and others in federal and state government are certain to contribute their share of new law. For the sake of the charitable community, I hope coming law changes are not too tough on fundraisers and those charitable organizations, they, which are a meaningful component of the nonprofit sector and our society in general; fundraising professionals are an important part of American philanthropy.

As a nonaccountant in the nonprofit field, I am glad to have *Not-for-Profit Accounting Made Easy* as a guide to the basics of the accounting rules and principles applicable to nonprofit organizations. I have once again tried to emulate Mr. Ruppel's work, to provide an equally valuable volume for the nonlawyer who needs a grounding in the law of charitable fundraising.

I extend my thanks to Natasha Andrews-Noel, senior production editor, and to Susan McDermott, senior editor, for their support and assistance in creating this book.

Bruce R. Hopkins
September 2009

About the Author

Bruce R. Hopkins is a senior partner in the law firm of Polsinelli Shughart PC, practicing in the firm's Kansas City, Missouri, and Washington, D.C., offices. He specializes in the representation of charitable and other nonprofit organizations. His practice ranges over the entirety of law matters involving tax-exempt organizations, with emphasis on fundraising law issues, charitable giving (including planned giving), the formation of nonprofit organizations, acquisition of recognition of tax-exempt status for them, the private inurement and private benefit doctrines, the intermediate sanctions rules, legislative and political campaign activities issues, public charity and private foundation rules, unrelated business planning, use of exempt and for-profit subsidiaries, joint venture planning, tax shelter involvement, review of annual information returns, and Internet communications developments.

Mr. Hopkins served as chair of the Committee on Exempt Organizations, Tax Section, American Bar Association; chair, Section of Taxation, National Association of College and University Attorneys; and president, Planned Giving Study Group of Greater Washington, D.C.

Mr. Hopkins is the series editor of Wiley's Nonprofit Law, Finance, and Management Series. In addition to *Fundraising Law Made Easy*, he is the author of *The Law of Fundraising, Fourth Edition; The Tax Law of Charitable Giving, Third Edition; The Law of Tax-Exempt Organizations, Ninth Edition; Planning Guide for the Law of Tax-Exempt Organizations: Strategies and Commentaries; IRS Audits of Tax-Exempt Organizations: Policies, Practices, and Procedures; The Tax Law of Associations; The Tax Law of Unrelated Business for Nonprofit Organizations; The Nonprofits' Guide to Internet Communications Law; The Law of Intermediate Sanctions: A Guide for Nonprofits; Starting and Managing a Nonprofit Organization: A Legal Guide, Fifth Edition; Nonprofit Law Made Easy; Charitable Giving Law Made Easy; Private Foundation Law Made Easy; 650 Essential Nonprofit Law Questions Answered; The First Legal Answer Book for Fund-Raisers; The Second Legal Answer Book for Fund-Raisers;*

The Legal Answer Book for Nonprofit Organizations; The *Second Legal Answer Book for Nonprofit Organizations*; and *The Nonprofit Law Dictionary*; and is the coauthor, with Jody Blazek, of *Private Foundations: Tax Law and Compliance, Third Edition*; also with Ms. Blazek, *The Legal Answer Book for Private Foundations*; with Thomas K. Hyatt, of *The Law of Tax-Exempt Healthcare Organizations, Third Edition*; with David O. Middlebrook, of *Nonprofit Law for Religious Organizations: Essential Questions and Answers*; with Douglas K. Anning, Virginia C. Gross, and Thomas J. Schenkelberg, of *The New Form 990: Law, Policy and Preparation*; and also with Ms. Gross, *Nonprofit Governance: Law, Practice, and Trends*. He also writes Bruce R. Hopkins' Nonprofit Counsel, a monthly newsletter, published by John Wiley & Sons.

Mr. Hopkins earned his JD and LLM degrees at George Washington University National Law Center, and his BA at the University of Michigan. He is a member of the bars of the District of Columbia and the state of Missouri.

Mr. Hopkins received the 2007 Outstanding Nonprofit Lawyer Award (Vanguard Lifetime Achievement Award) from the American Bar Association, Section of Business Law, Committee on Nonprofit Corporations. He is listed in *The Best Lawyers in America, Nonprofit Organizations/Charities Law*, 2007–2009.

FUNDRAISING LAW
MADE EASY

1

INTRODUCTION TO THE LAW OF FUNDRAISING FOR CHARITY

The purpose of this chapter is to provide a framework consisting of the fundamental elements in federal and state law that shape the rules concerning fundraising for charitable organizations. Thus, this chapter will:

- Provide a definition of the phrase *charitable fundraising.*
- Address the concept of *charitable sales.*
- Explore the definition of the phrase *charitable contribution.*
- Describe the various methods of fundraising.
- Discuss the controversial matter of fundraising costs.
- Summarize the commensurate test.
- Enumerate the several issues pertaining to fundraising compensation.
- Explain the trap that lurks in the step transaction doctrine.
- Summarize the law concerning the enforceability of charitable pledges.
- Correlate the applicability of the public policy doctrine to the charitable giving setting.

DEFINITION OF *CHARITABLE FUNDRAISING*

A common perception is that there is a single type of activity termed *fundraising*, just as there is a prevailing view that all charitable gifts are made in cash. Most state and local, as well as some federal, regulatory approaches seem founded on this perception. An assumption is made that the law amply defines *fundraising*, when in fact it does not. Yet, to raise funds in this setting is to solicit gifts.

State Law

State charitable solicitation acts (see Chapter 3) usually define the word *solicitation*. These definitions generally are encompassing. This fact is evidenced not only by the express language of the definition but also by an expansive definition of the term *charitable* and application of these acts to charitable solicitations conducted, in common parlance, "by any means whatsoever." A solicitation can be oral or written. It can take place by means of a variety of methods of communication (discussed ahead). Debate over the legal consequences of charitable solicitation over the Internet (discussed ahead) highlights the importance and scope of the word *solicitation*.

A most expansive, yet typical, definition of the term *solicit* states that it means any request, directly or indirectly, for money, credit, property, financial assistance, or other thing of any kind or value on the plea or representation that the subject of the gift is to be used to benefit a charitable organization or otherwise be used for a charitable purpose. Usually, the word *solicitation* is used in tandem with the word *contribution* (or gift) (discussed ahead). The term may, however, encompass the pursuit of a *grant* from a private foundation, other nonprofit organization, or a government department or agency. (About a dozen states exclude the process of applying for a government grant from the term *solicitation*; a few similarly exclude the seeking of private foundation grants.) There is no requirement that a solicitation be successful; a solicitation is a solicitation irrespective of whether the request actually results in the making of a gift.

A court created its own definition of the term *solicit* in this setting, writing that the "theme running through all the cases is that to solicit means to 'appeal for something,' 'to ask earnestly,' 'to make petition to,' 'to plead for,' 'to endeavor to obtain by asking,' and other similar expressions." (The court ruled that a state's charitable solicitation act did not apply to gambling activities held to generate funds destined for charitable purposes.)

Federal Lobbying Rules

At the federal level, the definition of fundraising that is most relevant (and accurate) in the charitable setting is found in an odd place: the tax laws restricting legislative activities by public charities. One of the law requirements is that these activities may not be substantial; an elective test provides allowable lobbying expenditures in terms of declining percentages of aggregate program (charitable purpose) expenditures. Exempt purpose expenditures, however, do not include amounts paid to or incurred for (1) a separate fundraising unit of the organization or (2) one or more other organizations, if the amounts are paid or incurred primarily for fundraising. Nonetheless, program expenditures include all other types of fundraising outlays.

An organization's first task in this context is to determine its direct fundraising costs. These costs include such items as payments to fundraising consultants, salaries to employees principally involved in fundraising, and fundraising expenses concerning travel, telephone, postage, and supplies. With respect to these direct items, there may have to be allocations, such as between the educational (program) aspects and the fundraising aspects, of the expenses of creating and delivering printed material. Then, an organization must ascertain its indirect costs, to be apportioned to fundraising, lobbying, and other factors. These costs include items such as salaries of supportive personnel, rent, and utilities.

For the purpose of these rules, the term *fundraising* includes the solicitation of (1) dues or contributions from members of the organization, persons whose dues are in arrears, or the public; (2) grants from businesses or other organizations, including charitable entities; and (3) grants from a governmental unit, or any agency or instrumentality of a governmental unit. (This is a strange definition of *fundraising*, in two respects: (1) normally, the solicitation of *dues* (including those in arrears) is not considered fundraising (dues not being gifts) and (2) businesses make gifts, not grants.)

Internal Revenue Service Reporting Rules

The Internal Revenue Service (IRS) has devised extensive requirements for the reporting of fundraising activities by tax-exempt, primarily charitable organizations (see Chapter 5). In this connection, the agency has defined the term *fundraising activities*. The fundraising profession has long differentiated among gifts of time, treasure, and talent (with only the solicitation of gifts of treasure constituting fundraising). The IRS, however, in its formulation of a sweeping definition of fundraising, has encompassed them all; according to the IRS, fundraising entails "activities undertaken to induce potential donors to contribute money, securities, services, materials, facilities, other assets, or time."

This definition of *fundraising activities* is far too broad (at least from a law standpoint). It is nonsensical to include the solicitation of services or time in a definition of *fundraising*. Fundraising pertains to the solicitation of money and/or other property; it does not relate to solicitations of services or time. If a charitable organization's president asks an individual to serve on the charity's board of trustees, the president has not engaged in fundraising. If a charitable organization's executive director asks an individual to volunteer to assist with a particular project (even a fundraising event), the executive director likewise has not undertaken a form of fundraising. The IRS has overlooked the fact that the concept underlying and the word *fundraising* not only contain the word *fund* but are predicated on it.

CONCEPT OF CHARITABLE SALES

A few state charitable solicitation acts include a definition of the term *sale* (or *sell* or *sold*). A statute may provide that a *sale* means the transfer of any property or the rendition of any service to any person in exchange for consideration. The word *consideration* is the critical element of this definition, inasmuch as it represents the principal dividing line between a sale and a contribution.

Consideration is the core component of a bona fide contract: Both parties to the bargain must, for the contract to be enforceable, receive approximately equal value in exchange for the participation of the other. Consideration is the reason one person enters into a contract with another; the contracting party is motivated or impelled by the benefit to be derived from the contract (goods or services), while the compensation to be received by the other contracting person is that person's inducement to the contract. A transaction that is not supported by adequate consideration cannot be a sale.

Correspondingly, a transaction that is completely supported by consideration cannot be a gift. Some transactions partake of both elements, where the consideration is less than the amount transferred, in which case only the portion in excess of the consideration is a gift. The most common types of these dual character transactions are quid pro quo contributions (see Chapter 8), and transfers by means of charitable remainder trusts and in the form of charitable gift annuities (see Chapter 6).

DEFINITION OF *CHARITABLE CONTRIBUTION*

A *contribution* (or gift or donation) basically is a transfer of money or property in the absence of consideration (discussed previously). The term may be defined in a charitable solicitation act as including a gift, bequest, devise, or other grant of money, credit, financial assistance, or property of any kind or value. The statutory definition may embrace promises to contribute (pledges).

The law on this point is the most developed in, not surprisingly, the federal income tax charitable giving setting. Many years ago, the U.S. Supreme Court observed that a contribution is a transfer motivated by "detached or disinterested generosity." Another observation from the Court was that a "payment of money [or transfer of other property] generally cannot constitute a charitable contribution if the contributor expects a substantial benefit in return." The Court has also referred to a contribution as a transfer made out of "affection, respect, admiration, charity or like impulses."

The Court has adopted use of the reference to consideration in determining what a contribution is. Thus, it wrote: "The *sine qua non* of a charitable contribution is a transfer of money or property without adequate consideration. The taxpayer, therefore, must at a minimum demonstrate that he purposefully contributed money or property in excess of the value of any benefit he received in return." The Court subsequently articulated essentially the same rule, when it ruled that an exchange having an "inherently reciprocal nature" is not a contribution.

Dues, being payments for services, are not contributions. The term *dues* embraces payments by members of an organization in the form of membership dues, fees, assessments, or fines, as well as fees for services rendered to individual members. A loan is not a contribution, including a loan to a charitable organization. If a person makes a loan to a charity and the amount of the loan, or a portion of it, is thereafter forgiven, the amount forgiven becomes a charitable contribution as of the date of the forgiveness.

Essentially, the concept in this context is that a contribution is a payment to a charitable organization where the donor receives nothing of material value in return. Thus, a court ruled that a state's charitable solicitation act did not apply to the solicitation of corporate sponsors for a marathon, stating that the transaction was a "commercial" one, was "not a gift," was a "corporate opportunity," and it had "nothing to do with philanthropy."

METHODS OF FUNDRAISING

Fundraising for charitable ends is a unique form of communication that simultaneously "promotes" and "sells" the product (the charitable cause) and "asks for the order" (the gift). Charitable organizations employ several methods and techniques to solicit contributions. Gifts can be in many forms—money, securities, tangible personal property, real property, and interests in property—all of which are embraced by the word *fundraising*. The one feature shared equally by all the ways to generate gifts is the objective—to ask for a gift that benefits someone else.

The asking part can entail many ways: in person, and by regular (old-fashioned) mail, facsimile, email, telephone, radio, television (and cable), and Web site. Organizing charitable entities to engage in fundraising is complex and requires the careful application and orchestration of many methods of solicitation by volunteers and employees. Each method of fundraising has its characteristics regarding suitability for use, public acceptance, potential or capacity for success, and cost-effectiveness. Likewise, the reporting and enforcement aspects of regulatory systems should, to be fair, distinguish between the varieties of fundraising techniques and their performance. The methods of asking are best understood by dividing them into three areas: annual giving, special-purpose, and estate planning.

Annual Giving Programs

The basic concept underlying charitable annual giving programs is to recruit new donors and renew (and perhaps upgrade) prior donors, whose gifts provide for annual operations. Some programs require a staff professional to manage; most programs require both staff and a volume of volunteer leaders and workers. Charities frequently conduct two or more forms of annual solicitation within a 12-month period; the net effect is to contact the same audience with multiple requests within the year. Some donors prefer one method of giving over the others. Multiple gift requests to present donors will increase net revenues faster than efforts to acquire new donors, inasmuch as present donors are the best prospects for added gifts and donor acquisition can be costly. An organization cannot use every fundraising method (chiefly because of donor resistance or saturation); rational selections are required.

Direct mail/donor acquisition fundraising uses direct mail response advertising (usually third class, bulk rate) in the form of letters to individuals who are not presently donors to the organization, inviting them to participate at modest levels. A small rate of return is likely. This type of "customer development" may require an investment of $1.25 to $1.50 to raise $1.00. The value of new donors is their potential for repeat gifts, and perhaps future leaders, volunteers, and even benefactors.

Direct mail/donor renewal is used to ask previous donors to give again. If there has been some contact since the prior gift, such as a report on the use of gifts, about 50 percent of these donors will give another time. Upgrading, that is, a request for a gift slightly higher than the last gift, works about 15 percent of the time, and has the added value of helping preserve the current giving level.

Telephone calls to prospects and donors permit dialogue and are more successful than direct mail. Response is not high, due in part to the intrusive nature of these calls. *Television solicitation* is, of course, more distant but is the best visual medium to convey the message. Both methods are expensive to initiate and require the instant response of donors.

Special and benefit events are social occasions that use ticket sales and underwriting to generate revenue but incur direct costs for production. While generally popular, these events are typically among the most expensive and least profitable methods of fundraising. Fundraising staff may deplore the energy and hours required to support an event; their great value, however, is in public relations visibility (which is why they are also termed "friend-raisers").

Support groups are used to organize donors in a quasi-independent entity affiliated with the charitable organization. Membership dues and event sponsorship are revenue sources. Valuable for their ability to develop committed annual donors, organize and train volunteers, and promote the charity in the community, support groups also require professional staff management.

Donor clubs and associations are donor-relations vehicles (similar to support groups) that are designed to enhance the link between donor and charity, thereby helping to preserve annual gift support. The clubs' selectivity and privileges (with imaginatively named gift levels) help justify the higher gifts, which are rewarded by access to top officials and other benefits.

Campaign committees are volunteer groups of peers using in-person solicitation methods to recruit the most important annual gifts. These committees are structured as a true campaign, with a chair and division leaders for individual and corporate prospects. Other annual giving methods involve:

Commemorative gifts

Gifts in kind

Advertisements (such as in newspapers and magazines)

Door-to-door solicitations

On-street solicitations

Sweepstakes and lotteries (where legal)

Las Vegas and Monte Carlo Nights

Mailings of unsolicited merchandise

In-plant solicitations

Federated campaigns

Special-Purpose Programs

A successful base of annual giving support permits the charitable organization to conduct more selective programs of fundraising that will secure major gifts, grants, and capital campaigns toward larger and more significant projects. A request for large gifts differs from annual gift solicitation because the request is for a one-time gift, allows for a multiyear pledge, and is directed toward a specific project or urgent need. Likely donors in this context are skillful "investors" who will respond to a major gift request only after researching the organization and determining whether the project justifies their commitment.

It takes courage to ask someone for a *major gift* (such as one million dollars). Current and committed donors are the best prospects. Before the request is made, the charity should engage in careful research to ascertain the prospect's financial capability, enthusiasm for the organization, preparedness to accept this special project, and likely response to the team assembled to make the call. Also important is early resolution of the donor recognition to be offered (such as a seat on the board or name on a building).

Separate skills and tools are required to succeed at *grant-seeking*. Grants are institutional decisions to provide support based on published policy and guidelines that demand careful observance of application procedures and deadlines. Usually, for a grant proposal to be accepted, the charitable organization and its project must perfectly match the goals of the grantor.

A *capital campaign* is clearly the most successful, cost-effective and enjoyable method of fundraising. Everyone is working together toward the same goal, the objective is significant to the future of the organization, major gifts are required, start and end dates are goal markers, and activities and excitement exist. A capital campaign is the culmination of years of effort, both in design and consensus surrounding the organization's master plan for its future, which depends on experienced volunteers and enthusiastic donors.

Planned Gift Programs

An increasingly active area of fundraising involves gifts made in the present, to be realized by the charitable organization in the future. The term *gift planning* best describes this concept. These gifts entail either transfers of assets to the charity at the time of the gift, in exchange for the donor's retention of income for life, or transfers (usually in trust) where the charity receives the remaining assets at the donor's death (or perhaps expiration of a period of time). This planning allows donors to remember their favorite charities in their estate and to plan gifts of their assets, in the present or at death. The four broad areas of planned giving are, from a law perspective, guided by income, gift, and estate tax considerations.

Donors may leave charitable gifts by means of bequests and devises made in their wills and/or trusts. These gifts may be outright transfers from an estate to one or more charitable organizations or may involve funding by means of a charitable trust. Trusts and similar arrangements can be utilized during lifetime or as part of an estate plan. Popular techniques are the use of charitable remainder trusts, charitable gift annuities, and perhaps charitable lead trusts (see Chapter 6).

An individual may name his or her favorite charity as a beneficiary, in whole or in part, of a life insurance policy. A charitable deduction is available for the surrender value of a policy contributed; in appropriate instances, the payments of premiums on a life insurance policy contributed to a charity are deductible gifts. Insurance is also used in the wealth replacement context; the donor uses annual income from a charitable remainder trust (and/or other tax savings induced by the charitable deduction) to purchase a life insurance policy, usually for the value of the asset(s) placed in trust, and names his or her heirs as beneficiaries, thus transferring to heirs the same value on the donor's death.

FUNDRAISING EXPENSES

One of the most important issues arising out of regulation of charitable solicitations, and an intense focus of the regulators' attention, is the matter of fundraising costs incurred by charities—internal expenses, and fees paid to fundraising consultants, professional fundraisers, professional solicitors, and/or other advisers in the realm of fundraising. The general standard is that fundraising expenses must be *reasonable*. Yet there is not much of a consensus as to how to evaluate, or measure, the reasonableness of fundraising costs. Many misstatements of the law are articulated in this context.

Disclosure Dilemma

One of the essential functions of most of the state charitable solicitation acts (see Chapter 3) is to promote disclosure of information to the public. A matter of principal concern among charitable groups, and thoughtful legislators and regulators, is the appropriate mode by which to achieve public disclosure by organizations soliciting financial support for charitable purposes. This issue basically has evolved around two conflicting positions, represented by the catch phrases *point-of-solicitation disclosure* and *disclosure-on-demand*.

Under the point-of-solicitation disclosure concept, certain information must be provided as part of the solicitation process, that is, in the solicitation materials. The solicitation-on-demand approach generally requires that a soliciting charitable organization provide information to the public on request; in some instances, the solicitation materials must bear notice of the availability of this information.

Proponents of the point-of-solicitation disclosure approach insist that it is the only effective way to ensure that the public has at least minimal information about a charitable organization at the time (or around the time) the decision as to whether to contribute is made. They assert that most people will not bother to seek information from charities, with the result being little, if any, meaningful disclosure. (This view, of course, is becoming anachronistic as considerable information about charitable organizations and fundraising by them is readily available by means of the Internet.) These advocates view this matter as one akin to consumer protection, with analogy made to labeling requirements on containers of food, medicine, and the like.

Opponents of the point-of-solicitation disclosure approach (including proponents of the disclosure-on-demand approach) insist that substantive information about a charitable organization (particularly financial data) cannot be presented, in a meaningful and balanced manner, as part of the solicitation process. They note that the purpose of a solicitation is to raise funds; they contend that cluttering a solicitation mailing, broadcast, and the like with statistical and other information only makes the fundraising confusing and less appealing, and hence generates fewer dollars, while simultaneously making the solicitation more expensive. They further assert that useful disclosure cannot be achieved by the mere provision of snippets of data and that this type of a requirement is counterproductive to the intent of the law by enhancing the likelihood that misleading information will be transmitted.

Thus, in designing or evaluating a charitable solicitation law, the mode of disclosure is a threshold issue. In part, the dispute over the two basic disclosure regimes can be resolved or mitigated by the outcome of the decision as to the items of information to be disclosed at the point of solicitation (if any). For example, even the most vehement opponents of general point-of-solicitation disclosure do not object to a requirement that the solicitation literature include a statement about the purpose of the soliciting charitable organization and the intended use of the contributions solicited. By contrast, any requirement that the solicitation materials state the organization's fundraising costs, and perhaps require that these costs be expressed as a percentage of contributions or other receipts, generates considerable controversy and opposition.

Fundraising Cost Percentages

Over 35 years ago, an expert on charitable fundraising observed that, "in the field today, there is no agreed-upon base for determining fundraising cost percentages." Nothing has changed in this regard in the interim. Nonetheless, a most common practice is to try to capture the essence of a charitable organization's fundraising costs in terms of a single percentage. (While it is illegal for a government to forbid a charity to fundraise because of its fundraising cost percentage (see Chapter 9), the watchdog groups whole-heartedly apply these percentages, touting them every chance they get (see Chapter 10).) These costs are usually expressed in relation to total receipts or charitable contributions, using the prior year's financial data.

   This approach is popular because it is simple. It is frequently the basis of comparison of charitable groups. For example, an individual reviewing financial data might see one charitable organization's annual gifts of $100,000 and fundraising costs of $15,000, and another charity's annual gifts of $100,000 and fundraising costs of $20,000, and conclude that the organization with fundraising costs of 15 percent is *more qualified* for gift support, or *more efficient*, or *better-managed* than the organization with fundraising costs at 20 percent. (This is the message sent, often quite successfully, by the watchdog groups and others who thrive on this percentage approach.) Moreover, this use of percentages readily lends itself to the disclosure-at-point-of-solicitation approach, inasmuch as a percentage can be easily displayed on solicitation material.

   The percentage approach, however, is deficient on two fundamental bases: (1) there is no universal standard for computing fundraising costs, thereby precluding the creation of fair percentages and meaningful comparisons of charitable organizations, and (2) a single percentage is a misleading factor to use in evaluating a charitable organization's fundraising practices and overall eligibility for contributions. For example, in the previous illustration, the organization with a 15 percent fundraising cost percentage may not be including in the base some allocable shares of indirect costs, while the 20 percent organization is doing so. Thus, were the same reporting system being followed, the first organization may have higher fundraising costs than the second. This is not a matter of fraud or cheating but rather a lack of uniformity and understanding about the expense elements to take into account in constructing the ratio.

There may be valid reasons, even assuming identical means of determining the fundraising cost percentages, as to why one organization's solicitation expenses exceed another's—reasons that have nothing to do with efficiency, cost effectiveness, or program merit. Fundraising practices are diverse and unique to various types of charitable organizations. An institution with an established donor base and a range of fundraising methods, including annual giving, planned giving, and a bequest program, will have a lower fundraising cost percentage than a new charity with heavy dependence on direct mail. Another type of organization may be spending most of its money in building a donor base (called *donor acquisition*), relying considerably on special-event fundraising, or championing an unpopular cause; these elements contribute to higher fundraising cost percentages.

An organization that is poorly managed and/or expending excessive sums on fundraising can nonetheless have a low fundraising cost percentage, attributable perhaps to one or more large charitable bequests or unexpected lifetime gifts, or low fundraising costs in one area that offset excessive costs in another area. Also, the fundraising costs for a multiyear capital campaign, which are normally largely incurred in the initial months of the campaign, or in relation to the establishment of a planned giving program, will introduce additional distortions relative to a single fundraising cost percentage based on a lone year's experience.

The realities of the costs of fundraising for charitable purposes are poorly understood by the public and in some instances by government regulators and legislators. The maxim that "it takes money to raise money" is frequently incompatible with the typical individual's view as to how a charitable dollar should be spent. Many charitable organizations understandably fear that the public uses the fundraising cost percentage approach as a ranking system by which to evaluate charities for giving purposes. Those holding this view insist that, at least until a uniform and equitable method for calculating the fundraising cost percentage is in place, such a "batting average" methodology is an inappropriate way to assess the relative worth of charitable entities.

Fundraising Cost Line Item Approach

Opponents of the fundraising cost percentage approach generally contend that the only suitable manner by which to present a charitable organization's fundraising costs is as part of its financial statements. This approach thus envisions an income and expense statement that displays fundraising costs as a line item, treated no differently from any other category of expenses. Proponents of line item treatment of charitable fundraising costs assert that mere fairness dictates this approach: (1) it enables an organization to present its fundraising costs in the context of its overall range of costs, and thus does not place undue emphasis on fundraising expenses by causing them to be evaluated in isolation, as is the case with the percentage approach, and (2) it avoids the unfair and misleading aspects of the percentage regime.

Again, this matter of the proper method of fundraising costs reporting and disclosure is inextricably entwined with the point-of-solicitation disclosure versus disclosure-on-demand conflict. It is much more difficult to graphically convey the amount of an organization's fundraising costs using the line-item approach rather than the percentage-approach, even if a meaningful financial statement is provided at the point of solicitation (which is likely to prove impractical in any event). It is also more difficult to make easy comparisons of organizations' fundraising costs when readers of financial statements have only aggregate sums to consider (although readers can, of course, construct their own fractions and percentages).

Advocates of the line-item approach say that this is as it should be, because fundraising costs computations are a complex and intricate matter, also that fast and easy fundraising expense calculations are not appropriate, and that fundraising cost disclosure cannot meaningfully be achieved at the point of solicitation.

Floating Average Approach

Those who understand the deficiencies of the fundraising cost percentage approach, yet believe that its virtues (principally, its usage in conjunction with point-of-solicitation disclosure) outweigh those of the fundraising cost line item approach, often seek to mitigate the excesses of the annual percentage approach by proposing a floating (or moving) average. This average might reflect fundraising expense performance over a three- or four-year period. Thus, for example, an organization that raised $100,000 in contributions in each of four consecutive years, and incurred fundraising costs of $70,000 in the first year, $50,000 in the second year, $30,000 in the third year, and $10,000 in the fourth year, would, when disclosing its fundraising costs in the fifth year, report that its costs during its previous four years averaged 40 percent rather than having to disclose in year two that its fundraising costs for the prior year were 70 percent.

In this fashion, the same essential facts would be disclosed but in a manner that eliminates (absent consistently "high" fundraising costs) the adverse consequences (such as a fall-off in giving, which exacerbates the problem) of disclosing only the initial months' cost. This approach would smooth out the distortions that can appear in a year-by-year evaluation, such as high start-up costs, unexpected and/or large gifts, and unanticipated gains or failures in the solicitation that can be unique to a single year. There is precedent for this approach in the federal tax law, such as the averaging period for calculating public support (discussed ahead) and the manner of calculating the threshold for the annual information return filing requirement (see Chapter 5).

A fundamental deficiency, however, separates the moving average idea from actual usage: a rule that does not require an organization to report fundraising costs until after, for example, two or three years of existence would be an open invitation for abuse by those who would simply create a new soliciting organization every few years and thus never report fundraising performance. Moreover, a rule that required annual percentage reporting until a floating average period was attained would likely defeat its purpose, particularly for new organizations.

Pluralization Approach

Much thinking has been devoted to the question of the proper method of measuring and reporting charitable fundraising costs. Among the more intriguing of the concepts to emerge is the idea that fundraising costs should be *pluralized* to be meaningful. This approach does not find fault so much with the idea of utilizing a percentage to display fundraising costs as it does with the idea that a true measure of fundraising costs can be captured in a single percentage. Blending in the moving average feature, the pluralization approach is based on the precept that a fair and productive understanding of a charity's fundraising costs, where more than one form of fundraising is used, can be achieved only by looking at the costs for each fundraising activity over a multiyear period (rather than the lumping of all costs over a measuring period).

In truth, there is no such thing as a single expense for something termed *fundraising* because there is, as noted, no lone activity that constitutes *fundraising.* There are many types of fundraising methods (discussed previously) and, while the precise parameters have yet to be documented, each effort carries with it a range of costs expressed as a percentage that may be considered reasonable. Thus, a fundraising cost that is considered reasonable for one fundraising method is not necessarily reasonable for another. The pluralization doctrine calls for a fundraising cost percentage to be assigned to each of an organization's fundraising methods and for abandonment of reliance on a bottom-line ratio.

The pluralization approach is predicated on the fact that there are fundamental categories of fundraising methods: donor acquisition by direct mail, donor renewal by direct mail, capital campaigns, special events, as well as planned giving and bequest programs. (Pluralization models have yet to incorporate website fundraising; those costs are quite low.) This approach postulates that these fundraising methods involve associated costs expressed (as illustrations) in the following reasonable percentages: donor acquisition, about 120 percent; donor renewal, about 10 percent; special events, about 50 percent; capital programs, about 15 percent; and planned giving and bequests programs, about 15 percent.

The singular contribution of the pluralization method of stating charitable fundraising costs is that it exposes the fundamental fallacy of the bottom-line ratio or single percentage approach. That is, the sole percentage disclosure mode can make the fundraising costs of certain organizations appear unreasonable when in fact they are reasonable and—in an outcome perversely counterproductive to the objective of disclosure—can make the fundraising costs of some organizations appear reasonable when in fact they are unreasonable.

The pluralization approach of reporting charitable fundraising costs, while a major contribution to the theory of fundraising costs disclosure, has not been widely adopted. The methodology has, however, facilitated greater understanding of the complexities of measuring and evaluating the fundraising costs of charitable organizations. It is a useful technique by which an organization can make an internal assessment of its fundraising performance. Perhaps of greatest importance is the availability of this approach for demonstrating to those concerned about the matter why a charitable organization's fundraising costs are reasonable in the face of a seemingly high single fundraising cost percentage.

Average Gift Size Factor

A well-intentioned and well-governed charitable organization that is adversely (and thus undoubtedly unfairly) affected by application of set percentage limitations on fundraising costs is likely to have low cost-per-gift and cost-per-solicitation factors. This type of organization, however, is also likely to depend on comparatively small contributions. Thus, an unfair comparison results when the fundraising cost ratios of this type of organization are compared with those of another charitable organization whose average gift size is much higher but whose fundraising cost ratios are relatively smaller when measured by the overall percentage of fundraising costs in relation to contributions. Thus, the former organization appears to have "high" costs of fundraising, while in fact the latter organization has higher fundraising costs per gift.

In illustration of this point, consider Charity A and Charity B, both of which received $1 million in contributions in the year under comparison. While A's total fundraising costs were $450,000, B's were $150,000. Consequently, B's single fundraising cost percentage is 15 percent and A's is 45 percent, perhaps placing A in considerable difficulty with prospective donors, the media, and watchdog agencies. But, this comparison is lacking inasmuch as it fails to reveal an additional and essential factor: the number of gifts, from which can be determined the average gift size and the cost per gift. Assume that Charity A received 200 gifts in the year under review, with an average gift of five dollars and a cost per gift of $2.25; Charity B received 30,000 gifts, with an average gift size of $33.33 and a cost per gift of five dollars.

It is thus inappropriate to compare Charities A and B in this manner. That is, using the single fundraising cost percentage factor as the basis of comparison, B appears more cost-effective than A, but this conclusion is misleading and unfair to A because it has a lower average gift. Conversely, a comparison on the basis of the cost-per-gift factor shows A as the charity that is more cost-effective, but this result is unfair to B because it has a higher average gift. Thus, it can be contended that disclosure of a charitable organization's number of gifts—by category—is essential for a complete and fair evaluation of fundraising costs, and that any comparisons of fundraising performance should occur only among organizations with similar constituencies, based on a number of factors, particularly average gift size.

Reasonableness of Fundraising Costs

There is consensus in some quarters (reflected, for example, in court opinions) as to the most effective means for determining fundraising costs and parameters for assessing the reasonableness of these costs. The law is filled with requirements that something be *reasonable;* how the term is defined in practice depends on the particular circumstances. The factors to be considered in determining the reasonableness of the annual fundraising expenses of a charitable organization include the following.

> *Period of Existence.* The period of time a charitable organization has been in existence needs to be taken into consideration in determining the reasonableness of its fundraising expenses. A new organization, or for that matter, an organization newly undertaking a solicitation, may incur fundraising expenses in the initial years of the solicitation that are higher, in relation to total annual receipts or contributions, than the costs incurred in subsequent years. Part of this aspect of the matter pertains to the development of an organization's donor base or constituency.

> *Purposes and Programs.* The nature of a charitable organization's purposes and programs are to be taken into account in this regard, with particular emphasis on whether the organization advocates one or more causes and disseminates substantive information to the public as part of the same process by which the organization solicits contributions (discussed ahead). Consideration should also be given to whether a charitable organization's purposes and programs involve a subject matter with general public appeal or are sufficiently controversial or unpopular that public support may not readily be forthcoming.

> *Constituency.* The nature and extent to which a charitable organization has an established constituency of donors is to be taken into account in determining the reasonableness of its fundraising expenses. This factor looks to whether the organization has established a broad base of public support or whether it must build such a base as part of its solicitation process.

> *Methods of Fundraising.* The method or methods selected by a charitable organization or available to it to implement its fundraising program (discussed previously) should be evaluated in this regard. Consideration should be given to those organizations that, for one or more

reasons, can conduct their fundraising by means of only one method of solicitation (such as direct mail).

Average Gift Size. The size of the average annual contribution received by a charitable organization (discussed previously) should be taken into consideration in determining the reasonableness of its fundraising expenses. The object of this factor is to ascertain the dependency of the organization on small contributions and whether it is nonetheless cost-effective in the management and expenditure of its receipts.

Unforeseen Circumstances. The extent to which the expenses of the solicitation effort or efforts of a charitable organization depend on or are otherwise materially affected by unforeseen circumstances should be taken into consideration in determining reasonableness.

Other Factors. The estimate by a charitable organization of its fundraising expenses and money as well as property to be raised or received during the immediately succeeding 12-month period, and its reasons for the estimate, including any program for reducing its annual fundraising expenses, should be acknowledged as factors. Also of relevance is the extent to which an organization is organized and operated to attract new and additional public or governmental support on a continuous basis (discussed ahead).

These concepts and factors are beginning to receive greater appreciation in the courts. One court was critical of a state's disclosure statute triggered when a charitable organization's program outlays were less than 70 percent of funds collected. This court observed that "many charities operate below the 70 percent threshold during the early years when they are engaged in building a substantial donor base." Also: "Their financial allocations to 'program services' may be low simply because they are just getting operations under way and attempting to fulfill a need that is unmet by other organizations." And: "Charities or nonprofit groups may also expend more on fundraising or management costs relative to program services because they serve unpopular causes." The court wrote that "it cannot be said that the organization [involved in the case] is either fraudulent or less 'efficient' in meeting charitable purposes than others with relatively low fundraising or management costs and consequently higher percentage allocations to program services."

This court placed this matter of fundraising costs in the constitutional law setting where, for law purposes, the issue festers the most (see Chapter 9). It stated that the "very organizations most deserving of First Amendment [free speech] protections—those involved in the dissemination of information, discussion, and advocacy of public issues ... are likely to have relatively high solicitation or fundraising costs (and therefore lower percentages of donations allocated to program services), not because they are fraudulent or any less efficient in furthering their causes than other nonprofit or charitable organizations, but because the very nature of their activities cause these costs to be high." The disclosure statute was held to be unconstitutional; the court wrote that, "[g]iven these fundamental flaws in the design and operation" of the contested provision, "it is only fortuitous that, in some of its applications, this statute might accomplish the State's goals of preventing fraud and providing information to prospective donors about the effectiveness of their contributions in furthering charitable purposes."

Cost Allocations

The accounting profession set forth financial accounting standards for properly accounting for costs associated with joint activities; these standards apply to all nonprofit organizations and all state and local governmental entities that solicit contributions (Statement of Position (SOP) 98-2, published by the American Institute of Certified Public Accountants).

The essence of SOP 98-2 is that costs associated with joint activities should be allocated between fundraising and the appropriate program or management function when the criteria of purpose, audience, and content are met for a particular joint activity. The criterion of purpose is met if the joint activity furthers the charity's program or management functions. Program functions may be accomplished when the activity requests specific action by the audience in furtherance of the charity's mission. Requests for contributions are not considered a specific action that furthers a charity's mission.

> *Purpose Criterion.* SOP 98-2 provides the following factors to consider when determining if the purpose criterion has been met: (1) whether compensation or fees for performing the activity are based on contributions raised; (2) whether a similar program or management and general activity is conducted separately and on a similar or greater scale; and (3) other evidence. These factors are to be considered in the order provided. The SOP provides further guidance as to what *other evidence* might be considered, including (1) measuring program results and accomplishments of the activity; (2) the medium—the program component of the joint activity calls for specific action by the recipient that will help accomplish the organization's mission and if the organization conducts the program component without a significant fundraising component in a different medium; (3) the relationship between evaluation and compensation; (4) evaluation of the measured results of the activity; (5) qualifications of those performing the joint activity; and (6) tangible evidence of intent.

> *Audience Criterion.* If the audience includes prior donors or is selected based on the ability or likelihood of the recipients to make a contribution to the charity, it is presumed that the audience criterion is

not met. To overcome this presumption, the audience must also be selected for one of the following reasons: (1) the audience's need to use or reasonable potential to take the specific action called for by the program's component of the joint activity; (2) the audience's ability to take specific action to assist the organization in meeting the goals of the program component of the joint activity; or (3) the organization's requirement to direct the management and general component of the joint activity to the particular audience or the audience has reasonable potential for use of the management and general component. The organization should compare the extent to which the audience was selected based on its ability or likelihood to contribute with the extent it was selected for one or more of the above-referenced factors to determine if the audience criterion has been met.

Content Criterion. If the joint activity supports program or management and general functions, then the criterion for content is satisfied. To support the program function, the joint activity must call for specific action that helps the organization accomplish its mission. To support the management and general function, a component of the joint activity must fulfill one or more of the organization's management and general responsibilities.

When an organization determines that allocation of costs for a joint activity is appropriate, it should apply the method of allocation in a reasonable and consistent manner. Organizations that allocate costs for joint activities should include the following in the notes to their financial statements: types of activities incurring joint costs; a statement that costs have been allocated; and the total amount allocated to each functional expense category.

As an illustration of the inconsistencies in reporting of fundraising costs, one of the watchdog agencies (see Chapter 10)—the American Institute of Philanthropy—refuses to follow the SOP 98-2 criteria, insisting that communications directed by a charity at donors can never simultaneously serve a fundraising purpose and a valid program purpose. (The Institute follows the criteria when it is applied to a tax-exempt social welfare agency.) Thus, when the Institute encounters charities that have allocated expenses between fundraising and program costs, it will disregard the allocation and apply all of the expenses to fundraising. The Institute's position in this regard is contrary to the views of other watchdog agencies, the IRS, and, of course, the accounting profession, all of which consider it a customary practice for a charity to apportion its expenses partly for program and partly for fundraising—particularly where the charity's communications serve a dual purpose of soliciting funds while simultaneously educating the public about the organization, its mission and programs, its accomplishments, as well as its goals.

COMMENSURATE TEST

A little-known, little-used standard in the federal tax law pertaining to tax-exempt, charitable organizations is termed the *commensurate test*. With this test, the fact-finder (the IRS or a court) assesses whether an organization is maintaining program activities at a level that is commensurate in scope with its revenue and assets. As the IRS stated, this test "requires that organizations have a charitable program that is both real and, taking the organization's circumstances and financial resources into account, substantial." When this rule was first articulated by the IRS (in 1964), the organization involved derived most of its income in the form of rents, yet was successful in preserving its exempt status because it satisfied the test, in that it was engaging in an adequate amount of charitable functions notwithstanding the extent of its rental activities.

The commensurate test has long been entangled with the matter of charitable fundraising expenses. On one extremely controversial occasion, the IRS revoked the tax-exempt status of a charitable organization using a variety of rationales, including the ground that its fundraising costs were too high. (Never before had the amount of fundraising costs been a criterion for eligibility for exemption.) The IRS concluded that the test was transgressed because the charity, during the two years examined, expended, according to the IRS, only about 1 percent of its revenue for charitable purposes; the balance was allegedly spent for fundraising (98 percent) and administration (1 percent). (This matter was ultimately resolved in court, albeit without application of the commensurate test.)

The IRS's lawyers have written that the commensurate test "does not lend itself to a rigid numerical distribution formula—there is no fixed percentage of income that an organization must pay out for charitable purposes." In each case, said the IRS, "it should be ascertained whether the failure to make real and substantial contributions for charitable purposes is due to reasonable cause." Therefore, the IRS continued, an organization that "raises funds for charitable purposes but consistently uses virtually all its income for administrative and promotional expenses with little or no direct charitable accomplishments cannot reasonably argue that its charitable program is commensurate with its financial resources and capabilities."

There have been a few IRS rulings over the years applying the commensurate test. In one, a charitable organization was allowed to retain its tax-exempt status while receiving 98 percent of its support from (passive) unrelated business income, since 41 percent of the organization's programs was charitable in nature. By contrast, an organization that began devoting a considerable portion of its efforts in conducting bingo games and generating gaming income, with little of it spent for charitable purposes, lost its exempt status.

The IRS is stepping up its use of the commensurate test. In late 2008, the agency announced, as one of its new compliance initiatives for fiscal year

2009, a *charitable spending initiative*. This is a "long-range study to learn more about sources and uses of funds in the charitable sector and their impact on the accomplishment of charitable purposes." The IRS said it will be looking at fundraising, contributions, grants, revenue from related and unrelated businesses, types and amounts of direct and indirect unrelated business expenses, and officer compensation, and the effect each of these elements has on funds available for charitable activities. The first stage of this initiative will focus on "organizations with unusual fundraising levels and organizations that report unrelated trade or business activity and relatively low levels of program service expenditures."

FUNDRAISING COMPENSATION ISSUES

The IRS and the courts tend to focus intently on the levels of compensation paid to executives and others by public charities. This concerns compensatory payments to employees and independent contractors (usually consultants). Consequently, compensation paid in the fundraising setting often is a matter of intense scrutiny from a federal tax law standpoint. There are three bodies of law that relate directly to this subject, all emphasizing the requirement that fundraising compensation must be *reasonable*.

Private Inurement

Charitable organizations must, to be tax-exempt, be operated so that they do not cause any inurement of their net earnings to certain persons in their private capacity. The private inurement doctrine is the principle of law that essentially separates nonprofit organizations from for-profit organizations. An organization that is operated *for profit* is one where the profits are destined for those who are the owners of the business, such as shareholders of a corporation who receive the profits of the enterprise (net earnings) by means of dividends. A nonprofit organization, by contrast, is expected to retain its profits (excess of revenue over expenses) at the entity level; to be exempt, a nonprofit organization cannot allow its net earnings to be passed along (inure) to those who control it (the substantive equivalent of owners). The private inurement doctrine is basically applicable only with respect to an exempt organization that it subject to the doctrine and those who have some special relationship to it (often referred to as *insiders*). A form of private inurement is the payment of excessive (unreasonable) compensation to a control person. The sanction for engaging in an act of private inurement is denial or revocation of exempt status. (See Chapter 2.)

Private Benefit

The private benefit doctrine derives from the rule that a charitable organization must be primarily organized and operated for the advancement of charitable ends. Operations for unwarranted private benefit obviously are not the conduct of activities that serve charitable objectives. This doctrine has greater breadth than the private inurement doctrine, principally because its application is not confined to those who are insiders with respect to an organization. The payment of excessive compensation is a form of private benefit; the sanction for engaging in an act of private benefit is denial or revocation of exempt status (*id.*).

Intermediate Sanctions

Pursuant to the intermediate sanctions rules, tax sanctions—structured as penalty excise taxes—may be imposed on the disqualified persons who improperly benefited from the transaction or arrangement and on the organization managers who participated in the transaction or arrangement knowing that it was improper. These rules, which basically require that the terms and conditions of a transaction or arrangement be reasonable, apply with respect to tax-exempt public charities and social welfare organizations (*id.*).

Fundraisers as Disqualified Persons

Generally, a fundraising executive is not a disqualified person with respect to the charitable organization being served. He or she is not normally in a position to exercise substantial influence over the affairs of the organization. This is usually the case where the fundraiser is an employee of the organization (such as a director of development) or a consultant to the organization.

There are, nonetheless, situations where the fundraising professional is a disqualified person. The fundraiser may be an organization manager. If the fundraising function is in a related entity, such as a foundation directly affiliated with a public charity, and the fundraiser is the chief executive officer of that foundation, he or she would be a disqualified person with respect to the foundation. Occasionally, a fundraiser will be a disqualified person by virtue of being a member of a family that includes a disqualified person.

An independent fundraising person may be considered a disqualified person. This is particularly the case where the person has control over a charitable organization's fundraising program that is a meaningful source of the organization's revenue. The fact that a person manages a discrete segment or activity of an organization, that represents a substantial portion of the activities, assets, income, or expenses of the organization, tends to lead to the conclusion that the person is a disqualified person.

Payment of Compensation

Because of these bodies of law, a charitable organization may not, without endangering its tax-exempt status or triggering other sanctions, pay a person engaged in fundraising for it (employee or consultant) an amount that is excessive or unreasonable. This matter of excessiveness of compensation is largely a question of fact. Whether a particular amount of compensation is excessive essentially depends on salaries or fees paid in the community for comparable services, the experience of the individual(s) involved, the individual's education and training, the type of fundraising, the resources and size of the charitable organization, and the nature (e.g., popularity or unpopularity) of the charitable cause.

Questions about the propriety of compensation to a fundraising employee or independent contractor may not have as much to do with the amount being paid as the manner in which it is determined. This is particularly true with respect to compensation that is ascertained on the basis of a percentage of the charitable organization's revenue stream or is otherwise cast as a commission. Although the IRS is suspicious of fundraising compensation that is based, in whole or in part, on percentages of contributions received, the courts are rather tolerant, sometimes supportive, of the practice.

In one instance, a compensation arrangement based on a percentage of gross receipts was held by a court to constitute private inurement, where the facts were somewhat egregious in nature and there was no upper limit as to total compensation. Nonetheless, this same court subsequently restricted the reach of its earlier decision by holding that private inurement did not occur when a tax-exempt organization paid its president a commission determined by a percentage of contributions obtained by him. The court held that the standard is whether the compensation is reasonable, not the manner in which it is ascertained.

In this latter case, fundraising commissions that are "directly contingent on success in procuring funds" were held to be an "incentive well-suited to the budget of a fledgling organization." In reaching this conclusion, the court reviewed states' charitable solicitation acts governing payments to professional solicitors (see Chapter 3), which the court characterized as "sanction[ing] such commissions and in many cases endors[ing] percentage commissions higher than" the percentage commission paid by the organization involved in the case. In another case, a court observed that "there is nothing insidious or evil about a commission-based compensation system." There, an arrangement whereby those who successfully procured contributions to a charitable organization were paid a percentage of the gifts received was judged "reasonable," despite the absence of any limit as to an absolute amount of compensation. Nonetheless, it is a good practice to ascertain the amount or range of fundraising compensation that is reasonable, then place a cap on the payment of compensation that may be in excess of that amount or range.

If the fundraising executive or consultant is a disqualified person with respect to a charitable organization, and excessive compensation is paid, the body of law most likely to be applied by the IRS is the intermediate sanctions regime. Some fundraisers are compensated, in whole or in part, on the basis of the revenue flow of the charitable organization involved. This arrangement may be structured as a commission or some other form of percentage-based compensation; this is certain to be a revenue-sharing arrangement. The fact that a revenue-sharing arrangement is subject to a cap is a relevant factor in determining the reasonableness of the compensation.

The initial contract exception can be of considerable utility in the fundraising setting. It is available when a charitable organization hires a fundraising professional, whether as an employee or independent contractor, where the person was not a disqualified person immediately before entering into the contract. When the parameters of this exception are satisfied, the compensation arrangement is totally exempted from the intermediate sanctions law penalties.

The rebuttable presumption of reasonableness can also be useful for the fundraising professional, particularly in circumstances where the initial contract exception cannot apply. The fundraiser, who is a disqualified person, should endeavor to be certain that the various elements of the presumption are satisfied, to shift the burden of proof, as to the reasonableness of compensation, to the IRS in the event of a challenge to the amount or method of calculation of the compensation.

It is sometimes said that the intermediate sanctions rules are a concern only to disqualified persons and not to the charitable organization involved or other persons who are not disqualified persons; this, however, is often not the case. From a fundraising perspective, a charitable organization embroiled in an excess benefit transaction is expected to report that transaction on its annual information return, which is a public document (see Chapter 8). The result, at a minimum, can be adverse publicity, which can harm the programs of the charity and perhaps fundraisers who are not disqualified persons.

If a fundraising professional, who is a disqualified person with respect to a charitable organization and hired by that charity, is paid excessive compensation, the arrangement would be a taxable excess benefit transaction, assuming inapplicability of the initial contract exception. Assume, as an illustration, that this fundraising professional was paid an annual compensation package of $200,000 for a three-year period. Following audit, the IRS concluded that this individual's services were worth only $100,000 annually. This fundraising executive would then owe initial excise taxes totaling $75,000 (a $25,000 tax per year on the excess benefit of $100,000). Also, this compensation arrangement would have to be corrected by the fundraiser, by means of payment of $300,000 to the charitable organization, plus suitable interest. If these steps were not timely taken, the fundraiser may have additional taxes imposed, totaling $600,000. The total obligation of the fundraiser would be $975,000, not including penalties, interest, and legal fees (presumably a stiff financial burden for one making $200,000 a year). A board member of this charity, who approved this compensation package, knowing it to be excessive, would be liable for $10,000 in taxes and perhaps the taxes of one or more other board members.

Statute of Limitations

In general, the statute of limitations for assessing an intermediate sanctions excise tax is three years. The statute of limitations begins to run, on the later of the dates the tax-exempt organization files the annual information return involved or the due date for the return.

Third-Party Summons

If a fundraising professional (or anyone else) is a disqualified person and the IRS is investigating the possibility of that person's participation in an excess benefit transaction, the IRS may issue a third-party summons to the charitable organization involved in pursuit of facts. The disqualified person may object to the summons if it is issued after the three-year statute of limitations has run. According to a court, that is not a basis for quashing the summons. All that is required to sustain the validity of the summons is that the IRS must show that, in the words of the U.S. Supreme Court in an earlier case, the "investigation will be conducted pursuant to a legitimate purpose, that the inquiry may be relevant to the purpose, that the information sought is not already within the [IRS's] possession, and that the administrative steps required by the [Internal Revenue] Code have been followed." Consequently, the court declined to quash a summons issued, after the statute of limitations with respect to a charitable organization had run, seeking information from the organization as to whether a disqualified person participated in an excess benefit transaction.

STEP TRANSACTION DOCTRINE

As a general rule, a contribution of appreciated capital gain property to a public charitable organization is deductible on the basis of the fair market value of the property and the capital gain element is not taxable to the donor (see Chapter 6). There is, however, a huge trap in this context, one that has snared many unsuspecting fundraisers and unwitting donors. This ambush is embedded in the *step transaction doctrine*.

It is all too easy for a donor and donee to succumb to these temptations. The charitable donee usually does not want to hold the gift property and thus is delighted that a prospective buyer is present. The donor may see the prearranged sale as a favor to the charity, saving the charity the need to pursue purchasers of the property. The step transaction doctrine is of no consequence in law to the charitable donee (absent fraud); the donor, however, can have what looks like a large appreciated property charitable deduction undone.

General Principles

If the donee charitable organization sells the property soon after the contribution is made, the donor may be placed in the position of having to recognize, for federal income tax purposes, the capital gain element. This can happen when, under the facts and circumstances surrounding the gift, the donee was legally obligated to sell the gift property to a purchaser that was prearranged by the donor. In this situation, the law regards the transaction as a sale of the property by the "donor" to the third-party purchaser and a gift of the after-tax sales proceeds to the charitable organization.

Pursuant to this step transaction doctrine, two or more ostensibly independent transactions (here, the gift to and subsequent sale by the donee) are consolidated and treated as a single transaction for federal tax purposes. The key to avoiding this tax-adverse outcome is to be certain that the charitable organization was not legally bound at the time of the gift to sell the property to the prospective purchaser.

This sidestep of the step transaction doctrine has its origins in a famous court case, where a gift of stock in a closely held corporation was made to a charitable organization, followed by a prearranged redemption. The transaction was not recharacterized as a redemption between the donor and the redeeming corporation and a later gift of the redemption proceeds to the charity. This was the outcome, although the donor held voting control over both the corporation and the charitable organization. The IRS lost this case because the charity was not legally bound to redeem the stock, nor was the corporation in a position to compel the redemption.

Illustrative Litigation

The step transaction rule has been and continues to be the subject of considerable litigation. Several court opinions illustrate the nature of this controversy. In one instance, a court ruled that a gift to a charitable organization of the long-term capital gains in certain commodity futures contracts gave rise to a charitable contribution deduction, and that the gifts and subsequent sales of the contracts were not step transactions within a unified plan.

This case concerned an individual who formed a private operating foundation in the early 1970s and had been president of it since it was established. From time to time, he contributed futures contracts to the foundation and claimed charitable contribution deductions for these gifts. In 1974, he obtained a private letter ruling from the IRS that the charitable contributions deductions were proper and that no gain need be recognized when the foundation sold the contracts.

In 1981, however, the federal tax law was changed. Beginning with that year, all commodities futures contracts acquired and positions established had to be marked to market at year-end and the gains (or losses) had to be characterized as being 60 percent long-term capital gains (or losses) and 40 percent short-term gains (or losses), regardless of how long the contracts had been held. This revision in the law posed a problem for this individual because the charitable deduction for a gift of short-term capital gain property is confined to the donor's basis in the property; there is no deduction for the full fair market value of the property (as there is for most gifts of long-term capital gain property). He solved the dilemma by donating only the long-term gain portion of the futures contracts.

In 1982, this individual entered into an agreement under which he contributed the long-term gains of selected futures contracts from his personal accounts at a brokerage house and retained for himself the short-term capital gains. For the most part, the selected contracts were sold on the same day the gift was made, and the portions of the proceeds representing the long-term capital gains were transferred to an account of the foundation at the same brokerage house. The donor chose the futures contracts to be donated according to the funding needs of the foundation and the amount of unrealized long-term capital gains inherent in the contracts. Once the contracts were transferred to a special account, they were to be immediately sold, pursuant to a standing instruction. On audit for 1982, the IRS took the position that the full amount of the capital gains on the sales of these contracts was includable in this individual's taxable income; the IRS also disallowed the charitable deductions for that year and prior years. The IRS's position rested on two arguments: (1) the transfers of a portion of the gain to the foundation were a taxable anticipatory assignment of income; and (2) the step transaction doctrine should apply, thereby collapsing separate interrelated transactions into a single transaction for tax purposes.

The step transaction doctrine was inapplicable in this instance, the individual argued, because no prearrangements were made with respect to the gifts. He maintained that he donated all of his interest in the long-term capital gain portions of the futures contracts, free and clear. The IRS, by contrast, contended that the gift transfers should be treated together with the later future sales and division of proceeds as a single transaction. The government argued that this individual's plan was to meet the foundation's operating needs by selling selected futures contracts with unrealized appreciation of equal amounts. Rather than donating cash, this argument went, he tried to donate the futures contracts with a restriction that he would keep the short-term capital gains on their sale.

The court said that the question in the case was "[h]ow related were the decisions to sell the futures to their donation?" The court looked to the matter of control and found that the donation agreements and powers of attorney executed by the individual supported his position that the trustees of the foundation had control over the sale of the futures contracts once they were transferred into the broker's special account. Thus, the court concluded that the issue of the donor's control over the sale of the contracts "was not such that the donations and sales could be viewed as step transactions encompassed within a unified plan."

As this case illustrated, the question posed by the step transaction doctrine involves the relationship among various seemingly independent transactions. In this case, the question was: How related were the decisions to sell the futures contracts to the contributions of them? Had some pre-arrangement existed by which the individual donated selected contracts to cover the charitable organization's operating expenses, and had he received in return short-term gains without having to pay taxes on the full amount of the futures contracts, the transfers could have been viewed as a step transaction within a larger plan. In this connection, one court held that "if, by means of restrictions on a gift to a charitable donee, either explicitly formulated or implied or understood, the donor so restricts the discretion of the donee that all that remains to be done is to carry out the donor's prearranged plan for designation of the stock, the donor had effectively realized the gain inherent in the appreciated property."

As to this case, the individual claimed that the sales were not prearranged but rather were the prudent acts of the trustees of a charitable organization in need of operating funds. The IRS argued that the standing instruction reflected a prearranged plan to use the charity to sell the futures contracts, cover its needs with the long-term gains, and enable the individual to keep the short-term gains without having to pay taxes on the entire proceeds of the sale. The court held, however, that there was no evidence to suggest that the individual was the source of the standing instruction, and thus that his control over the sale of the contracts was not such that the contributions and sales could be viewed as step transactions encompassed within a unified plan.

In a similar case, a court held that contribution of appreciated futures contracts to a charitable organization controlled by an individual did not result in income to the individual when the contracts were sold shortly after they had been donated. The court dismissed the importance of control between the business and the recipient charitable organization and the fact that everyone involved anticipated that the gifted property would be sold or otherwise liquidated. The court wrote: "Only through such a step could the purpose of the charitable contribution be achieved."

In another instance, an individual made annual gifts, for ten consecutive years, to a university of closely held stock in a corporation of which he was the majority shareholder, an officer, and a director. He retained a life interest in the gift property and confined his charitable contribution deduction to the value of the remainder interest (see Chapter 6). Each year the university tendered stock to the corporation for redemption; each year the corporation redeemed it. There was no contract evidencing this cycle of events. The university invested the redemption proceeds in income-producing securities and made quarterly disbursements to the donor.

The IRS asserted that the donor employed the university as a tax-free conduit for withdrawing funds from the corporation and that the redemption payments by the corporation to the university were in reality constructive dividend payments to the donor. The court on appeal nicely framed the dispute: "Our aim is to determine whether [the donor's] gifts of the [c]orporation's shares [to the university] prior to redemption should be given independent significance or whether they should be regarded as meaningless intervening steps in a single, integrated transaction designed to avoid tax liability by the use of mere formalisms."

The IRS wanted the court to "infer from the systematic nature of the gift-redemption cycle" that the donor and donee had "reached a mutually beneficial understanding." But the court declined to find any informal agreement between the parties; it also refused to base tax liability on a "fictional one" created by the IRS. The court so held even though the donor was the majority shareholder of the corporation, so that his vote alone was sufficient to ensure redemption of the university's shares. The court wrote that "foresight and planning do not transform a nontaxable event into one that is taxable."

In still another instance, an individual donated promissory notes issued by a company he controlled to three charitable foundations several weeks prior to redemption of the notes. A court held that he did not realize income in connection with these gifts or the subsequent redemption of the notes by the company. The court observed: "A gift of appreciated property does not result in income to the donor so long as he gives the property away absolutely and parts with title thereto before the property gives rise to income by way of a sale."

In one more instance involving facts of this nature, a court took note of the fact that the concept of a charitable organization originated before and independently of the sale, the deed of trust for the property contributed was executed before and independent of the sale, and at the time the deed of trust was executed, "no mutual understanding or meeting of the minds or contract existed between the parties."

There are cases to the contrary, however, holding that the transfer of the property to a charitable organization "served no business purpose other than an attempt at tax avoidance."

In the end, perhaps the matter of the step transaction doctrine comes down to this observation by a court: "Useful as the step transaction doctrine may be in the interpretation of equivocal contracts and ambiguous events, it cannot generate events which never took place just so an additional tax liability might be asserted."

IRS Rulings

The step transaction doctrine occasionally appears in IRS private letter rulings. In one instance, an individual planned to fund a charitable remainder trust (see Chapter 6) with a significant block of stock of a corporation. It was anticipated that the trust would sell most, if not all, of this stock in order to diversify its assets. The stock first had to be offered to the corporation to redeem the stock for its fair market value. The donor was the sole initial trustee of the trust.

The IRS focused, in this instance, on whether the trust would be legally bound to redeem the stock. Although it did not answer that question, the agency assumed that to be the case and also assumed that the trust could not be compelled by the corporation to redeem the stock. Thus, the IRS held that the transfer of the stock by the donor to the trust, followed by the redemption, would not be recharacterized for federal income tax purposes as a redemption of the stock by the corporation followed by a contribution of the redemption proceeds to the trust. The IRS also held that the same principles would apply if the stock were sold rather than redeemed. This holding assumed that the donor had not prearranged a sale of the stock before contributing it to the trust under circumstances in which the trust would be obligated to complete the sales transaction.

In another situation, an individual planned to contribute a musical instrument to a charitable remainder trust. The instrument was used in the donor's profession; the donor was not a dealer in this type of instrument, nor was the instrument depreciated for tax purposes. Again, the issue was presented: If the trust subsequently sold the instrument for a gain, would that gain have to be recognized by the donor? The IRS presumed that there was no prearranged sales contract legally requiring the trust to sell the instrument following the gift. With this presumption, the IRS was able to hold that any later gain on a sale of the instrument would not be taxable to the donor.

CHARITABLE PLEDGES

The making of a charitable pledge—a promise to make a charitable contribution—does not give rise to an income tax charitable contribution deduction. Any deduction that is occasioned by the pledge, such as it may be, is determined at the time the pledge is satisfied.

The enforceability of a charitable pledge is a matter of state law. Some states require the existence of consideration as a prerequisite to the existence of an enforceable pledge. Other states will enforce a charitable pledge on broader, social grounds, such as reliance. A typical circumstance concerning the latter approach arises where a person pledges a significant gift to a charity for a building and the charity commences construction of it in reliance on the forthcoming gift.

Usually, a pledge is made by a potential donor in the form of a written statement—a promise to the potential charitable donee of one or more contributions to be made sometime in the future. Pursuant to a *funding agreement,* a person may commit in writing to make multiple contributions to a charitable organization over a stated period for purposes such as general operations or endowment; the charitable contribution (and resulting deduction) arises in each year of actual payment. A variation on this approach is a pledge to charity of a stock option. The pledge then produces an income tax charitable deduction in the year in which the charitable donee, having acquired the option, exercises it.

PUBLIC POLICY CONSIDERATIONS

A doctrine in the law of nonprofit organizations states that an entity cannot be tax-exempt as a charitable one if it engages in an activity that is contrary to public policy. For example, the U.S. Supreme Court held that it is contrary to federal public policy for a private school to engage in racially discriminatory practices as to its student body and faculty; this type of discrimination was found to bar tax exemption of the school as a charitable or educational organization. This doctrine is occasionally applied in the charitable giving setting.

In one case, an individual contributed certain Native American artifacts to a museum; a portion of the collection consisted of items covered by eagle and migratory bird protection laws. The IRS contended that there should not be any charitable deduction for these gifts, on the ground that acquisition of the items was contrary to public policy. Nonetheless, a court held that these donors had a sufficient ownership interest in these items to contribute them to the museum, even though the donors may have violated federal law when they acquired the items.

There are other aspects of the public policy doctrine; one concerns the efficacy of the imposition of certain conditions subsequent on the terms and conditions of a gift. In the principal case, an individual transferred certain property interests to a trust benefiting his children. The instrument making the gift provided that, should there be a final determination that any part of the transfer was subject to gift tax, all the parties agreed that the excess property decreed to be subject to the tax would automatically be deemed not included in the conveyance and be the sole property of the individual, free of trust.

The court held that this provision was a condition subsequent that was void because it was contrary to public policy. It wrote that "[w]e do not think that the gift tax can be avoided by any such device as this." A contrary holding, wrote the court, would mean that, "upon a decision that the gift was subject to tax, the court making such decision must hold it not a gift and therefore not subject to tax." This holding would be made in the context of litigation to which the donees of the property were not parties, so the decision would not be binding on them and they would be able to enforce the gift notwithstanding the court's decision. Then wrote the court: "It is manifest that a condition which involves this sort of trifling with the judicial process cannot be sustained."

This condition subsequently was found to be contrary to public policy for three reasons. First, "it has a tendency to discourage the collection of the [gift] tax by the public officials charged with its collection, since the only effect of an attempt to enforce the tax would be to defeat the gift."

Second, the "effect of the condition would be to obstruct the administration of justice by requiring the courts to pass upon a moot case." That is, if the condition "were valid and the gift were held subject to tax, the only effect of the holding would be to defeat the gift so that it would not be subject to tax." The consequence would be that the donor "would thus secure the opinion of the court as to the taxability of the gift, when there would be before the court no controversy whatever with the taxing authorities which the court could decide, the only possible controversy being as to the validity of the gift and being between the donor and persons not before the court."

Third, the condition "is to the effect that the final judgment of a court is to be held for naught because of the provision of an indenture necessarily before the court when the judgment is rendered." The court noted that gift tax liability cannot be the subject of a federal court declaratory judgment. The condition thus "could not be given the effect of invalidating a judgment which had been rendered when the instrument containing the condition was before the court, since all matters are merged in the judgment." The court rephrased its distress with the voided condition: The condition "is not to become operative until there has been a judgment; but after the judgment has been rendered it cannot become operative because the matter involved is concluded by the judgment."

In a similar case, a husband and wife transferred shares of stock to their three children. At the time of the gifts, these individuals executed a gift adjustment agreement that was intended to ensure that the parents' gift tax liability for the stock transfers would not exceed the unified credit against tax to which they were entitled at the time. This agreement stated that, if it should be finally determined for federal gift tax purposes that the fair market value of the transferred stock either was less than or greater than $2,000 per share, an adjustment would be made to the number of shares conveyed, so that each donor would have transferred $50,000 worth of stock to each donee.

The court in this case declined to give effect to the gift adjustment agreement, inasmuch as honoring the agreement would run counter to public policy concerns. It wrote that a "condition that causes a part of a gift to lapse if it is determined for Federal gift tax purposes that the value of the gift exceeds a given amount, so as to avoid a gift tax deficiency," involves a "trifling with the judicial process." If valid, this type of condition would "compel" the court to "issue, in effect, a declaratory judgment as to the stock's value, while rendering the case moot as a consequence." Yet there was "no assurance that the [parents] will actually reclaim a portion of the stock previously conveyed to their sons, and our decision on the question of valuation in a gift tax suit is not binding upon the sons, who are not parties to this action." The sons, the court added, "may yet enforce the gifts."

There is another line of law, captured by this quotation: "The purpose of Congress in providing deductions for charitable gifts was to encourage gifts for charitable purposes; and in order to make such purposes effective, there must be a reasonable probability that the charity actually will receive the use and benefit of the gift, for which the deduction is claimed." A dissenting opinion in a court case stitched these aspects of the case law together in an attempt to defeat charitable contributions that the dissenter viewed as caused by an increase in value of property facilitated by the court majority. The dissent concluded that the "possibility of an increased charitable deduction serves to discourage [the IRS] from collecting tax on the transaction because any attempt to enforce the tax due on the transaction is of no advantage to the fisc." It argued that the charity involved would never be able to benefit from the gifts, and characterized the charitable deduction as "against public policy" and "plainly wrong."

Perhaps the best application of the public policy doctrine in the charitable giving setting occurred when the IRS issued regulations concerning charitable lead trusts (see Chapter 6) in an effort to stop the practice of using the lives of seriously ill individuals to measure the income interest period, so as to move income and assets away from charitable beneficiaries prematurely and to private beneficiaries instead. The IRS observed that, "similar to the vulture, the promoters of this form of charitable lead trust circle in on mortally ill people," thus giving rise to the term *vulture* or *ghoul* charitable lead trust. The agency stated: "Marketing schemes that exploit the misfortunes of some for the benefit of others are contrary to public policy."

SUMMARY

This chapter provided an introduction to the law of fundraising for charitable organizations, with a summary of the concepts of charitable fundraising and charitable sales, a definition of *charitable contribution*, a description of the methods of fundraising, an analysis of the matter of fundraising expenses, a summary of the commensurate test, a survey of fundraising compensation issues, a discussion of the step transaction doctrine, a summary of the law on charitable pledges, and an analysis of the public policy considerations that can apply in the charitable fundraising setting.

2

FUNDRAISERS' LAW PRIMER

A professional fundraiser is not necessarily a lawyer, yet usually is expected to understand (and cope with) many bodies of law, including the federal tax law pertaining to tax-exempt status, public charity status (see Chapter 4), and charitable giving (see Chapter 6). The principal bodies of these laws, with which the fundraiser should be generally familiar, are summarized in this chapter. Specifically, this chapter will:

- Discuss the matter of the organization's *form.*
- Summarize the *organizational tests.*
- Summarize the *operational test.*
- Discuss the *primary purpose rule.*
- Summarize the principles of fiduciary responsibility.
- Inventory the various *charitable* purposes and activities.
- Discuss the concept of *recognition* of tax exemption.
- Summarize the doctrine of *private inurement.*
- Summarize the doctrine of *private benefit.*
- Briefly integrate the *intermediate sanctions* rules.
- Summarize the federal tax rules concerning *lobbying.*
- Summarize the federal tax rules concerning political campaign activities.
- Discuss the law concerning *prohibited tax shelter transactions.*
- Discuss the law concerning *personal benefit contracts.*

- Summarize the various policies a charitable organization should consider adopting.

FORM OF ORGANIZATION

Every tax-exempt organization must have a legal form; this is basically a matter of state law. Tax-exempt, nonprofit organizations generally are of three types: corporation, unincorporated association, and trust.

Generically, the document by which a tax-exempt organization is created is known, in the parlance of the federal tax law, as the *articles of organization*. There usually is a separate document containing rules by which the organization conducts its affairs; this document is most often termed *bylaws*. The organization may develop other documents governing its operations, such as various policies and procedures, an employee handbook, a conflict-of-interest policy (although that may be part of the bylaws), and/or a code of ethics.

The types of articles of organization for each of the principal types of tax-exempt, nonprofit organizations are:

- Corporation: articles of incorporation.

- Unincorporated association: constitution.

- Trust: declaration of trust or trust agreement.

The contents of a set of articles of organization should include the following:

- The name of the organization.

- A statement of its purposes (discussed ahead).

- The name(s) and address(es) of its initial directors or trustees.

- The name and address of the registered agent (if a corporation).

- The name(s) and address(es) of its incorporator(s) (if a corporation).

- A statement as to whether the entity has members (a private foundation is unlikely to have members).

- A statement as to whether the entity can issue stock (if a corporation).

- Provisions reflecting any other state law requirements.

- Provisions reflecting any other federal tax law requirements.

- A dissolution clause (discussed ahead).

The bylaws of a nonprofit organization (if any) will usually include provisions with respect to:

- The organization's purposes.

- The origins (e.g., election) and duties of its directors.

- The origins and duties of its officers.

- The role of its members (if any).

- Meetings of members and directors, including dates, notice, quorum, and voting.

- The role of executive and other committees.

- The role of its chapters (if any).

- The organization's fiscal year.

- A conflict-of-interest policy (if not separately stated).

- Reference to (any) affiliated entities.

- Restatement of the federal tax law requirements.

ORGANIZATIONAL TESTS

In theory, every type of tax-exempt organization must adhere to an *organizational test*. As the name implies, this test looks to the manner in which the entity was organized. Compliance with this test is determined by what is in and is not in the organization's articles of organization (discussed previously). The elements of an organizational test are the most developed in the case of charitable organizations.

Basically, for charitable organizations, the organizational test requires a suitable statement of purposes and mandates a *dissolution clause*. This clause is a provision in the organizing document that dictates where the organization's net income and assets (if any) will be distributed should the organization liquidate or otherwise dissolve. Permissible recipients are one or more other charitable organizations or governmental agencies.

Some tax-exempt charitable organizations have additional operational tests to satisfy. These include private foundations, which generally must incorporate the private foundation rules (see Chapter 4) in their articles of organization. Supporting organizations (*id.*) also have additional requirements as to their articles.

OPERATIONAL TEST

Likewise, in theory, every type of tax-exempt organization must adhere to an *operational test*. Again, as the name implies, this test looks to the manner in which the entity is operated, and concerns whether the organization is in fact operated for exempt purposes. The elements of an operational test are the most developed in the case of charitable organizations. Generally, defects in an entity's articles of organization cannot be cured by complete adherence to the operational test.

Charitable organizations, to be tax-exempt, must, of course, have charitable purposes and engage in the appropriate activities to advance those purposes. These purposes must, at a minimum, be the organization's primary purposes (discussed ahead). There are basically 18 discrete ways an organization can serve charitable purposes (discussed ahead).

PRIMARY PURPOSE RULE

The appropriate category of tax exemption (if any) for a nonprofit organization, is dictated by application of the *primary purpose rule.* Also, an organization's primary purpose can change; this development may cause the organization to evolve into a different type of exempt entity (or, in rare cases, to lose exempt status). The law, however, tolerates incidental nonexempt purposes.

The general rule, as stated by the Supreme Court, is that the "presence of a single . . . [nonexempt] purpose, if substantial in nature, will destroy the exemption regardless of the number or importance of truly [exempt] purposes." A federal court of appeals held that nonexempt activity will not result in loss or denial of tax-exemption where it is "only incidental and less than substantial" and that a "slight and comparatively unimportant deviation from the narrow furrow of tax approved activity is not fatal." In the words of the IRS, the rules applicable to charitable organizations in general have been "construed as requiring all the resources of the organization [other than an insubstantial part] to be applied to the pursuit of one or more of the [allowable] exempt purposes."

There is no definition of the term *insubstantial* in this context. Thus, application of these rules is an issue of fact to be determined under the facts and circumstances of each case. In some instances, this is a matter of weighing the relative importance of purposes. For example, an organization with some charitable and educational purposes will not qualify for exemption as a charitable organization if its predominate purposes are social and recreational; an organization in this situation will be classified as a social club.

Nonprofit organizations should, therefore, frame their statement of purposes with care. Also, it is prudent to revisit the statement from time to time to be certain that it accurately reflects the entity's contemporary activities and objectives.

PRINCIPLES OF FIDUCIARY RESPONSIBILITY

Out of the common law of charitable trusts has evolved the concept that a director of a tax-exempt organization, particularly a charitable entity, is a fiduciary of the organization's resources and a facilitator of its mission. Consequently, the law imposes on directors of exempt organizations standards of conduct and management that comprise *fiduciary responsibility*.

Most state laws, by statute or court opinion, impose the standards of fiduciary responsibility on directors of nonprofit organizations. A summary of this aspect of the law stated: "In many cases, nonprofit corporation fiduciary principles govern the actions of the organization's directors, trustees, and officers, and charitable trust law governs the use and disposition of the assets of the organization." This summary added: "These laws generally address issues such as the organization's purposes and powers, governing instruments (such as articles of organization and bylaws), governance (board composition, requirements for board action, and duties and standards of conduct for board members and officers), and dedication of assets for charitable uses (including a prohibition against the use of assets or income for the benefit of private individuals)." Thus, personal liability can result when a director (or officer or key employee) of a nonprofit organization breaches the standards of fiduciary responsibility.

One of the principal responsibilities of board members is to maintain financial accountability and effective oversight of the organization they serve. Board members are guardians of the organization's assets, and are expected to exercise due diligence to see that the organization is well-managed and has a financial position that is as strong as is reasonable under the circumstances. Fiduciary duty requires board members of exempt organizations to be objective, unselfish, responsible, honest, trustworthy, and efficient. Board members, as stewards of the organization, should always act for its good and betterment, rather than for their personal benefit. They should exercise reasonable care in their decision-making, and not place the organization under unnecessary risk.

The distinction as to legal liability between the board as a group and the board members as individuals relates to the responsibility of the *board* for the organization's affairs and the responsibility of *individual board members* for their actions personally. The board collectively is responsible and may be liable for what transpires within and happens to the organization. As the ultimate authority, the board should ensure that the organization is operating in compliance with the law and its governing instruments. If legal action ensues, it is often traceable to an inattentive, passive, and/or captive board. Legislators and government regulators are becoming more aggressive in demanding higher levels of involvement by and accountability of board members of tax-exempt organizations; this is causing a dramatic shift in thinking about board functions, away from the concept of mere oversight and toward the precept that board members should be far more involved in policy setting and review, employee supervision, in addition to overall management. Consequently, many boards of exempt organizations are becoming more vigilant and active in implementing and maintaining sound policies.

In turn, the board's shared legal responsibilities depend on the actions of individuals. Each board member is liable for his or her acts (commissions and omissions), including those that may be civil law or even criminal law offenses. In practice, this requires board members to hold each other accountable for deeds that prove harmful to the organization.

The board of a tax-exempt organization, particularly a public charity (see Chapter 4), is, according to the American National Red Cross Governance Modernization Act of 2007, collectively responsible for:

- Reviewing and approving the organization's mission statement
- Approving and overseeing the organization's strategic plan and maintaining strategic oversight of operational matters
- Selecting, evaluating, and determining the level of compensation of the organization's chief executive officer
- Evaluating the performance and establishing the compensation of the senior leadership team and providing for management succession
- Overseeing the financial reporting and audit process, internal controls, and legal compliance
- Ensuring that the chapters of the organization are geographically and regionally diverse
- Holding management accountable for performance
- Providing oversight of the financial stability of the organization
- Ensuring the inclusiveness and diversity of the organization
- Providing oversight of the protection of the brand of the organization
- Assisting with fundraising on behalf of the organization

CHARITABLE PURPOSES AND ACTIVITIES

The federal tax law recognizes 18 *charitable* (using that term in its most expansive sense) purposes and activities:

1. Relief of the poor
2. Relief of the distressed
3. Promotion of health
4. Lessening the burdens of government
5. Promotion of social welfare

6. Advancement of education

7. Advancement of science

8. Advancement of religion

9. Promotion of the arts

10. Protection of the environment

11. Promotion of patriotism

12. Promotion of sports for youth

13. Prevention of cruelty to children or animals

14. Certain forms of economic development

15. Operation of formal educational institutions (such as schools, colleges, universities, and museums)

16. Operation of scientific organizations, including research entities

17. Operation of religious organizations (such as churches, conventions or associations of churches, and religious orders)

18. Operation of certain cooperative investment entities or charitable risk pools

RECOGNITION OF TAX EXEMPTION

An organization's tax-exempt status may be *recognized* by the IRS; this is done by issuance of a determination letter or ruling, following the filing by the organization of an application for recognition of exemption. As a general rule, a charitable organization must, to be tax-exempt, have its exemption recognized by the IRS; the application to be filed in this regard is Form 1023. Private foundations and supporting organizations (see Chapter 4) must, to be exempt, have their exemptions so recognized. Churches and certain small organizations are exempt from this requirement.

PRIVATE INUREMENT DOCTRINE

The doctrine of private inurement, which is the essential principle of law distinguishing nonprofit and for-profit organizations, is applicable to nearly all types of tax-exempt organizations. It is most pronounced and developed, however, for charitable organizations, including private foundations. By contrast, for a few types of nonprofit organizations, forms of private benefit are the exempt function.

Charitable Organizations

The federal law of tax exemption for charitable organizations requires that each such entity be organized and operated so that "no part of [its] net earnings . . . inures to the benefit of any private shareholder or individual." Literally, this means that the profits of a charitable organization (and any other type of entity subject to the doctrine) may not be passed along to individuals or other persons in their private capacity, in the way that dividends are paid to shareholders. In actual fact, the private inurement rule, as expanded and amplified by the IRS and the courts, means much more.

The contemporary concept of private inurement is broad and wide-ranging. Lawyers for the IRS advised that inurement is "likely to arise where the beneficial benefit represents a transfer of the organization's financial resources to an individual solely by virtue of the individual's relationship with the organization, and without regard to accomplishing exempt purposes." That description is essentially correct for today's private inurement doctrine but it is a substantial embellishment of the original (and antiquated) statutory rule.

The essence of the private inurement concept is to ensure that a charitable organization is serving public, not private, interests. To be tax-exempt, an organization must establish that it is not organized and operated for the benefit of private interests—designated individuals, the creator of the entity or his or her family, shareholders of the organization, persons controlled (directly or indirectly) by private interests, or any persons having a personal and private interest in the activities of the organization.

Insiders

The federal securities laws that govern for-profit business corporations target the notion of the *insider*—someone who has a special and close relationship with a corporation, frequently because he or she is a director, officer, and/or significant shareholder. Thus, for example, the securities laws prohibit insider trading. The private inurement rules, using the odd phrase *private shareholder or individual,* mirror the concept of the insider. In the intermediate sanctions context (discussed ahead) and in the private foundation setting, the term is *disqualified person* (see Chapter 4).

An insider for private inurement purposes includes an organization's directors, trustees, and officers. It also encompasses key employees, particularly where they have duties or responsibilities normally vested in officers. Further, the family members of insiders and entities controlled by insiders (such as corporations, partnerships, trusts, and estates) are covered. Indeed, the contemporary version of the term *insider* in the exempt organizations context is that it is any person who is in a position to exercise control over a significant portion of the affairs of an organization. It is not necessary that this control in fact be exercised.

The inurement doctrine prohibits a transaction between a tax-exempt organization subject to the rule and a person who is an insider, where the latter is able to cause the organization's net earnings to be turned to private purposes as the result of his, her, or its control or influence. The IRS once observed that, as a general rule, an organization's "trustees, officers, members, founders, or contributors may not, by reason of their position, acquire any of its funds." Stating its view another way, the IRS has rather starkly said that the "prohibition of inurement, in its simplest terms, means that a private shareholder or individual cannot pocket the organization's funds."

Standard of Reasonableness

Persons can receive private benefits in many ways; private inurement can take many forms. Still, a charitable organization may incur ordinary and necessary operating expenditures without losing its tax-exempt status. It may pay compensation, rent, interest, and maintenance costs without penalty, because these expenses, even if paid to insiders, further the organization's exempt purposes. The costs, however, must be justifiable and be for reasonable amounts.

The matter of *reasonableness* is one of *fact*, not *law*. The exercise in determining what is reasonable is closely akin to *valuation*. In complex instances, the services of an independent, competent consultant may be warranted. The law that is developing in the intermediate sanctions setting (discussed ahead) is helping to define the parameters of the term *reasonable*.

Compensation

The most common form of private inurement involving nonprofit organizations is excessive and unreasonable compensation. When a charitable organization pays an employee a salary, it is paying a portion of its earnings to an individual in his or her private capacity. Payment of reasonable compensation, however, is allowable; it is not private inurement. Payment of compensation becomes private inurement when the amount is excessive—and is made to an insider (discussed previously). In this context, *compensation* is not confined to payment of a salary or wage. It also includes bonuses, commissions, royalties, expense accounts, insurance coverages, deferred compensation, and participation in retirement plans,

Whether compensation paid by a nonprofit organization is reasonable is, as noted, a question of fact, to be decided in the context of each case. Generally, allowable compensation is ascertained by comparing the compensation paid to individuals who have similar responsibilities and expertise, serving organizations of comparable type and size, in the same or similar communities. (Where similar entities are operating in the for-profit sector, compensation paid by them can be included in the evaluation.) Other factors are the need of the organization for a particular individual's services, the amount of time devoted to the job, and whether an independent or captive board approved the compensation.

Thus, individuals (and other persons) serving charitable (and other) tax-exempt organizations are allowed, by the law, fair compensation for their efforts. A federal court observed that the "law places no duty on individuals operating charitable organizations to donate their services; they are entitled to reasonable compensation for their services." Likewise, a congressional committee report contained the observation that "an individual need not necessarily accept reduced compensation merely because he or she renders services to a tax-exempt, as opposed to a taxable, organization."

Three aspects of compensation can make it unreasonable. One is the sheer amount of the compensation, in absolute terms. A federal court, in finding private inurement because of excessive compensation, characterized the salaries as being "substantial" amounts. Other courts, however, tolerate substantial amounts of compensation where the employees' services and skills warrant the level of payment.

The second aspect is extraordinary jumps (or spikes) in the level of compensation. An amount of compensation that might otherwise be reasonable can be suspect if there is a sudden significant increase in pay. A case in point: Two individuals who for years received annual compensation of $20,000 were each awarded a $700,000 bonus; the IRS and two courts found that level of compensation to be unreasonable. Another telling factor is whether the spike in compensation level causes the recipient to enjoy far more compensation than anyone else on the payroll.

The third aspect of compensation that can lead to private inurement is the manner in which the amount is calculated. The IRS may challenge, and courts may agree with the agency, compensation arrangements that are predicated on a percentage of the revenue flow of the tax-exempt organization employer. Case law on this point is inconsistent and unclear but the prevailing view seems to be that private inurement will not be found simply because a commission system is used; the important fact is the reasonableness of the compensation. Private inurement has been found in a compensation arrangement based on a percentage of gross receipts, where an upper limit (a cap) was not placed on total compensation. In another instance, a court focused on the reasonableness of the percentage, not the reasonableness of the resulting compensation. The IRS has recently been rather tolerant of these forms of compensation, particularly in the health care area, where various forms of *gainsharing* have become prevalent.

Prompted by media reports of ostensible excess compensation paid by nonprofit organizations to insiders, the IRS in 2004 launched an enforcement effort to "identify and halt" the practice. The agency initiated contact with what is expected to ultimately be about 2,000 charitable organizations to seek information about the compensation they pay. The IRS terms this undertaking its Tax-Exempt Compensation Enforcement Project.

Rents and Loans

A charitable organization generally may lease property and pay rent. The private inurement doctrine, however, requires that where the landlord is an insider—the rental arrangement must be beneficial to and suitable for the organization, and that the rental payments must also be reasonable in amount. Loans between charitable organizations and their insiders are subject to the same standard.

Rental arrangements and terms of a loan involving a charitable organization should be financially advantageous to the organization and in line with its exempt purposes. Where a charity is the borrower and an insider is the lender, the interest charges, amount of security, repayment period, terms of repayment, and other aspects of the loan must be reasonable. The scrutiny will heighten where an insider is borrowing from the charity (assuming state law permits the transaction). If a loan from a charity is not timely repaid, questions of private inurement may be raised. A federal court observed that the "very existence of a private source of loan credit from [a charitable] organization's earnings may itself amount to inurement of benefit."

Some charitable organizations are called on to guarantee the debt of another entity, such as a related nonprofit or even a for-profit organization. The terms of such an arrangement should be carefully reviewed, particularly where an insider is involved. If the loan guarantee does not advance exempt purposes or cannot be characterized as part of a reasonable investment, private inurement may be occurring.

Joint Ventures

Charitable organizations are increasingly involved in partnerships with individuals and/or other joint ventures with individuals or for-profit entities. In a general partnership, all of the partners are subject to liability for the acts committed in the name of the partnership. In a limited partnership, which will have at least one general partner, the limited partners are essentially investors; their liability is confined to the extent of their investment. The general partner(s) in a limited partnership has the responsibility to operate the partnership in a successful manner; this includes efforts to enable the limited partners to achieve an economic return that is worth the commitment of their capital.

In this structure and set of expectations, there is the potential for private inurement. In its worst light, a limited partnership with a charitable organization at the helm can be construed as the running of a business for the benefit of private interests (the limited partners), particularly where the limited partners include or are insiders. This has rarely been the case in the nonprofit organizations context. A partnership (general or limited) basically is an entity formed to attract financing—it is a means to an end. In this fashion, a charitable organization is able to secure the funds of others for a legitimate purpose. As long as involvement in the partnership does not deter the charity from advancing its exempt ends and as long as the limited partners' return on their investment is reasonable, there will not be private inurement—notwithstanding the participation of any insiders.

The IRS is having some success in situations where a tax-exempt charitable organization is involved in a joint venture (usually where the venture vehicle is a limited liability company) to the extent that the entirety of the entity is in the venture. If the charitable organization loses control of its resources to (or, as one court put it, "cedes its authority" to) one or more for-profit companies, the charity will lose its tax-exempt status. This may, however, entail application of the private benefit doctrine (discussed ahead) rather than the private inurement doctrine.

Sanction

The sanction for violation of the private inurement doctrine is loss or denial of the organization's tax-exempt status. There is no other penalty; there is no sanction imposed on the insider who received the unwarranted benefit.

The private inurement doctrine and the intermediate sanctions rules (discussed ahead) have much in common. The general expectation is that the IRS will first apply intermediate sanctions, and invoke private inurement principles (i.e., pursue revocation of tax exemption) only in egregious cases. Nonetheless, it is certainly possible for the IRS to simultaneously apply both bodies of law, thus penalizing both the insider and/or insiders who obtained the excess benefit and the tax-exempt organization that provided it.

PRIVATE BENEFIT DOCTRINE

The body of law that concerns *private benefit* is somewhat different from the law encompassed by the doctrine of *private inurement*. The private benefit doctrine, created largely by the courts, is the more sweeping of the two; it covers a wider range of activities. Most significantly, the private benefit rule does not require involvement of an insider (discussed previously)—this fact alone accounts for its breadth. The law tolerates incidental private benefit. The private benefit doctrine is applicable only to tax-exempt charitable organizations, including private foundations.

The private benefit rule was illustrated by a case involving a nonprofit school, which satisfied all of the federal tax statutory law for exempt status. Individuals were trained there to become political campaign consultants but the graduates of the school seemed to always end up working for candidates and organizations of the same political party. The school's instructional activities did not constitute political campaign activity (discussed ahead). The judge in the case, offended by the fact that all of the school's graduates gravitated to this party's candidates and campaigns, decided to deny tax-exempt status to the school. Thus, he ruled that the school could not be exempt because it provided private benefits in the form of assistance to political candidates by the school's alumni.

The private benefit doctrine has, in recent years, emerged as a potent force in the law concerning charitable organizations. The doctrine is not applied only where individuals are benefited. Private benefit can also occur where the beneficiary is a for-profit corporation, as joint venture law developments attest. Indeed, it is in this context that the doctrine has grown to be so expansive; the very involvement of a for-profit entity in connection with the operations of a charitable organization can trigger application of the doctrine. A federal appellate court wrote: "The critical inquiry is not whether particular contractual payments to a related for-profit organization are reasonable or excessive, but instead whether the entire enterprise is carried on in such a manner that the for-profit organization benefits substantially from the operation of" the nonprofit organization.

In the case that is regarded as on the outer reaches of all this, several for-profit organizations were found to be exercising "considerable control" over the nonprofit entity in question. The for-profit entities set fees that the nonprofit organization charged the public for training sessions, required the nonprofit organization to carry on certain types of educational activities, and provided management personnel paid for by and responsible to one of the for-profit organizations. Because of these and other facts, a court concluded that the nonprofit organization was "part of a franchise system which is operated for private benefit and ... its affiliation with this system taints it with a substantial commercial purpose." The "ultimate beneficiaries" of the nonprofit organization's activities were found to be the for-profit corporations; the nonprofit organization was portrayed as "simply the instrument to subsidize the for-profit corporations and not vice-versa." The nonprofit organization was held to not be operating primarily for charitable purposes.

Indeed, the IRS, supported to some degree by a court, has aggressively begun finding impermissible private benefit conferred by charitable entities on other types of tax-exempt organizations. The court held that an educational foundation affiliated with an exempt business league could not be tax-exempt because its training activities conferred undue private benefit on the association and its members. It is also the view of the IRS that foundations established to provide scholarships to participants in beauty pageants cannot qualify for tax exemption by reason of provision of impermissible private benefit to the exempt social welfare organizations (*id.*) that sponsor the pageants.

The private benefit doctrine posits a proverbial trap for the unwary. The private inurement doctrine (discussed previously) may not apply because of lack of involvement of an insider. The intermediate sanctions rules (discussed ahead) may be inapplicable because there is no disqualified person in the transaction or an exception is available. Nonetheless, the private benefit doctrine may be applicable.

As is the case with the private inurement doctrine, the sole sanction for transgression of the private benefit doctrine is loss or denial of the organization's tax-exempt status.

INTERMEDIATE SANCTIONS

The intermediate sanctions rules are designed to curb and punish abuses in the arena of private inurement using an enforcement mechanism other than revocation of tax-exempt status. These rules are applicable with respect to all tax-exempt public charitable organizations (see Chapter 4) and all exempt social welfare organizations. For this purpose, these two categories of entities are termed *applicable tax-exempt organizations*.

The heart of this body of tax law is the *excess benefit transaction*. A transaction is considered an excess benefit transaction if an economic benefit is provided by an applicable tax-exempt organization directly or indirectly to, or for the use of, a disqualified person (discussed ahead), if the value of the economic benefit provided exceeds the value of the consideration received by the exempt organization for providing the benefit.

The concept of the excess benefit transaction includes any transaction in which the amount of any economic benefit provided to, or for the use of, a disqualified person is determined in whole or in part by the revenues of one or more activities of the organization, where the transaction is reflected in tax regulations and it results in private inurement.

One of the principal aspects of intermediate sanctions is application of them to instances of unreasonable compensation—where a person's level or type of compensation is deemed to be in excess of the value of the economic benefit derived by the organization from the person's services. In that regard, an economic benefit may not be treated as compensation for the performance of services unless the exempt organization clearly indicated its intent to so treat the benefit. When that intent is not properly evidenced, the provision of the benefit is an *automatic excess benefit transaction*.

A *disqualified person* is any person, member of the family of such an individual, or a controlled entity who was, at any time during the five-year period ending on the date of the transaction, in a position to exercise substantial influence over the affairs of the organization. This term is closely akin to the concept of *disqualified person* in the private foundation context (*id.*).

A disqualified person who inappropriately benefited from an excess benefit transaction is subject to an initial tax equal to 25 percent of the amount of the excess benefit. (The intent or good faith of the parties is irrelevant to this determination.) Moreover, this person will be required to return the excess benefit amount (generally in cash) to the tax-exempt organization—this is known as *correction*. An *organization manager* (usually a trustee, director, or officer) who participated in an excess benefit transaction, knowing that it was such a transaction, is subject to a tax of 10 percent of the excess benefit.

An additional tax may be imposed on a disqualified person where the initial tax was imposed and the appropriate correction of the excess benefit transaction did not occur. In this situation, the disqualified person is subject to a tax equal to 200 percent of the excess benefit involved.

A major exception to the intermediate sanctions rules is the *initial contract* exception. These rules do not apply to a fixed payment made by an applicable tax-exempt organization to a disqualified person pursuant to the first contract between the parties. A *fixed payment* is an amount of money or other property specified in the contract involved, or determined by a fixed formula specified in the contract, which is to be paid or transferred in exchange for the provision of specified services or property. An *initial contract* is a binding written contract between an applicable tax-exempt organization and a person who was not a disqualified person immediately prior to entering into the contract.

If a transaction creating a benefit was approved by an independent board of an applicable tax-exempt organization, or an independent committee of the board, a presumption arises that the terms of the transaction are reasonable. This presumption also requires a showing that the board or committee acted on the basis of appropriate data as to comparability and properly documented the transaction. When these three elements are met, the burden of proof shifts to the IRS, which has to overcome (rebut) the presumption to prevail.

In many respects, the concept of the excess benefit transaction will be based on existing law concerning private inurement. The statute, however, expressly states, as noted, that an excess benefit transaction also may include any transaction in which the amount of any economic benefit provided to a disqualified person is determined, at least in part, by the revenue flow of the organization. These transactions are referenced in the legislative history underlying the intermediate sanctions rules as *revenue-sharing transactions.*

The IRS and the courts have determined that a variety of revenue-sharing arrangements do not constitute private inurement. This includes arrangements where the compensation of a person is ascertained, in whole or in part, on the basis of the value of contributions generated, as well as other forms of incentive compensation. The legislative history of the intermediate sanctions rules states that the agency is not bound by these prior determinations when interpreting and applying intermediate sanctions.

The final tax regulations on this subject having been issued, IRS enforcement of the intermediate sanctions rules has begining. Private letter rulings and technical advice memoranda are begin to appear; litigation is underway. This body of law may be expected to be one of the most active components of the overall federal law of nonprofit organizations in the coming years.

LEGISLATIVE ACTIVITIES

Organizations that are tax-exempt because they are charitable must, to preserve the exemption, adhere to a variety of requirements (including those previously summarized). One of these is that "no substantial part of the activities" of the organization may constitute "carrying on propaganda, or otherwise attempting, to influence legislation." This is known as the *substantial part test.* Another set of rules applicable to public charities is the *expenditure test* (discussed ahead); this test, which applies in lieu of the substantial part test, must be elected.

A charitable organization that has lobbying as a substantial activity is an *action organization.* Excessive lobbying can cause a charitable organization to pay excise taxes. In some instances, too much lobbying results in revocation of tax-exempt status.

Lobbying

Legislative activities can take many forms. Some constitute *direct* lobbying, which occurs when one or more representatives of an organization make contact with a legislator and/or his or her staff, and/or the staff of a legislative committee. Direct lobbying includes office visits, presentation of testimony at hearings, correspondence, publication and dissemination of material, email and other Internet communications, as well as entertainment.

Grass-roots (indirect) lobbying is another form. This type of lobbying occurs when the organization urges the public, or a segment of the public, to contact members of a legislative body or their staffs for the purpose of proposing, supporting, or opposing legislation.

Generally, the federal tax rules concerning lobbying and political campaign activities (discussed ahead) are separate, discrete bodies of law. If, however, a nonprofit organization engages in lobbying, particularly grass-roots lobbying, doing so in the context of a political campaign, so that the advocacy of the issue(s) involved can be tied to the political fortunes of a candidate (such as an incumbent legislator pursuing reelection), the lobbying activity can also be regarded as political campaign activity. Undertakings of this nature are known as *public policy advocacy communications*; they are said to have a *dual character.*

The federal tax law prohibition comprising the substantial part test does not differentiate between direct and indirect lobbying, nor does it distinguish between lobbying that is related to an organization's exempt purposes and lobbying that is not. The function remains lobbying; the various types of it are subject to the proscription. A charitable organization, however, that does not initiate any action with respect to pending legislation but merely responds to a request from a legislative committee to testify is not, solely because of that activity, considered an action organization. Also, a charitable organization can engage in nonpartisan analysis, study, as well as research, and publish the results. Even where some of the plans and policies formulated can only be carried out through legislative enactments, as long as the organization does not advocate the adoption of legislation or legislative action to implement its findings, it escapes classification as an action organization.

There can be a fine line between nonpartisan analysis, study, or research, and lobbying. A charitable organization may evaluate proposed or pending legislation and present an objective analysis of it to the public, as long as it does not participate in the presentation of suggested bills to a legislature and does not engage in any campaign to secure passage of the legislation. If the organization's primary objective can be attained only by legislative action, however, it is an action organization.

Legislation

Because these rules obviously apply to legislative activities—activities undertaken in connection with the championing or opposing of legislation—it is necessary to know what does and does not constitute *legislation*. The term *legislation* refers principally to action by the U.S. Congress, a state legislative body, a local council, or similar governing body, and by the general public in a referendum, initiative, constitutional amendment, or similar procedure.

Legislation generally does not include action by an executive branch of a government, such as the promulgation of rules and regulations, nor does it include action by independent regulatory agencies. Litigation activities, including the filing of amicus curiae briefs, also do not entail action with respect to legislation.

Substantiality

The most important concept under these rules is the meaning of the word *substantial*. The law offers no general formula for computing *substantial* or *insubstantial* legislative undertakings.

There are at least three ways to measure *substantiality* in this context:

1. Determine what percentage, of an organization's annual *expenditures*, is devoted to efforts to influence legislation.

2. Apply a percentage to legislative *activities*, in relation to total activities.

3. Ascertain whether an organization had a substantial *impact* on or *influence* over a legislative process simply by virtue of its prestige or because of significant information provided during consideration of legislation.

The true measure of substantiality in the lobbying setting remains elusive. In reports accompanying tax legislation over the years, the Senate Finance Committee characterized this state of affairs well. In 1969, the Committee wrote that the "standards as to the permissible level of [legislative] activities under the present law are so vague as to encourage subjective application of the sanction." In 1976, the Committee portrayed the dilemma this way: "many believe that the standards as to the permissible level of [legislative] activities under present law are too vague and thereby tend to encourage subjective and selective enforcement."

Lobbying Taxes

To give the general restriction on lobbying by charities more strength, there is a system of excise taxes on excess lobbying outlays. If a charitable organization loses its tax exemption because of attempts to influence legislation, a tax of 5 percent of the *lobbying expenditures* is imposed on the organization. This tax, however, does not apply to an organization that is under the expenditure test (discussed ahead) or that is ineligible to make this election.

A separate 5 percent tax is applicable to each of the organization's managers (directors, officers, key employees) who agreed to the lobbying expenditures, knowing they were likely to result in revocation of exemption, unless the agreement was not willful and was due to reasonable cause. The burden of proof as to whether a manager knowingly participated in the lobbying expenditure is on the IRS.

The IRS has, in every instance involving a charitable organization's excessive lobbying, the discretion as to whether to revoke tax-exempt status, impose these taxes, or do both.

Expenditure Test

The *expenditure test* regarding permissible lobbying by charitable organizations arose from a desire to clarify the substantial part test. That is, the purpose of this test is to offer charitable entities some reasonable certainty concerning how much lobbying they can undertake without endangering their tax-exempt status. The test is a safe-harbor guideline.

The expenditure test rules provide definitions of terms such as *legislation, influencing legislation, direct lobbying,* and *grass-roots lobbying.* These terms are essentially the same as those used in connection with the substantial part test. In an attempt to define when the legislative process commences (and, therefore, when a lobbying process begins), however, the expenditure test offers a definition of legislative *action*: the "introduction, amendment, enactment, defeat, or repeal of Acts, bills, resolutions, or similar items."

The expenditure test measures permissible and impermissible legislative activities of charitable organizations in terms of sets of declining percentages of total exempt purpose expenditures. (These expenditures do not include fundraising expenses.) The basic permitted level of expenditures for legislative efforts (termed the *lobbying nontaxable amount*) is 20 percent of the first $500,000 of an organization's expenditures for an exempt purpose (including legislative activities), plus 15 percent of the next $500,000, ten percent of the next $500,000, and 5 percent of any remaining expenditures. The total amount spent for legislative activities in any year by an electing charitable organization may not exceed $1 million. A separate limitation—amounting to 25 percent of the foregoing amounts—is imposed on grassroots lobbying expenditures.

A charitable organization that has elected these limitations and exceeds either the general lobbying ceiling amount or the grass-roots lobbying ceiling amount becomes subject to an excise tax of 25 percent of the excess lobbying expenditures. The tax falls on the greater of the two excesses. If an electing organization's lobbying expenditures normally (on average over a four-year period) exceed 150 percent of either limitation, it will forfeit its tax-exempt status as a charitable organization.

The expenditure test rules contain exceptions for five categories of activities. Consequently, the term *influencing legislation* does not include:

1. Making available the results of nonpartisan analysis, study, or research.

2. Providing technical advice or assistance in response to a written request by a governmental body.

3. Appearances before, or communications to, any legislative body in connection with a possible decision of that body that might affect the existence of the organization, its powers and duties, its tax-exempt status, or the deductibility of contributions to it.

4. Communications between the organization and its bona fide members regarding legislation or proposed legislation that is of direct interest to them, unless the communications directly encourage the members to influence legislation or to urge nonmembers to influence legislation.

5. Routine communications with government officials or employees.

The third of these exceptions is known as the *self-defense exception*. Sheltered by this exception is all lobbying by a public charity, as long as it can be reasonably rationalized as coming within one or more of the allowable forms of lobbying.

The expenditure test contains a method of aggregating the expenditures of affiliated organizations. The intent of these rules is to forestall the creation of numerous organizations for the purpose of avoiding the expenditure test.

Lobbying by Other Nonprofit Organizations

The federal tax law pertaining to tax-exempt status does not impose lobbying restrictions on nonprofit organizations other than charitable ones. The only constraint is that the organization must pursue its exempt functions as its primary purpose (discussed previously) and that any lobbying it may do (other than an insubstantial amount) must further that principal requirement.

Basically, then, entities such as social welfare organizations, labor organizations, business and professional associations, and veterans' organizations may lobby without restriction. Special rules can cause members' dues to not be fully deductible in an instance of lobbying by associations (business leagues). Legislative activities are not normally exempt functions for political organizations.

POLITICAL CAMPAIGN ACTIVITIES

Congress has flatly decreed that charitable organizations may not engage in political campaign activity. In fact, however, these organizations, frequently religious entities, often participate directly and indirectly in political campaigns.

General Rules

The federal tax law states that charitable organizations must "not participate in, or intervene in (including the publishing or distributing of statements), any political campaign on behalf of or in opposition to any candidate for public office." Although this prohibition is framed as an absolute one, minor involvement in politics may not result in loss of tax exemption. As a court observed, a "slight and comparatively unimportant deviation from the narrow furrow of tax approved activity is not fatal."

The concept of an *action organization* (discussed previously) is used in the political campaign context. An action organization includes an entity that participates or intervenes, directly or indirectly, in any political campaign on behalf of or in opposition to a candidate for public office; an action organization cannot qualify as a tax-exempt charitable one. Thus, an exempt charitable organization cannot make a contribution to a political campaign, endorse or oppose a candidate, or otherwise support a political candidacy.

Most of the law amplifying the political campaign proscription for charitable organizations is in IRS rulings. These determinations have, over the years, been uniformly rigid in their finding that nearly any activity relating to a political process will prevent charitable organizations from being tax-exempt. For example, the evaluation of candidates, the administration of a fair campaign practices code, and even assistance to individuals immediately after they have been elected to public office have been found to be prohibited activities.

In recent years, the IRS has relented somewhat, with the agency ruling that voter education activities are permissible for charitable organizations. As an illustration, a charitable organization can prepare and disseminate a compilation of the voting records of legislators on a variety of subjects, as long as there is no editorial comment and no approval or disapproval of the voting records implied. A charitable organization may also conduct public forums where there is a fair and impartial treatment of political candidates.

Some charitable organizations have cautiously entered the political milieu, as part of the process of advancing education (discussed previously). For example, charitable organizations have been permitted to assemble and donate to libraries the campaign speeches, interviews, and other materials of a candidate for a historically important elective office, and to conduct public forums at which debates and lectures on social, political, and international questions are considered. In performing this type of educational activity, however, charitable organizations are expected to present a balanced view of the pertinent facts. Members of the public must be permitted to form their own opinions and conclusions independent of any presented by the organization.

Taxation of Political Expenditures

Federal law levies taxes in situations where a charitable organization makes a political expenditure. Generally, a *political expenditure* is any amount paid or incurred by a charitable organization in any participation or intervention (including the publication or distribution of statements) in any political campaign, on behalf of or in opposition to any candidate for public office.

In an effort to discourage ostensibly educational organizations from operating in tandem with political campaigns, the term *political expenditure* also applies with respect to an organization "which is formed primarily for purposes of promoting the candidacy (or prospective candidacy) of an individual for public office (or which is effectively controlled by a candidate or prospective candidate and which is availed of primarily for such purposes)."

A political expenditure can trigger an initial tax, payable by the organization, of 10 percent of the amount of the expenditure. An initial tax of 2.5 percent of the expenditure can also be imposed on each of the organization's managers (such as directors and officers), where these individuals knew it was a political expenditure, unless the agreement to make the expenditure was not willful and was due to reasonable cause. The IRS has the authority to abate these initial taxes where the organization is able to establish that the violation was due to reasonable cause and not to willful neglect, and timely corrects the violation.

An additional tax can be levied on a charitable organization, at a rate of 100 percent of the political expenditure, where the initial tax was imposed and the expenditure was not timely corrected. Such a tax can also be levied on an organization's manager, at a rate of 50 percent of the expenditure, where the additional tax was imposed on the organization and the manager refused to agree to part or all of the expenditure.

The IRS has, in every instance involving a charitable organization's involvement in political campaign activity, the discretion as to whether to revoke tax-exempt status, impose these taxes, or do both.

Under certain circumstances, the IRS is empowered to commence an action in federal district court to enjoin a charitable organization from making further political expenditures and for other relief to ensure that the assets of the organization are preserved for charitable purposes. If the IRS finds that a charitable organization has flagrantly violated the prohibition against political expenditures, the IRS is required to immediately determine and assess any income and/or excise tax(es) due, by terminating the organization's tax year.

PROHIBITED TAX SHELTER TRANSACTIONS

An excise tax is imposed on most tax-exempt organizations (including private foundations) and/or organization managers that participate in prohibited tax shelter transactions as accommodation parties. This tax can be triggered in three instances: (1) an exempt organization is liable for the tax in the year it becomes a party to the transaction and any subsequent year or years in which it is such a party; (2) an exempt organization is liable for the tax in any year it is a party to a subsequently listed transaction; and (3) an exempt organization manager is liable for the tax if the manager caused the organization to be a party to a prohibited tax shelter transaction at any time during a year and knew or had reason to know that the transaction is such a transaction.

A *prohibited tax shelter transaction* is of two types: a listed transaction and a prohibited reportable transaction. A *listed transaction* is a reportable transaction that is the same as, or is substantially similar to, a transaction specifically identified by the IRS as a tax avoidance transaction. A *reportable transaction* is a transaction as to which information is required to be included with a tax return or statement because the transaction is of a type that the IRS determined has a potential for tax avoidance.

A *prohibited reportable transaction* is any confidential or otherwise contractually protected transaction that is a reportable transaction. A *subsequently listed transaction* is a transaction to which a tax-exempt entity is a party and which is determined by the IRS to be a listed transaction at any time after the entity has become a party to the transaction.

In conjunction with these rules, the IRS requires disclosure of arrangements that it classifies as *transactions of interest*. Unfortunately, the first two of these transactions identified by the IRS arose in the context of charitable giving. One of these transactions concerns a charitable contribution deduction scheme involving transfers of property to charity by means of limited liability companies, in the form of successor member interests designed to (artificially) inflate the value of the donated property to in turn inflate (improperly) the amount of the charitable deduction. The second of these transactions involved charitable remainder trusts (see Chapter 6), where the scheme involved the receipt of the value of the income interest by the grantor, on the sale of the trust's interests, while claiming to not have to recognize any gain, by manipulation of the tax law basis rules.

PERSONAL BENEFIT CONTRACTS

Charitable split-dollar insurance plans, whereby life insurance was the underpinning for forms of endowment-building investment vehicles for charitable organizations, have been effectively outlawed by the federal tax law. That is, the federal tax law denies an income tax charitable contribution deduction for, and imposes excise tax penalties on, transfers associated with use of these plans.

Specifically, there is no federal charitable contribution deduction for a transfer to or for the use of a charitable organization, if, in connection with the transfer, (1) the organization directly or indirectly pays, or has previously paid, any premium on any personal benefit contract with respect to the transferor; or (2) there is an understanding or expectation that any person will directly or indirectly pay any premium on this type of a contract with respect to the transferor. A *personal benefit contract*, with respect to a transferor, is any life insurance, annuity, or endowment contract, where any direct or indirect beneficiary under the contract is the transferor, any member of the transferor's family, or any other person (other than a charitable organization) designated by the transferor.

GOVERNANCE POLICIES

The matter of *governance* has become, for a variety of reasons, the hottest topic in the realm of the law of tax-exempt organizations, primarily public charities. The forces driving this development include congressional investigations into the operations and finances of public charities and other tax-exempt organizations, and the leadership of the component of the IRS that is responsible for overseeing the nonprofit sector (see Chapter 10). One of the principal outcomes of governance developments is the pressure for charitable organizations to promulgate various policies. The fundraiser will rarely be called on to prepare these policies but can become caught up in their requirements.

New Annual Information Return

One of the principal features of the redesigned annual information return (see Chapter 5) is the structuring of the form so that pointed questions are answered by checking a "yes" box or a "no" box, with a check in a "no" box often plummeting the tax-exempt organization into a morass of difficult and uncomfortable questions. Consequently, the organization is not so subtly encouraged to look good in the eyes of the IRS, the public, and the media by having checked only "yes" boxes.

This annual return (Form 990), however, is signed under penalties of perjury, so an organization preparing it is well-advised to be truthful when checking a box "yes." What does it take to check all these "yes" boxes? The answer: adoption of a battery of policies, processes, and procedures, all picked up by the IRS from the efforts of the many undertakings to formulate good governance principles (see Chapter 10):

- A conflict-of-interest policy (Form 990, Part VI, Section B, line 12).

- A whistleblower policy (*id.*, line 13).

- A document retention and destruction policy (*id.*, line 14).

- A process for determining executive compensation (*id.*, line 15).

- A policy or procedure concerning participation in a joint venture arrangement (*id.*, line 16).

- A policy regarding documentation of meetings (Part VI, Section A, line 8).

- A policy or procedure concerning activities of affiliates (*id.*, line 9).

- A process used to review the Form 990 (*id.*, line 10).

- A gift acceptance policy (Schedule M, line 31).

- A policy concerning the acceptance and maintenance of conservation easements (Schedule D, Part II, line 5).

- Procedures regarding international grantmaking (Schedule F, Part I).

- If a hospital, a policy as to charity care (Schedule H,).

- If a hospital, a policy on debt collections (*id.*).

Although not reflected in the Form 990, the IRS also encourages an investment policy and a fundraising policy. Many of the good governance principles advocate adoption of a code of ethics and an expense reimbursement policy.

Fundraising Policy

The Evangelical Council on Financial Accountability (ECFA) best practices standards require that, in fundraising materials, representations of fact, descriptions of the organization's financial condition, and narrative about events be "current, complete, and accurate." "Material omissions or exaggerations of fact" are not permitted. Member organizations are exhorted to "not create unrealistic donor expectations of what a donor's gift will accomplish." Organizations are asked to make efforts to "avoid accepting a gift from or entering into a contract with a prospective donor which would knowingly place a hardship on the donor, or place the donor's well-being in jeopardy." The ECFA practices address the compensation paid to outside fundraisers, require the organization to honor statements made in fundraising appeals, and include adoption of a policy concerning donor confidentiality.

Along these lines, the Standards of Excellence Institute's standards state that solicitation materials should be "accurate and truthful and should correctly identify the organization, its mission, and the intended use of the solicited funds." All statements made by a charitable organization in its fundraising appeals "about the use of a contribution should be honored." A charitable organization "must honor the known intention of a donor regarding the use of donated funds." Charitable organizations should respect the privacy of donors and "safeguard the confidentiality of information that a donor reasonably would expect to be private." These standards likewise address the topic of fundraisers' compensation, including a prohibition on compensation on the basis of a "percentage of the amount raised or other commission formula," and mandate that a charitable organization should contract only with those persons who are "properly registered with applicable regulatory authorities."

The IRS's draft of good-governance principles, which observed that "success at fundraising requires care and honesty" (regrettably, a dubious assumption), stated that the board of directors of a charitable organization "should adopt and monitor policies to ensure that fundraising solicitations meet federal and state law requirements and [that] solicitation materials are accurate, truthful, and candid." Charities "should keep their fundraising costs reasonable." In selecting paid fundraisers, a charity "should use those that are registered with the state and that can provide good references." Performance of professional fundraisers "should be continuously monitored."

The position of the Panel on the Nonprofit Sector is that solicitation materials and other communications addressed to prospective donors and the public "must clearly identify the organization and be accurate and truthful." The Panel stated that a prospective donor "has the right to know the name of anyone soliciting contributions, the name and location of the organization that will receive the contribution, a clear description of its activities, the intended use of the funds to be raised, a contact for obtaining additional information, and whether the individual requesting the contribution is acting as a volunteer, employee of the organization, or hired solicitor." (The derivation of this right, ostensibly possessed by prospective contributors, to know the names of everyone soliciting contributions is not clear.)

The Panel's view is that contributions "must be used for purposes consistent with the donor's intent, whether as described in the relevant solicitation materials or as specifically directed by the donor." The Panel stated that solicitations should "indicate whether the funds they generate will be used to further the general programs and operations of the organization or to support specific programs or types of programs." The Panel advised charitable organizations to "carefully review the terms of any contract or grant agreement before accepting a donation."

An organization must, according to the Panel, "provide donors with specific acknowledgments of charitable contributions, in accordance with [federal tax law] requirements, as well as information to facilitate the donor's compliance with tax law requirements." The Panel noted that, not only is this type of acknowledgment generally required by law, "it also helps in building donors' confidence in and support for the activities they help to fund."

Gift Acceptance Policy

The standards of the Standards for Excellence Institute state that a charitable organization should have policies governing the acceptance and disposition of charitable gifts, including procedures to determine any limits on individuals or entities from which the organization will accept a gift, the purposes for which contributions will be accepted, the type of property that will be accepted, and whether an "unusual or unanticipated" gift will be accepted in view of the organization's mission and "organizational capacity."

The IRS launched an examination program pertaining to charitable contributions of certain successor member interests, involving the questionable use of limited liability companies, ostensibly done to inflate the value of contributed property for deduction purposes (discussed previously). In this connection, the agency developed a prototype document that it is sending to various charities, asking pointed questions that charitable organizations should ponder when considering whether to accept an "unconventional" charitable contribution. These questions include a request for a summary of the economic rights the charity anticipates, the nature of the legal advice obtained in connection with the gift, whether the organization has "guidelines" for accepting "unusual" gifts, and whether the gift transaction was reviewed by the organization's board.

Conservation Easements Policy

Few charitable organizations have the need for a policy as to conservation easements, simply because it is not common for entities to receive this type of property by gift. For a charitable contribution of a conservation easement (or certain other conservation properties) to be deductible, however, the charitable donee must be *qualified* to receive and maintain the property. A policy in this context, therefore, will focus on the organization's ability to properly maintain the conservation property and enforce the terms of the easement (and perhaps other restrictions) placed on it.

Mission Statement Policy

Many aspects of a nonprofit organization's operations can be the subject of a policy (or a procedure or process). Take, for example, the matter of an entity's mission statement (discussed previously). In the summary portion of the annual information return, which is Part I of the return, an organization can describe either its mission or its most significant activity for the year. An organization *must*, however, describe its mission in Part III of the return but can do this only if it has a mission statement that has been adopted by its governing body. Thus, an organization may consider it important to adopt a policy of having a mission statement that has been approved and periodically reviewed by its board.

Conflict-of-Interest Policy

The most venerable of the policies in the bundle of emerging good governance practices involving nonprofit organizations (and the one most heartily insisted on by the IRS) is the *conflict-of-interest policy*. There has long been inherent tension in this area, between the view that conflicts of interest should be prohibited (a wholly unrealistic notion) and the approach that calls for disclosure (and, if necessary, resolution) of one or more conflicts of interest. The conflict-of-interest policy is a manifestation of the latter view.

The Better Business Bureau standards reflect the first of these views, in that they forbid "transaction(s) in which any board or staff members have material conflicting interests with the charity resulting from any relationship or business affiliation." Factors that are considered in determining whether a transaction entails a *conflict of interest* and if so whether the conflict is *material* include "any arm's length procedures established by the charity; the size of the transaction relative to like expenses of the charity; whether the interested party participated in the board vote on the transaction; if competitive bids were sought [;] and whether the transaction is one-time, recurring or ongoing." These standards, however, hint at the utility of a conflict-of-interest policy in the reference to "arm's length procedures established by the charity."

By contrast, the Evangelical Council on Financial Accountability opts for the other approach. One of its best practices requires the organization's members to "avoid conflicts of interest." Having said that, members are allowed to engage in transactions with related parties if (1) a material transaction is fully disclosed in the audited financial statements of the organization, (2) the related party is excluded from the discussion and approval of the transaction, (3) a competitive bid or comparable valuation exists, and (4) the organization's board has demonstrated that the transaction is in the best interest of the entity. The ECFA best practices include (1) adoption of a conflict-of-interest policy covering the governing board and key executives, (2) annual documentation of any potential related-party transactions, and (3) all significant related-party transactions should be initially approved and, if continuing, annually reapproved by the board.

Similarly, the standards of the Standards for Excellence Institute state that a nonprofit organization should have a conflict-of-interest policy applicable to "all board members and staff, and to volunteers who have significant independent decision making authority regarding the resources of the organization." This policy "should identify the types of conduct or transactions that raise conflict of interest concerns, should set forth procedures for disclosure of actual or potential conflicts, and should provide for review of individual transactions by the uninvolved members of the board of directors." The policy should include a statement that provides "space for the board member, employee, or volunteer to disclose any known interest that the individual, or a member of the individual's immediate family, has in any business entity, which transacts business with the organization." This statement should be signed by board members, staff, and volunteers, "both at the time of the individual's initial affiliation with the organization and at least annually thereafter."

The IRS, in a draft of good-governance principles, stated that the duty of loyalty imposed on directors of charitable organizations "requires a director to avoid conflicts of interest that are detrimental to the charity." According to these principles, the board of a charitable organization "should adopt and regularly evaluate an effective conflict of interest policy" that "requires directors and staff to act solely in the interests of the charity without regard for personal interests," includes "written procedures for determining whether a relationship, financial interest, or business affiliation" results in a conflict of interest, and prescribes a "certain course of action in the event a conflict of interest is identified." Directors and staff "should be required to disclose annually in writing any known financial interest that the individual, or a member of the individual's family, has in any business entity that transacts business with the charity."

The Panel on the Nonprofit Sector stated in its principles for good governance and ethical practices for charitable organizations that an organization should "adopt and implement policies and procedures to ensure that all conflicts of interest, or the appearance thereof, within the organization and the board are appropriately managed though disclosure, recusal, or other means." A conflicts-of-interest policy "must be consistent with the laws of the state in which the nonprofit is organized and should be tailored to specific organizational needs and characteristics." This policy "should require full disclosure of all potential conflicts of interest within the organization" and "should apply to every person who has the ability to influence decisions of the organization, including board and staff members and parties related to them."

Whistleblower Policy

The IRS, in its draft of good governance principles, stated that the board of directors of a charitable organization "should adopt an effective policy for handling employee complaints and establish procedures for employees to report in confidence suspected financial impropriety or misuse of the charity's resources."

The Panel on the Nonprofit Sector stated that an organization "should establish and implement policies and procedures that enable individuals to come forward with information on illegal practices or violations of organizational policies." This whistleblower policy "should specify that the organization will not retaliate against, and will protect the confidentiality of, individuals who make good-faith reports." The Panel recommended that "[i]nformation on these policies . . . be widely distributed to staff, volunteers and clients, and should be incorporated both in new employee orientations and ongoing training programs for employees and volunteers." These policies "can help boards and senior managers become aware of and address problems before serious harm is done to the organization" and "can also assist in complying with legal provisions that protect individuals working in charitable organizations from retaliation for engaging in certain whistle blowing activities."

Document Retention and Destruction Policy

The IRS's draft of good-governance principles stated that an "effective charity" will "adopt a written policy establishing standards for document integrity, retention, and destruction." (A charitable organization, however, can be effective, presumably programmatically, in the absence of a document retention and destruction policy.) According to the IRS, this type of policy, which "should include guidelines for handling electronic files," should "cover backup procedures, archiving of documents, and regular checkups of the reliability of the system."

The Panel on the Nonprofit Sector stated that an organization should "establish and implement policies and procedures to protect and preserve the organization's important documents and business records." The Panel observed that a document-retention policy "is essential for protecting the organization's records of its governance and administration, as well as business records that are required to demonstrate legal compliance." This type of policy "also helps to protect against allegations of wrongdoing by the organization or its directors and managers."

Executive Compensation Policy

The ECFA best practices include adoption of an "executive compensation philosophy statement." According to the Standards for Excellence Institute, the board or a committee of it "should hire the executive director, set the executive's compensation," and "periodically review the appropriateness of the overall compensation structure of the organization."

The IRS's draft of good-governance principles stated that a "successful charity pays no more than reasonable compensation for services rendered." (Again, however, there is no correlation between the success of a charitable organization, presumably from a program standpoint, and whether the compensation it pays is reasonable; a charity can pay excessive compensation to, for example, its chief executive and nonetheless be a successful organization in terms of program outcomes.) Charities, said the IRS, "may pay reasonable compensation for services provided by officers and staff."

The Panel on the Nonprofit Sector stated that the board of a charitable organization should "hire, oversee, and annually evaluate the performance of the chief executive officer of the organization, and should conduct such an evaluation prior to any change in that officer's compensation," unless a multi-year contract is in force or the change consists solely of routine adjustments for inflation or the cost of living. The Panel stated that "[o]ne of the most important responsibilities of the board ... is to select, supervise, and determine a compensation package that will attract and retain a qualified chief executive." The organization's governing documents should require the full board to evaluate the executive's performance and approve his or her compensation.

Meetings Documentation Policy

The ECFA best practices include the standard that the organization should "properly document the proceedings of all board and board committee meetings in order to protect the organization" and board minutes "should identify all voting board members as present or absent to clearly document a quorum."

From the perspective of the IRS, the agency will be looking to see whether the meetings of the governing board and any committee with authority to act on behalf of the board are the subject of minutes or a written unanimous consent document. The IRS will also inquire as to whether this documentation is *contemporaneous*.

Annual Information Return Review Policy

The IRS requires an organization to describe, in its annual information return, the process, if any, it uses to have the return reviewed (presumably before it is filed). This review may be by one or more members of the board, one or more officers, one or more staff members, and/or the organization's lawyer. A question on the annual return inquires as to whether a copy of the return was provided to the organization's governing body in advance of its filing.

International Grantmaking Policy

If a charitable organization engages in international grantmaking activities, it should consider adoption of a procedure summarizing the substance of these activities and the grantees involved, including their location. Grantmaking includes awards, prizes, cash allocations, stipends, scholarships, fellowships, and research grants. Grantees can be foreign organizations, governments, and/or individuals. Program services in this context include the provision of assistance, such as food, shelter, clothing, medical assistance, or supplies. This type of policy should be formulated taking into account the concerns of the federal government that U.S. charitable dollars may be funneled to terrorist organizations.

Investment Policy

Oddly, none of the organizations that promulgate good-governance principles have focused on the terms of a nonprofit organization's investment policy. The closest in this regard is the Panel on the Nonprofit Sector standards, which state that the board of a charitable organization "must institute policies and procedures to ensure that the organization (and, if applicable, its subsidiaries) manages and invests its funds responsibly, in accordance with all legal requirements." This two-part admonition is not particularly helpful.

An investment policy should primarily address two elements. One concerns the nature of the organization's portfolio, stating the vehicles and properties in which the organization will invest (or, in some instances, will not invest). This includes stocks, bonds, real estate, partnerships, and investment funds. The other element is the general balance of the portfolio, stipulating the percentages of investments in equities, interest-bearing instruments, foreign investment property, and the like.

Code of Ethics

The ECFA best practices standards include a requirement that the organization adopt a "stewardship philosophy statement." The IRS, in its draft of good-governance principles, stated that the public "expects a charity to abide by ethical standards that promote the public good." According to the IRS, the board of directors of a charitable organization "bears the ultimate responsibility for setting ethical standards and ensuring [that] they permeate the organization and inform its practices." To that end, the board "should consider adopting and regularly evaluating a code of ethics that describes behavior it wants to encourage and behavior it wants to discourage." This code of ethics "should be a principal means of communicating to all personnel a strong culture of legal compliance and ethical integrity."

The Panel on the Nonprofit Sector, in its good-governance principles for charitable organizations, stated that an organization should have a "formally adopted, written code of ethics with which all of its directors or trustees, staff and volunteers are familiar and to which they adhere." This principle is predicated on the thought that "[a]dherence to the law provides a minimum standard for an organization's behavior." The adoption of a code of ethics "helps demonstrate the organization's commitment to carry out its responsibilities ethically and effectively." The code should be "built on the values that the organization embraces, and should highlight expectations of how those who work with the organization will conduct themselves in a number of areas, such as the confidentiality and respect that should be accorded to clients, consumers, donors, and fellow volunteers and board and staff members."

Other Policies

The ECFA standards include adoption of policies concerning board confidentiality and ownership of intellectual property. Some sets of good-governance principles provide that a nonprofit organization have a policy of compliance with all applicable federal, state, and local laws.

The Panel on the Nonprofit Sector, as part of its battery of proposed policies, stated that a charitable organization's board "should ensure that the organization has adequate plans to protect its assets—its property, financial and human resources, programmatic content and material, and its integrity and reputation—against damage or loss." The board "should review regularly the organization's need for general liability and directors' and officers' liability insurance, as well as take other actions necessary to mitigate risks." The Panel noted that the board is "responsible for understanding the major risks to which the organization is exposed, reviewing those risks on a periodic basis, and ensuring that systems have been established to manage them." It was observed that the "level of risk to which the organization is exposed and the extent of the review and risk management process will vary considerably based on the size, programmatic focus, geographic location, and complexity of the organization's operations."

Other policies that a tax-exempt organization should contemplate are:

- A joint venture policy (if it engages in these ventures).
- A policy concerning affiliates (if it has chapters, branches, and the like).
- An expense reimbursement policy (if it is an exempt hospital).
- A charity care and debt collection policy (*id.*).

Policies for Typical Charity

An organization is highly unlikely to need all of these policies. The typical charitable organization, particularly if it is a public charity, should consider having, at a minimum, the following policies in place:

- A policy as to creation and review of the entity's mission statement.
- A conflict-of-interest policy.
- A whistleblower policy.
- A document retention and destruction policy.
- An expense reimbursement policy.

If the charity engages in fundraising, it should consider a fundraising policy and perhaps a gift acceptance policy. Other policies to contemplate are a meetings documentation policy, an investment policy, and an annual information return review policy.

SUMMARY

This chapter provided summaries of the basic federal tax laws applicable to tax-exempt charitable organizations that members of the fundraising community should know, namely, the rules as to form, the organizational and operational tests, the primary purpose test, the various ways an organization can be charitable, the concept of recognition of exemption, private inurement and private benefit, intermediate sanctions, legislative and political campaign activities, prohibited tax shelter transactions, and personal benefit contracts. The chapter concluded with a summary of the various good-governance policies that charitable organizations should consider adopting, including a fundraising policy and a gift acceptance policy.

3

STATE REGULATION OF CHARITABLE FUNDRAISING

Those who manage or advise charitable organizations are often unaware of all of the law—federal, state, and local—that is applicable to the organizations and the individuals involved. Nowhere are the gaps in knowledge more pronounced than in the field of fundraising regulation. The sheer magnitude of state governments' regulation of charitable gift solicitation is often underestimated, even unknown. The purpose of this chapter is to summarize the state laws that regulate the process of fundraising for charitable purposes. (The role of the federal government in this regard is the subject of Chapters 5–8, 10, and 11.) Specifically, this chapter will:

- Survey the scope of state regulation of charitable fundraising.

- Inventory the elements of typical state charitable solicitation acts.

- Survey the various exemptions from state charitable solicitation acts.

- Discuss the powers of state attorneys general in the charitable fundraising setting.

- Summarize the sanctions that these charitable solicitation acts can impose.

- Address developments pertaining to unified registration and like efforts.

- Examine the law issues raised in connection with fundraising by means of the Internet.

FUNDRAISING REGULATION AT STATE LEVEL

Government regulation of fundraising for charitable objectives has tradition-ally been at the state level. Forty-six states have some form of a *charitable solicitation act*—a statute regulating the charitable fundraising process (dis-cussed ahead). Many counties, cities, and towns compound the regulatory requirements with comparable ordinances. Recently, the federal government has also become heavily involved in the regulation of fundraising for charitable purposes.

Most fundraising charitable organizations realize that they must comply with the charitable solicitation act (if any) in effect in the state in which they are principally located. These laws also frequently mandate compliance by pro-fessional fundraisers, commercial co-venturers, and others who assist in fundraising endeavors. Many charities, however, seem to not realize that they are expected to adhere to the law in *each state* in which they are soliciting funds. A charitable organization that is fundraising nationwide should be in annual compliance with these 46 laws. Enforcers of county and city ordinances on fundraising often expect the national charities to comply with their rules as well.

Compliance in this setting varies from state to state, but essentially the term means that a charity must obtain permission from the appropriate reg-ulatory authorities before a fundraising effort can begin. This permission is usually termed a permit or license, acquired as the result of filing a registration statement. Most states also require a filing fee, a bond, and/or the registra-tion of professional fundraisers and others who will assist in the effort. The registration is usually updated by annually filing a report on the fundraising program, including financial information.

This process would be amply difficult if the registration and annual reporting requirements were uniform. The staff time and expense required to obtain, maintain, and disseminate the information throughout the states can be enormous. Historically, there has not been uniformity; recent years have brought limited progress toward use of a uniform registration form by several states (often accompanied nonetheless with schedules requiring varying infor-mation). Charities must constantly face differing registration and reporting forms, accounting methods, due dates, enforcement attitudes, and other sub-stantial twists in the states' statutes, regulations, and forms. All of this becomes much more complex when fundraising by means of the Internet is contem-plated, because then the charity is (presumably) soliciting funds in every state, county, township, city, and town (discussed ahead).

CHARITABLE SOLICITATION ACTS

What follows is an analysis of this type of law, based on the principal features of these acts as found in the majority of these statutes.

Definition of *Charitable*

The obvious purpose of the states' solicitation statutes is to regulate the process of fundraising for charitable purposes. Thus, the definition of the word *charitable* in this context is a major factor in establishing the parameters of these laws. (To a lesser extent, the boundaries of these laws are also set by the scope of the terms *solicit* and *contribution* (discussed ahead).) The meaning of *charitable* in the fundraising law setting is usually much broader than the meaning used for federal tax exemption purposes (see Chapter 2).

The word *charitable*, as employed with respect to state charitable solicitation acts, is sufficiently encompassing to embrace all categories of organizations that are regarded as charitable entities for federal tax exemption and deduction purposes. Therefore, the range of the term includes churches, and conventions, associations, integrated auxiliaries, and similar organizations involving churches; other religious organizations; schools, colleges, universities, libraries, and museums; other educational organizations; hospitals, hospital systems, clinics, homes for the aged, other health care providers, and medical research organizations; other health care organizations; publicly supported charities; and supporting organizations. (See Chapters 2 and 4.)

The state legislatures, however, in defining the term *charitable* for purposes of regulating charitable (or other) fundraising, often additionally sweep within the ambit of these laws some or all of the following purposes: philanthropic, benevolent, eleemosynary, public interest, social service, social advocacy, humane, voluntary, cultural, environmental, artistic, welfare, patriotic, and recreational.

There are states' laws that expressly incorporate within the reach of a charitable solicitation act one or more purposes that otherwise would not be covered under the most reasonably expansive definition of the term *charitable*. Thus, one of these statutes may include within its purview solicitations for *police, law enforcement, legal defense,* or *labor* purposes. This phenomenon may also be reflected in a statute's exemptions, such as a law exempting unions from the registration requirement imposed on charitable organizations.

Some solicitations by nonprofit organizations for contributions lie outside the range of a state's charitable solicitation act because the gifts are not to be used for charitable purposes (again, as that term is reasonably defined). An illustration of this is solicitation of contributions by political organizations or for political campaign purposes. For the most part, these unencompassed solicitations are implicit in a reading of a statute on its face. Sometimes, however, a statute recognizes this fact by means of an exclusion; about ten of these laws are not applicable to solicitations for political purposes.

Some fundraising is undertaken for the benefit of a named individual. It is common for this type of solicitation to be excluded from one or more aspects of this type of regulation. Also, although state regulators disagree on the point, a respectable argument can be made that fundraising for the benefit of one individual is not fundraising for a charitable objective because of the private benefit inherent in the effort. (For federal income tax purposes, an organization benefiting only one individual cannot be a tax-exempt charitable entity.) This issue arises most frequently at the state level when there is public fundraising for a legal defense fund in support of an individual.

No court opinion generally delineates the ultimate scope of these laws, from the standpoint of the boundaries of the term *charitable*. In general, the government officials interpreting these statutes accord the concept of *charitable* great latitude when determining their jurisdiction over fundraising regulation matters.

Definition of *Solicitation*

Another key term usually defined in a charitable solicitation act is the word *solicitation*. This term is generally broadly defined. This fact is evidenced not only by the express language of the definition but also by application of these acts to charitable solicitations conducted, in common terminology, "by any means whatsoever." A solicitation can be oral or written. It can take place by means of an in-person request, postal mail, email, facsimile, advertisement, other publication, television, radio, telephone, cable, Web site, or other medium (see Chapters 1, 5). Contemporary debate over the consequences in law of charitable solicitation by means of the Internet (discussed ahead) highlights the importance and scope of the word *solicitation*.

A most encompassing, yet typical, definition of the term *solicitation*, in the charitable fundraising context, reads as follows: the term *solicit* means any request, directly or indirectly, for money, credit, property, financial assistance, or other thing of any kind or value on the plea or representation that such money, credit, property, financial assistance, or other thing of any kind or value is to be used for a charitable purpose or benefit a charitable organization (discussed previously).

Usually, the word *solicitation* is used in tandem with the word *contribution* (discussed ahead). The term may, however, encompass the pursuit of a grant from a private foundation, other nonprofit organization, or government department or agency. About a dozen states exclude the process of applying for a government grant from the term *solicitation*. Occasionally, state law will provide that the word *contribution* includes a grant from a governmental agency or will exclude the pursuit of a grant from a private foundation. Thus, a charitable organization seeking this type of financial assistance should explore the need to register pursuant to one or more state charitable solicitation acts before submitting the grant proposal.

It is clear, although few solicitation acts expressly address the point, that the definition of *solicitation* entails the *seeking* of a charitable gift (or perhaps, grant). There is no requirement that the solicitation be successful—that is, that the request actually results in the making of a contribution.

One court created its own definition of the term *solicit* in this setting, writing that the "theme running through all the cases is that to solicit means 'to appeal for something,' 'to ask earnestly,' 'to make petition to,' 'to plead for,' 'to endeavor to obtain by asking,' and other similar expressions." This court held that a state's charitable solicitation act did not apply to the conduct of gambling activities held to generate funds destined for charitable purposes.

Definition of *Membership*

The states' charitable solicitation acts often define the words *membership* or *member*. The general purpose, when this definition is provided, is to define the term in relation to the exclusion for solicitations that are confined to the membership of the soliciting charitable organization (discussed ahead).

The statute may define the term *membership* to mean those persons to whom, for payment of dues, fees, assessments, and the like, an organization provides services and confers a bona fide right, privilege, professional standing, honor, or other direct benefit, in addition to the right to vote, elect officers, and/or hold offices.

This type of statutory definition is likely to add the point that the concept of *membership* does not extend to those persons who are granted membership status as a consequence of making a contribution as the result of a solicitation (a ploy that would balloon the exception to the point of hollowing the statute).

Other Definitions

The typical state charitable solicitation act opens with a series of definitions. A fundraising professional is often termed a *professional fundraiser* or a *fundraising counsel*, frequently defined as a person who, for compensation, "plans, manages, advises, consults, or prepares material for" the solicitation in the state of contributions for a charitable organization. This type of person does not "employ, procure, or engage" any compensated person to solicit contributions on behalf of the charity involved. Volunteers or salaried employees of a charitable organization are not a fundraising counsel, nor are lawyers, investment counselors, or bankers.

A *paid solicitor* is often defined as a person who, for compensation, performs for a charitable organization any service, in connection with which contributions are or will be solicited in the state by that person or by any other compensated person the solicitor employs, procures, or engages, directly or indirectly, to solicit. There is often an exclusion from this definition for officers, employees, and volunteers of charitable organizations.

Other terms often defined in these laws are *contribution* (see Chapter 1), *sale* (*id.*), *professional fundraisers, solicitors, commercial co-venturer*, and *charitable sales promotion* (discussed ahead).

Regulation of Charitable Organizations

Generally, every charitable organization desiring to solicit contributions in a state must, in advance, file a registration statement with the appropriate state agency. This requirement applies whether the charity is to solicit on its own behalf or have funds solicited for it by another organization, or be the recipient of gifts generated through the services of a commercial co-venturer or paid solicitor.

If the organization is in compliance, the state issues a certificate of registration; the solicitation can then proceed. The statement must be filed in every year in which the charitable organization is soliciting in the state. A registration fee is imposed.

A charitable organization usually is also required to file an annual financial report with the state. An organization with gross support and revenue not exceeding a certain amount (which varies from state to state) is, however, often excused from filing an annual financial report. Submission of a copy of the annual information return filed with the IRS (see Chapter 5) may sometimes be a satisfactory way to supply this financial information. Where the gross support and revenue of a charitable organization exceeds a certain amount (again, it varies), the organization must submit audited financial statements.

Churches, other religious organizations, and charitable organizations closely affiliated with them usually are exempt from the registration requirements (because of constitutional law concerns). Also often exempt from registration are organizations that engage in small annual solicitations—that is, they do not receive gifts in excess of a certain amount or do not receive gifts from more than a few persons—but sometimes only if all of their functions (including fundraising) are carried on by persons who are not paid for their services.

Under some of these laws, every charitable organization engaged in a solicitation in the state must disclose, at the point of solicitation, its name, address, telephone number, a "full and fair" description of the charitable program that is the subject of the fundraising campaign, and the fact that a financial statement is available on request. Where the services of a paid solicitor are utilized, additional disclosures at the point of solicitation are required (discussed ahead).

Regulation of Professional Fundraisers

Many state charitable solicitation acts go beyond the regulation of fundraising charities and impose obligations on professional fundraisers. The definition of this term varies considerably, thus being an additional source of confusion generated by these laws.

Conceptually, a *professional fundraiser* is a person (an individual consultant or a company) retained by a charity that does not solicit contributions but, rather, designs and oversees implementation of a fundraising program. (As noted, employees of charitable organizations are usually excluded from professional fundraiser status for purposes of these laws.) Normally, they do not take custody of charitable gifts. They are usually paid a fixed fee for their advice and services in structuring a fundraising program.

Thus, under this conceptualization, the actual asking for and receipt of charitable gifts are the functions of others. In the contemporary era, however, this definition has collapsed and the roles overlap. Those who plan may also solicit. Thus, the confusion in these laws mirrors reality.

The registration of professional fundraisers is annual, for a fee. The application contains such requests for information as the state deems appropriate. The bond requirement and amount varies from state to state. Within a stated period (such as 90 days) following the completion of a solicitation, and on the anniversary of the commencement of a fundraising campaign longer than one year, the professional fundraiser must account in writing to the charitable organization for all income received and expenses paid.

Often, every contract between a charitable organization and a professional fundraiser must be in writing. The professional fundraiser must file it with the state prior to performing any material services. From the contract, the state regulator must be able to identify the nature of the services the professional fundraiser is to provide.

Regulation of Paid Solicitors

Confusion as to the regulation of solicitors also reigns throughout the states. A paid solicitor is often required to register annually with the state prior to any activity—using an application containing the information the state may require—and to pay a fee. At that time, the solicitor almost certainly will have to post a bond.

A *paid solicitor* conceptually is an (perhaps the) active participant in the gift solicitation process. He or she literally asks for gifts. This can be done by any form of communication, most likely in person (as in door-to-door or on a street corner), by telephone, or by letter. Other modes are other publications (such as a newsletter or journal), fax, or Internet (as to the latter, see section ahead). Again, however, this fine distinction is often obliterated in modern charitable fundraising.

In many instances, prior to a solicitation campaign, the paid solicitor must file with the state a copy of his, her, or its contract with the charitable organization. In addition, the paid solicitor will likely have to file a solicitation notice with the state. In a typical requirement, the notice must include a copy of the contract, the projected dates when the solicitation will commence and terminate, the location and telephone number from where the solicitation will be conducted, the name and residence address of each person responsible for directing and supervising the conduct of the campaign, a statement as to whether the paid solicitor will at any time have custody of contributions, and a full and fair description of the charitable program for which the solicitation campaign is being carried out.

Often, every contract between a paid solicitor and a charitable organization must be in writing. More than one state patronizingly requires that this document "clearly state the respective obligations" of the parties. The contract may have to provide for a fixed percentage of the gross revenue (or a reasonable estimate of it) from the solicitation effort, which is the amount the charitable organization will (or is expected to) receive. The stated minimum percentage may not include the expenses of the solicitation paid by the charity.

Many of these charitable solicitation acts impose a point-of-solicitation requirement, for which paid solicitors are responsible. Under versions of this rule, before a verbal request or as part of a written request for a contribution, the potential donor must be advised that the solicitor is a paid solicitor and that the charitable organization will receive a percentage of gross receipts as stipulated in the contract. The disclosure must be "clear" and "conspicuous." In an oral solicitation, a written receipt must be sent to the contributor within a short period (such as five days), and it must include a clear and conspicuous disclosure of the point-of-solicitation items.

Following completion of a solicitation campaign (such as within 90 days), and on the anniversary of the start of a solicitation campaign longer than one year, the paid solicitor may be required to file with the state a financial report for the fundraising campaign.

A paid solicitor may be required to maintain certain information during each solicitation campaign and for a significant period of time (such as three years) afterward. This information is likely to include the name and address of each contributor, the date and amount of each contribution, the name and residence address of each employee or other person involved in the solicitation, and all expenses incurred during the course of the solicitation campaign.

Monies collected by a paid solicitor may have to be deposited in a bank account in a timely manner; the account almost certainly will have to be in the name of the charitable organization involved. The charity may have to have sole control over withdrawals from the account.

Special rules may be applicable in situations where paid solicitors represent that tickets to an event will be donated for use by other persons. These rules include limitations on solicitations for donated tickets and record-keeping requirements.

Regulation of Commercial Co-Venturers

Under the laws of some states, every charitable sales promotion must be the subject of a written contract, when a charitable organization enters into an arrangement with a commercial co-venturer. In these instances, a copy of the contract will likely have to be filed with the state prior to the start of the promotion.

The law defines a *commercial co-venturer* as a person who for profit is regularly and primarily engaged in trade or commerce (other than in connection with charitable fundraising) and who conducts a charitable sales promotion. A *charitable sales promotion* is an advertising or sales campaign, conducted by a commercial co-venturer, where there is a representation that the purchase or use of goods or services offered by the commercial co-venturer will benefit, in whole or in part, a charitable organization or purpose. Example: Fast-food restaurant A, located in city B, advertises (by television, radio, and newspapers) that, during weekend C, every time there is a purchase of sandwich D, five cents of the sales amount will be paid to charity E. The promotion is undertaken both to encourage sales and to benefit a charity—hence the term *co-venture.*

The charitable sales promotion contract must include a statement of the goods or services to be offered to the public, the geographic area where the promotion will occur, the starting and ending dates of the promotion, the manner in which the name of the charitable organization will be used (including the representation to be made to the public as to the amount or percent per unit of goods and services purchased or used that will benefit the charitable organization), a provision for a final accounting on a per-unit basis by the commercial co-venturer to the charitable organization, and the date by when and the manner in which the benefit will be conferred on the charitable organization.

The commercial co-venturer is required to disclose in each advertisement for the charitable sales promotion the amount per unit of goods or services purchased or used that will benefit the charitable organization or purpose. This amount may be expressed as a dollar amount or percentage.

The final accounting will probably have to be retained by the commercial co-venturer for a period of time (such as three years) and must be made available to the state authorities on request.

Solicitation Notice Requirements

One of the contemporary trends in the development of state charitable solicitation acts is the growing number and stringency of requirements applicable to professional (or paid) solicitors. The emphasis has been on increased reporting and other forms of disclosure to a government agency, to the charitable organization involved, and/or to the solicited public, particularly by means of a *solicitation notice.*

A typical requirement obligates a professional solicitor to file a solicitation notice with the regulatory body within a relatively short period (such as 20 days) prior to the commencement of a solicitation. This notice, which must be under oath, must include a description of the solicitation event or campaign, the location and telephone number from which the solicitation is to be conducted, the names and residence address of all employees, agents, or other persons who are to solicit during the campaign, and the account number(s) and location of all bank accounts where receipts from the campaign are to be deposited. Copies of campaign solicitation literature, including the text of solicitation to be made orally, must be attached to the solicitation notice. The charitable organization on whose behalf the solicitor is acting must certify that the solicitation notice and accompanying material are "true and complete."

In other states, the solicitation notice may require additional items of information, such as whether the solicitor will at any time have custody of the contributions received, a "full and fair" description of the charitable program for which the solicitation is being conducted, the fundraising materials to be used, the dates when the solicitation will commence and terminate, and information concerning any investigation or litigation regarding the professional solicitor's solicitation activities within the previous six years. Some states also require that a copy of the contract between the charitable organization and the professional solicitor (discussed previously) be attached to the solicitation notice.

Using a somewhat similar approach, a few states require a professional solicitor to provide the charitable organization involved with an accounting after the conclusion of a solicitation. Some states require a solicitor to carry a *solicitation card* that contains certain information and to display the card to prospective donors.

Prohibited Acts

Nearly all of the state charitable solicitation acts contain a list of one or more types of conduct—often termed *prohibited acts*—that may not be lawfully engaged in by a charitable organization (and perhaps not by a professional fundraiser, paid solicitor, and/or commercial co-venturer).

For example, state law may provide that a person may not, for the purpose of soliciting charitable contributions, use the name of another person without consent. Or, a person may not, for gift solicitation purposes, use a name, symbol, or statement so closely related to that used by a charitable organization or government agency that it would tend to confuse or mislead the public.

Other examples of a prohibited act are to lead the public to believe that registration with the state constitutes an endorsement of the fundraising organizations by the state or to represent that a solicitation is for a charitable organization without proper authorization from the organization.

Contracts

Many of the state charitable solicitation acts require that the relationship between a fundraising charitable organization and a professional fundraiser and/or paid solicitor be evidenced in a written agreement. This contract must be filed with the state soon after the document is executed. A few of the states with laws pertaining to commercial co-venturers have a like requirement with respect to contracts between charitable organizations and business enterprises.

Several state charitable solicitation acts contain rules that mandate certain provisions in a contract involving a fundraising charitable organization. The law may require that these contracts (whether with a fundraiser, solicitor, or co-venturer) contain (1) a concise and accurate statement of the charitable organization's right to cancel and of the period during which the contract can be canceled; (2) the address to which any notice of cancellation is to be sent; (3) the address of the state official to whom a copy of the cancellation notice is to be sent; and (4) a statement of the financial arrangement between the parties.

Availability of Records

The information filed in accordance with a state's charitable solicitation act, whether contained in an application for registration, annual reports, contracts, or other documents, is almost certain to be a matter of public record. This requirement encompasses information filed by charitable organizations, professional fundraisers, professional solicitors, and commercial co-venturers.

This type of provision is frequently buttressed by a record-keeping requirement. In almost all instances, this record-keeping obligation is imposed on the soliciting charitable organization. In some states, however, the requirement is confined to professional fundraisers, paid solicitors, and/or commercial co-venturers.

Many of these laws require that the information be maintained, by the regulators and/or the regulated, for a stated period (usually three years). Where the records must be maintained by a regulated entity, such as a charitable organization or a paid solicitor, the law also often requires that the information be open to inspection at all reasonable times by the appropriate state officials.

Fiduciary Relationships

A recent category of provision to emerge in state charitable solicitation acts is the one adopted in a few states, which statutorily (as opposed to by means of the common law) makes professional fundraisers and/or professional solicitors fiduciaries with respect to the charitable organization involved. This designation, among other outcomes, increases the liability under the law of these persons. A typical provision of this nature states that every person soliciting, collecting, or expending contributions for charitable purposes, and every trustee, director, officer, and employee of any such person concerned with the solicitation, collection, or expenditure of such contributions is deemed to be acting in a fiduciary capacity.

Reciprocal Agreements

The law may authorize the state to enter into reciprocal agreements with other states or the federal government for the purpose of exchanging or receiving information filed by a charitable organization in another state, instead of requiring the organization to file under the particular state's law.

EXEMPTIONS FROM SOLICITATION ACTS

Most of the states' charitable solicitation acts provide some form of exemption from their requirements. These laws, however, vary widely with respect to the exemptions available for organizations and types of solicitations. The basic definition of the term *charitable* is sufficiently broad to initially encompass all categories of charitable and other organizations (discussed previously). Therefore, these laws are applicable to fundraising religious, educational, health care, and other charitable organizations, unless an exemption is expressly available to them.

These statutory exemptions may be available for an organization because of the nature of the entity or for an organization to the extent it engages in a particular type of solicitation. The exemption may be from the entirety of the statute or merely a portion of it. In some states, an exemption is not effective until the organization applies for it and is recognized by the state as being eligible to have it.

Exemptions from state charitable solicitation acts are controversial. The policy underlying the exemptions (other than constitutional law concerns in the case of religious organizations) is often questioned, in relation to the fundamental policy that gave rise to these statutes, which is to protect the public against deceptive fundraising. These bodies of law are intended to ward off misrepresentation in charitable giving by ensuring an appropriate flow of information to prospective and actual donors, thus preventing them from being duped into giving in circumstances where the contributions are diverted to noncharitable ends. In this regard, these laws are compared to state and federal securities laws, designed to protect investors against fraudulent sales of stocks and bonds. From this perspective, there ought not be exceptions to state charitable solicitation acts (other than, as noted, for religious entities).

The countervailing view is that these exemptions are valid, inasmuch as those being solicited by the exempted organizations are not *the public*, but rather are members of a class or group—a constituency—that already have trust in, knowledge of, and ample access to information about the fundraising charity. Thus, this line of thinking goes, those who are the subject of these fundraising efforts do not need the protection (afforded by reporting and disclosures) of the charitable solicitation acts. Constituencies of this nature include individuals who are members of an organization, students and their families, and patrons of libraries and museums. These solicitations are seen as *private* ones; to continue with the analogy to securities laws, these statutes differentiate between regulated sales of securities to the public and somewhat unregulated private offerings of securities. (A court held that a state's charitable solicitation act was inapplicable with respect to giving to private foundations, for the reason that the "obvious intent" of the statute is to "regulate those charitable organizations who solicit or accept contributions from persons or corporations *outside the charitable entity*" (emphasis added).)

These competing views often lead to a compromise: exemption of a category of organization from the registration requirements of a state charitable solicitation act, with the organizations in that category subject to the balance of the statute (e.g., reporting and disclosures).

Churches

Churches and their closely related entities are often exempted from the entirety of the states' charitable solicitation acts, in reflection of the view that constitutional law precepts dictate the exemptions. A typical state's fundraising regulation statute accords total exemption to any church or convention or association of churches, where they are primarily operated for nonsecular purposes and no part of the net income of which, inures to the direct benefit of any individual. In many of these states, this exemption is not found within the portion of the statute providing for exemptions but instead is located in the definition of *charitable* entities.

Some states' charitable solicitation laws grant this exemption only to churches and like organizations that have been classified as such by the IRS. These organizations, however, are not required by the federal tax law to obtain recognition of tax-exempt or church status (see Chapters 2, 4) and thus some of them do not have this type of classification; technically, then, these religious organizations are ineligible for this exemption.

Other Religious Organizations

Many states provide an exemption for religious organizations in general from the totality of their charitable solicitation acts. A state law may exclude a corporation sole or other religious corporation, trust or organization incorporated or established for a religious purpose, any agency or organization established for charitable, hospital, or educational purposes and engaging in effectuating one or more of such purposes, that is affiliated with, operated by, or supervised or controlled by a corporation sole or other religious corporation, trust or organization incorporated or established for religious purposes, and other religious agencies or organizations which serve religion by the preservation of religious rights and freedom from persecution or prejudice or fostering religion, including the moral and ethical aspects of a particular religious faith.

It is less common for an exemption for religious organizations to be confined to the registration or other requirements as to preapproval. Some states provide religious organizations with exemption from their registration, and sometimes reporting or like requirements.

Educational Institutions

Some states exempt at least certain types of educational institutions (often with emphasis on higher education) from the entirety of their charitable solicitation acts. Usually, this exemption is applicable only where the institution is accredited. The more common practice is to exempt educational institutions from only the registration or other preapproval, and sometimes reporting requirements.

States may, either as an alternative to or in addition to the foregoing approach, exempt from the registration and reporting requirements educational institutions that confine their gift solicitations to their "constituency." Thus, a state's law may provide an exemption from registration for any other educational institution confining its solicitation of contributions to its student body, alumni, faculty, and trustees, and the members of their families. On occasion, a state may exempt solicitations by educational institutions of their constituency from the entirety of their charitable solicitation laws.

Many schools, colleges, and universities undertake their fundraising by means of related foundations. Foundations functioning on behalf of educational institutions that are operated by state governments are recognized in the federal tax law as public charities. Foundations operating for the benefit of nongovernmental educational institutions are also public charities, either as publicly supported organizations or supporting organizations. (See Chapter 4.)

Several states expressly provide exemption, in tandem with whatever exemption their laws extend to formal educational institutions, to these supporting foundations. (These exemptions raise the question, in the law of the states that do not have them, as to whether these foundations must register even though the institutions they serve are not required to do so.) Some states exempt, from the registration requirements, parent-teacher associations affiliated with an educational institution, alumni organizations, and various types of student groups.

Libraries

Some states exempt nonprofit libraries from the registration and reporting requirements of their charitable solicitation acts. Where an act fails to expressly exempt libraries from its purview, these entities may be able to secure exemption as educational institutions.

Museums

Rarely does a state exempt nonprofit museums from the registration requirements of their charitable solicitation act. A museum may be able to acquire exemption from a state's charitable solicitation act as an educational institution, where express provision has not been made for it in the exemption clauses.

Health Care Institutions

Some states exempt charitable hospitals from the registration or reporting requirements of their charitable solicitation acts. A state may similarly exempt foundations that are related to and supportive of hospitals (discussed previously). A few states exempt nonprofit hospitals from the entirety of their charitable solicitation acts; a state may likewise exempt hospital-related foundations.

Other Health Care Provider Organizations

A few state fundraising laws provide exemption from registration for volunteer rescue associations. A state charitable solicitation act may exempt volunteer ambulance organizations from its registration requirements. A rare exemption from the registration requirements is for licensed medical care facilities, mental health organizations, and mental retardation centers. An exemption from charitable solicitation act registration and reporting requirements may be available for nonprofit organizations that operate facilities for the aged and chronically ill or nursing care facilities. Other exemptions may be in the law for volunteer health organizations and licensed health care service plans.

Membership Organizations

Charitable solicitation acts are designed to apply to solicitations of the public to protect citizens from fundraising fraud and other misuses of charitable dollars (discussed previously and in the discussion of states' *police power* in Chapter 9). In reflection of this rationale, many states exempt organizations (or, in some instances, only certain categories of organizations)—but only from the registration or like requirements—that confine their solicitation to their membership. The boundaries of this exemption are marked by the definition accorded the term *member* or *membership* (discussed previously).

A few jurisdictions exempt organizations soliciting only their membership from the entirety of their charitable solicitation acts. These exemptions are often limited, such as where the solicitation is conducted solely by the members.

Small Solicitations

For administrative convenience and to alleviate the burdens of regulation that would otherwise be imposed, many of the state charitable solicitation acts exempt small solicitation efforts from the registration or similar requirements. The definition as to what constitutes *small*, however, varies considerably from state to state.

A typical provision in a state charitable solicitation act exempts from registration those charitable organizations that do not intend to solicit and receive, and do not actually solicit or receive, contributions from the public in excess of a stated amount (frequently, $10,000) during a calendar year. While there are variations in the phrasing of these provisions, some states provide for this exemption with the threshold set at $25,000; a few states have this type of provision with limitations of $8,000, $5,000, $4,000, $3,000, and $1,500.

Often, this type of exemption is accompanied by a provision that triggers applicability of the registration requirement should contributions exceed the annual threshold amount. Thus, the state statute may include the rule that, if a charitable organization that does not intend to solicit or receive contributions from the public in excess of a stipulated amount during a calendar year does in fact solicit or receive contributions in excess of that amount, the organization shall, within a stated period (e.g., 30 days) after the date the contributions amount reached the limitation amount, register with and report to the appropriate agency.

This exemption may be confined to organizations in which fundraising is conducted wholly by volunteers. A few states provide for this exemption in relation to the entirety of their solicitation acts.

As another approach to the exclusion of small solicitations, some states exempt organizations that do not intend to annually receive or do not receive contributions from more than a stated number of persons (frequently, ten) during a calendar year. On a rare occasion, a solicitation by a charitable organization is exempt where up to as many as 100 persons were solicited.

Solicitations for Specified Individuals

Many states exempt from the registration and reporting requirements of their charitable solicitation acts solicitations that are solely for the benefit of specified individuals. Thus, a charitable solicitation statute may make this type of exemption available for persons requesting contributions for the relief of an individual specified by name at the time of the solicitation when all of the contributions collected without any deductions are turned over to the named beneficiary for his or her use. As this phraseology indicates, this type of exemption is usually voided where professional fundraising assistance is used.

This type of exemption is often in conflict with the concept of solicitations for *charitable* purposes, in that, under the federal tax law, an organization benefiting a named (or specified) individual cannot be a charitable entity. In any event, rarely will this category of solicitations be exempt from the totality of the charitable solicitation act.

Political Organizations

Some states exempt political organizations from the entirety of their charitable solicitation acts. Others exempt political organizations from the registration and reporting requirements of these statutes. This is one of these exemptions that need not be stated, inasmuch as fundraising for political campaign purposes is not fundraising for charitable purposes (see Chapter 1), and thus is always outside the ambit of the states' charitable solicitation acts.

Named Organizations

Some state charitable solicitation acts provide exemption—usually only from the registration requirements—for organizations identified by name. (These provisions are of dubious legality (see Chapter 9).) This practice is evidenced in provisions granting this type of exemption to the American National Red

Cross, named boys' and girls' clubs, named educational institutions, Boy Scouts and Girl Scout organizations, the Junior League, Young Men's and Young Women's Christian Associations, and (in one instance) a named children's trust fund.

Other Categories of Exempted Organizations

The state charitable solicitation acts contain exemptions—usually from the registration requirements—for a variety of other categories of charitable or other nonprofit organizations. The scope of these exemptions is vast; some expressly mandate a filing requirement for the exemption, solicitations only by volunteers to so qualify, an absence of private inurement (see Chapter 2), solicitations only of members, and other limitations and conditions.

This type of exemption, albeit with some restrictions in some states, may include:

- Firefighting organizations

- Fraternal and veterans' organizations

- Social clubs and like groups

- Patriotic organizations

- Historical societies

- Civic organizations

- Nonprofit nurseries or other children's groups

- Certain organizations receiving an allocation from community chests, united funds, and the like

- Federally chartered organizations

- Law enforcement groups

- Community service organizations

- Youth organizations

- Labor unions (like the one for political organizations (discussed previously), an exemption that need not be stated), business and professional associations (same)

- Senior citizen centers

- Grange organizations

- Civil defense organizations

- Civil rights organizations

- Fraternities and sororities associated with a variety of organizations

- Debt counseling agencies
- State-based charitable trusts
- Persons seeking contributions and grants only from corporations and private foundations

One state has an exemption, from the totality of its statute, for all organizations described in section 501(c)(3) of the Internal Revenue Code, that is, for nearly all charitable organizations. This is one of these statutory exemptions that is sufficiently capacious as to leave little for applicability of the general rule.

POWERS OF ATTORNEYS GENERAL

Frequently, a state charitable solicitation act invests the state's attorney general (or, occasionally, another government official) with specific powers in connection with administration and enforcement of the statute. Usually, the attorney general's office is authorized to investigate the operations or conduct of charitable organizations, professional fundraisers, professional solicitors, and others who are subject to the statute, and to issue orders having the force and effect as a subpoena.

The attorney general is often empowered to initiate an action in court to enjoin, preliminarily or permanently, a charitable organization, professional fundraiser, paid solicitor, and the like who engages in a method or practice in violation of the statute or a rule or regulation promulgated in connection with the statute, or employs or uses in a solicitation of charitable contributions a device, scheme, or artifice to defraud, or to obtain money or property by means of a false premise, deception, representation, or promise.

Occasionally, the attorney general is collaterally granted some or all of this authority with respect to individuals or organizations masquerading as charitable organizations or as charitable organizations that are entitled to an exemption from the statutory requirements. Thus, the statute may empower the state's attorney general to institute legal action against a charitable organization or person which or who operates under the guise or pretense of being an organization or person exempted by the act and is not in fact an organization or person entitled to the exemption.

These state statutes usually include the obligatory provision that they may not be construed to limit or restrict the exercise of powers or performance of duties of the attorney general that he or she otherwise is authorized to exercise or perform under any other provision of law. The charitable solicitation act is likely to explicate this principle, by providing that the attorney general must enforce the due application of funds given or appropriated to public charities within the state and prevent breaches of trust in that regard.

SANCTIONS

The means of enforcing a state charitable solicitation act are plentiful. The principal enforcement mechanisms, which come into play on the occurrence of one or more violations of the act, are the following: authorization of the revocation, cancellation, or denial of a registration; authorization of an investigation by the appropriate government officials; authorization of injunctive proceedings; authorization of the levying of fines and other penalties; and authorization of the imposition of criminal penalties (including imprisonment). Many states characterize violations of these statutes as misdemeanors, with specific penalties referenced elsewhere in the state's code of laws.

In some states, a violation of the state's charitable solicitation act simultaneously constitutes a violation of the state's unfair practices or deceptive practices law. In all of the jurisdictions, a person may be found to have committed a fraud against the public, in the setting of the solicitation of charitable gifts.

UNIFIED REGISTRATION

The National Association of State Charity Officials (NASCO) and the National Association of Attorneys General undertook a project to standardize, simplify, and economize the process of registration pursuant to the states' charitable solicitation laws. This project was manifested in the Unified Registration Statement (URS). The URS is part of a larger effort by these organizations to consolidate the information and data requirements of all states that require registration by charitable organizations engaged in fundraising.

The URS effort consists of three phases: (1) compilation of an inventory of registration information demands from all of the states, (2) production of a format (or form) that incorporates all or most of these demands, and (3) encouragement of the states to accept this standardized format as an alternative to their own forms.

Most of the states with charitable solicitation acts are participating in this project. This enterprise is marred to some degree, as a number of states are requesting additional information, entailing supplementary forms, which leads to more complexity.

The URS project addresses only the matter of registration. Once registered, even under this uniform approach, a fundraising charitable organization is on its own in connection with annual reporting and other compliance with these laws. Nonetheless, a project is underway to produce some form of uniform annual report in the fundraising context.

In the interim, it is ironic that the advent of the Internet as a powerful tool for charitable fundraising and charitable giving (discussed ahead) has yet to bring about much registration and reporting in this context by means of this technology. All would be much simpler if there were uniform fundraising registration and reporting, done electronically.

FUNDRAISING BY MEANS OF INTERNET

The Internet has greatly expanded the number of charitable organizations capable of carrying out, and actually engaged in the practice of, multi-state gift solicitation activities. Essentially, to reach potential donors in all of the states, an organization needs nothing more than a computer and an account with an Internet service provider. Once established, the organization's charitable appeal can instantly be sent or made available to the entire Internet community. The large national and international charities with the resources necessary to assure compliance with the various state regulatory regimes are thus no longer the only ones affected by the state charitable solicitation laws. Instead, even the smallest organizations are beginning to tap the national contribution market. Thus, today's technology is altering the nature of communication in the charitable solicitations context—it renders these communications inexpensive.

General Precepts

One of the most difficult of contemporary issues in the nonprofit law setting is whether fundraising by charitable organizations by means of the Internet constitutes fundraising in every state and locality. Current thinking is that, technically, it does. If states asserting jurisdiction over Internet fundraising are justified in doing so (none have made that move to date), the result would be that even the smallest organizations—those too small to afford multistate solicitation efforts using any other medium—would be required to register and report under tens, maybe hundreds, of state and local charitable solicitation laws simply by virtue of utilizing the new communications technology to seek contributions. If they do not or cannot assure state-law compliance, they will be forced to decide between risking adverse legal action in several states or refraining from engaging in this form of speech altogether. The question thus is whether, under this unfolding mix of facts, state laws enforced in this fashion would impermissibly restrict speech protected by free speech principles (see Chapter 9).

There is another question that needs to be addressed. From a legal perspective, should Internet fundraising appeals be treated any differently simply because they take place via the Internet? That is, should communication over this newest medium be treated as anything other than communication, for which there already is a rich regulatory regime? For federal tax purposes, the answer to this question from the IRS is no.

To determine whether the various state charitable solicitation schemes unduly intrude on the protected speech interest in this type of solicitation, the existing regulatory framework must be applied to the new set of facts. The first step in this analysis is to ascertain whether the act of an organization in placing an appeal for funds in a document on a computer in one state subjects the organization to the jurisdiction of one or more other states. There is as yet no law directly on this subject. Nonetheless, while not directly on point, a court opinion sheds some light on the matter.

A federal court of appeals had the opportunity to discuss the legal status of computer-borne communications in the First Amendment context. Two individuals operated an adult-oriented bulletin board service from their home. This site was accessible to others around the nation via modems and telephone lines.

Working with a U.S. Attorney's office in another state, a postal inspector purchased a membership in this bulletin board service and succeeded in downloading allegedly obscene images from the bulletin board. The U.S. Attorney's office filed criminal charges against these individuals for, among other reasons, transmitting obscenity over interstate telephone lines from their computer. The images involved were found by a jury to constitute obscene materials; the couple was convicted.

On appeal, this federal appellate court affirmed the convictions, holding that the crime of "knowingly us[ing] a facility or means of interstate commerce for the purpose of distributing obscene materials" did not require proof that the defendants had specific knowledge of the destination of each transmittal at the time it occurred. Of interest in the Internet setting, in determining that the crime occurred in the second state, the court placed considerable weight on its finding that "substantial evidence introduced at trial demonstrated that the . . . [bulletin board service] was set up so members located in other jurisdictions could access and order [obscene] files which would then be instantaneously transmitted in interstate commerce."

If state courts follow the reasoning of this appellate court, it appears that communication via computer constitutes sufficient contact with foreign states to subject the communicator to local law requirements. Applied in the charitable solicitation regulation context, then, the import of this court decision is clear: Soliciting funds by means of the Internet, where users residing in foreign jurisdictions download Web pages, in all likelihood will constitute sufficient contact to subject the organization to the jurisdiction of the foreign state or states and therefore to the foreign charitable solicitation regulatory regime or regimes.

It must next be determined whether interstate communication of this nature constitutes solicitation encompassed by the fundraising regulations laws of the states. Although a definite answer cannot be divined from the language of any one statute, a brief survey of some state laws strongly indicates that Internet solicitation will be held in many jurisdictions to be subject to regulation.

For example, in one state, *solicitation* embraced by the charitable solicitation act is defined as the making of a fundraising request "through any medium," regardless of whether any contribution is actually received. In another state, the charitable solicitation law applies to all "request[s] of any kind for a contribution." The statutory scheme in another state applies to "any request, plea, entreaty, demand or invitation, or attempt thereof, to give money or property, in connection with which . . . any appeal is made for charitable purposes." In still another state, the law applies to organizations "soliciting or collecting by agents or solicitors, upon ways or in and other public places within the [state] to which the public have a right of access."

Certainly it is difficult to see how Internet fundraising is not encompassed by any of these strikingly broad provisions. As currently written, then, the statutes of at least five states can easily be construed to reach Internet charitable fundraising.

Indeed, it is likely that most, if not all, of the state charitable fundraising regulation regimes could be so construed and that these statutes that fail as currently written can be appropriately amended without much trouble.

Charleston Principles

If the assumption is that the solicitation of funds (and perhaps other property) by charitable and other nonprofit organizations by means of the Internet constitutes, as a matter of law, fundraising in every state (and municipality), then, as suggested, the charitable community is facing an enormous burden. Many in the regulatory sector realize that, if this technically is the law, some form of relief for charities that solicit gifts by means of the Internet is warranted.

To this end, the NASCO developed guidelines to assist state regulators, charitable organizations that solicit contributions, and their fundraisers, in deciding whether it is necessary to register fundraising efforts in one or more states when the solicitations are made by email or on the organizations' Web sites. These guidelines are a product of discussion initiated at a NASCO conference in Charleston, South Carolina; hence the guidelines are termed the "Charleston Principles" (Principles). The Principles are not law but, rather, nonbinding guidance to NASCO members.

The Principles rest on this proposition: "Existing registration statutes generally, of their own terms, encompass and apply to Internet solicitations." An unstated assumption is that it is untenable to require registration and reporting of all charities soliciting gifts solely by means of the Internet, and their fundraisers, in all of the states with reporting requirements. Thus, the scope of potential registration must be narrowed or, as the Principles put it, state charity officials should "address the issue of who has to register where."

The Principles differentiate between entities that are domiciled in a state and those that are domiciled outside the state. (An entity is *domiciled* in a state if its principal place of business is in that state.)

An entity that is domiciled in a state and uses the Internet to conduct charitable solicitations in that state must, according to the Principles, register in that state. This position reflects the prevailing view that the Internet is a form of communication and the law does not make a distinction between that type of communication and another (such as use of regular mail). The rule applies "without regard to whether the Internet solicitation methods it uses are passive or interactive, maintained by itself or another entity with which it contracts, or whether it conducts solicitations in any other manner."

Matters become more complex in situations where an entity is fundraising, using the Internet, in a state in which it is not domiciled. Registration in the state is nonetheless required if:

- The organization's non-Internet activities alone are sufficient to require registration.
- It solicits contributions through an interactive Web site.
- The entity
  - Specifically targets persons physically located in the state for solicitation.
  - Receives contributions from donors in the state on a repeated and ongoing basis or a substantial basis through its Web site.
  - The entity solicits contributions through a site that is not interactive but either specifically invites further offline activity to complete a contribution or establishes other contacts with that state, such as sending email messages or other communications that promote the Web site, and the entity engages in one of the foregoing two activities.

Often considerable line drawing will be required in the application of these guidelines. The matter becomes more intricate when some definitions are factored in.

An *interactive Web site* is a site that "permits a contributor to make a contribution, or purchase a product in connection with a charitable solicitation, by electronically completing the transaction, such as by submitting credit card information or authorizing an electronic fund transfer." These sites include those through which a donor "may complete a transaction online through any online mechanism processing a financial transaction even if completion requires the use of linked or redirected sites." A Web site is considered *interactive* if it has this capacity, irrespective of whether donors actually use it.

The phrase specifically targets persons physically located in the state for solicitation means to engage in one of two practices:

1. Include on the Web site an express or implied reference to soliciting contributions from persons in that state.

2. Otherwise affirmatively appeal to residents of the state, such as by advertising or sending messages to persons located in the state (electronically or otherwise) when the entity knows, or reasonably should know, that the recipient is physically located in the state.

Charities operating on a "purely local basis" or within a "limited geographic area" do not target states outside their operating area if their Web site makes clear in context that their fundraising focus is limited to that area, even if they receive contributions from outside that area on less than a repeated and ongoing basis or on a substantial basis.

To receive contributions from a state on a *repeated and ongoing basis* or a *substantial basis* means "receiving contributions within the entity's fiscal year, or relevant portion of a fiscal year, that are of sufficient volume to establish the regular or significant (as opposed to rare, isolated, or insubstantial) nature of these contributions."

States are encouraged to set, and communicate to the regulated entities, "numerical [sic] levels at which it [sic] will regard this criterion as satisfied." These levels should, the Principles provide, define *repeated and ongoing* in terms of a number of contributions and *substantial* in terms of a dollar amount of contributions or percentage of total contributions received by or on behalf of the charity. The meeting of one of these thresholds would give rise to a registration requirement but would not limit an enforcement action for deceptive solicitations.

Another Principle is that an entity that solicits via email in a particular state is to be treated the same as one that solicits by means of telephone or direct mail, if the soliciting party knew or reasonably should have known that the recipient was a resident of or was physically located in that state.

The Principles address the circumstance as to whether a charity is required to register in a particular state when the operator of a Web site, through which contributions for that charity are solicited or received, is required to register but the charity does not independently satisfy the registration criteria. If the law of the state does not universally require the registration of all charities on whose behalf contributions are solicited or received through a commercial fundraiser, commercial co-venturer, or fundraising counsel who is required to register, then the state should independently apply the criteria to each charity and only require registration by charities that independently meet the tests. If, however, the law of the state universally requires registration of all charities under these circumstances, the state should consider whether, as a matter of "prosecutorial discretion, public policy, and the prioritized use of limited resources," it would take action to enforce registration requirements as to charities that do not independently meet the criteria.

Still another Principle is that solicitations for the sale of a product or service that include a representation that some portion of the price shall be devoted to a charitable organization or charitable purpose (commercial co-venturing, charitable sales promotion, or cause-related marketing) shall be governed by the same standards as otherwise set out in the Principles governing charitable solicitations.

There are two exclusions from the registration requirements. One is that maintaining or operating a Web site that does not contain a solicitation of contributions but merely provides program services, by means of the Internet, does not, by itself, invoke a requirement to register. This is the case even if unsolicited contributions are received.

The other exclusion is for entities that solely provide administrative, supportive, or technical services to charities without providing substantive content or advice concerning substantive content; they are not required to register. These entities include Internet service providers and organizations that do no more than process online transactions for a separate firm that operates a Web site or provide similar services. This exclusion does not encompass professional fundraisers, fundraising counsel, or commercial co-venturers.

The Principles provide that state charity officials "recognize that the burden of compliance by charitable organizations and their agents, professional fundraisers, commercial co-venturers and/or professional fundraising counsel should be kept reasonable in relation to the benefits to the public achieved by registration." Projects to create "common forms," such as the unified registration statement (discussed previously), are "strongly encouraged."

State charity offices are also "strongly encouraged" to publish their registration and reporting forms, their laws and regulations, and other related information on the Internet to facilitate registration and reporting by charitable organizations and their agents.

The Principles encourage development of information technology infrastructure to facilitate electronic registration and reporting. Also encouraged is Internet posting by charitable organizations of their application for recognition of tax-exempt status, their IRS determination letter, their most recent annual information returns, and their state registration statement(s). (This posting practice is also encouraged by the federal tax law, which obviates the need to provide hard copies of these federal documents to requestors when they are made available on the Internet (see Chapter 8).)

IMPACT ON FEDERAL REGULATION

Occasionally, the interpretation of state law fundraising concepts can have implications for federal law enforcement. For example, in a case brought on behalf of the Federal Trade Commission (FTC), filed in the fall of 2007, the federal government asserted that a for-profit organization violated an FTC order that it not misrepresent the use of charitable contributions. The outcome of this case will be determined, in part, on whether the organization is considered to be a fundraising consultant or a solicitor.

SUMMARY

One of the most frustrating bodies of law pestering charitable organizations is fundraising regulation by the state governments. This chapter surveyed the scope of state regulation of charitable fundraising and summarized the elements of typical state charitable solicitation acts, including the law regulating professional fundraisers, paid solicitors, and commercial co-venturers. The chapter surveyed the various exemptions from state charitable solicitation acts, discussed the powers of state attorneys general in the charitable fundraising setting, and summarized the sanctions that these charitable solicitation acts can impose. The chapter also addressed developments pertaining to unified registration and like efforts. It concluded by analyzing fundraising by means of the Internet—and the host of new legal issues that are being raised.

4

PUBLIC CHARITIES AND PRIVATE FOUNDATIONS

The principal purpose of this chapter is to explain the distinctions between *private foundations* and *public charities*. This subject is critical to the fundraiser. Fundamentally, a private foundation is not likely to engage in much, if any, fundraising. Public charities, however, often solicit contributions; the fundraiser needs to know the public charity status of the entity he, she, or it is serving, particularly in the charitable giving context (see Chapter 6). There are, moreover, various types of public charities and likewise different types of private foundations. Specifically, this chapter will:

- Provide a generic and a technical definition of the term *private foundation*.

- Explain the terms *private operating foundations, exempt operating foundations, conduit private foundations,* and *nonexempt charitable trusts*.

- Summarize the private foundation rules.

- Explain the concept of a *public charity*.

- Define the public charities that are the *institutions*.

- Define the public charities that are the *donative publicly supported charities*.

- Define the public charities that are the *service provider publicly supported charities*.

- Provide a comparative analysis of publicly supported charities.

- Define the public charities that are *supporting organizations*.

- Define the public charities that *test for public safety*.

- Explain the significance of the private foundation–public charity dichotomy.

- Review some of the most recent IRS statistics on these subjects.

PRIVATE FOUNDATION DEFINED

A *private foundation* is a form of tax-exempt charitable organization. In this context, the term *charitable* includes program undertakings that are classified as educational, scientific, and religious. Generically, however, a private foundation typically has four other characteristics:

1. A private foundation is usually funded from a single source, often an individual, a family, or a corporation.

2. This funding is usually a one-time occasion, by means of a sizeable charitable contribution. While a private foundation may receive an ongoing flow of gifts, that is a rarity.

3. The year-by-year revenue derived by a private foundation is almost always in the form of investment income earned on their assets (also known as *principal* or *corpus*).

4. The typical private foundation makes grants for charitable purposes to other persons (individuals and/or organizations), rather than conduct its own programs.

The *private* aspect of the concept of a private foundation, then, principally reflects the nature of its financial support, particularly its initial funding. The *private* nature of a foundation, however, is often reflected in its governing board structure.

Because private foundations are generally exempt from federal income tax, the term *private foundation* appears in the Internal Revenue Code. This technical tax law definition, however, does not match the generic definition. Congress could have crafted a definition of private foundation in accord with the four unique attributes of foundations but it elected another approach. The reason for this distinction is rooted in the history of private foundation law, which came into being in 1969.

When most of the law as to private foundations was created in that year, Congress was in a horrific anti-foundation mood. The antipathy toward foundations at that time was substantial, largely because members of Congress were being regaled with tales of foundation abuse (mostly apocryphal) and many were in a populist mindset, with foundations seen as playthings (and pocketbooks) of the wealthy. Consequently, when fashioning a definition of the term

private foundation, Congress was careful to write it in such a way as to minimize the likelihood that crafty tax lawyers would find ways around the foundation laws.

Thus, the technical definition of *private foundation* has two key characteristics. One, despite the fact that the Internal Revenue Code purports to define
the term, it does not. Instead, the Code defines what a private foundation is
not. (A private foundation is a tax-exempt charitable organization that is not
a public charity.) Two, a unique feature in the law causes every tax-exempt
charity in the United States to be *presumed* to be a private foundation. Among
other outcomes, this forces nearly all charities that are not private foundations
to convince the Internal Revenue Service of that fact and be officially classified
as public entities. Put another way, a charitable organization that cannot, or
subsequently fails to, qualify as a public charity is, by operation of law, a private
foundation.

PRIVATE OPERATING FOUNDATIONS

As noted, one of the characteristics of a conventional private foundation is
that it is a grantmaker. That is, the typical foundation serves as a funder of
the charitable programs of other organizations. There are some private foundations, however, that, instead of grantmaking, use their funds principally to
administer their own charitable programs. This type of private foundation
is known as a *private operating foundation*, with the word *operating* intended
to convey this feature of internal program operations (rather than external
funding). (These foundations are exempt from the standard income distribution requirement imposed on most foundations (discussed ahead).) Some
museums, libraries, housing and health care facilities, and scientific research
entities, for example, are structured as private operating foundations.

To qualify as an operating foundation, a private foundation must meet
an income test and one of three other tests: an assets test, an endowment test,
or a support test.

A private foundation satisfies the *income test* if it expends at least 85 percent of the lesser of its (1) *minimum investment return* (which is an amount equal
to 5 percent of the value of the foundation's investment assets) or (2) adjusted
net income for the direct, active conduct of charitable activities. *Adjusted net
income* is the amount of income from charitable functions, investment activities, set-asides, unrelated business, and short-term capital gains that exceeded
the cost incurred in earning the income.

To meet the *assets test*, a private foundation must directly use at least 65
percent of its assets for the active conduct of charitable activities. Satisfaction of
the *endowment test* requires that the foundation regularly make distributions for
the active conduct of charitable activities in an amount not less than two-thirds
of its minimum investment return. To meet the *support test*, a private foundation
must regularly receive substantially all of its support (other than from gross

investment income) from the public or from five or more qualifying exempt organizations; receive no more than 25 percent of its support (other than from gross investment income) from any one qualifying exempt organization; and receive no more than 50 percent of its support in the form of gross investment income.

EXEMPT OPERATING FOUNDATIONS

Certain private operating foundations are exempt from the excise tax on net investment income paid by most private foundations (discussed ahead). This type of operating foundation must maintain public support for a minimum of ten years; maintain a governing body at all times that is broadly representative of the public, where no more than 25 percent of that board consists of disqualified individuals; and not have at any time during the year an officer who is a disqualified individual. These foundations are also exempt from the expenditure responsibility requirements.

CONDUIT FOUNDATIONS

A *conduit private foundation* is not a separate category of private foundation; it is a standard private foundation that, under certain circumstances, is regarded as a public charity for charitable contribution deduction purposes. A foundation functions as a conduit when it makes qualifying distributions that are treated as distributions from its corpus in an amount equal to 100 percent of all contributions received in the year involved, whether as money or property. These distributions, to qualify, must be made not later than the 15th day of the third month after the close of the foundation's tax year in which the contributions were received. The foundation must not have any remaining undistributed income for the year.

These distributions are treated as made first out of contributions of property and then out of contributions of money received by the private foundation in the year involved. The distributions cannot be made to an organization controlled, directly or indirectly, by the distributing foundation or by one or more disqualified persons with respect to the foundation or to a private foundation that is not a private operating foundation (discussed previously).

NONEXEMPT CHARITABLE TRUSTS

Nonexempt charitable trusts are trusts that are not tax-exempt but are treated as private foundations for federal tax law purposes. These trusts are funded and operated in nearly identical fashion as exempt private foundations. This type of trust has exclusively charitable interests; donors to them are allowed to claim a tax deduction for charitable contributions. Unlike private foundations, nonexempt charitable trusts are required to pay an annual tax on income that is not distributed for charitable purposes.

PRIVATE FOUNDATION RULES

Private foundations are subject to several unique rules. A number of them are predicated on an understanding of persons who are *disqualified persons* with respect to the foundation. These persons are foundation trustees, directors, officers, and key employees, as well as members of these individuals' families. Disqualified persons also include substantial contributors and certain controlled entities (such as corporations, trusts, and estates). In general, a *substantial contributor* is a person who contributes, grants, or bequeaths an aggregate amount of more than $5,000 to a charitable organization, where that amount is more than 2 percent of the total contributions, grants, and bequests received by the organization before the close of its tax year in which the contribution or the like from the person is received.

The private foundation rules are underlain with a series of penalty taxes. These rules essentially prohibit most forms of self-dealing between a private foundation and a disqualified person with respect to it, require foundations to adhere to a mandatory payout formula (an amount equal to 5 percent of the value of the organization's noncharitable assets), forbid holdings in nearly all business enterprises, place limits on forms of investment activity, and prohibit forms of expenditures, such as those for most forms of lobbying and political campaign activities and for other noncharitable purposes. Private foundations must pay an excise tax (usually 2 percent) on their net investment income.

CONCEPT OF PUBLIC CHARITY

The dichotomy thus established in the Internal Revenue Code forces every U.S. charity to be classified as a public charity or a private foundation. This is by no means an equal division, in that, while there are millions of public charities, there are about 80,000 private foundations (discussed ahead). (This disparity as to numbers, however, is not reflected in any balancing of the volume of federal tax law concerning charitable organizations; there are many pages of rules in the Internal Revenue Code that are applicable only to private foundations.)

As noted, a private foundation is a tax-exempt charitable organization that is not a public charity. The Code "definition" of *private foundation* focuses on the meaning of the term *public charity*. There are many categories of public charities. From a big-picture standpoint, however, there are four types of public charities: the *institutions, publicly supported charities, supporting organizations,* and (of minor import) *public safety testing organizations.*

As will be seen, public charities tend to be organizations with inherently *public* activity, entities that are financially supported by the public, or entities that have a close operating relationship with one or more other public charities. The term *public* can, however, be misleading; it is not used in the sense of a governmental entity (department, agency, and the like). The confusion is emblematic in the notion that a private school is a public charity. (Governmental entities are public charities.)

Most private foundations confine their grantmaking to public charities. Therefore, it is essential (to avoid tax penalties) that foundations having that approach understand the various ways in which a tax-exempt charitable organization can also be a public charity.

INSTITUTIONS

A category of public charity is loosely defined as *institutions*. These are entities that have inherently public activity. Embraced by the ambit of the institutions are churches, certain other religious organizations, schools, colleges, universities, hospitals, medical research organizations, and governmental units.

Churches

A *church* (including a synagogue and a mosque) is a public charity. The federal tax law is imprecise in defining this term, largely due to constitutional law (First Amendment) constraints. Although the term is not defined in the Internal Revenue Code, the IRS formulated criteria that it uses to ascertain whether a religious organization constitutes a *church*. Originally, these criteria (unveiled in 1977) were in a list of 14 elements, not all of which needed to be satisfied. These elements include:

- A distinct legal existence
- A recognized creed and form of worship
- An ecclesiastical government
- A formal code of doctrine and discipline
- A distinct religious history
- A literature of its own
- Established places of worship
- Regular congregations
- Regular religious services
- Schools for the religious instruction of youth and preparation of its ministers

Over the ensuing years, however, the IRS has added criteria and become more rigid (and inconsistent) in its interpretation of the term *church*. It is currently the position of this agency that, to be a church, an organization must—in addition to being *religious*—have a defined congregation of worshippers, an established place of worship, and regular religious services. Some of the criteria in the original 14-element list have been downgraded in importance, as being common to tax-exempt organizations in general.

Associations and Conventions of Churches

Some religious entities are public charities because all of their members are churches. An *association of churches* is a church-membership entity where the membership is confined to churches in a state. A *convention of churches* is a church-membership entity where the membership embraces a multistate region of the United States or perhaps the entire nation.

Educational Institutions

An *educational institution* is a public charity. The concept of what is *educational* is much broader than *educational institution*, so it is insufficient for these purposes that an organization is merely educational in nature. To be an educational institution, an organization must normally maintain a regular faculty and curriculum, and normally have a regularly enrolled body of pupils or students in attendance at the place where its educational activities are regularly carried on. This type of institution is generically a *school*; consequently, it must have as its primary function the presentation of formal instruction.

Educational institutions that qualify for public charity status include primary, secondary, preparatory, and high schools, in addition to colleges and universities. (Public schools are public charities by virtue of being units of government (discussed ahead).) An organization cannot achieve public charity status as an operating educational institution where it is engaged in both educational (institution-type) and educational (non-institution-type) activities, unless the latter activities are merely incidental to the former. For example, an organization cannot qualify as this type of public charity if its primary function is the operation of a museum, rather than the presentation of formal instruction.

A *university* generally is an institution of higher learning with teaching and research facilities, comprising an undergraduate school that awards bachelor's degrees and a graduate school and professional schools that award master's or doctor's degrees. A *college* is generally referred to as a school of higher learning that grants bachelor's degrees in liberal arts or sciences; the term is also frequently used to describe undergraduate divisions or schools of a university that offer courses and grant degrees in a particular field. The term *school* is defined as a division of a university offering courses of instruction in a particular profession; the term is also applicable to institutions of learning at the primary and secondary levels of education.

An organization may be regarded as presenting formal instruction even though it lacks a formal course program or formal classroom instruction. For example, an organization that conducted a survival course was classified as a public charity, even though its course periods were only 26 days and it used outdoor facilities more than classrooms; it had a regular curriculum, faculty, and student body. By contrast, an organization, the primary activity of which was providing specialized instruction by correspondence and a five- to ten-day seminar program of personal instruction for students who completed the correspondence course, did not qualify as an operating educational institution.

Even if an organization qualifies as a school or other type of formal educational institution, it will not be able to achieve public charity (or tax-exempt) status if it maintains racially discriminatory admissions policies or if it benefits private interests to more than an insubstantial extent. As an illustration of the latter, an otherwise qualifying school that trained individuals for careers as political campaign professionals was denied exempt status because of the private benefit accruing to a national political party and its candidates, inasmuch as nearly all of the school's graduates became employed by or consultants to the party's candidates.

Hospitals

A tax-exempt organization, the principal purpose or functions of which are the provision of medical or hospital care, medical education, or medical research, if the organization is a hospital, is a public charity. The term *hospital* includes exempt federal government hospitals, state, county, and municipal hospitals that are instrumentalities of governmental units, rehabilitation institutions, outpatient clinics, extended care facilities, or community mental health or drug treatment centers, and cooperative hospital service organizations. This term does not include convalescent homes, homes for children or the elderly, or institutions the principal purpose or function of which is to train disabled individuals to pursue a vocation, nor does it include free clinics for animals. The term *medical care* includes the treatment of any physical or mental disability or condition, whether on an inpatient or outpatient basis, as long as the cost of the treatment is deductible by the individual treated.

Medical Research Organizations

A *medical research organization* directly engaged in the continuous active conduct of medical research in conjunction with a public charity hospital can qualify as a public charity. The term *medical research* means the conduct of investigations, experiments, and studies to discover, develop, or verify knowledge relating to the causes, diagnosis, treatment, prevention, or control of physical or mental diseases and impairments of human beings. To qualify, an organization must have the appropriate equipment and professional personnel necessary to carry out its principal function. *Medical research* encompasses the associated disciplines spanning the biological, social, and behavioral sciences.

An organization, to be a public charity under these rules, must have the conduct of medical research as its principal purpose or function and be primarily engaged in the continuous active conduct of medical research in conjunction with a qualified hospital. The organization need not be formally affiliated with an exempt hospital to be considered primarily engaged in the active conduct of medical research in conjunction with the hospital. There must, however, be a joint effort on the part of the research organization and the hospital to maintain close cooperation in the active conduct of the medical research. An organization is not considered to be primarily engaged directly in the continuous active conduct of medical research unless it, during a computation period, devotes more than one-half of its assets to the continuous active conduct of medical research or it expends funds equaling at least 3.5 percent of the fair market value of its endowment for the continuous active conduct of medical research.

If an organization's primary purpose is to disburse funds to other organizations for the conduct of research by them or to extend research grants or scholarships to others, it is not considered directly engaged in the active conduct of medical research.

Public College Support Foundations

Public charity status is accorded to certain organizations providing support for public (governmental) colleges and universities. This type of organization must normally receive a substantial part of its support (exclusive of income received in the performance of its tax-exempt activities) from the United States and/or direct or indirect contributions from the public. It must be organized and operated exclusively to receive, hold, invest, and administer property and to make expenditures to or for the benefit of a college or university that is a public charity and that is an agency or instrumentality of a state or political subdivision of a state, or that is owned or operated by a state or political subdivision or by an agency or instrumentality of one or more states or political subdivisions.

These expenditures include those made for any one or more of the regular functions of these colleges and universities, such as the acquisition and maintenance of real property comprising part of the campus; the construction of college or university buildings; the acquisition and maintenance of equipment and furnishings used for or in conjunction with regular functions of these colleges and universities; or expenditures for scholarships, libraries, and student loans.

Governmental Units

The United States, possessions of the United States, the District of Columbia, states, and their political subdivisions are classified as *governmental units*, which are public charities. This type of a unit qualifies as a public charity without regard to its sources of support, partly because it is responsive to all citizens.

The concept of a governmental unit also embraces government instrumental-ities, agencies, and entities referenced by similar terms.

Other Institutions

One of the many anomalies of the federal tax law is that some of the charita-ble institutions in U.S. society that are not generically private foundations are not accorded a public charity classification, unlike churches, schools, hospi-tals, and the like. Organizations in this position include museums, libraries, and organizations that operate orchestras and operas. To be public charities, these entities must be publicly supported or (much less likely) be structured as supporting organizations (discussed ahead). Some of these types of orga-nizations are private operating foundations or exempt operating foundations (discussed previously).

DONATIVE PUBLICLY SUPPORTED ORGANIZATIONS

A way for a tax-exempt charitable organization to be a public charity is to receive its financial support from a suitable number of sources. A publicly supported charity is the antithesis of a private foundation, in that a foundation customarily derives its funding from one source, whereas a publicly supported charitable organization is (by definition) primarily or wholly supported by the public. One type of publicly supported charity—the *donative* type—is an organization, the revenues of which are in the form of a range of contributions and grants.

General Rules

An organization is a donative publicly supported entity if it is a tax-exempt char-itable organization that normally receives a substantial part (defined below) of its support (other than income from the performance of one or more exempt functions) from a governmental unit or from direct or indirect contributions from the public. It is this focus on support in the form of gifts and grants that causes this type of organization to be considered a *donative* one.

Organizations that qualify as donative publicly supported entities gen-erally are organizations such as museums of history, art, or science; libraries; community centers to promote the arts; organizations providing facilities for the support of an opera, symphony orchestra, ballet, or repertory drama group; organizations providing some other direct service to the public; and organizations such as the American National Red Cross or that conduct fed-erated fundraising campaigns.

The principal way for an organization to be a publicly supported charity under these rules is for it to normally derive at least one-third of its financial support from qualifying contributions and grants. (This one-third threshold is the definition of the phrase *substantial part* in this context.) Thus, an organization classified as this type of publicly supported charity must maintain a *support fraction*, the denominator of which is total gift and grant support received during the computation period (discussed ahead) and the numerator of which is the amount of support qualifying in connection with the one-third standard from eligible public and/or governmental sources for the period.

Two Percent Rule

A 2 percent ceiling is generally imposed on contributions and grants in determining public support. Only this threshold amount of a particular gift or grant is counted as public support, under this rule, irrespective of whether the contributor or grantor is an individual, corporation, trust, private foundation, or other type of entity (taking into account amounts given by related parties). In computing public support in this manner, the IRS has traditionally used a four-year measuring period, consisting of the organization's most recent four years. Beginning with the 2008 tax year, however, the measuring period is the organization's most recent five years.

An illustration will undoubtedly be helpful. Consider a charitable organization that received total gift and grant support in the amount of $1 million during the measuring period. In that instance, all contributions and grants up to $20,000 each are counted as public support (the total of them being the numerator of the support fraction). The amount of all gifts and grants during the period comprises the denominator of that fraction. If a person gave, for example, $80,000 during the measuring period, only $20,000 is public support from that source for that period. This organization thus must receive, during the period, at least $333,334 in contributions or grants of $20,000 or less each. It could receive $666,666 from one source and $10,000 each from 34 sources, or $20,000 each from 17 sources, for example.

A meaningful exception to this rule is available. Support received by a donative publicly supported charity from governmental units and/or other donative publicly supported charities is considered to be a form of *indirect* contributions from the public (in that these grantors are regarded as conduits of direct public support). This type of support is public support in its entirety. That is, this form of funding is not limited by the 2 percent rule. The same is true with respect to support from charitable organizations that satisfy the donative publicly supported organization definition even though they are classified as some other form of public charity (such as a church).

For these purposes, the legal nature of the donors and/or grantors is not relevant. That is, in addition to individuals, charities, and governments, public support can be derived from for-profit entities (such as corporations and partnerships) and nonprofit entities (including various forms of charitable and noncharitable tax-exempt organizations). In another example of the English language failing in this regard, private foundations can be sources of public support. Generally, the fact that contributions or grants are restricted or earmarked does not detract from their qualification as public support.

Nonetheless, the 2 percent limitation applies with respect to support received from a donative publicly supported charitable organization or governmental unit if the support represents an amount that was expressly or impliedly earmarked by a donor or grantor to the publicly supported organization or unit of government as being for or for the benefit of the organization asserting status as a publicly supported charitable organization.

Support Test

A matter that can be of considerable significance in determining whether a charitable organization can qualify as a donative publicly supported entity is the meaning of the term *support*. For this purpose, *support* means amounts received in the form of, as noted, contributions (including corporate sponsorships) and grants, along with net income from unrelated business activities (see Chapter 7), gross investment income, tax revenues levied for the benefit of the organization and paid to or expended on behalf of the organization, and the value of services or facilities (exclusive of services or facilities generally furnished to the public without charge) furnished by a governmental unit to the organization without charge. All of these items comprise the denominator of the support fraction. (The larger the denominator, the greater the amount of public support that is allowed by the 2 percent threshold.) *Support* does not include gain from the disposition of property, that is, gain from the sale or exchange of a capital asset; the value of exemption from any federal, state, or local tax or any similar benefit; or funding in the form of a loan.

In constructing the support fraction, an organization must exclude from the numerator and the denominator any amounts received from the exercise or performance of its exempt purpose or function and contributions of services for which a charitable contribution deduction is not allowable. An organization will not be treated as meeting this support test, however, if it receives *almost all* of its support in the form of gross receipts from related activities and an insignificant amount of its support from governmental units and/or the public. Moreover, the organization can exclude from the numerator and the denominator of the support fraction an amount equal to one or more unusual grants (discussed ahead).

Concept of *Normally*

In computing the support fraction, the organization's support that is *normally* received must be reviewed. This means that the organization must meet the one-third support test for a period encompassing the five tax years immediately preceding the year involved, on an aggregate basis. (Prior to 2008, this measuring period was four years.) When this is accomplished, the organization is considered as meeting the one-third support test for its current tax year and for the tax year immediately succeeding its current tax year. For example, if an organization's current tax year is calendar year 2009, the computation period for measuring public support pursuant to these rules is calendar years 2004–2008; if the support fraction requirement is satisfied on the basis of the support received over this five-year period, the organization satisfies this support test for 2009 and 2010. (A five-year period for meeting this support test is available for organizations during the initial five years of their existence.)

Unusual Contributions or Grants

Under the *unusual grant* rule, a contribution or grant may be excluded from the public support fraction. A gift or grant is *unusual* if it is an unexpected and substantial amount attracted by the public nature of the organization and received from a disinterested party. (Thus, this term is somewhat of a misnomer. The exception is not confined to grants and the operative word should be *unexpected*, not *unusual*.)

A number of factors are taken into account in this regard; no single factor is determinative. The positive factors follow, with their opposites (negative factors) in parentheses:

- The contribution or grant is from a person with no connection to the charitable organization. (The contribution or grant is received from a person who created the organization, is a substantial contributor to it, is a board member, an officer, or is related to one of these persons.)

- The gift or grant is in the form of cash, marketable securities, or property that furthers the organization's exempt purposes. An example of the latter is a gift of a painting to a museum. (The property is illiquid, difficult to dispose of, and/or not suitable in relation to the organization's functions.)

- No material restrictions or conditions are placed on the transfer.

- The organization attracts a significant amount of support to pay its operating expenses on a regular basis, and the gift or grant adds to an endowment or pays for capital items. (The gift or grant is used for operating expenses for several years; nothing is added to an endowment.)

- The gift is a bequest. (The gift is an *inter vivos* (lifetime) transfer.)

- An active fundraising program attracts significant public support. (Gift and grant solicitation programs are limited or unsuccessful.)

- A representative and broad-based governing body controls the organization. (Related parties are in control.)

- Prior to the receipts of the unusual grant, the organization qualified as a publicly supported entity. (The unusual grant exclusion was relied on in the past to satisfy the test.)

Facts-and-Circumstances Test

One of the defects of the donative organization support rules is that organizations that are not private foundations in a generic sense, because they have many of the attributes of a public organization, may nonetheless be classified as private foundations because they cannot meet the somewhat mechanical one-third support test. Charitable organizations with this dilemma can include entities such as museums and libraries that heavily rely on their endowments for financial support and thus have little or no need for contributions and grants. Although the statutory law is silent on the point, the tax regulations somewhat ameliorate this rigidity of the general rule by means of a *facts-and-circumstances test*.

The history of an organization's programmatic and fundraising efforts, and other factors, can be considered as an alternative to the rather strict mechanical formula for qualifying as a public charity under the general donative publicly supported charitable organization rules. These factors must be present for this test to be met:

- Public support (computed pursuant to the general rule) must be at least 10 percent of the total support, and the higher the better.

- The organization must have an active "continuous and bona fide" fundraising program designed to attract new and additional public and governmental support. Consideration will be given to the fact that, in its early years of existence, the charitable organization may limit the scope of its gift and grant solicitations to those persons deemed most likely to provide seed money in an amount sufficient to enable it to commence its charitable activities and expand its solicitation program.

- Other favorable factors must be present, such as:

  ○ The composition of the organization's governing board is representative of broad public interests.

  ○ Support is derived from governmental and other sources representative of the public.

  ○ Facilities and programs are made available to the public.

  ○ The organization's programs appeal to a broad range of the public.

As to the governing board factor, the organization's public charity status will be enhanced where it has a governing body that represents the interests of the public, rather than the personal or private interests of a limited number of donors. This can be accomplished by the election of board members by a broad-based membership or by having the board composed of public officials, individuals having particular expertise in the field or discipline involved, community leaders, and the like.

As noted, one of the important elements of this facts-and-circumstances test is the availability of facilities or services to the public. Examples of entities meeting this standard are a museum that holds its building open to the public, a symphony orchestra that gives public performances, a conservation organization that provides services to the public through the distribution of educational materials, and a home for the elderly that provides domiciliary or nursing services for members of the public.

Issues

Nine issues can arise in computing the public support component (the numerator) of the support fraction for donative publicly supported organizations. They are:

1. Proper calculation of the denominator of the support fraction.

2. Whether a payment constitutes a contribution or a grant.

3. Whether a membership fee can be treated as a contribution rather than a payment for services.

4. Whether a payment pursuant to a contract is a grant rather than revenue from a related activity (exempt function revenue).

5. Whether a grant is from another donative publicly supported charity (or a charity *described in* the rules).

6. Whether a grant from a publicly supported charity or governmental unit is a pass-through transfer from another grantor.

7. Whether a grant constitutes an unusual grant.

8. Whether an organization is primarily dependent on gross receipts from related activities.

9. Whether the organization needs to rely on the facts-and-circumstances test.

The fourth item warrants additional mention. When the term *contract* is used in this context, it usually connotes a payment for services rendered or goods provided, which means that the funds involved are exempt function revenue and thus must be excluded from the support fraction. Confusion can arise because a grant is often the subject of a contract, although in that setting the term used usually is *agreement*. While sometimes it is difficult to differentiate between the two, a *grant* is a payment made to a charitable organization to enable it to operate one or more programs, while a payment pursuant to a contract is for the acquisition of a good or service.

The principal point with these issues is that the resolution of them can materially affect the construct of the support fraction and thus the public support percentage. Sometimes, an organization will want to exclude a large amount from the fraction (such as a payment made in accordance with a contract) so as to increase the support percentage. It is not uncommon for a support fraction to be improperly computed, so that the resulting public support percentage is below the one-third threshold. It can be great joy for a tax lawyer to review a draft of an anemic public support fraction calculation, and discover, for example, that a grant that was limited by the 2 percent threshold can in fact be counted in full as public support (issue five) or that a large grant can in fact be excluded from the fraction as an unusual grant (issue seven), thereby enabling the charitable organization to report a public support ratio that is considerably in excess of the one-third minimum.

Community Foundations

In the world of charities, the term *foundation* is often used in conjunction with an organization that is not a *private foundation*. An illustration of this word interplay is the *community foundation*, which usually is a donative publicly supported charity. These foundations almost always attract, receive, and depend on financial support from members of the public on a regular, recurring basis. Community foundations are designed to attract large contributions of a capital or endowment nature, with the gifts often received and maintained in separate trusts or funds. These entities are generally identified with a particular community and are controlled by a representative group of persons in that area.

For classification as a public charity, however, a community foundation wants to be regarded as a single entity, rather than an aggregation of funds. To be treated as a component part of a community foundation, a trust or fund must be created by gift or similar transfer and may not be subjected by the transferor to any material restriction. A community foundation must, to be considered a single entity, be appropriately named, be so structured as to subject its funds to a common governing instrument, have a common governing body, and prepare periodic financial reports that treat all funds held by the foundation as its assets. The board of a community foundation must have the power to modify any restriction on the distribution of funds where it is inconsistent with the charitable needs of the community, must commit itself to the exercise of its powers in the best interests of the foundation, and must commit itself to seeing that the funds are invested in accordance with standards of fiduciary conduct.

A private foundation may make a grant to a designated fund within a community foundation (often a donor-advised fund). The private foundation can receive a payout credit for this type of grant, even though it acquires the ability to make recommendations as to distributions to other charitable organizations from the fund, as long as there are no prohibited material restrictions. Grants of this nature are regarded as made to the community foundation as an entity and not to a discrete fund.

SERVICE PROVIDER PUBLICLY SUPPORTED ORGANIZATIONS

The second way that a tax-exempt charitable organization can be a publicly supported entity is to be a *service provider* organization. As is the case with the donative organization rules, qualification for public charity status focuses on sources of revenue, although there are considerable differences between the two ways to compute public support. Public support in this context includes gifts and grants, but also includes forms of exempt function revenue. Thus, this type of publicly supported charity usually has a major portion of its support in the form of fees and like charges derived from the conduct of its programs, such as exempt dues-based entities, theaters, arts organizations, educational publishers, day care centers, and animal shelters.

A two-part support test must be met for an organization to qualify as this type of publicly supported charity:

1. Investment income cannot exceed one-third of total support. *Total support* basically is all of the organization's gross revenue normally received (discussed ahead), other than capital gains and the value of exemptions from local, state, and federal taxes.

2. More than one-third of total support must be a combination of:

   ○ Contributions, grants, and membership dues from sources other than disqualified persons.

   ○ Admission fees to exempt function facilities or activities, such as payments for theater tickets, access to a museum or historical site, seminars, lectures, and athletic events.

   ○ Fees for performance of services, such as day care fees, counseling fees, testing fees, laboratory fees, library fines, animal neutering charges, and athletic activity fees.

   ○ Sales of merchandise related to the organization's exempt purpose, including books and other educational literature, pharmaceuticals and medical devices, handicrafts, reproductions and copies of original works of art, byproducts of a blood bank, and goods produced by disabled workers.

Exempt function revenue from one source may not be treated as public support to the extent it is in excess of $5,000 or 1 percent of the total support of the organization, whichever is higher.

Permitted Sources

Generally, to be public support under these rules, the support must be derived from *permitted sources*. Consequently, a charitable organization seeking to qualify as a publicly supported entity under these rules must construct a support fraction, with the amount of support from permitted sources constituting the numerator of the fraction and the total amount of support being the fraction's denominator.

Permitted sources are certain public and publicly supported charitable organizations, governmental units, and persons other than disqualified persons with respect to the organization. Thus, in general, support (other than from disqualified persons) from another service provider publicly supported organization, a supporting organization (discussed ahead), any other tax-exempt organization (other than the institutions and donative publicly supported organizations (discussed previously)), a for-profit organization, or an individual constitutes public support for this type of organization, albeit limited in some instances (discussed ahead).

Support

The term *support* means (in addition to the categories of public support, which may include corporate sponsorships) (1) net income from any unrelated business (see Chapter 7), (2) gross investment income, (3) tax revenues levied for the benefit of the organization and either paid to or expended on behalf of the organization, and (4) the value of services or facilities (other than services or facilities generally furnished to the public without charge) furnished by a governmental unit. These items of support are combined to constitute the denominator of the support fraction.

The concept of support does not include (1) any gain from the disposition of a capital asset, (2) the value of local, state, and/or federal tax exemptions or similar benefits, and (3) the proceeds of a loan.

Limitations on Support

The support taken into account in determining the numerator of the support test under these rules must come from permitted sources. Thus, transfers from disqualified persons cannot qualify as public support under the service provider publicly supported organizations rules. The fact that a contribution or grant is restricted or earmarked does not detract from its qualification as public support.

In determining the amount of support in the form of gross receipts that is allowable in calculating the numerator of this support fraction, gross receipts from related activities (other than membership fees) from any person or from any bureau or similar agency of a governmental unit are includible in any tax year only to the extent that these receipts do not exceed the greater of $5,000 or 1 percent of the organization's total support for that year.

The phrase *bureau or similar agency* of a government means a specialized operating (rather than a policymaking or administrative) unit of the executive, judicial, or legislative branch of a government, usually a subdivision of a department of a government. Therefore, an organization receiving gross receipts (a grant) from both a policymaking or administrative unit of a government (for example, the Agency for International Development) and an operational unit of a government's department (for example, the Bureau for Latin America, an operating unit within AID) is treated as receiving gross receipts from two sources, with the amount from each agency separately subject to the $5,000/1 percent limitation.

A somewhat similar *permitted sources* limitation excludes support from a disqualified person, including a substantial contributor. As noted, however, grants from governmental units and certain public charities are not subject to this limitation.

The federal tax law defines and distinguishes the various forms of support referenced in the service provider publicly supported organizations rules: *contributions* or *gross receipts*, *grant* or *gross receipts*, *membership fees*, *gross receipts* or *gross investment income*, and *grant* or *indirect contribution*. For example, the term *gross receipts* means amounts received from the conduct of an activity related to an exempt function where a specific service, facility, or product is provided to serve the direct and immediate needs of the payor; a *grant* is an amount paid to confer a direct benefit for the public. A payment of money or transfer of property without adequate consideration generally is a *contribution* or a *grant*. The furnishing of facilities for a rental fee or the making of loans in furtherance of an exempt purpose will likely give rise to *gross receipts* rather than *gross investment income*. The fact that a membership organization provides services, facilities, and the like to its members as part of its overall activities will not result in the fees received from members being treated as *gross receipts* rather than *membership fees*.

Investment Income Test

An organization, to be classified as a service provider publicly supported charity, must normally receive no more than one-third of its support from (1) gross investment income, including interest, dividends, royalties, rent, and payments with respect to securities loans, and (2) any excess of the amount of unrelated business taxable income over the amount of tax on that income. To qualify under this test, an organization must construct a *gross investment income fraction*, with the amount of gross investment income and any unrelated income (net of the tax paid on it) constituting the numerator of the fraction and the total amount of support being the denominator. On occasion, there may be an issue as to whether a revenue item is a *gross receipt* from the performance of an exempt function or is *gross investment income*.

Concept of *Normally*

These public support and investment income tests are computed on the basis of the nature of the organization's *normal* sources of support. An organization is considered as *normally* receiving at least one-third of its support from permitted sources and no more than one-third of its support from gross investment income for its current tax year and immediately succeeding tax year if, for the *measuring period,* the aggregate amount of support received over the period from permitted sources is more than one-third of its total support and the aggregate amount of support over the period from gross investment income is not more than one-third of its total support.

In computing support under these rules, the IRS has traditionally used a four-year measuring period, involving the organization's most recent years. Beginning with the 2008 tax year, however, the measuring period is the organization's most recent five years. For example, if an organization's current tax year is calendar year 2009, the computation period for measuring support pursuant to these rules is calendar years 2004–2008; if the support fraction is satisfied on the basis of the support received over this five-year period, the organization satisfies this support test for 2009 and 2010. (A five-year period for meeting these support tests has long been available for organizations during the initial five years of their existence.)

Issues

The issues that arise in connection with calculation of public support under the service provider publicly supported organization rules are somewhat the same as those that can emerge in the donative publicly supported organization context (discussed previously). Of the nine issues in that setting, numbers one through four and seven apply equally here. (A facts-and-circumstances test is not available for service provider entities.) There are five other potential issues (and thus a total of ten issues) for service provider publicly supported organizations:

1. Accurate identification of the organization's disqualified persons

2. Correct computation of exempt function revenue

3. Correct application of the 1 percent rule

4. Whether a grant is from another service provider publicly supported organization (or a charity described in the rules)

5. Correct ascertainment of gross investment income

COMPARATIVE ANALYSIS OF PUBLICLY SUPPORTED CHARITIES

The two principal types of publicly supported charities can simultaneously meet both public support tests if they have a broad base of financial support in the form of contributions and grants. Indeed, many charities can easily satisfy either test at any time.

A significant deviation arises, however, concerning the matter of *exempt function revenue.* In the case of donative publicly supported charities, exempt function revenue is omitted from the fraction and too much of it can prevent or cause loss of public charity status. By contrast, some or all of exempt function revenue can be public support for service provider publicly supported charities. This distinction is one of the principal determinants for a charitable organization in deciding which category of publicly supported charity is appropriate. A dues-based charitable organization, for example, would almost always select the service provider publicly supported charity classification.

There are other considerations. The donative publicly supported charity calculates its public support using a rather mechanical formula, while the service provider publicly supported charity must go through the machinations of determining whether any of its financial support has been derived from disqualified persons. The donative publicly supported charity status has a preferred aura, if only because the service provider publicly supported charity (usually being fee-based) can appear too commercial in nature. Most service provider publicly supported charities are not permitted to maintain a pooled income fund (see Chapter 6), although today this is not much of a distinction because these funds are out of favor.

SUPPORTING ORGANIZATIONS

A category of tax-exempt charitable organization that is a public charity is the *supporting organization*. Charitable supporting organizations usually are entities that do not qualify as *institutions* or *publicly supported charities* (discussed previously) but are sufficiently related to one or more charitable organizations that are institutions or are publicly supported organizations so that the requisite degree of public control and involvement is considered present. Certain types of noncharitable tax-exempt organizations also may be supported organizations (discussed ahead).

A supporting organization must be organized, and at all times operated, exclusively for the benefit of, to perform the functions of, or to carry out the purposes of one or more eligible supported organizations. Also, a supporting organization must be operated, supervised, or controlled by one or more qualified supported organizations, supervised or controlled in connection with one or more such organizations, or operated in connection with one or more such organizations. A parsing of this rule has led to a quadruple classification of supporting organizations:

- Parents and subsidiaries (also known as Type I supporting organizations)
- Commonly controlled organizations (Type II)
- Functionally integrated organizations (Type III)
- Nonfunctionally integrated organizations (also Type III)

A third fundamental requirement is that a supporting organization must not be controlled, directly or indirectly, by one or more disqualified persons (other than foundation managers or eligible supported organizations).

A supporting organization may be created by one or more donors or by an organization that becomes the supported organization. To qualify as a supporting organization, a charitable entity must meet an organizational test and an operational test.

Organizational Test

A supporting organization must be organized exclusively to support or benefit one or more specified public institutions, publicly supported charitable organizations, or certain noncharitable organizations. Its articles of organization must limit its purposes to one or more of the purposes that are permissible for a supporting organization, may not expressly empower the organization to engage in activities that are not in furtherance of these purposes, must state the specified entity or entities on behalf of which it is to be operated, and may not expressly empower the organization to operate to support or benefit any other organization.

To qualify as a supporting organization, an organization's stated purposes may be as broad as, or more specific than, the purposes that are permissible for a supporting organization. Thus, an organization that is formed "for the benefit of "one or more eligible supported organizations will meet this organizational test, assuming the other requirements are satisfied. An organization that is *operated, supervised, or controlled by* (a Type I entity) or *supervised or controlled in connection with* (Type II) one or more qualified supported organizations to carry out their purposes will satisfy these requirements if the purposes stated in the articles of organization are similar to, but no broader than, the purposes stated in the articles of the supported organization or organizations.

An organization will not meet this organizational test if its articles of organization expressly permit it to operate to support or benefit any organization other than its specified supported organization or organizations. The fact that the actual operations of the organization have been exclusively for the benefit of one or more specified eligible supported organizations is not sufficient to permit it to satisfy this organizational test.

Operational Test

A supporting organization must be operated exclusively to support or benefit one or more specified qualified supported organizations. Unlike the definition of the term *exclusively* as applied in the context of charitable organizations generally, which has been held by the courts to mean *primarily* (see Chapter 3), the term *exclusively* in the supporting organization context means *solely*.

A supporting organization must engage solely in activities that support or benefit one or more eligible supported organizations. One way to do this, although it is not mandated but will be in certain instances, is for the supporting organization to make grants to the supported organization; this is often done, for example, where the supporting organization houses an endowment for the benefit of a supported organization. Another form of support or benefit occurs where a supporting organization carries on a discrete program or activity on behalf of a supported organization. In one instance, a tax-exempt hospital wanted a facility near the hospital in which patients about to undergo serious surgery, and their families and friends, could stay in immediate advance of the surgical procedure; the hospital created a supporting organization, which purchased a nearby motel and converted it into the facility the hospital needed. In another case, a supporting organization, supportive of the academic endeavors of the medical school at an exempt university, was used to operate a faculty practice plan in furtherance of the teaching, research, and service programs of the school. A supporting organization may engage in fundraising activities, such as solicitation of contributions and grants, special events, and unrelated business, to raise funds for one or more supported organizations or other permissible beneficiaries.

The allowable activities of a supporting organization may include making payments to or for the use of, or providing services or facilities for, members of the charitable class benefited by the charitable supported organization. A supporting organization may make a payment indirectly through an unrelated organization to a member of a charitable class benefited by a supported charitable organization but only where the payment constitutes a grant to an individual rather than a grant to the organization.

A supporting organization has many characteristics of a private foundation, such as the absence of any requirement that it be publicly supported. Thus, like a private foundation, a supporting organization can be funded entirely by investment income. It can satisfy this organizational test by engaging solely in investment activity, assuming charitable ends are being served.

Specification Requirement

As noted, a supporting organization must be organized and operated to support or benefit one or more *specified* supported organizations. This specification must be in the supporting organization's articles of organization, although the manner of the specification depends on which of the types of relationships with one or more eligible supported organizations are involved.

Generally, it is expected that the articles of organization of the supporting organization will designate (that is, *specify*) each of the supported organizations by name. If the relationship is one of *operated, supervised, or controlled by* (Type I) or *supervised or controlled in connection with* (Type II), however, designation by name is not required as long as the articles of organization of the supporting organization require that it be operated to support or benefit one or more beneficiary organizations that are designated by class or purpose and that include one or more supported organizations, as to which there is one of these two relationships, or organizations that are closely related in purpose or function to supported organizations as to which there is one of the two relationships (in either instance, where there is no designation of the organization(s) by name). If the relationship is one that is *operated in connection with* (Type III), the supporting organization must designate the supported organization or organizations by name.

A supporting organization is deemed to meet the specification requirement, even though its articles of organization do not designate each supported organization by name—irrespective of the nature of the relationship—if there has been a historical and continuing relationship between the supporting organization and the supported organizations and, by reason of that relationship, there has developed a substantial identity of interests between the organizations.

Nonetheless, in practice, it is common to specify the supported organization or organization in the supporting organization's articles of organization, irrespective of the type of supporting organization.

Required Relationships

As noted, to meet these requirements, an organization must be operated, supervised, or controlled by or in connection with one or more eligible supported organizations. Thus, if an organization does not stand in at least one of the required relationships with respect to one or more eligible supported organizations, it cannot qualify as a supporting organization. Regardless of the applicable relationship (Type I, II, or either of the IIIs), it must be ensured that the supporting organization will be *responsive* to the needs or demands of one or more eligible supported organizations and that the supporting organization will constitute an *integral part* of or maintain a *significant involvement* in the operations of one or more qualified supported organizations.

Operated, Supervised, or Controlled By

The distinguishing feature of the relationship between a supporting organization and one or more eligible supported organizations encompassed by the phrase *operated, supervised, or controlled by* is the presence of a substantial degree of direction by one or more supported organizations in regard to the policies, programs, and activities of the supporting organization. This is a relationship comparable to that of a parent and subsidiary (Type I).

Supervised or Controlled in Connection With

The distinguishing feature of the relationship between a supporting organization and one or more eligible supported organizations encompassed by the phrase *supervised or controlled in connection with* is the presence of common supervision or control by the persons supervising or controlling the supporting organization(s) and the supported organization(s) to ensure that the supporting organization(s) will be responsive to the needs and requirements of the supported organization(s). Therefore, in order to meet this requirement, the control or management of the supporting organization(s) must be vested in the same individuals who control or manage the supported organization(s) (Type II).

Operation in Connection With

Qualification as a supporting organization by reason of the *operated in connection with* relationship entails the least intimate of the relationships between a supporting organization and one or more supported organizations. This relationship usually is more of a programmatic one than a governance one. This type of relationship (Type III), prevalent for example in the health care field, is often structured so as to avoid legal liability, from the standpoint of a supported organization, for something done by the supporting organization.

The distinguishing feature of the relationship between a supporting organization and one or more supported organizations encompassed by this phrase is that the supporting organization must be responsive to and significantly involved in the operations of the supported organization or organizations. Generally, to satisfy the criteria of this relationship, a supporting organization must meet a *responsiveness test* and an *integral part test.*

Noncharitable Supported Organizations

Certain tax-exempt organizations that are not charitable entities qualify as supported organizations; this means that a charitable organization that is supportive of one or more of these noncharitable entities constitutes a supporting organization. These eligible supported organizations are exempt social welfare organizations (501(c)(4) entities), labor, agricultural, and horticultural organizations (501(c)(5) entities), and business leagues, such as trade associations (501(c)(6) entities). The principal requirement is that these organizations have to satisfy the one-third support test applicable to service provider publicly supported organizations. These organizations frequently meet this support requirement because they have a membership that pays dues.

This rule is principally designed to facilitate public charity status for related foundations and other funds (such as scholarship, award, and research funds) operated by the specified noncharitable organizations. This type of supporting organization can be in an awkward position: It must be charitable in function to be tax-exempt, yet be supportive of a noncharitable entity to be a public charity.

Substitutions

The federal tax law is vague as to how a supported organization with respect to a supporting organization can be changed (substituted), without loss of the supporting organization's public charity status. In what may be the only example of this type of substitution to date, the IRS ruled that a tax-exempt entity could retain its status as a supporting organization, notwithstanding a transaction in which a supported organization was substituted. An exempt university caused a related supporting organization to become affiliated with another entity that also functioned to support and benefit the university. This ruling is of limited utility in understanding the bounds of supported organization substitution, however, because, under the facts of the ruling, the functions of the supporting organization remained essentially the same and it continued to indirectly support the university.

An organization that is *operated in connection with* one or more eligible supported organizations can satisfy the specification requirement (discussed previously) even if its articles of organization permit an eligible supported organization that is designated by class or purpose to be substituted for the supported organizations designated by name in its articles but only if the substitution is conditioned on the occurrence of an event that is beyond the control of the supporting organization. This type of event includes, as to a supported organization, loss of tax exemption, substantial failure or abandonment of operations, or dissolution of the entity.

Limitation on Control

As noted, one or more disqualified persons with respect to a supporting organization, other than its officers and the like (technically termed *foundation managers*) cannot (without jeopardizing its public charity status), directly or indirectly, control the organization. An individual who is a disqualified person with respect to a supporting organization does not lose that status because a beneficiary supported organization appoints or designates him or her to be a foundation manager of the supporting organization, to serve as a representative of the supported organization.

A supporting organization is considered *controlled* if the disqualified persons, by aggregating their votes or positions of authority, may require the organization to perform an act that significantly affects its operations or may prevent the supporting organization from performing this type of an act. Generally, control exists if the voting power of these persons is 50 percent or more of the total voting power of the organization's governing body or if one or more disqualified persons have the right to exercise veto power over the actions of the organization. All pertinent facts and circumstances, including the nature, diversity, and income yield of an organization's holdings, the length of time particular securities or other assets are retained, and the manner of exercising its voting rights with respect to securities in which members of its governing body also have an interest, are taken into consideration in determining whether a disqualified person does in fact indirectly control an organization.

Caution needs to be exercised in this context. The IRS can find indirect control of a supporting organization by disqualified persons by going beyond the foregoing rules. One such instance involved a charitable organization that made distributions to a tax-exempt university. The organization's board of directors was composed of a substantial contributor to the organization, two employees of a business corporation of which more than 35 percent of the voting power was owned by the disqualified person, and an individual selected by the university. None of the directors had veto power over the organization's actions. Conceding that disqualified persons did not directly control the organization, the IRS said that "one circumstance to be considered is whether a disqualified person is in a position to influence the decisions of members of the organization's governing body who are not themselves disqualified persons." Thus, the IRS concluded that the two directors who were employees of the disqualified person corporation should be considered the equivalent of disqualified persons for purposes of applying the 50 percent control rule. This position led to the conclusion that the organization was indirectly controlled by disqualified persons and, therefore, could not be a public charity by virtue of being a qualified supporting organization.

PUBLIC SAFETY TESTING ORGANIZATIONS

Another category of organization that is deemed to be a public charity is an organization that is organized and operated exclusively for testing for public safety. Although these entities are considered public charities, they are not eligible to receive tax-deductible charitable contributions.

IMPORT OF PUBLIC–PRIVATE DICHOTOMY

As a general proposition—and this is from a law standpoint—public charity status is preferable to private foundation status. That is, again, purely from the perspective of the law, there is no advantage to a charitable organization in being a private foundation. (There is nothing inherently wrong in being a private foundation, of course, and about 80,000 of them (discussed ahead) function quite nicely in that capacity.)

The biggest disadvantage of classification as a private foundation is that a charitable organization is subject to and expected to comply with the private foundation rules concerning mandatory payouts, self-dealing, excess business holdings, jeopardizing investments, and prohibited expenditures (discussed ahead). Public charities are generally not caught up in this barrage of restrictions and requirements.

Having said that, however, some of the private foundation rules are being applied in the public charity setting. The excess business holdings rules are applicable to certain supporting organizations. Congress and the IRS are working on mandatory payout requirements for some supporting organizations. Although the self-dealing rules do not apply to public charities, rules as to excess benefit transactions apply in connection with public charities (see Chapter 2); in several instances, the requirements are the same.

Certain basic principles of the law, such as the private inurement and private benefit doctrines (*id.*) are applicable to both categories of charitable organizations.

Another disadvantage to private foundation status is that the charitable giving rules (see Chapter 6) considerably favor public charities. This problem (if there is one) usually is presented at the time a private foundation is initially funded, either because percentage limitations restrict the extent of a charitable contribution deduction or because a deduction for a gift of property is confined to the donor's basis in the property.

SOME STATISTICS

The IRS collects data on private foundations and nonexempt charitable trusts, based on information in these organizations' annual information returns (see Chapter 5). The most recent year for which the IRS has developed these statistics is 2004.

For that year, the total number of returns filed by private foundations was 76,897; nonexempt charitable trusts filed 3,511 returns. The fair market value of foundations' assets for that year was $509.9 billion; the asset value for charitable trusts was about $5.6 billion. Private foundations disbursed $32.1 billion, of which $27.6 billion was in the form of grants; charitable trusts distributed $332 million. Private foundations had $58.7 billion in total revenue in 2004; nonexempt charitable trusts had total revenue in the amount of $502 million. Private foundations had $34 billion in net investment income; the net investment income of nonexempt charitable trusts was $304 million.

Large private foundations—those with $50 million or more in fair market value of total assets at the end of tax year 2004—accounted for the majority of financial activity by the annual return filers. Although they represented less than 2 percent of the filers (including nonexempt charitable trusts), they held 67 percent of the aggregate fair market value of total assets. Nearly 60 percent of all assets were held by the 610 private foundations with assets valued at $100 million or more. Large foundations received 57 percent of the revenue and distributed 55 percent of the grants.

For 2004, ten private foundations held nearly one-fifth of private foundations' assets, totaling $97.1 billion. The largest of these foundations held $28.8 billion in assets; the tenth of these foundations held $5 billion in assets. The largest private foundation grantmaker distributed $1.3 billion in 2004; the tenth largest grantmaker made grants totaling $210 million.

SUMMARY

This chapter provided basic information as to the distinctions between public charities and private foundations. The various types of public charities were discussed, as were the different types of private foundations. Particular emphasis was placed on the ways a tax-exempt charitable organization can qualify as a publicly supported entity and on the types of supporting organizations. A summary of the unique rules applicable to private foundations was provided. The chapter included a comparative analysis of publicly supported charities and explained the significance of the private foundation–public charity dichotomy. The chapter concluded with a summary of the IRS's statistics concerning private foundations and nonexempt charitable trusts.

5

FEDERAL ANNUAL REPORTING REQUIREMENTS

The purpose of this chapter is to summarize the federal tax law annual reporting requirements imposed on charitable (and other) tax-exempt organizations, from a fundraising perspective. For decades, these organizations have been subject to a considerable amount of annual reporting. Beginning with the general annual information return filed for 2008, however, the reporting requirements have been dramatically intensified, including significant new reporting mandates in connection with charitable giving and fundraising. Specifically, this chapter will:

- Describe the principal federal tax law filing requirements for charitable organizations.

- Inventory the various types of annual information and other returns.

- Identify the portions of the redesigned annual information return with special significance to fundraising.

- Summarize the new fundraising reporting rules.

- Summarize the little federal tax law there is concerning gaming (or gambling).

- Summarize the new gaming reporting rules.

- Summarize the new rules concerning noncash contributions.

- Summarize the rules pertaining to the disclosure of contributions and grants.

- Inventory the various penalties and other sanctions in this context.

FEDERAL TAX LAW REPORTING BASICS

Nearly every organization that is exempt from federal income taxation must file an annual information return with the IRS. This return generally calls for the provision of much information, some of it financial and some in prose form. This document, being an *information return* rather than a *tax return*, is available for public inspection (see Chapter 8).

Various Forms

For most tax-exempt organizations, the information return that must be filed annually is Form 990. Private foundations, however, file an information return that is uniquely styled for them: Form 990-PF. Small organizations (other than supporting organizations and private foundations (see Chapter 4) file Form 990-EZ. Traditionally, entities that have gross receipts that are less than $100,000 and total assets that are less than $250,000 in value at the end of the reporting year filed Form 990-EZ.

In the context of publication of the redesigned Form 990 for 2008, the IRS announced a graduated three-year transition period for annual information return filings. For the 2008 tax year (returns filed in 2009), organizations with gross receipts of more than $1 million or total assets in excess of $2.5 million are required to file the Form 990. For the 2009 tax year (returns filed in 2010), organizations with gross receipts over $500,000 or total assets over $1.25 million are required to file the Form 990. Tax-exempt organizations below these thresholds are allowed to file the Form 990-EZ (with the option to file the new Form 990 if they wish). The filing threshold will be permanently set, beginning with the 2010 tax year, at $200,000 in gross receipts and $500,000 in total assets.

Tax-exempt organizations with gross receipts that are normally less than $25,000 annually are required to file, electronically, the Form 990-N—the e-postcard. Starting with the 2010 tax year, the filing threshold for organizations required to file the Form 990-N will be increased to $50,000. Exempt organizations with unrelated business taxable income that is in excess of $1,000 are required to file the Form 990-T—the unrelated business income tax return.

Filing Exceptions

The requirement for the filing of an annual information return does not apply to:

- Churches (including interchurch organizations of local units of a church)

- Integrated auxiliaries of churches

- Conventions or associations of churches

- Financing, fund management, or retirement insurance program management organizations functioning on behalf of the foregoing organizations

- Certain other entities affiliated with a church or convention or association of churches

- Most religious orders (to the exclusive extent of their religious activities)

- State and local institutions

- Certain schools and mission societies

- Governmental units

- Affiliates of governmental units (which can include nonprofit, tax-exempt organizations)

- Organizations (other than supporting organizations and private foundations) that have gross receipts that normally are not in excess of $25,000 annually

- Foreign organizations (other than private foundations) that normally do not receive more than $25,000 in gross receipts annually from sources within the United States and that do not have any significant activity (including lobbying or political activity) in the United States.

Filing Due Dates

The annual information return is due on or before the 15th day of the fifth month following the close of the organization's tax year. Thus, the return for a calendar-year organization should be filed by May 15 of each year. One or more extensions may be obtained. These returns are filed with the IRS service center in Ogden, Utah.

The filing date for an annual information return may fall due while the organization's application for recognition of tax-exempt status is pending with the IRS. In that instance, the organization should nonetheless file the information return (rather than a tax return) and indicate on it that the application is pending.

Penalties

Failure to timely file the annual information return, without reasonable cause or an exception, can generally give rise to a $20-per-day penalty. The organization must pay for each day the failure continues, up to a maximum of $10,000. For larger organizations (those with annual gross receipts in excess of $ 1 million), the per-day penalty is $100 and the maximum penalty is $50,000.

An additional penalty can be imposed, at the same rate and up to the same maximum, on the individual(s) responsible for the failure to file, absent reasonable cause. Other fines and even imprisonment can be imposed for willfully failing to file returns or for filing fraudulent returns and statements with the IRS.

IMPORT OF REDESIGNED FORM 990

The redesigned Form 990 is no ordinary information return and, for that matter, is no ordinary government form. This is a significant, complex, and extraordinary document. It is, in many ways, (from a lawyer's viewpoint) a work of art, in that it captures the requirements of a large amount of statutory law, much of it recently enacted. At the same time, because of its size and complexity, many organizations will be engaging in considerable effort (measured in terms of time and money) to create needed documents, maintain records, and properly prepare and timely file the return.

From a law perspective, the new return has, as noted, enormous implications for tax-exempt organizations, for two reasons.

1. The form in various places and ways has the effect of creating much new law. A dramatic example of this fact is the portion on governance (see Chapter 10).

2. The form is designed to induce certain behavior by the management of nonprofit, tax-exempt organizations by in essence forcing organizations to check "yes" boxes (or avoid checking "no" boxes). The import of this "shaming technique" can be seen, for example, in the requirements as to development of various policies and dissemination to the public of various documents (see Chapter 2).

SUMMARY OF PARTS OF REDESIGNED FORM 990

The redesigned Form 990 includes an 11-page "core form." There is a one-page summary of the organization (Part I), followed by 10 additional parts (II–XI). Part II is the signature block. This core return is accompanied by 16 schedules (discussed ahead).

Part I (Summary)

The summary requests, in line 1, a brief description of the organization's mission or most significant activities. The organization has the choice as to which it wishes to highlight. This summary asks for the number of voting members of the organization's governing body (line 3), the number of these board members who are independent (line 4), the number of employees (line 5), and the number of volunteers (line 6). Other questions concern the amount of contributions and grants (line 8), program service revenue (line 9), investment income (line 10), other revenue (line 11), total gross unrelated business income (line 7a), total revenue and expenses (lines 12 and 18), grants and similar amounts paid (line 13), compensation (line 15), professional fundraising expenses (line 16a), other expenses (line 17), and total assets and liabilities (lines 20 and 21).

A box is to be checked (line 2) if the organization discontinued its operations or disposed of more than 25 percent of its assets. That is, this box is to be checked if the organization answered "yes" to lines 31 or 32 of Part IV and thus completed Schedule N, Parts I or II.

As to volunteers (line 6), the organization is required to provide the number of volunteers, full time and part time, who provided services to the organization during the reporting year. Organizations that do not keep track of this information in their books and records or report this information elsewhere (such as in annual reports or grant proposals) may provide a "reasonable estimate [of this number], and may use any reasonable basis for determining this estimate." Organizations may, but are not required to, provide an explanation on Schedule O as to how this number was determined as well as the types of services or benefits provided by their volunteers.

As to unrelated business taxable income (line 7b), if the organization is not required to file a Form 990-T for the tax year, it should enter "0." If the organization has not yet filed Form 990-T for the tax year, it should provide an estimate of the amount it expects to report on that return (line 34) when it is filed. (See Chapter 7.)

Lines 8 to 19 require reporting of prior-year (2007) revenue and expense amounts. This list should be used to determine what to report on these lines for prior-year revenue and expense amounts from the 2007 Form 990:

- Contributions and grants (line 8) (2007 Form 990, Part I, line 1e)

- Program service revenue (line 9) (2007 Form 990, Part I, lines 2 and 3)

- Investment income (line 10) (2007 Form 990, Part I, lines 4, 5, and 7, less any royalties reported on line 7, and 8d)

- Other revenue (line 11) (2007 Form 990, Part I, lines 6c, 9c, 10c, and 11, plus any royalties reported in line 7)

- Total revenue (line 12) (2007 Form 990, Part I, line 12)

- Grants and similar amounts paid (line 13) (2007 Form 990, Part II, lines 22a–23, column (A))

- Benefits paid to or for members (line 14) (2007 Form 990, line 24, column (A))

- Salaries, other compensation, employee benefits (line 15) (2007 Form 990, Part II, lines 25a-28, column (A))

- Professional fundraising expenses (line 16) (2007 Form 990, Part II, line 30, column (A))

- Other expenses (line 17) (2007 Form 990, Part II, lines 29 and 31–43g, column (A))

- Total expenses (line 18) (2007 Form 990, Part II, line 44, column (A))

- Revenue less expenses (line 19) (2007 Form 990, Part I, line 18)

The IRS, in its instructions, advises organizations that, because Part I generally reflects information reported elsewhere in the new Form 990, completion of this part (Summary) should be deferred until completion of the other parts of the return.

Part II (Signature Block)

To make the new Form 990 complete, an officer of the filing organization authorized to sign the return must sign it in the space provided. For a corporation or unincorporated association, this officer may be the president, vice president, treasurer, assistant treasurer, chief accounting officer or other corporate or association officer, such as a tax officer. A receiver, trustee, or assignee must sign any return he or she files for a corporation or an association. For a trust, the authorized trustee(s) must sign the return.

Generally, anyone who is paid to prepare the return must sign in the Paid Preparer's Use Only area. The paid preparer must (1) sign the return in the space provided for the preparer's signature, (2) enter the preparer information (other than the preparer taxpayer identification number and the employer identification number blocks, except as described next), and (3) provide a copy of the return to the organization. The paid preparer, however, must enter the preparer taxpayer identification number and the preparer's firm's employer identification number only if filing the Form 990 for a nonexempt charitable split-interest trust that is not filing Form 1041. The paid preparer's space is to be left blank if a regular employee of the filing organization prepared the return.

On the last line of Part II, the organization should check the "yes" box if the IRS may contact the paid preparer who signed the return to discuss the return. By checking this box "yes," the organization is authorizing the IRS to contact the paid preparer to discuss any matter relating to this return. The "no" box is to be checked if the IRS is to contact the organization or its principal officer rather than the paid preparer.

Part III (Program Service Accomplishments)

Part III of the redesigned Form 990 concerns the filing organization's program service accomplishments. It is required to describe its mission, new significant program services, any significant changes in the way it conducts a program, a cessation of any activity, and the exempt purpose achievements for each of its three largest program services by expenses. Charitable and social welfare organizations are required to report the amount of grants and allocations to others, total; expenses; and any revenue for each program service reported.

Part IV (Schedules)

Part IV of the redesigned Form 990 is a checklist of (potentially) required schedules. This schedule references 44 questions and 16 schedules (discussed ahead).

Part V (Other IRS Filings)

Part V of the Form 990 pertains to a variety of activities and IRS filings. As to activities, there are questions about unrelated business income, involvement in a prohibited tax shelter transaction, use of supporting organizations, use of donor-advised funds, and payments with respect to personal benefit contracts (see Chapters 2, 4). As to IRS filings, there are questions about the filing of seven forms (990-T, 1096, 1098-C, 8282, 8886-T, W-2G, and W-3).

Part VI (Governance)

Part VI of the Form 990 concerns governance, management, policies, and disclosure (see Chapters 2, 10). As to the governing body and management (Section A), questions concern the number of the voting members of the governing body and the number of board members who are "independent." Inquiry is made as to whether the organization has conflict-of-interest, whistle-blower, and document retention and destruction policies, as well as policies governing the activities of chapters, affiliates, and branches (Section B). Additional questions pertain to various disclosures (Section C). (See Chapter 8.)

Part VII (Compensation)

Part VII of the Form 990 focuses on compensation of insiders and independent contractors. The persons currently in their positions must be listed (irrespective of compensation), along with a list of the organization's five highest compensated employees (other than insiders) who received compensation of more than $100,000 from the organization and any related organizations during the year; the organization's former officers, key employees, or highest compensated employees who received more than $100,000 of compensation from the organization and any related organizations during the year; and the organization's former directors or trustees who received (in that capacity) more than $10,000 of compensation from the organization and any related organizations during the year.

Parts VIII to XI (Financial Information)

Part VIII of the Form 990 is a revenue statement, Part IX is a statement of expenses (including functional reporting), Part X is a balance sheet, and Part XI concerns financial statements.

ANNUAL RETURN SCHEDULES

The redesigned Form 990 includes the following 16 schedules.

Schedule A

Schedule A of the Form 990 is used by charitable organizations to report their public charity status (see Chapter 4). Specific questions about supporting organizations include identification of the organization's type, a certification as to lack of control by disqualified persons, contributions from disqualified persons, and information about supported organizations.

Separate public support schedules are provided for the basic types of publicly supported charitable organizations. The public support computation period has been lengthened to five years, which makes it consistent with the advance ruling period public support test. An organization can claim public charity status on the basis of the facts-and-circumstances test on this schedule. (*id.*)

Schedule B

Schedule B is the schedule used to report charitable contributions and grants. It is the same as the preexisting Schedule B.

Schedule C

Schedule C comprises questions concerning political campaign and lobbying activities, principally by charitable organizations. Filing organizations are required to describe their direct and indirect political campaign activities, including the amounts of political expenditures and volunteer hours. There are separate parts for lobbying charitable organizations that are under the substantial part test and the expenditure test. Certain other types of tax-exempt entities must prepare additional parts of this schedule.

Schedule D

Schedule D is used to report supplemental financial information, such as for investments, liabilities, conservation easements, donor-advised funds, art collections, trust accounts, and endowment funds.

Schedule E

Schedule E is filed by organizations that constitute tax-exempt private schools. Most of this schedule relates to the requirement that the organization cannot, to be exempt, maintain a racially discriminatory policy. A question inquires as to whether the organization receives any financial aid or other assistance from a governmental agency.

Schedule F

The essence of Schedule F is the reporting of activities outside the United States. These activities, such as program services, grantmaking, and fundraising, are reported on a per-region basis. Grantmakers are required to describe their procedures for monitoring the use of grant funds. Information must be supplied if a grantee or other recipient of assistance is related to any person with an interest in the grantmaking organization. Additional details are required in instances of grants or other assistance to organizations or individuals.

Schedule G

Schedule G largely concerns fundraising activities (discussed ahead). The filing organization indicates the type or types of fundraising in which it is engaged and provides information about any fundraising contracts (including those with insiders). The organization is required to list the jurisdictions in which it is authorized to solicit funds (see Chapter 3). A part of this schedule focuses on fundraising events; another part solicits details about gaming activities.

Schedule H

Schedule H is filed by tax-exempt hospitals. The first part of this schedule (Part I) is a "community benefit report." The filing hospital indicates whether it provides free or discounted care to low-income individuals or those who are "medically indigent." The hospital reports on its charity care (such as care provided at cost, unreimbursed Medicaid services, and other unreimbursed costs in connection with government programs) and other community benefits (such as health improvement services, health professions education, subsidized health services, and research). The organization is asked whether it prepares an annual community benefit report and to describe its charity care policy.

The second part of this schedule (Part II) inquires as to the hospital's "community building" activities. These activities include physical improvements and housing, economic development, community support, environmental improvements, leadership development and training for community members, coalition building, community health improvement advocacy, and workforce development.

Another part (Part III) pertains to bad debt, Medicare, and collection practices. A fourth part asks questions about the use of management companies and involvement in joint ventures. A fifth part (Part V) seeks information about the hospital's facilities. The schedule (Part VI) requests a description of how the organization assesses the health care needs of the communities it serves and how the organization informs patients about their eligibility for assistance under federal, state, or local government programs or under its charity care policy.

Schedule I

Schedule I is used to solicit information about the organization's domestic grant and other assistance programs. For example, the organization is asked whether it maintains records to substantiate the amount of its assistance, and about the organization's selection criteria and grantees' eligibility. Information is required for grants of more than $5,000 to organizations and all grants to individuals.

Schedule J

Schedule J is used to solicit supplemental information about compensation. The organization must indicate (in Part I) if it provides to its insiders, payments or items in forms such as first class or charter travel, a discretionary spending account, a housing allowance, or health or social club dues; it is asked whether it follows a written policy in connection with such payments (or reimbursements) or items. The organization is asked how it determines certain executive compensation and, in the case of charitable and social welfare organizations, whether it provided any form of nonfixed payments.

The organization reports information concerning compensation paid to trustees, directors, officers, key employees, and highly compensated employees (Part II). There is a breakdown as to base compensation, bonus and incentive compensation, deferred compensation, and nontaxable benefits.

Schedule K

Schedule K is used to solicit information about tax-exempt bond issues (Part I) and the use of the proceeds (Part II). Questions are posed about private use rules (Part III) and arbitrage (Part IV).

Schedule L

Schedule L concerns excess benefit transactions and loans to and from interested persons (see Chapter 2). Information sought includes the name of the debtor/creditor, original principal amount, balance due, the purpose of the loan, and whether there is a written agreement. Questions are also asked about grants or other forms of assistance benefiting, and business transactions involving, interested persons.

Schedule M

The focus of Schedule M is on noncash contributions (discussed ahead). Thus, information is sought about gifts of art (including fractional interests), books, clothing and household goods, automobiles, airplanes, boats, intellectual property, securities, qualified conservation property, real estate, collectibles, food inventory, drugs and medical supplies, taxidermy, historical artifacts, scientific specimens, and archaeological artifacts.

This schedule inquires as to the number of Forms 8283 (see Chapter 8) received by the organization for contributions for which the organization completed the donee acknowledgment portion; whether the organization received any property that it must hold for at least three years from the date of its contribution, which is not required to be used for exempt purposes during the entire holding period; whether the organization has a gift acceptance policy that requires the review of nonstandard contributions; and whether the organization used third parties or related organizations to solicit, process, or sell noncash distributions.

Schedule N

Schedule N pertains to liquidations, terminations, dissolutions, and significant disposition of assets. Inquiries include a description of the assets involved, their value, and the method of determining the value, the date of the distribution, as well as the name and address of the recipient. Other questions concern the involvement of an insider with the successor or transferee organization, notification of one or more state officials, and other compliance with state laws. Additional information is sought concerning transfers of more than 25 percent of the organization's assets.

Schedule O

Filing organizations use Schedule O to provide additional information for responses to specific questions in the Form 990 and/or its schedules and to provide additional information.

Schedule R

Schedule R has as one of its purposes the identification of disregarded entities and related tax-exempt organizations. Related organizations taxable as a partnership and as a corporation or trust must also be identified. A series of questions about transactions with related organizations and unrelated organizations taxable as partnerships is posed.

FEDERAL AND STATE REGULATION OF GAMING

Federal tax law is generally silent on the matter of gaming by tax-exempt organizations; the little law there is (which should be understood in relation to the preparation of Schedule G (discussed ahead)) consists of the IRS's instructions accompanying the redesigned Form 990 and the exception from treatment as unrelated business for qualified bingo games (see Chapter 7).

Definitions

The IRS's Form 990 instructions provide that *gaming* includes "bingo, pull tabs/instant bingo (including satellite and progressive bingo), Texas Hold-Em Poker and other card games, raffles, scratch-offs, [use of] charitable gaming tickets, break-opens, hard cards, banded tickets, jar tickets, pickle cards, Lucky Seven cards, Nevada Club tickets, casino nights, Las Vegas nights, and coin-operated gambling devices." *Coin-operated gambling devices* include "slot machines, electronic video slot or line games, video poker, video blackjack, video keno, video bingo, [and] video pull tab games."

These instructions define *bingo* as follows: A "game of chance played with cards that are generally printed with five rows of five squares each. Participants place markers over randomly called numbers on the cards in an attempt to form a pre-selected pattern such as a horizontal, vertical, or diagonal line, or all four corners. The first participant to form the pre-selected pattern wins the game. To be a 'bingo' game, the game must be of the type described in which wagers are placed, winners are determined, and prizes or other property are distributed in the presence of all persons placing wagers in that game."

The instructions define *pull-tabs/instant bingo/progressive bingo* as follows: This phrase includes "games in which an individual places a wager by purchasing preprinted cards that are covered with pull-tabs. Winners are revealed when the individual pulls back the sealed tabs on the front of the card and compares the patterns under the tabs with the winning patterns preprinted on the back of the card. Included in the definition of pull-tabs are 'instant bingo', 'mini bingo', and other similar scratch-off cards. Satellite, Internet and Progressive bingo are games conducted in many different places simultaneously and the winners are not all present when the wagers are placed, the winners are determined and the prizes are distributed. Revenue and expenses associated with satellite, internet and progressive bingo should be included under this category."

The instructions define the phrase *partnership formed to administer charitable gaming* to mean "two or more organizations that are authorized under state law to conduct bingo or other gaming at the same location joining together to account for and/or share revenues, authorized expenses, and inventory related to bingo and gaming operations."

Law in General

The principal focus of the IRS in this regard, principally in the contexts of examinations, is on bingo and pull-tab games. Bingo games are excluded from the definition of unrelated business. Generally, however, the regular operation by a tax-exempt organization of gambling activities (including instant bingo, pull-tab games, and the like) is the conduct of an unrelated business, particularly where the activities involve the public. A gaming activity conducted entirely by volunteers may be exempt from unrelated business taxation.

In some instances, gaming activities can be substantially related activities, such as when conducted by a tax-exempt organization for social or recreational purposes for its members and their bona fide guests. These exempt organizations include social clubs, fraternal beneficiary societies, domestic fraternal societies, and veterans' organizations. Gaming activities involving only members and their guests directly furthers exempt purposes in these instances.

A *nonmember*, in this context, is defined in the instructions as an "individual who is not a member of the organization but who participates in recreational activities sponsored by the organization or receives services or goods from the organization and pays for the services or goods received." These instructions continue: "Such an individual, even when accompanied by a member, is generally considered to be the principal in a business transaction with the organization. Gaming open to the general public may result in unrelated business income tax (UBIT) or adversely affect exempt status."

Many states have gaming laws that identify the types of organizations that are allowed to conduct gaming activities and the conditions pursuant to which the games may be conducted (such as a requirement that volunteers be utilized or a limit on the number of nights in a week a tax-exempt organization can conduct gaming activity). If there is an IRS examination of an exempt organization as to gaming, it should be expected that the examining agent(s) will be aware of the state's agency in charge of gaming activities enforcement, policy memoranda, and reporting requirements.

IRS Examination Practices

An IRS examiner will likely ask questions such as (1) What types of gaming activities does the organization conduct, (2) who conducts the activities, (3) who owns the facility where the gaming is conducted, (4) how are the games advertised, (5) who supplied the gaming equipment and/or supplies, (6) how long has the gaming been conducted, (7) what is the size and extent of the gaming activity (on an income, expense, and time basis), and (8) has the manner in which the games have been conducted changed over time? The examiner will review board minutes and contracts, and interview current and past employees. Among the issues on the examiner's mind will be private inurement and private benefit.

An IRS examiner of bingo activity will determine whether the operation has a system of internal controls to adequately safeguard the revenue generated from the games. He or she will monitor the bingo game while it is underway, probably as an unannounced visit. A bingo game gross receipts analysis will be conducted, looking for unreported revenue. An expense analysis will be undertaken, such as where a charitable organization raises funds from gaming activities and makes payments to other charitable organizations.

An examination of pull-tab activity will likely entail a review of the tax-exempt organization's inventory of pull-tab supplies, comparing the boxes of pull-tabs to supplier invoices (the absence of which may indicate diversion of the exempt organization's funds). The examiner will monitor the pull-tab sales, and will undertake a pull-tab gross receipts and expense analysis.

Gaming activities may adversely affect a tax-exempt organization's exempt status, such as where a charitable organization engages in these activities for nonexempt purposes and the activities are substantial. If, however, an exempt charitable organization has a program of making grants to other charities from its gaming activities revenue, the commercial or business aspects of the gaming may be considered incidental to the charitable purposes. A gaming activity that is illegal may jeopardize the exempt organization's tax-exemption on the ground that it is contrary to public policy. Gaming activities may endanger exemption if they violate the doctrines of private inurement or private benefit; these activities may transgress the intermediate sanctions rules.

The receipt of gaming income may have an adverse effect on a charitable organization's public charity status if it is a publicly supported charity. This determination turns, in large part, on whether the income is unrelated business income. In ascertaining whether a charitable organization qualifies as a donative type publicly supported charity, gross receipts from activities that do not constitute unrelated business (including nontaxable bingo receipts) are excluded from the computation of public support. In determining whether a charitable organization is a service provider publicly supported charity, gross receipts, if not unrelated business income, are likely to qualify as public support.

An IRS examiner will attempt to identify related entities. That is, the gaming operation may have related management, real estate, supply, equipment, or concession companies. Agreements (including subleases) will be reviewed, with the examiner searching for excessive compensation, lengthy contract terms, penalties on the tax-exempt organization in case of termination of an agreement, and lack of open bidding in selection of the gaming operator. If related entities are found, the examiner will determine the nature of the relationship between the parties: agency, joint venture, sales, license, or other arrangement.

The examiner will review the books and records of the tax-exempt organization conducting the gaming operations, examine the exempt organization's returns (and correlate them with the returns filed by gaming operators (Forms 1040, 1120)), and issuance of a tax form of prize winners (Form W-2G), to determine if the organization is liable for federal excise taxes on wagering, and in compliance with the rules as to employment taxes and tip income.

Preparation of Form 990 Schedule G

Form 990, Schedule G, concerns fundraising and/or gaming activities by tax-exempt organizations (principally public charities). This schedule is comprised of three parts: Part I pertaining to fundraising in general, Part II pertaining to special-event fundraising, and Part III pertaining to gaming.

A tax-exempt organization is required to complete some or all of Schedule G if the organization answers "yes" to one or more of these questions:

- The organization reported payment of more than $15,000 in the form of professional fundraising fees (see Form 990, Part IV, line 17; Form 990, Part IX, line 11e).

- The organization reported receipt of more than $15,000 in revenue from fundraising events (see Form 990, Part IV, line 18; Form 990, Part VIII, line eight (a)).

- The organization reported receipt of more than $15,000 in revenue from gaming (see Form 990, Part IV, line 19; Form 990, Part VIII, line nine (a)).

Part I (Professional Fundraising Expenses)

Part I of Schedule G must be completed by organizations that reported, for the year, payment of more than $15,000 in professional fundraising expenses. This requires an understanding of the IRS's definition of the term *professional fundraising services* (see Chapter 1). This definition, however, rests on the definition of the term *fundraising activities* accorded it by the IRS: "activities undertaken to induce potential donors to contribute money, securities, services, materials, facilities, other assets, or time."

The organization must indicate (in response to question one, by checking a box in front of each method of fundraising used) whether it raised funds by means of one or more of the following seven fundraising methods:

1. Mail solicitations

2. Email solicitations

3. Telephone solicitations

4. In-person solicitations

5. Solicitation of nongovernment grants

6. Solicitation of government grants

7. Special fundraising events

This list is not a complete inventory of the various methods pursuant to which fundraising by tax-exempt organizations takes place (see Chapter 1). For example, the IRS's list does not include solicitations posted on Web sites. It is not clear how gifts received as the result of a charitable sales promotion (see Chapter 3) are reported.

The organization is asked whether it has a written or oral agreement with any individual (including trustees, directors, officers, or key employees (see Form 990, Part VII)) or entity in connection with professional fundraising activities (line two (a), ending in "yes" or "no" boxes). This question does not apply with respect to trustees, directors, officers, or key employees of the organization, such as a development officer.

If the answer to this question is "yes," the organization must list the ten highest paid individuals or entities where the fundraiser is to be compensated at least $5,000 in the year by the organization (question two (b)). In this list, the organization must provide the following information:

- The name of the individual or entity (fundraiser) (column (i)).

- A summary of the type of fundraising activity with respect to which the fundraiser performed services (column (ii)).

- Whether the fundraiser has custody or control of contributions (column (iii), "yes" or "no" boxes); *custody or control* means possession of the funds or the ability to deposit, direct the use of, or use the funds; any such custody or control should be described in Schedule O.

- Gross receipts that the organization collected or the fundraiser collected on behalf of the organization or in connection with the fundraising activity of the organization during the tax year (column (iv)).

- Amount of fees paid to or retained (the instructions use the word *withheld*) by the fundraiser for its services (column (v)); if the arrangement also provides for the payment by the organization of fundraising expenses (such as printing, paper, envelopes, postage, mailing list rental, and equipment rental), the organization must report those amounts paid during the year in Schedule O and describe how the arrangement distinguishes payments for professional fundraising services from expense reimbursements; the organization must also describe in Schedule O whether it entered into any arrangements under which payments were made exclusively for such expenses and no payment was made for professional fundraising services.

- Amount paid to or retained by the organization (column (vi)); this equals the amount in column (v) less the amount in column (iv).

The filing organization must list all states in which it is registered or licensed to solicit funds or has been notified that it is exempt from such registration or licensing (question three) (see Chapter 3). The IRS's instructions state that, if the filing organization is registered, licensed, or exempted from registration or licensing "in all 50 States, it may answer 'All 50 States.'" This outcome, however, is impossible inasmuch as not all states have registration, licensing, or exemption laws.

Part II (Fundraising Events)

Part II of Schedule G must be completed by organizations that reported, for the year, receipt of more than $15,000 in revenue from fundraising events. There is an anomaly here. Despite this opening threshold of $15,000, Part II requires the listing of events the gross receipts of which are greater than $5,000. What does an organization do if it had, for example, five fundraising events during the year, each of which grossed $4,000? The $15,000 threshold is exceeded but not the $5,000 threshold.

The table in Part II is to be completed by listing the two largest fundraising events (#1 and #2), as measured by gross receipts, in columns (a) and (b) by indicating the name (the instructions state *type*); in column (c), the organization reports the total number of other events that occurred. The organization also reports, as to these two events and the summary of the others (if any), the following:

- *Gross receipts from the event(s)* (line 1). The organization enters the total amount the organization received from each of the two largest events during the year (without subtracting any costs or expenses or charitable contributions received in connection with the event) (columns (a) and (b)). The total amount the organization received from all other events during the year (without any offsets) is also reported (column (c)). The sum of line 1, columns (a)–(c) is reported in column (d).

- *Charitable contributions received in connection with the event(s)* (line 2). The total amount of contributions and similar amounts (including the total value of any noncash contributions (discussed ahead) received by the organization for the two largest events during the year is separately reported (columns (a) and (b)). The total amount of contributions and the like received by the organization from the other events during the year is also reported (column (c)). The sum of line 2, columns (a)–(c) is reported in column (d). This amount is also entered in Form 990, Part VIII, line (c).

- *Gross revenue from the event (gross receipts minus contributions)* (line 3). The total amount of gross revenue received by the organization from the two largest events during the year (without reduction for catering, entertainment, cost of goods sold, compensation, fees or other expenses) is separately reported (columns (a) and (b)). The total amount of gross revenue received by the organization from the other events during the year is also reported (column (c)). The sum of line 3, columns (a)–(c) is reported in column (d). This amount is also entered in Form 990, Part VIII, line (a).

- *The total amount of cash prizes paid out* (line 4). The prize amounts for the two largest events are separately reported (columns (a) and (b)). The prize amounts for the other events are also reported (column (c)). The sum of line 4, columns (a)–(c) is reported in column (d).

- *The total amount (fair market value) of noncash prizes paid out* (line 5). The prize amounts for the two largest events are separately reported (columns (a) and (b)). The prize amounts for the other events are also reported (column (c)). The sum of line 5, columns (a)–(c) is reported in column (d).

- *Total expenses paid or incurred for the rent of property and/or other facilities* (line 6). The rent/facility costs for the two largest events are separately reported (columns (a) and (b)). The rent/facility costs for the other events are also reported (column (c)). The sum of line 6, columns (a)–(c) is reported in column (d).

- *Total other direct expenses* (line 7). This is the sum of other direct expense items not included on lines 4–6, including catering and entertainment expenses. The other direct expenses for the two largest events are separately reported (columns (a) and (b)). The prize amounts for the other events are also reported (column (c)). The sum of line 7, columns (a)–(c) is reported in column (d).

- *The IRS, in its instructions, requires the filing organization to retain in its records a schedule providing an itemized listing of all other direct expenses not included on lines 4–6.* For labor costs and wages, the organization should include the total amount of compensation paid to special event workers or paid to independent contractors for labor costs.

- *A summary of direct expenses for all reported events* (line 8). This is the sum of line 8, columns (a)–(c), reported in column (d). The organization should enter this amount in Form 990, Part VIII, line (b).

- *A net income summary for all reported events (gross revenue less direct expenses)* (line 9). This amount (reported in line 9, column (d)) is the difference between the amount on line 3, column (d), and the amount on line 8, column (d). The organization should enter this amount in Form 990, Part VIII, line (c).

Part III (Gaming)

Part III of Schedule G must be completed by organizations that reported (Form 990, Part VIII, line (a)), for the year, receipt of more than $15,000 in revenue from gaming. This part differentiates among bingo (column (a)), pull-tabs/instant bingo/progressive bingo (column (b)), and other forms of gaming (column (c)). The IRS's instructions state that "certain consolation bingo games within a progressive bingo game should be included in column (a)." There is no monetary threshold in connection with the reporting of discrete gaming operations.

For each gaming operation, the organization must report:

- *Gross revenue* (line 1). The amount of gross revenue from gaming activities, for each type of gaming conducted is reported (columns (a)–(c)), with the total in column (d). This amount should not be reduced by any amount of cash or noncash prizes, cost of goods sold, compensation, fees, or other expenses.

- *Total amount of cash prizes paid out* (line 2). This must be reported for each of the types of gaming reported on line 2 (columns (a)–(c)) and totaled (column (d)).

- *Total fair market value of non-cash prizes provided* (line 3). This must be reported for each of the types of gaming reported on line 3 (columns (a)–(c)) and totaled (column (d)).

- *Expenses paid or incurred for the rent of property and/or other facilities* (line 42). These expenses must be reported for each of the types of gaming reported on line 4 (columns (a)–(c)) and totaled (column (d)).

- *Other direct expenses* (line 5). The organization must report the amount of other direct expenses (expenses not included on lines 2–4). These expenses should include labor costs and wages (including the total amount of compensation paid to gaming workers or paid to independent contractors for labor costs), employment taxes (including the amount of federal, state, and local payroll taxes paid for the year associated with gaming workers but only those that are imposed on the organization as an employer), and excise taxes. The foregoing includes the employer's share of social security and Medicare taxes, the federal unemployment tax, state unemployment compensation taxes, and other state and local payroll taxes. These expenses must be reported for each of the types of gaming reported on line 5 (columns (a)–(c)) and totaled (column (d)).

- The organization should not include in line 5 taxes withheld from the employees' salaries and paid to various governmental units, such as federal and state income taxes, and the employees' share of social security and Medicare taxes.

- The IRS's instructions require the organization to retain in its records a schedule providing an itemized listing of all other direct expenses.

- *Gaming activities may be subject to a wagering excise tax*, imposed on the amount of the wager, and an occupational tax, imposed on the persons engaged in receiving wagers.

- *Use of any volunteer labor, by "yes" or "no" boxes* (if there is such labor, the percentage of it must be reported) (line 6). If the organization uses volunteer labor, where substantially all of the work is performed without compensation, to conduct gaming, one or more of the appropriate "yes" boxes is to be checked and the percentage of total labor performed by volunteers for each type of gaming conducted is to be reported. This percentage is determined by comparing the number of individuals who receive direct compensation for their services provided in the conduct of the gaming activity with the total number of workers used by the organization, whether paid or unpaid. For this purpose, the word *compensation* includes tips and noncash benefits. These answers and percentages (if any) must be reported for each of the types of gaming reported on line 6 (columns (a)–(c)); column (d) is to be left blank.

- *A summary of direct expenses for all gaming* (line 7). This amount is the sum of the amounts on lines 2, column (d), through 7, column (d), and reported on line 7, column (d).

- *A summary of net gaming income for all gaming* (line 8). This amount is the difference between the amount on line 1, column (d), and on line 7, column (d).

- *For organizations filing the new Form 990*, the amounts in column (d) of line 1, column (d) of line 7, and column (d) of line 8 must equal the amounts reported on Form 990, Part VIII, lines 9(a), 9(b), and 9(c), respectively.

The organization must identify the states in which it operated gaming activities during the tax year (question 9); if additional space is needed, the organization should utilize Schedule O. The organization is asked whether it is licensed to operate gaming activities in each of these states (question 9(a), "yes" or "no" boxes); if the answer to this question is "no," the organization must provide a narrative statement of explanation, preferably using Schedule O (question 9 (b)).

The organization is asked whether any of its gaming licenses were revoked, suspended, or terminated during the year (question 10(a), "yes" or "no" boxes). If the answer to this question is "yes," the organization must provide a narrative statement of explanation for each state in which there was a revocation or the like during the tax year, preferably using Schedule O (question 10(b)). The organization is asked whether it operates gaming activities with nonmembers (question 11, "yes" or "no" boxes). The organization is asked if it is a grantor, beneficiary, or trustee of a trust or a member of a partnership or other entity formed to administer charitable gaming (question 12, "yes" or "no" boxes).

Part III of Schedule G seeks additional information in connection with gaming activities:

- The percentage of gaming activity operated in the organization's facility and/or an outside facility (question 13).

- The name and address of the person who prepares the organization's gaming/special events books and records (question 14).

- Whether the organization has a contract with an entity from which it receives gaming revenue (question 15a, "yes" or "no" boxes). If the answer to this question is "yes," the organization must report the amount of gaming revenue it received and the amount of gaming revenue retained by the entity (question 15b). Also, if the answer to this question is "yes," the organization must provide the entity's name and address (question 15c). Schedule O is available if additional space is needed, such as where there is more than one third-party operator.

- Gaming manager information, that is, information about the person who has overall supervision and management of the gaming operation (question 16). Generally, this person has responsibilities that may include record-keeping, money counting, hiring and firing of workers, and making bank deposits for the gaming operation. The information to be reported is the manager's name, compensation, services provided, and whether the manager is, with respect to the organization, a director, officer, employee, and/or independent contractor. If more than one person shares these responsibilities, Schedule O is available to report that information.

- Whether the organization is required under state law to make charitable distributions from the gaming proceeds in order to retain its state gaming license (question 17a, "yes" or "no" boxes).

- The amount of distributions required under state law to other tax-exempt organizations or spent in furtherance of the organization's exempt activities during the year (question 17b). A breakdown of required distributions, by each state, must be provided in Schedule O.

PREPARATION OF FORM 990 SCHEDULE M

Schedule M consists of many questions pertaining to contributions to public charities and other categories of tax-exempt organizations, of types of property, other than money (*noncash contributions*). This schedule must be completed by exempt organizations that report, as revenue, more than an aggregate of $25,000 of noncash contributions on Form 990 (Part IV, line 1 (g)). This schedule must also be filed by organizations that received during the year any contributions of art, historical treasures, or other similar assets, or qualified conservation contributions. At the top of this schedule, the filing organization must enter its name and employer identification number.

Introduction

Organizations filing this schedule are likely to be *charitable* entities (see Chapter 1), namely, entities that may receive deductible noncash contributions:

- Charitable organizations (other than private foundations or organizations that test for public safety)

- Domestic fraternal organizations that use charitable contributions exclusively for charitable purposes

- Cemetery companies

- Qualified veterans' organizations

As noted, however, the Schedule M filing requirement is applicable to all exempt organizations that received one or more noncash gifts and applies irrespective of the availability of a charitable contribution deduction.

Questions 1 to 24 of Schedule M pertain to specific types of contributed property. Contributed items that are not identified on the schedule by category of property must be reported separately as *other* items beginning with line 25.

In Schedule M, Part I, Column (a), the filing organization must check each box that relates to the type of property referenced in the schedule (even if the number of contributions need not be reported).

In Schedule M, Part I, Column (b), the filing organization must enter, for each type of property received during the year, the number of contributions or the number of items, interests, collections, properties, and the like received during the year, determined in accordance with the organization's recordkeeping practices. The organization must explain in Schedule M, Part II, whether the organization is reporting the number of contributions or the number of items received.

For each security, the organization must treat each separate gift (rather than each share received) as an item for this purpose. For all other types of property, the organization must provide the number of items contributed to it. If precise numbers are not regularly kept by the organization, a good-faith estimate will suffice. This requirement, however, is inapplicable (because of the recordkeeping burdens) with respect to contributions of books and publications, clothing, and household goods.

In Schedule M, Part I, Column (c), the organization must enter any revenue as reported elsewhere on the Form 990 (Part VIII, line 1(g)) for the appropriate type of property. Museums and other organizations, however, often do not report contributions of art, historical treasures, and similar items as revenue, as is permitted under generally accepted accounting principles. Organizations in this circumstance should enter "0" in Column (c). A museum, for example, may explain in Part II of Schedule M that a zero amount was reported because, as allowed by accounting principles, it does not capitalize its collections.

In Schedule M, Part I, Column (d), the organization must describe the method it used to determine revenue amount (such as cost or selling price of the contributed property, sale of comparable properties, replacement cost, or an opinion of an expert). An organization that is permitted to enter "0" in Column (c) should leave the accompanying Column (d) blank.

Questions One to Three (Works of Art)

Questions 1 to 3 of Schedule M pertain to contributions to tax-exempt organizations of types of works of art. These questions concern gifts of historical treasures, gifts of fractional interests in art, and all other types of art. *Art* does not include collectibles, which are reported on line 18. For each of these types of art, the filing organization must check the box in Column (a) if applicable, and report the number of the work or works of art contributed (Column (b)), the amount of any of these gift(s) reported as revenue (Form 990, Part IV, line 1g) (Column (c)), and (if applicable) the method of determining revenues.

In the case of a contribution of a fractional interest in a work of art, in the Column (b) reporting, the organization should report the fractional interest received in each year with respect to the underlying work of art.

It should be reiterated that the Form 990 inquires as to whether the filing organization maintains collections of works of art, historical treasures, or other similar assets for "public exhibition, education, or research in furtherance of public service rather than for financial gain" (Part VII, line 5). If the answer to this question is "yes," the filing organization must complete a portion of another schedule (Schedule D, Part X). In this schedule, the organization must: indicate whether it reported as revenue any contributions of art; indicate whether it capitalized any contributions of art in the reporting of prior years and reported those amounts on the Form 990 (Part VI); and provide the text of the footnote to the organization's audited financial statements that discusses the organization's holdings of art, historical treasures, and other similar assets.

Question 4 (Books and Publications)

Question 4 of Schedule M pertains to contributions to tax-exempt organizations of books and publications. Books and other publications may be contributed to a charitable organization; the gift may give rise to a charitable contribution deduction. Rare books and manuscripts are treated as works of art (discussed previously); they may also be collectibles (discussed ahead). For these contributions, the filing organization must check the line 4 box. The number of these contributions need not be reported. If applicable, the amount of the gift(s) reported as revenue (Form 990, Part VIII, line 1g) and the method of determining revenues must be reported.

Question 5 (Clothing and Household Goods)

Question 5 of Schedule M pertains to contributions of clothing and/or household goods that were in good used condition or better. For these two categories of items, the filing organization must check the box. The number of these contributions need not be reported. If applicable, the organization must report the amount of the gift(s) reported as revenue (Form 990, Part VIII, line 1g) and the method of determining revenues. Clothing items and/or household goods that were not in good used condition or better are reported as *other*.

Questions 6 and 7 (Vehicles)

Questions 6 and 7 of Schedule M concern contributions of vehicles, such as automobiles, boats, and airplanes. Vehicles that constitute inventory are to be reported as such (discussed ahead). For these types of vehicles, the filing organization must check the box and report the number of the vehicle or vehicles contributed, the amount of the gift(s) reported as revenue (Form 990, Part VIII, line 1g), and the method of determining revenues.

The response to the question on line 6 should include only contributions of motor vehicles manufactured primarily for use on public streets, roads, and highways.

The organization is required to file Form 1098-C for certain of these contributions reported on these lines. See Form 990, Part V, line 7h.

Question 8 (Intellectual Property)

Question 8 of Schedule M pertains to charitable and other contributions of intellectual property. For this type of property, the filing organization must check the box and report the number of the intellectual property or properties contributed, the amount of the gift(s) reported as revenue (Form 990, Part VIII, line 1g), and the method of determining revenues.

Certain contributions of intellectual property may require the organization to file Form 8889 with the donor and the IRS with respect to the contribution. See Form 990, Part V, line 7g.

Questions 9 to 12 (Securities)

Questions 9 to 12 of Schedule M pertain to charitable and other contributions of securities, differentiating among publicly traded securities, closely held stock, securities in the form of partnership or trust interests, and other types of securities. For each of these categories of securities, the filing organization must check the box and report the number of securities contributed, the amount of the gift(s) reported as revenue (Form 990, Part VIII, line), and the method of determining revenues. For each security, the filing organization should treat each separate gift (rather than each share received) as a contribution for this purpose.

Questions 13 and 14 (Qualified Conservation Contributions)

Questions 13 and 14 of Schedule M pertain to qualified conservation contributions, distinguishing between gifts involving historic structures and other conservation contributions. For each of these types of contributions, the filing organization must check the box and report the number of the property or properties contributed, the amount of the gift(s) reported as revenue (Form 990, Part VIII, line 1g), and the method of determining revenues.

On line 13, the filing organization should enter information about contributions of a qualified real property interest that is a restriction with respect to the exterior of a certified historic structure. Line 14 is used to report information about qualified conservation contributions other than those referenced in connection with line 13; this includes conservation easements to preserve land areas for outdoor recreation by or for the education of the public, to protect a relatively natural habitat or ecosystem, to preserve open space, or to preserve an historically important land area.

Questions 15 to 17 (Real Estate)

Questions 15 to 17 of Schedule M concern charitable and other contributions of real estate, differentiating among, gifts of residential real estate, commercial real estate, and other categories of real estate. For each of these types of properties, the filing organization must check the box and report the number of the property or properties contributed, the amount of the gift(s) reported as revenue (Form 990, Part VIII, line 1g), and the method of determining revenues.

On line 15, the filing organization enters information about contributions of residential real estate. This entry should include any information about contributions (not in trust) of a remainder interest in a personal residence that was not the donor's entire interest in the property. On line 16, the organization enters information about contributions of commercial real estate, such as a commercial office building. This entry should include any information about contributions (not in trust) of a remainder interest in a farm that was not the donor's entire interest in the property. Line 17 is used to enter information about any real estate interests not reported on lines 15 or 16.

Question 18 (Collectibles)

Question 18 of Schedule M pertains to charitable and other contributions of collectibles. For this type of gift, the filing organization must check the box and report the number of collectibles contributed, the amount of the gift(s) reported as revenue (Form 990, Part IV, line 1g), and the method of determining revenues.

Question 19 (Food Inventory)

Question 19 of Schedule M pertains to charitable and other contributions of food items, including food inventory contributed by corporations and other businesses. For this type of gift, the filing organization must check the box and report the number of the inventory property contributed, the amount of the gift(s) reported as revenue (Form 990, Part VIII, line 1g), and the method of determining revenues.

Question 20 (Drugs and Medical Supplies)

Question 20 of Schedule M concerns charitable and other contributions of drugs, medical supplies, and similar items contributed by businesses that manufactured or distributed these items. For this type of gift, the filing organization must check the box and report the number of the drugs or supplies contributed, the amount of the gift(s) reported as revenue (Form 990, Part VIII, line 1g), and the method of determining revenues.

Question 21 (Taxidermy)

Question 21 pertains to contributions of taxidermy. For this type of gift, the filing organization must check the box and report the number of taxidermy items contributed, the amount of the gift(s) reported as revenue (Form 990, Part VIII, line 1g), and the method of determining revenues.

Question 22 (Historical Artifacts)

Question 22 of Schedule M pertains to contributions of historical artifacts. For this type of gift, the filing organization must check the box and report the number of historical artifacts contributed, the amount of the gift(s) reported as revenue (Form 990, Part VIII, line 1g), and the method of determining revenues. This entry should not include works of art or historical treasures (discussed previously) or archeological artifacts.

Question 23 (Scientific Specimens)

Question 23 of Schedule M pertains to contributions of scientific specimens. For this type of gift, the filing organization must check the box and report the number of scientific specimens contributed, the amount of the gift(s) reported as revenue (Form 990, Part VIII, line 1g), and the method of determining revenues.

Question 24 (Archaeological Artifacts)

Question 24 of Schedule M pertains to contributions of archaeological ethnological artifacts. For this type of gift, the filing organization must check the box and report the number of archaeological artifacts contributed, the amount of the gift(s) reported as revenue (Form 990, Part VIII, line 1g), and the method of determining revenues. This entry should not include information about works of art, historical treasures, or historical artifacts (discussed previously).

Questions 25 to 28 (Other Types of Property)

Questions 25 to 28 of Schedule M enable the filing organization to report as to any other types of noncash contributions received. For each of these types of gift, the filing organization must check the box and report the number of property(ies) contributed, the amount of the gift(s) reported as revenue (Form 990, Part VIII, line 1g), and the method of determining revenues.

Question 29 (Forms 8283)

The filing organization is required, pursuant to question 29 of Schedule M, to report the number of Forms 8283 that it received during the reporting year for contributions as to which the organization completed Part IV of the form(s). If the organization does not keep complete records of these forms, it should not provide an estimate but rather leave line 29 blank.

Question 30 (Contribution Holding Period)

The filing organization must, in response to question 30a of Schedule M, report ("yes" or "no") whether, during the reporting year, it received a con-tribution of property, reported in Part I of the schedule, that it is required, by the terms of the gift or otherwise, to hold for at least three years from the date of the initial contribution, where it is not required that the property be used for exempt purposes for the entire holding period. If the answer to this question is "yes," the arrangement must be described in Schedule M, Part II (line 30b).

Tax-exempt organizations should be cautious when considering accep-tance of property with this condition. The IRS will assume that the purpose of the condition is to sidestep the three-year reporting requirement rule.

Question 31 (Gift Acceptance Policy)

The filing organization must, in response to question 31 of Schedule M, report ("yes" or "no") whether it has a gift acceptance policy that requires the review of any nonstandard contributions.

Question 32 (Service Providers)

The filing organization must, in response to question 32a of Schedule M, report ("yes" or "no") whether it hired or otherwise used third parties or related organizations to solicit, process, or sell contributed noncash property. If the answer to this question is "yes," the matter must be described in Schedule M, Part II (line 32b).

Question 33 (Explanation of Nonrevenue Treatment)

The filing organization must, if it did not report revenues in Part I, Column (c) for a type of property for which Column (a) is checked, explain the matter, in response to question 33 of Schedule M, in Schedule M, Part II.

PREPARATION OF SCHEDULE B

Schedule B of the redesigned Form 990 (and Forms 990-EZ and 990-PF) is used to provide information, about contributors, received by the filing organization during the reporting year. (This schedule is the same as the Schedule B that accompanied prior Forms 990.) For this purpose, a *contributor* (or *grantor*) is any donating person, whether it is an individual, fiduciary, corporation, trust, partnership, or tax-exempt organization. The term *contribution* means contributions, grants, bequests, devises of money or property, whether for charitable purposes or other like purposes (such as political contributions). Contributions do not include fees received for the performance of services.

A *cash contribution* includes contributions paid by cash, credit card, check, money order, electronic fund or wire transfers, and other charges against funds on deposit at a financial institution. The phrase *charitable deduction property* means property other than money or certain publicly traded securities.

Part I. Generally, an organization must list in Part I of Schedule B every contributor who, during the year, gave the organization, directly or indirectly, money, securities, or other type of property aggregating $5,000 or more. In determining the $5,000 threshold, the organization totals all of the contributor's gifts only if they are $1,000 or more for the year.

If the filing organization is a donative type publicly supported charity (see Chapter 4), under the general rules (that is, not just pursuant to the facts-and-circumstances test), it lists in Part I only those contributors whose contribution of $5,000 or more is greater than 2 percent of its total support during the public support measuring period (see Form 990, Part VIII, line 1h). As an example, Charity X, a donative type public charity, reported $700,000 in contributions, grants, and the like for its public support measuring period. Two percent of $700,000 is $14,000. Thus, a contributor who gave $11,000 to X during the year would not be reported on Schedule B of X's Form 990. This is the case even though this contributor's contribution(s) for the year was in excess of $5,000.

In the case of contributions to tax-exempt social clubs, and fraternal beneficiary and domestic fraternal societies, which were not for an exclusively charitable purpose, the organizations lists each contributor who, during the year, contributed $5,000 or more, as determined above. In the case of contributions to these organizations that were for exclusively religious purposes, the organization reports each contributor whose aggregate contributions were more than $1,000 during the year (taking into account contributions of all amounts).

These three types of tax-exempt organizations provide further information on these contributions of more than $1,000 during the year in Part III of Schedule B, and show the total amount received in the case of contributions that were for $1,000 or less during the year. If one of these organizations did not receive a contribution of more than $1,000 during the year for exclusively charitable purposes, and thus was not required to complete Parts I–III of Schedule B, it need only check the correct *Special Rules* box applicable to that organization on the front of Schedule B and enter, in the space provided, the total contributions it received during the year for exclusively charitable purposes.

In Part I of Schedule B, contributors are to be numbered consecutively (column (a)). The contributor's name and address (column (b)), aggregate contributions for the year (column (c)), and the type of contribution (column (d)) must be reported. If a cash contribution came directly from a contributor, the "person" box is to be checked. The "payroll" box is to be checked if an employer forwarded an employee's contributions. The "noncash" box is to be checked in an instance of a contribution of property other than cash. The checking of a "noncash" box triggers the requirement to file Part II of Schedule B.

A central (parent) organization with a group ruling that files a group Form 990 must file a separate Form 990 for itself (unless it is exempt from filing Form 990 (discussed previously)). With respect to Schedule B, however, a central organization has two choices—it may file:

1. A Schedule B for itself with its Form 990 and a separate Schedule B with the group return

2. A consolidated Schedule B for itself and all included subordinates with the group return

The same information must be reported whichever method of reporting is used; the information is just formatted differently and appears in different returns.

The central organization must indicate, in Schedule O, which method of reporting it has adopted. Once a method is used, it cannot be changed without the consent of the IRS.

Part II. In column (a) of this Part II, the filing organization shows the number that corresponds to the contributor's number in Part I. Column (b) is used to describe the noncash contribution received by the organization.

The fair market value of the contributed property is reported in column (c). If the organization immediately sells gifted securities, the contribution nonetheless must be reported as a gift of property (with the value being the net proceeds of the sale plus any broker's fees and other expenses). If contributed securities are not immediately sold, and they are marketable securities registered and listed on a recognized securities exchange, the market value is measured by the average of the highest and lowest quoted selling prices (or the average between the bona fide bid and asked prices) on the contribution date.

When fair market value of an item of contributed property cannot be readily determined, the filing organization is to use, according to the IRS's instructions, an "appraised or estimated" value. To determine the amount of a noncash contribution that is subject to debt, the organization subtracts the amount of the debt from the property's fair market value.

The date the property was received by the organization is reported in column (d) (assuming the transaction is, in fact, a completed gift).

If the organization received a partially completed Form 8283 (see Chapter 8) from a donor, the organization should complete it and return it to the donor to enable the donor to obtain a charitable contribution deduction. The organization should retain a copy of this form for its records. Original and successor donee organizations must file Form 8282 if they sell, exchange, consume, or otherwise dispose of charitable deduction property within three years after the date the original donee received the property.

Part III. Tax-exempt social welfare and fraternal organizations that received contributions for exclusively charitable purposes must complete Parts I–III of Schedule B for those persons whose contributions totaled more than $1,000 for the year. The filing organization must also show, in the heading of Part III, total gifts to these organizations that were $1,000 or less for the year and were for an exclusively charitable purpose. This latter item of information is to be completed only on the first Part III page.

If an amount is set aside for an exclusively charitable purpose, the filing organization must describe, in column (d), how the amount is held. For example, a set-aside amount may be commingled with amounts held for other purposes. If the organization transferred the gift to another organization, the filing organization should report the name and address of the transferee organization, and explain the relationship between the two organizations, in column (e).

Disclosure Considerations. For organizations that file Form 990, the names and addresses of contributors are not open to public inspection. If an organization files a copy of its Form 990 with one or more states, it should not include its Schedule B in the filing, unless the state requires a schedule of contributors. States that do not require the information might inadvertently make the schedule available for public inspection.

PREPARATION OF OTHER PARTS OF FORM 990

In addition to Schedules G and M, other parts of the new Form 990 pertain to fundraising reporting.

Part I, Line 16a (Professional Fundraising Expenses)

On line 16a of Part I, the filing organization reports its professional fund-raising expenses. This is the amount that also appears in Part IX, line 11e, column (A).

Part IV, Line 14b (Fundraising Outside U.S.)

On line 14b of Part IV, the filing organization reports whether it has aggregate revenues or expenses of more than $10,000 from fundraising activities outside the United States.

Part VIII, Lines 1c, 8a, and 9a (Fundraising Events)

On line 1c of Part VIII, the filing organization reports the amount of contributions received from fundraising events. On line 8a of Part VIII, the filing organizations reports the amount of revenue derived from fundraising events, other than contributions. On line 9a of Part VIII, the filing organization reports the amount of its gross income from gaming activities. (See Part IV, lines 18 and 19.)

Part IX, Line 11e (Professional Fundraising Expenses)

On Part IX, line 11e, the filing organization reports the amount of its professional fundraising expenses. (See Part IV, line 17.)

SUMMARY

This chapter described the principal federal tax law filing requirements for charitable organizations and inventoried the various types of annual information and other returns. The portions of the redesigned annual information return having special significance to fundraising were identified and summarized, with emphasis on the reporting on fundraising and gaming (Schedule G), noncash contributions (Schedule M), and contributions and grants (Schedule B). The chapter also inventoried the various penalties and other sanctions in this context.

6

CHARITABLE GIVING RULES

The purpose of this chapter is to summarize the basics of the federal tax law rules concerning deductible charitable giving that every fundraising professional should know. A seemingly simple subject, the law pertaining to the making of and deductibility of gifts to charitable organizations is complex. This is particularly the case with respect to planned giving. Specifically, this chapter will:

- Analyze the elements of a charitable gift.
- Summarize the concept of qualified donees.
- Summarize the rule as to contributions for the use of charity.
- Explain the deductibility of conditional gifts.
- Discuss the advantages of gifts of property.
- Summarize the rules as to valuation of contributed property.
- Summarize the percentage limitations on deductibility.
- Explain the deduction reduction rules.
- Summarize the rules as to qualified appreciated stock.
- Address the twice-basis deductions rules.
- Summarize the rules as to gifts of partial interests in property.
- Summarize the rules as to charitable gifts using insurance.
- Discuss the planned giving rules and techniques.

BASIC CONCEPTS

The basic concept of the federal income tax deduction for a charitable contribution is this: Corporations and individuals who itemize their deductions can deduct on their annual tax returns, within certain limits (discussed ahead), an amount equivalent to the amount contributed (money) or to the value of a contribution (property) to a qualified donee. A *charitable contribution* for income tax purposes is a gift to or for the use of one or more qualified donees.

Deductions for charitable gifts are also allowed under the federal gift tax and estate tax laws. A charitable estate tax deduction is allowed for the value of all transfers from a decedent's estate to or for the use of charitable organizations. A charitable gift tax deduction is available for transfers by contribution to or for the use of charitable organizations. The extent of these charitable deductions is not dependent on whether the charitable donee is a public charity or a private foundation (see Chapter 4); percentage limitations do not apply to these deductions.

Donors and the charitable organizations they support commonly expect gifts to be in the form of outright transfers of money or property. In more sophisticated situations, however, a gift may be part of a larger transaction or be of a partial interest in an item of property (discussed ahead). For both parties (donor and donee), a gift is usually a unilateral transaction, in a financial sense: The donor parts with the contributed item and the charity acquires it (assuming acceptance of the gift).

The advantages to the donor, from the making of a charitable gift, generally are the resulting charitable deduction and the gratification derived from the giving. Planned giving (discussed ahead) provides additional financial and tax advantages to the donor. Overall, these are the economic advantages that can result from a charitable gift:

- A federal, state, and/or local tax deduction
- Avoidance of capital gains taxation
- Creation of or an increase in cash flow
- Improved tax treatment of income
- Free professional tax and investment management services
- Opportunity to transfer property between the generations of a family
- Receipt of benefits from the charitable donee

In some instances, there can be additional advantages. The best example of this is a contribution to a private foundation. This is because a contributor to a foundation usually is a founder of the foundation, and likely also is a trustee and officer of it. Thus, the contributor, in the case of a foundation gift, usually retains control over the money and/or property that is the subject of the gift. This is not to countenance or advocate wrongdoing; it is merely a statement of fact that gives rise to unique circumstances not normally found in the charitable giving setting. Indeed, in this context, the contributor (and/or one or more family members) may also be an employee of the donee foundation. (These types of arrangements are impermissible when the charitable donee is a supporting organization or a donor-advised fund (see Chapter 4).)

DEFINING *CHARITABLE GIFT*

A fundamental requirement of the charitable contribution deduction law is that the cash or property transferred to a charitable organization must be transferred (in whole or in part) in the form of a *gift*. Just because money is paid or property is transferred to a charity does not necessarily mean that the payment or transfer is a gift. When a tax-exempt university's tuition, an exempt hospital's health-care fee, or an exempt association's dues are paid, there is no gift and thus no charitable deduction for the payment. (In some settings, however, a business expense deduction is available.)

Basically, a gift has two elements: It involves a transfer that is *voluntary* and is motivated by something other than *consideration* (something received in return for a payment). Where payments are made to receive something in exchange (education, health care, and the like), the transaction is a purchase. The law places more emphasis on what is received by the payor than on the payment or transfer. The income tax regulations state that a transfer is not a contribution when made "with a reasonable expectation of financial return commensurate with the amount of the transfer." A single transaction, however, can be partially a gift and partially a purchase (discussed ahead); when a charity is the payee, only the gift portion is deductible.

The U.S. Supreme Court, in a famous pronouncement, observed that a gift is a transfer motivated by "detached or disinterested generosity." The Court also characterized a gift as a transfer stimulated "out of affection, respect, admiration, charity, or like impulses." Thus, the focus in this area for the most part has been an objective analysis, comparing what the "donee" parted with and what (if anything) the "donor" received net in exchange.

Another factor, that of *donative intent*, is sometimes taken into consideration. A set of tax regulations states that, for any part of a payment made in the context of a charity auction to be deductible as a charitable gift, the patron must have donative intent. More broadly, a congressional committee report contains this statement: "The term 'contribution or gift' is not defined by statute, but generally is interpreted to mean a voluntary transfer of money or other property without receipt of adequate consideration and with donative intent. If a taxpayer receives or expects to receive a quid pro quo in exchange for a transfer to charity, the taxpayer may be able to deduct the excess of the amount transferred over the fair market value of any benefit received in return provided the excess payment is made with the intention of making a gift."

A federal court of appeals described the matter as to what is a gift this way: It is a "particularly confused issue of federal taxation" law. The statutory law on the subject, said this court, is "cryptic," and "neither Congress nor the courts have offered any very satisfactory definitions" of the terms *gift* and *contribution* (which are, for these purposes, basically synonymous).

QUALIFIED DONEES

Qualified donees are charitable organizations (including educational, religious, and scientific entities), certain fraternal organizations, certain cemetery companies, and most veterans' organizations. Contributions to both private foundations and public charities (see Chapter 4) are deductible; the law favors gifts to public charities.

Federal, state, and local governmental bodies are charitable donees. State or local law, however, may preclude a governmental entity from accepting charitable gifts. In most jurisdictions, a charitable organization can be established to solicit deductible contributions for and make grants to governmental bodies. This is a common technique for public schools, colleges, universities, and hospitals.

An otherwise nonqualifying organization may be allowed to receive a deductible charitable gift, where the gift property is used for charitable purposes or received by an agent for a charitable organization. An example of the former is a gift to a trade association that is earmarked for a charitable fund within the association. Examples of an agent for a charity are a title-holding company that holds a property for charitable purposes and a for-profit company that acquires and disposes of vehicles as part of a charity's used-vehicle donation program.

GIFTS FOR THE USE OF CHARITY

Most deductible charitable gifts are made *to* a charitable organization. It is possible, however, for a deductible charitable contribution to be *for the use of* a charity. There is little law on this latter point.

A court had occasion to peruse the legislative history of the law that added this phrase to the statutory law (in 1921) and concluded that the words mean "roughly the equivalent of" the words "in trust for." Previously, the then Bureau of Internal Revenue ruled that charitable deductions could not be taken for contributions to trusts, community chests, and other types of charitable foundations, on the ground that these organizations were not organized and operated for charitable purposes but served merely as conduits of contributions to charitable organizations.

This matter was taken to the U.S. Supreme Court, in connection with an issue as to whether funds transferred by parents to their children while the children served as full-time, unpaid missionaries for a church are deductible as charitable contributions. Inasmuch as the gifts were not to the church, the argument advanced by the parents turned on whether the gifts were for the use of the church. The Court, in reaffirming that the words mean "in trust for," concluded that the payments were not deductible charitable contributions because the church lacked the requisite legal rights with respect to the disposition of donated funds.

CONDITIONAL GIFTS

A donor may make a contribution to a charitable organization but place one or more conditions on the gift. Depending on the type of condition, there may not be a charitable deduction for the transfer, at least not until the condition is satisfied. Conversely, a condition may not preclude deductibility of the charitable gift.

There are three types of conditions in this regard:

1. A condition (sometimes termed a *contingency*) that is material, so that the transfer is not considered complete until the condition is satisfied

2. A condition involving a possible occurrence, when the likelihood of the event occurring is so remote as to be negligible, in which case the condition is disregarded for purposes of determining deductibility

3. A condition that is material but that is in furtherance of a charitable purpose, so that the condition is more in the nature of a *restriction* (and the charitable deduction is allowed)

Material Conditions—Nondeductibility

As to the first two of the above categories, the standard is as follows: If, as of the date of a gift, a transfer for charitable purposes is dependent on the performance of some act or the happening of a precedent event in order that it might become effective, a charitable deduction is not allowable unless the possibility that the charitable transfer will not become effective is so remote as to be negligible. If the possibility is not negligible, if it occurs, and if the charitable transfer becomes effective, the charitable deduction arises at the time the condition is satisfied or eliminated.

For example, a charitable organization wishes to construct a building to be used entirely in advancement of its program purposes. It developed a building fund that is sufficient to cover 90 percent of the construction costs of this building; the organization will seek the balance of these funds from the public. The organization represents to prospective donors that, if the contributions are not sufficient to meet the remaining costs of construction, the contributions will be returned. The charity also represents that, should the contributions received exceed the necessary amount, the organization will retain the excess funds for its general program purposes. Thus, as of the date of the gifts, the transfers for charitable purposes depend on the performance of an act or the happening of a precedent event to become effective. Furthermore, whether the contributions will be returned depends solely on whether the donors contribute the 10-percent-of-construction-costs amount. Under these circumstances, the possibility that the charitable transfers will not become effective is not so remote as to be negligible. Consequently, the gifts are not deductible as of the time of the transfers; they will become deductible at the time the condition is satisfied (and thus eliminated).

A condition or battery of conditions may be so extensive that the matter goes to the question of the donor's intent. In one instance, a gift of land was burdened with so many conditions, including sale of the property, that a court concluded that the "donor," at best, had an intent to make a gift of future land sales proceeds rather than an intent to make a present gift of the land.

Negligible Conditions

As noted, a condition that is *so remote as to be negligible* is ignored for gift deductibility purposes. This phrase has been defined as a "chance which persons generally would disregard as so highly improbable that it might be ignored with reasonable safety in undertaking a serious business transaction." It has also been characterized as a "chance which every dictate of reason would justify an intelligent person in disregarding as so highly improbable and remote as to be lacking in reason and substance."

If it is determined that a condition is a negligible one, the amount of the gift for deduction purposes may have to be discounted by the present value of the condition.

Material Conditions—Deductibility

One type of material condition that will not defeat a charitable deduction and, indeed, must be satisfied if the deduction is to be allowed, is a condition that the gift be used for one or more charitable program (see Chapter 2) purposes. As noted, this is frequently termed a *restricted gift*. The following are examples of these gifts:

- A gift to an educational organization restricted to use for scholarships

- A gift to a university restricted to a fund endowing a chair or underlying a particular department

- A gift to a tax-exempt museum restricted to its endowment fund

- A gift to a tax-exempt hospital restricted to the institution's building fund

These types of conditions or restrictions will not cause a charitable contribution deduction to be disallowed.

GIFTS OF PROPERTY IN GENERAL

Aside from the eligibility of the gift recipient, the other basic element in determining whether a charitable contribution is deductible is the nature of the property given. Essentially, the distinctions are between outright giving and planned giving, also between gifts of cash and gifts of property. In many instances, the tax law differentiates between personal property and real property, as well as tangible property and intangible property (securities).

The federal income tax treatment of gifts of property is dependent on whether the property is capital gain property. The tax law makes a distinction between *long-term capital gain* and *short-term capital gain*. Property that is not capital gain property is *ordinary income property*. These three terms are based on the tax classification of the type of revenue that would be generated on sale of the property. Short-term capital gain property is generally treated the same as ordinary income property. Therefore, the actual distinction is between capital gain property (really long-term capital gain property) and ordinary income property.

Capital gain property is a capital asset that has appreciated in value and, if sold, would give rise to long-term capital gain. To result in long-term capital gain, property must be held for at least 12 months. Most forms of capital gain property are securities and real estate.

The charitable contribution deduction for capital gain property is often equal to its fair market value or at least is computed using that value. Thus, a critical determination in ascertaining the extent of a charitable deduction can be the value of the property. In general, the fair market value of an item of property is the price at which the property would change hands between a willing buyer and a willing seller, neither being under any compulsion to buy or sell and both having reasonable knowledge of relevant facts. The IRS amplified this rule, holding that the "most probative evidence of fair market value is the price at which similar quantities of . . . [the property] are sold in arms'-length transactions." The IRS also determined that the fair market value of gift property is determined by reference to the "most active and comparable marketplace at the time of the donor's contribution." (The fair market value of an item of property is frequently the subject of litigation.)

Inasmuch as the charitable deduction for a gift of property is often based on the fair market value of the property, a donor can be economically benefited where the property has increased in value since the date on which the donor acquired the property. Property in this condition has *appreciated* in value; it is known as *appreciated property*. This gain is the amount that would have been recognized for tax purposes had the donor sold the property; it is sometimes referred to as the *appreciation element*.

Gifts of ordinary income property generally produce a deduction equivalent to the donor's cost basis in the property. The law provides exceptions to this basis-only rule; an example is a gift by a corporation out of its inventory (discussed ahead). A charitable deduction based on the full fair market value of an item of appreciated property (with no recognition of the built-in capital gain) is a critical feature of the federal tax law incentives for charitable giving. This incentive is limited in the case of contributions of appreciated property to private foundations (discussed ahead).

VALUATION OF PROPERTY

Charitable gifts are frequently made of property. These gifts to charity may be outright contributions of property or of a partial interest in an item of property (discussed ahead). The gift may entail a reduction of the otherwise deductible amount or may implicate one of the percentage limitations. The property may be personal property or real property, tangible property or intangible property.

Whatever the circumstances, the determination of a federal income tax charitable contribution deduction for a gift of property to charity will require valuation of the property. Appraisal requirements apply in instances of larger charitable contributions, and the value of gift property is an integral part of the quid pro quo contribution rules (see Chapter 8).

As a general rule, the *fair market value* of an item of property is the price at which the property would change hands between a willing buyer and a willing seller, neither being under any compulsion to buy or sell and both having reasonable knowledge of the relevant facts. The valuation standards for charitable contribution deduction purposes generally are the same as those used in the estate tax context.

The valuation of property often is not confined to good faith estimates by charitable organizations or the work of appraisers. There can be controversy in this area between contributors and the IRS, with the matter taken into court for resolution. The issue of the value of an item of property is one of fact, not law. In this type of litigation, it is common for both sides to use expert witnesses in an attempt to convince the court of the merits of a particular value. The court may rely on the expertise of one or more of these witnesses or may disregard all of them and set a value on the basis of its own belief as to value. As with any witness, the credibility of an expert witness (and the donor) in the eyes of a judge is critical in formulating the outcome. A finding by a trial court of the value of an item of property is to be set aside on appeal, and the case remanded, only if the finding of the value is clearly erroneous.

LIMITATIONS ON DEDUCTIBILITY

The extent of charitable contributions that can be deducted for a particular tax year is limited to a certain amount, which for individuals is a function of the donor's *contribution base*—essentially, an amount equal to the individual's adjusted gross income. This level of allowable annual deductibility is determined by five percentage limitations. They are dependent on several factors, principally the nature of the charitable recipient and the nature of the property contributed. The examples used below assume an individual donor with an annual contribution base of $100,000.

The first three limitations apply to gifts to public charities and to private operating foundations.

First, there is a percentage limitation of 50 percent of the donor's contribution base for gifts of cash and ordinary income property. A donor with a $100,000 contribution base may, in a year, make deductible gifts of these items up to a total of $50,000. If an individual makes contributions that exceed the 50 percent limitation, the excess generally may be carried forward and deducted in 1 to 5 subsequent years. Thus, if this donor gave $60,000 to public charities in year 1 and made no other charitable gifts in that year, he or she would be entitled to a deduction of $50,000 in year 1 and the remaining $10,000 would be available for deductibility in year 2.

The second percentage limitation is 30 percent of the donor's contribution base for gifts of capital gain property. A donor thus may, in a year, contribute up to $30,000 of qualifying stocks, bonds, real estate, and like property, and receive a charitable deduction for that amount. Any excess (more than 30 percent) of the amount of these gifts is subject to the carryforward rule. If a donor gave $50,000 in capital gain property in year 1 and made no other charitable gifts that year, he or she would be entitled to a charitable contribution deduction of $30,000 in year 1 and the $20,000 would be available in year 2.

A donor who makes gifts of cash and capital gain property to public charities (and/or private operating foundations) in any one year generally is limited by a blend of these percentage limitations. For example, if the donor in year 1 gives $50,000 in cash and $30,000 in appreciated capital gain property to a public charity, his or her charitable deduction in year 1 is $30,000 of capital gain property and $20,000 of the cash (to keep the deduction within the overall 50 percent ceiling); the other $30,000 of cash would be carried forward to year 2 (or to years 2 through 5, depending on the donor's circumstances).

The third percentage limitation allows a donor of capital gain property to use the 50 percent limitation, instead of the 30 percent limitation, where the amount of the contribution is reduced by all of the unrealized appreciation in the value of the property. This election is usually made by donors who want a larger deduction in the year of the gift for an item of property that has not appreciated in value to a great extent. Once made, this election is irrevocable.

The fourth and fifth percentage limitations apply to gifts to private foundations and certain other charitable donees (other than public charities and private operating foundations). These other donees are generally veterans' and fraternal organizations.

Under the fourth percentage limitation, contributions of cash and ordinary income property to private foundations and other entities may not exceed 30 percent of the individual donor's contribution base. The carryover rules apply to this type of gift. If the donor gives $50,000 in cash to one or more private foundations in year 1, his or her charitable deduction for that year (assuming no other charitable gifts) is $30,000, with the balance of $20,000 carried forward into subsequent years (up to 5).

The carryover rules blend with the first three percentage limitations. For example, if in year 1 a donor gave $65,000 to charity, of which $25,000 went to a public charity and $40,000 to a private foundation, his or her charitable deduction for that year would be $50,000: $30,000 for the gift to the private foundation and $20,000 for the gift to the public charity. The remaining $10,000 of the gift to the foundation and the remaining $5,000 of the gift to the public charity would be carried forward into year 2.

The fifth percentage limitation is 20 percent of the contribution base for gifts of capital gain property to private foundations and other charitable donees. There is a carryforward for any excess deduction amount. For example, if a donor gives appreciated securities, having a value of $30,000, to a private foundation in year 1, his or her charitable deduction for year 1 (assuming no other charitable gifts) is $20,000; the remaining $10,000 may be carried forward.

Deductible charitable contributions by corporations in any tax year may not exceed 10 percent of pretax net income. Excess amounts may be carried forward and deducted in subsequent years (up to 5). For gifts by corporations, the federal tax laws do not differentiate between gifts to public charities and gifts to private foundations. As an illustration, a corporation that grosses $1 million in a year and incurs $900,000 in expenses in that year (not including charitable gifts) may generally contribute to charity and deduct in that year an amount up to $10,000 (10 percent of $100,000); in computing its taxes, this corporation would report taxable income of $90,000. If the corporation contributed $20,000 in that year, the numbers would remain the same, except that the corporation would have a $10,000 charitable contribution carryforward.

A corporation on the accrual method of accounting can elect to treat a contribution as having been made in a tax year if it is actually donated during the first $2\frac{1}{2}$ months of the following year. Corporate gifts of property are generally subject to the deduction reduction rules (discussed ahead).

A business organization that is a *flow-through entity* generates a different tax result when it comes to charitable deductions. (These organizations are partnerships, other joint ventures, small business (S) corporations, and limited liability companies.) Entities of this nature, even though they may make charitable gifts, do not claim charitable contribution deductions. Instead, the deduction is passed through to the partners, members, or other owners on an allocable basis and they claim their share of the deduction on their tax return.

Thus, aside from these percentage limitations, the ability in instances of gifts of property, to base a charitable deduction on the full fair market value of the property often turns on this public charity/private foundation dichotomy. As a general rule, the only time the deduction can be based on the property's fair value (and enable the contributor to avoid recognition of the appreciation element (capital gain)) is when the charitable donee is a public charity or a private operating foundation. By contrast, where a contribution is made to a charitable organization that is a private foundation, a deduction reduction rule usually applies (discussed ahead), unless the contributed property is qualified appreciated stock (discussed ahead).

DEDUCTION REDUCTION RULES

A donor (individual or corporation) who makes a gift of *ordinary income property* to a charitable organization (public or private) must confine the charitable deduction to an amount equal to the donor's cost basis in the property. The deduction is not based on the fair market value of the property; it must be reduced by the amount that would have been gain (ordinary income) if the property had been sold. As an example, if a donor gave to a charity an item of ordinary income property having a value of $1,000, for which he or she paid $600, the resulting charitable deduction would be $600.

Any donor who makes a gift of *capital gain property* to a public charity generally can compute the charitable deduction using the property's fair market value at the time of the gift, regardless of the basis amount and with no taxation of the appreciation (the capital gain inherent in the property). Suppose, however, a donor makes a gift of capital gain tangible personal property (such as a work of art) to a public charity and the use of the gift property by the donee is unrelated to its tax-exempt purposes (see Chapter 7). The donor must reduce the deduction by an amount equal to all of the long-term capital gain that would have been recognized had the donor sold the property at its fair market value as of the date of the contribution.

Generally, a donor who makes a gift of capital gain property to a private foundation must reduce the amount of the otherwise allowable deduction by all of the appreciation element (built-in capital gain) in the gift property. An individual, however, is allowed full fair market value for a contribution to a private foundation of certain publicly traded stock (known as *qualified appreciated stock*).

QUALIFIED APPRECIATED STOCK

A significant exception to the deduction reduction rule that is unique to private foundations is that it does not apply where the contribution is of qualified appreciated stock. That is, where this exception is applicable, the charitable contribution deduction for a contribution of stock to a foundation is based on the fair market value of the stock at the time of the gift.

The term *qualified appreciated stock* means any stock:

- For which, as of the date of contribution, market quotations are readily available on an established securities market

- That is capital gain property (discussed previously)

Market quotations are readily available on an established securities market, according to the tax regulations, if:

- The security is listed on the New York Stock Exchange, the American Stock Exchange, or any city or regional exchange where quotations are published on a daily basis.

- The security is regularly traded in the national or a regional over-the-counter market, for which published quotations are available.

- The security is a share of an open-ended investment company (that is, a mutual fund) for which quotations are published on a daily basis in a newspaper of general circulation throughout the United States.

Securities are not considered publicly traded if (1) the securities are subject to restrictions that materially affect the value of the securities to the donor or prevent the securities from being freely traded or (2) if the amount claimed or reported as a deduction with respect to the contribution of the securities is different from the amount listed in the market quotations that are readily available on an established securities market.

The IRS, applying the first of these two rules, held that stock that cannot be sold or exchanged by reason of the federal securities law rules, confining sales of control stock to small portions (Securities and Exchange Commission Rule 144), cannot qualify as qualified appreciated stock. Moreover, the IRS ruled that stock traded by means of the Over-the-Counter Bulletin Board Service is not qualified appreciated stock because market quotations are not readily available, in that they can be obtained only by consulting a broker, subscribing to a service, or obtaining a copy of the one newspaper that lists the stock.

By contrast, in one of the most enlightened and well-reasoned rulings ever issued by the IRS in the tax-exempt organizations context, the IRS held (in 2007) that stock to be contributed to a private foundation was qualified appreciated stock, because the market quotations for the stock were readily available due to accessibility of the information on Internet sites. Having determined, by reviewing daily trade data for the stock on Internet financial sites for a one-year period, that the stock was *regularly traded*, the IRS contemplated the phrase *published quotations are available*. The agency concluded that the trades in the stock were posted on Internet sites immediately following the transaction (so that *quotations are available*) and that "virtually anyone in the world with access to the Internet" can "view current and historical market quotations" for this stock (so that the quotations were *published*). The IRS smartly observed that the tax regulations were written (in 1988) "before access to the Internet was universal and before availability of financial information on the Internet was as extensive as now."

One court case addressed the concept of qualified appreciated stock. The court held that stock contributed to a private foundation did not give rise to a charitable contribution deduction based on its fair market value, because the stock did not constitute qualified appreciated stock. The stock involved was that of a bank holding company. The shares were not listed on the New York Stock Exchange, the American Stock Exchange, or any city or regional stock exchange; the shares were not regularly traded in the national or any regional over-the-counter market for which published quotations were available. The shares were not those of a mutual fund. A brokerage firm occasionally provided a suggested share price based on the net asset value of the bank. The procedure for someone wishing to purchase or sell shares of this corporation was to contact an officer of the bank or a local stock brokerage firm specializing in the shares. An attempt would be made to match a potential seller with a potential buyer; the shares were not sold frequently. The court held that the stock did not constitute qualified appreciated stock because the market quotations requirement was not satisfied.

Further, qualified appreciated stock does not include any stock contributed to a private foundation to the extent that the amount of stock contributed (including prior gifts of stock by the donor) exceeds 10 percent (in value) of all of the outstanding stock of the corporation. In making this calculation, an individual must take into account all contributions made by any member of his or her family. The fact that a foundation disposed of qualified appreciated stock is irrelevant in making this computation.

In applying this limitation with respect to future contributions of qualified appreciated stock, the values of prior contributions of the same stock are based on the value of the stock at the time of their contribution. That is, for this purpose, the prior contributions of stock are not revalued each time there is another contribution of the same stock.

TWICE-BASIS DEDUCTIONS

As a general rule, when a corporation makes a charitable gift of property from its inventory, the resulting charitable deduction cannot exceed an amount equal to the donor's cost basis in the donated property. In most instances, this basis amount is rather small, being equal to the cost of producing the property. Under certain circumstances, however, corporate donors can receive a greater charitable deduction for gifts out of their inventory. Where the tests are satisfied, the deduction can be equal to cost basis plus one-half of the appreciated value of the property. The charitable deduction may not, in any event, exceed an amount equal to twice the property's cost basis.

Five requirements have to be met for this twice-basis charitable deduction to be available:

1. The donated property must be used by the charitable donee for a related use.

2. The donated property must be used solely for the care of the ill, the needy, or infants.

3. The property may not be transferred by the donee in exchange for money, other property, or services.

4. The donor must receive a written statement from the donee representing that the use and disposition of the donated property will be in conformance with these rules.

5. Where the donated property is subject to regulation under the Federal Food, Drug, and Cosmetic Act, the property must fully satisfy the Act's requirements on the date of transfer and for the previous 180 days.

For these rules to apply, the donee must be a public charity; that is, it cannot be a standard private foundation or a private operating foundation (see Chapter 4).

Similarly computed charitable deductions are available for contributions of scientific property used for research and contributions of computer technology and equipment for educational purposes.

GIFTS OF VEHICLES

Special rules apply with respect to contributions to charity of motor vehicles, boats, and airplanes—collectively termed *qualified vehicles*. These requirements include special substantiation rules (that supplant the general gift substantiation rules (see Chapter 8)) where the claimed value of the gifted property is in excess of $500.

Pursuant to these rules, a federal income tax charitable contribution deduction is not allowed unless the donor substantiates the contribution by a contemporaneous written acknowledgment of it by the donee organization and includes the acknowledgment with the donor's income tax return reflecting the deduction.

GIFTS OF INTELLECTUAL PROPERTY

Statutory Regime

Contributions of certain types of intellectual property have been added to the list of gifts that give rise to a charitable contribution deduction that is confined to the donor's basis in the property, although in instances of gifts of intellectual property, there may be one or more subsequent charitable deductions (discussed ahead). This property consists of patents, copyrights (with exceptions), trademarks, trade names, trade secrets, know-how, software (with exceptions), or similar property, or applications or registrations of such property. Collectively, these properties are termed *qualified intellectual property* (except in instances when contributed to standard private foundations (see Chapter 4)).

A person who makes this type of gift, denominated a *qualified intellectual property contribution*, is provided a charitable contribution deduction (subject to the annual percentage limitations (discussed previously)) equal to the donor's basis in the property in the year of the gift and, in that year and/or subsequent years, a charitable deduction equal to a percentage of net income that flows to the charitable donee as the consequence of the gift of the property. For a contribution to be a qualified intellectual property contribution, the donor must notify the donee at the time of the contribution that the donor intends to treat the contribution as a qualified intellectual property contribution for deduction and reporting purposes. The net income involved is termed *qualified donee income.*

Thus, a portion of qualified donee income is allocated to a tax year of the donor, although this income allocation process is inapplicable to income received by or accrued to the donee after ten years from the date of the gift, the process is also inapplicable to donee income received by or accrued to the donee after the expiration of the legal life of the property.

The amount of qualified donee income that materializes into a charitable deduction, for one or more years, is ascertained by the *applicable percentage*, which is a sliding-scale percentage determined by the following table that appears in the Internal Revenue Code:

Donor's Tax Year	Applicable Percentage
1st	100
2nd	100
3rd	90
4th	80
5th	70
6th	60
7th	50
8th	40
9th	30
10th	20
11th	10
12th	10

Thus, if, following a qualified intellectual property contribution, the charitable donee receives qualified donee income in the year of the gift, and/or in the subsequent tax year of the donor, that amount becomes, in full, a charitable contribution deduction for the donor (subject to the general limitations). If this income is received by the charitable donee eight years after the gift, for example, the donor receives a charitable deduction equal to 40 percent of the qualified donee income. As this table indicates, the opportunity for a qualified intellectual property deduction arising out of a qualified intellectual property contribution terminates after the donor's 12th tax year that ends after the date of the gift.

Notification Requirement

A donor satisfies the notification requirement if the donor delivers or mails to the donee, at the time of the contribution, a statement containing:

- The donor's name, address, and taxpayer identification number
- A description of the intellectual property in sufficient detail to identify it
- The date of the contribution
- A statement that the donor intends to treat the contribution as a qualified intellectual property contribution

GIFTS OF CLOTHING AND HOUSEHOLD ITEMS

A federal income tax deduction is not allowed for a charitable contribution of clothing or a household item unless the subject of the gift is in good used condition or better. The IRS is authorized to deny, by publication of regulations (which has not happened), a deduction for a contribution of clothing or a household item that has minimum monetary value, such as used socks and used undergarments. *Household items* include furniture, furnishings, electronics, appliances, and linens; the term does not embrace food, paintings, antiques, other objects of art, jewelry, gems, and collections.

A deduction may be allowed for a charitable contribution of an item of clothing or a household item not in good used condition or better if the amount claimed, as a deduction, for the item is more than $500 and the donor includes with the donor's income tax return a qualified appraisal (see Chapter 8) with respect to the property.

GIFTS OF TAXIDERMY

The amount allowed as a deduction for a charitable contribution of taxidermy property, contributed by the person who prepared, stuffed, or mounted the property, is the lesser of the person's basis in the property or the fair market value of the property. A person who makes a charitable contribution of taxidermy property for a use related to the donee's exempt purposes must, in determining the amount of the charitable deduction, reduce the fair market value of the property by the amount of gain that would have been long-term capital gain (discussed previously) if the property contributed had been sold by the person at its fair market value. Special rules apply in computing basis in this context. *Taxidermy property* is any work of art that is the reproduction or preservation of an animal, in whole or in part; is prepared, stuffed, or mounted for purposes of creating one or more characteristics of the animal; and contains a part of the body of the dead animal.

PARTIAL INTEREST GIFTS

Most charitable gifts are of all ownership of a property: The donor parts with all right, title, and interest in the property. A gift of a *partial interest*, however, is also possible—a contribution of less than a donor's entire interest in the property.

As a general rule, charitable deductions for gifts of partial interests in property, including the right to use property, are not available. The exceptions, which are many, are:

- Gifts made in trust form (using a *split-interest trust*)

- Gifts of an outright remainder interest in a personal residence or farm

- Gifts of an undivided portion of the donor's entire interest in an item of property

- Gifts of a lease on, option to purchase, or easement with respect to real property granted in perpetuity to a public charity exclusively for conservation purposes

- A remainder interest in real property granted to a public charity exclusively for conservation purposes

Contributions of income interests in property in trust are basically confined to the use of charitable lead trusts. Aside from a charitable gift annuity and gifts of remainder interests, there is no charitable deduction for a contribution of a remainder interest in property unless it is in trust and is one of three types: a charitable remainder annuity trust, a charitable remainder unitrust, or a pooled income fund (discussed ahead).

Defective charitable split-interest trusts may be reformed to preserve the charitable deduction where certain requirements are satisfied.

GIFTS OF OR USING INSURANCE

Another type of charitable giving involves life insurance. To secure an income tax charitable deduction, the gift must include all rights of ownership in a life insurance policy. Thus, an individual can donate a fully paid-up life insurance policy to a charitable organization and deduct (for income tax purposes) its value. Or, an individual can acquire a life insurance policy, give it to a charity, pay the premiums, and receive a charitable deduction for each premium payment made.

For the donation of an insurance policy to be valid, the charitable organization must be able to demonstrate that it has an insurable interest in the life of the donor of the policy (unless state statutory law eliminates the requirement). From an income tax deduction standpoint, it is not enough for a donor to simply name a charitable organization as the or a beneficiary of a life insurance policy. There is no income tax charitable contribution deduction for this philanthropic act. Although the life insurance proceeds become part of the donor's estate, however, there will be an offsetting estate tax charitable deduction.

There is a use of life insurance in the charitable giving context that essentially has been outlawed and thus is to be avoided. This use is embodied in the charitable split-interest insurance plan.

PLANNED GIVING

Planned giving is the most sophisticated form of charitable giving. For the most part, planned gifts are partial interest gifts (discussed previously). In a broader sense, planned giving encompasses contributions made via decedent's estates and by use of life insurance (discussed previously). Planned gifts are common in the public charity and private foundation contexts, particularly those made by means of charitable remainder trusts and charitable lead trusts (discussed ahead).

Introduction

There are two basic types of planned gifts. One type is a legacy: Under a will, a gift comes out of an estate (as a bequest or a devise). The other type is a gift made during a donor's lifetime, using a trust or other agreement.

These gifts once were termed *deferred gifts* because the actual receipt of the contribution amount by the charity is deferred until the happening of some event (usually the death of the donor or subsequent death of the donor's spouse). This term, however, has fallen out of favor. Some donors (to the chagrin of the gift-seeking charities) gained the impression that it was their tax benefits that were being deferred.

A planned gift usually is a contribution of a donor's interest in money or an item of property, rather than an outright gift of the money or property in its entirety. (The word *usually* is used because gifts involving life insurance do not neatly fit this definition and because an outright gift of property, in some instances, is treated as a planned gift.) Technically, this type of gift is a conveyance of a partial interest in property; planned giving is (usually) partial interest giving.

An item of property conceptually has within it two interests: an income interest and a remainder interest. The *income interest* within an item of property is a function of the income generated by the property. A person may be entitled to all of the income from a property or to some portion of the income—for example, income equal to 6 percent of the fair market value of the property, even though the property is producing income at the rate of 9 percent. This person is said to have the (or an) income interest in the property. Two or more persons (such as spouses or siblings) may have income interests in the same property; these interests may be held concurrently or consecutively.

The *remainder interest* within an item of property is equal to the projected value of the property, or the property produced by reinvestments, at some future date. Put another way, the remainder interest in property is an amount equal to the present value of the property (or its offspring) when it is to be received at a subsequent point in time.

These interests are measured by the value of the property, the age of the donor(s), and the period of time that the income interest(s) will exist. The actual computation is made by means of actuarial tables, usually those promulgated by the Department of the Treasury.

An income interest or a remainder interest in property may be contributed to charity, but a deduction is almost never available for a charitable gift of an income interest in property. (This is more of an estate planning technique.) By contrast, the charitable contribution of a remainder interest in an item of property will—assuming all of the technical requirements are satisfied—give rise to a (frequently sizable) charitable deduction.

When a gift of a remainder interest in property is made to a charity, the charity will not acquire that interest until the income interest(s) in the property have expired. The donor receives the charitable contribution deduction for the tax year in which the recipient charity's remainder interest in the property is established. On the occasion of a gift of an income interest in property to a charity, the charity acquires that interest immediately and retains it until such time as the remainder interest commences.

Basically, under the federal tax law, a planned gift must be made by means of a trust if a charitable contribution deduction is to be available. The trust used to facilitate a planned gift is known as a *split-interest trust* because it is the mechanism for satisfying the requirements involving the income and remainder interests. In other words, this type of trust is the medium for—in use of a legal fiction—splitting the property into its two component categories of interests. Split-interest trusts are charitable remainder trusts, pooled income funds, and charitable lead trusts (discussed ahead).

There are some exceptions to the general requirements as to the use of a split-interest trust in the planned giving context. The principal exception is the charitable gift annuity, which entails a contract rather than a trust. Individuals may give a remainder interest in their personal residence or farm to charity and receive a charitable deduction without utilizing a trust. Other exceptions are listed above (in the discussion of partial interest gifts).

A donor, although desirous of financially supporting a charity, may be unwilling or unable to fully part with property, either because of a present or perceived need for the income that the property generates and/or because of the capital gains taxes that would be experienced if the property were sold. The planned gift is likely to be the solution in this type of situation: The donor may satisfy his or her charitable desires and yet continue to receive income from the property (or property that results from reinvestment). The donor also receives a charitable deduction for the gift of the remainder interest, which will reduce or eliminate the tax on the income from the gift property. There is no tax imposed on the capital gain inherent in the property. If the gift property is not throwing off sufficient income, the trustee of the split-interest trust may dispose of the property and reinvest the proceeds in more productive property. The donor may then receive more income from the property in the trust than was received prior to the making of the gift.

The various planned giving vehicles are explored next.

Charitable Remainder Trusts

The most widespread form of planned giving involves a split-interest trust known as the *charitable remainder trust*. The term is nearly self-explanatory: The entity is a trust by which a remainder interest destined for charity has been created. Each charitable remainder trust is designed specifically for the particular circumstances of the donor(s), with the remainder interest in the gift property designated for one or more charities. Occasionally, because of miscommunication with the donor(s), lack of skill in use of a word processor, or incompetence, a remainder trust will be drafted that is the wrong type (discussed ahead). The IRS generously characterizes these trusts as the product of *scrivener's error*, and will recognize the qualification of the corrected trust, which must be undertaken by court-supervised reformation.

A qualified charitable remainder trust must provide for a specified distribution of income, at least annually, to or for the use of one or more beneficiaries (at least one of which is not a charity). This flow of income must be for life or for a term of no more than 20 years, with an irrevocable remainder interest to be held for the benefit of the charity or paid over to it. The beneficiaries are the holders of the income interests and the charity has the remainder interest.

How the income interests in a charitable remainder trust are ascertained depends on whether the trust is a *charitable remainder annuity trust* (income payments are in the form of a fixed amount, an annuity) or a *charitable remainder unitrust* (income payments are in the form of an amount equal to a percentage of the fair market value of the assets in the trust, determined annually). Recently promulgated tax regulations have changed the concept of *trust income*, doing away with the traditional precepts of income and principal, with as-yet-unknown consequences for some charitable remainder unitrusts.

There are four types of charitable remainder unitrusts. The one described above is known as the *standard charitable remainder unitrust* or the *fixed percentage charitable remainder unitrust*. There are two types of unitrusts that are known as *income exception charitable remainder unitrusts*. One of these types enables income to be paid to the income interest beneficiary once there is any income generated in the trust; this is the *net income charitable remainder unitrust*. The other type of income exception unitrust is akin to the previous one, but can make catch-up payments for prior years' deficiencies once income begins to flow; this is the *net income make-up charitable remainder unitrust*. The fourth type of unitrust is allowed to convert (flip) once from one of the income exception methods to the fixed percentage method for purposes of calculating the unitrust amount; this is the *flip charitable remainder unitrust*.

The income payout of both of these types of trusts is subject to a 5 percent minimum. That is, the annuity must be an amount equal to at least 5 percent of the value of the property initially placed in the trust. Likewise, the unitrust amount must be an amount equal to a least 5 percent of the value of the trust property, determined annually. These percentages may not be greater than 50 percent. Also, the value of the remainder interest in the property must be at least 10 percent of the value of the property contributed to the trust.

Nearly any kind of property can be contributed to a charitable remainder trust. Typical gift properties are cash, securities, and/or real estate. Yet, a charitable remainder trust can accommodate gifts of artworks, collections, and just about any other forms of property. One of the considerations must be the ability of the property (or successor property, if sold) to generate sufficient income to satisfy the payout requirement with respect to the income interest beneficiary or beneficiaries.

All categories of charitable organizations—public charities and private foundations—are eligible to be remainder interest beneficiaries of as many charitable remainder trusts as they can muster. The amount of the charitable deduction will vary for different types of charitable organizations, however, because of the percentage limitations (discussed previously).

Often, a bank or other financial institution serves as the trustee of a charitable remainder trust. The financial institution should have the capacity to administer the trust, make appropriate investments, and timely adhere to all income distribution and reporting requirements. It is not unusual, however, for the charitable organization that is the remainder interest beneficiary to act as trustee. If the donor or a related person is named the trustee, the *grantor trust* rules may apply: The gain from the trust's sale of appreciated property is taxed to the donor.

Conventionally, once the income interest expires, the assets in a charitable remainder trust are distributed to the charitable organization (or organizations) that is(are) the remainder interest beneficiary(ies). If the assets (or a portion of them) are retained in the trust, the trust will be classified as a private foundation, unless it can qualify as a public charity (most likely, a supporting organization) (see Chapter 4).

There have been some abuses in this area. One problem has been the use of short-term (such as a term of two years) charitable remainder trusts to manipulate the use of assets and payout arrangements for the tax benefit of the donors. Certain of these abuses were stymied by legislation creating some of the above-referenced percentage rules. The tax regulations were revised in an attempt to prevent transactions by which a charitable remainder trust is used to convert appreciated property into money while avoiding tax on the gain from the sale of the assets. (Some of these arrangements were so audacious that the vehicles garnered the informal name *chutzpah trust*.)

Inasmuch as charitable remainder trusts are split-interest trusts, they are subject to at least some of the prohibitions that are imposed on private foundations, most notably the rules concerning taxable expenditures and self-dealing. For example, the IRS has an informal procedure for the premature termination of a charitable remainder trust, where the termination does not give rise to self-dealing because the procedure devised for allocation of the trust's assets to beneficiaries is reasonable.

A qualified charitable remainder trust generally is exempt from federal income taxation. For many years, however, the law was that, in any year in which a remainder trust had unrelated business taxable income (see Chapter 7), the trust lost its tax-exempt status. Beginning in 2007, that rule no longer applies. Now, when one of these trusts has unrelated business taxable income, it must pay an excise tax of 100 percent on that income, but otherwise it retains its tax exemption.

Pooled Income Funds

Another planned giving technique involves gifts to charity via a *pooled income fund*. Like a charitable remainder trust, a pooled income fund is a form of split-interest trust.

A donor to a qualified pooled income fund receives a charitable deduction for giving the remainder interest in the donated property to charity. The gift creates income interests in one or more noncharitable beneficiaries; the remainder interest in the gift property is designated for the charity that maintains the fund.

The pooled income fund's basic instrument (a trust agreement or a declaration of trust) is written to facilitate gifts from an unlimited number of donors, so the essential terms of the transactions must be established in advance for all participants. The terms of the transfer cannot be tailored to fit any one donor's particular circumstances (as is done with the charitable remainder trust). The pooled income fund constitutes, literally, a pool of gifts.

Each donor to a pooled income fund contributes an irrevocable remainder interest in the gift property to (or for the use of) an eligible charitable organization. Each donor creates an income interest for the life of one or more beneficiaries, who must be living at the time of the transfer. The properties transferred by the donors must be commingled in the fund (thereby creating the necessary pool of gifts).

Each income interest beneficiary must receive income at least once each year. The pool amount is determined by the rate of return earned by the fund for the year. Beneficiaries receive their proportionate share of the fund's income. The dollar amount of the income share is based on the number of units owned by the beneficiary; each unit must be based on the fair market value of the assets when transferred. Thus, a pooled income fund is essentially an investment vehicle whose funding is motivated by charitable intents.

A pooled income fund must be maintained by one or more charitable organizations. Usually, there is only one charity per fund. The charity must exercise control over the fund; it does not have to be the trustee of the fund (although it can be), but it must have the power to remove and replace the trustee. A donor or an income beneficiary of the fund may not be a trustee. A donor may be a trustee or officer of the charitable organization that maintains the fund, however, as long as he or she does not have the general responsibilities with respect to the fund that are ordinarily exercised by a trustee.

Unlike other forms of planned giving, a pooled income fund is restricted to only certain categories of charitable organizations. Most types of public charities can maintain a pooled income fund; private foundations and some other charities cannot.

Charitable Lead Trusts

Most forms of planned giving have a common element: The donor transfers to a charitable organization the remainder interest in an item of property, and one or more noncharitable beneficiaries retain the income interest. A reverse sequence may occur, however – and that is the essence of the *charitable lead trust*.

The property transferred to a charitable lead trust is apportioned into an income interest and a remainder interest. Like the charitable remainder trust and the pooled income fund, this is a split-interest trust. An income interest in property is contributed to a charitable organization, either for a term of years or for the life of one individual (or the lives of more than one individual). The remainder interest in the property is reserved to return, at the expiration of the income interest (the *lead period*), to the donor or pass to some other noncharitable beneficiary or beneficiaries. Often, the property passes from one generation (the donor's) to another.

The tax regulations limit the types of individuals whose lives can be used as *measuring lives* for determining the period of time the charity will receive the income flow from a charitable lead trust. The only individuals whose lives can be used as measuring ones are those of the donor, the donor's spouse, and/or a lineal ancestor of all the remaining beneficiaries. This regulation project is designed to eliminate the practice of using the lives of seriously ill individuals to move assets and income away from charitable beneficiaries prematurely and, instead, to private beneficiaries. These trusts are sometimes referred to as *vulture trusts* or *ghoul trusts*.

The charitable lead trust can be used to accelerate into one year a series of charitable contributions that would otherwise be made annually. There can be a corresponding single-year deduction for the "bunched" amount of charitable gifts.

In some circumstances, a charitable deduction is available for the transfer of an income interest in property to a charitable organization. There are stringent limitations, however, on the deductible amount of charitable contributions of these income interests.

Charitable Gift Annuities

Still another form of planned giving is the *charitable gift annuity*. It is not based on use of a split-interest trust. Instead, the annuity is arranged in an agreement between the donor and the charitable donee. The donor agrees to make a gift and the donee agrees, in return, to provide the donor (and/or someone else) with an annuity.

With one payment, the donor is engaging in two transactions: the purchase of an annuity and the making of a charitable gift. The contribution gives rise to the charitable deduction. One sum is transferred; the money in excess of the amount necessary to purchase the annuity is the charitable gift portion. Because of the dual nature of the transaction, the charitable gift annuity transfer constitutes a bargain sale.

The annuity resulting from the creation of a charitable gift annuity arrangement (like an annuity generally) is a fixed amount paid at regular intervals. The exact amount paid depends on the age of the beneficiary, which is determined at the time the contribution is made. Frequently, the annuity payment period begins with the creation of the annuity payment obligation. The initiation of the payment period can be postponed to a future date; this type of arrangement is termed the *deferred payment charitable gift annuity*.

A portion of the annuity paid is tax-free because it is a return of capital. Where appreciated securities (or other capital gain property) are given, there will be capital gain on the appreciation that is attributable to the value of the annuity. If the donor is the annuitant, the capital gain can be reported ratably over the individual's life expectancy. The tax savings occasioned by the charitable contribution deduction may, however, shelter the capital gain (resulting from the creation of a charitable gift annuity) from taxation.

Inasmuch as the arrangement is by contract between the donor and donee, all of the assets of the charitable organization are subject to liability for the ongoing payment of the annuities. (With most planned giving techniques, the resources for payment of the income are confined to those in a split-interest trust.) That is why some states impose a requirement that charities must establish a reserve for the payment of gift annuities—and why many charitable organizations are reluctant to embark on a gift annuity program. Charities that are reluctant to commit to the ongoing payment of annuities can eliminate the risk by reinsuring them.

ADMINISTRATIVE MATTERS

Despite compliance with the foregoing rules, the availability of (and/or the extent of) a federal income tax charitable deduction will hinge on compliance with a host of recordkeeping, substantiation, disclosure, and/or appraisal requirements (all of which are discussed in Chapter 8).

SUMMARY

This chapter provided a summary of the federal tax charitable giving rules, including an analysis of the elements of a charitable gift, identification of the nonprofit organizations that are eligible to receive a deductible charitable contribution, and discussion of the rule as to contributions for the use of property. It explained the deductibility of conditional gifts, discussed the advantages of gifts of property, summarized the rules as to valuation of contributed property, explained the law concerning the limitations on deductibility of charitable contributions, and discussed gifts of qualified appreciated stock. Federal tax law in this context is additionally complicated because of the deduction reduction rules and the twice-basis deductions rules; both sets of rules are explained in the chapter. The chapter also summarized the rules as to gifts of partial interests in property and charitable gifts using insurance. The chapter concluded with an analysis of the rules as to planned giving, including underlying principles and the use of charitable remainder trusts, pooled income funds, charitable lead trusts, and charitable gift annuities. The non-lawyer may be surprised to find that something as seemingly simple as giving to charity can spawn these exceedingly complex bodies of law.

7

UNRELATED BUSINESS RULES

The purpose of this chapter is to explain the federal tax rules concerning the conduct of unrelated business by charitable organizations and the application of these rules in the fundraising context. Many find it surprising that what looks like a charitable solicitation undertaking is in fact a taxable unrelated business. Often, charities are spared this taxation regime when fundraising, because of one or more exceptions to the unrelated business rules. Specifically, this chapter will:

- Summarize the unrelated business law rules.

- Discuss *regularly carried on* businesses.

- Discuss the concepts of *related* and *unrelated* businesses.

- Explain the exceptions from the unrelated business tax scheme.

- Explain how the unrelated business rules apply in the charitable fundraising setting.

- Discuss donor recognition programs, including corporate sponsorships.

- Summarize the commerciality doctrine.

- Discuss the tax law rules concerning the sale of services.

UNRELATED BUSINESS LAW STATUTORY FRAMEWORK

For nearly 60 years, the federal tax law has categorized the activities of tax-exempt organizations as those that are related to the performance of exempt functions and those that are not. The revenue occasioned by the latter type of activities, *unrelated activities*, is subject to tax. In computing unrelated business taxable income, the organization is entitled to deduct expenses incurred that are directly related to the conduct of the unrelated business. In the case of organizations that are incorporated, the net revenue from unrelated activities is subject to the regular federal corporate income tax. The federal tax on the income of individuals applies to the unrelated activities of organizations that are not corporations (usually, trusts).

To decide whether any of its activities are taxable, an otherwise tax-exempt organization must first ascertain whether a particular activity is a business, then determine whether it is regularly carried on, then whether activities are related or unrelated, and then (if necessary) whether one or more exceptions are available. The judgments that go into assigning activities into these two categories are at the heart of one of the greatest controversies facing nonprofit organizations.

The objective of the unrelated business income tax is to prevent unfair competition between tax-exempt organizations and for-profit, commercial enterprises. The rules are intended to place the unrelated business activities of an exempt organization on the same tax basis as those of a nonexempt business with which it competes.

To be tax-exempt, a nonprofit organization must be organized and operated *primarily* for exempt purposes. The federal tax law allows an exempt organization to engage in a certain amount of income-producing activity that is unrelated to its exempt purposes. Where the organization derives net income from one or more unrelated business activities, known as *unrelated business taxable income*, a tax is imposed on that income. A nonprofit organization's tax exemption may be denied or revoked if an appropriate portion of its activities is not promoting one or more of its exempt purposes.

Business activities may preclude the initial qualification of an otherwise tax-exempt organization. If the organization is not being operated principally for exempt purposes, it will fail the *operational test*. If its articles of organization empower it to carry on substantial activities that are not in furtherance of its exempt purpose, it will not meet the *organizational test*.

A nonprofit organization may still satisfy the operational test, even when it operates a business as a substantial part of its activities, as long as the business promotes the organization's exempt purpose. If the organization's primary purpose is carrying on a business for profit, it is denied exempt status, perhaps on the ground that it is a *feeder organization*.

Occasionally, the IRS will assume a different stance toward the tax consequences of one or more unrelated businesses when it comes to qualification for tax exemption. That is, the IRS may conclude that a business is unrelated to an organization's exempt purpose and thus is subject to the unrelated business income tax. Yet, the IRS may also agree that the purpose of the unrelated business is such that the activity helps further the organization's tax-exempt function (by generating funds for exempt purposes), even if the business activity is more than one-half of total operations. In this circumstance, an exempt organization can be in the anomalous position of having a considerable amount of taxable business activity—and still be exempt.

AFFECTED TAX-EXEMPT ORGANIZATIONS

Nearly all types of tax-exempt organizations are subject to the unrelated business rules. They include religious organizations (including churches), educational organizations (including universities, colleges, and schools), health care organizations (including hospitals), scientific organizations (including major research institutions), private foundations, and similar organizations. Beyond the realm of charitable entities, the rules are applicable to social welfare organizations (including advocacy groups), labor organizations (including unions), trade and professional associations, fraternal organizations, employee benefit funds, and veterans' organizations.

Special rules tax all income not related to exempt functions (including investment income) of social clubs, homeowners' associations, and political organizations.

Some exempt organizations are not generally subject to the unrelated income rules, simply because they are not allowed to engage in any active business endeavors. The best example of this is private foundations, where the operation of an active unrelated business (internally or externally) would likely trigger application of the excess business holdings restrictions. Generally, an exempt title holding company cannot have unrelated business taxable income; an exception permits such income in an amount up to 10 percent of its gross income for the tax year, where the income is incidentally derived from the holding of real property.

Instrumentalities of the United States, like governmental agencies, generally, are exempt from the unrelated business rules. These rules are, however, applicable to colleges and universities that are agencies or instrumentalities of a government, as well as to corporations owned by such institutions of higher education.

CONDUCT OF BUSINESS

For purposes of the federal tax rules, the term *trade or business* includes any activity that is carried on for the production of income from the sale of goods or the performance of services. Most activities that would constitute a trade or business under basic tax law principles are considered a trade or business for the purpose of the unrelated business rules. That definition is a statutory one; courts occasionally ignore that definition and compose their own, such as by holding that the activity simply does not rise to the level of business functions.

This definition of the term *trade or business*—often referred to simply as *business*—embraces nearly every activity of a tax-exempt organization; only passive investment activities and the provision of administrative services among related organizations generally escape this classification. In this sense, a non-profit organization is viewed as a bundle of activities, each of which is a business. (It must be emphasized that this term has nothing to do with whether a particular business is related or unrelated; there are related businesses and unrelated businesses.)

The IRS is empowered to examine each of a nonprofit organization's activities in search of unrelated business. Each activity can be examined as though it existed wholly independently of the others; an unrelated activity cannot, as a matter of law, be hidden from scrutiny by tucking it in among a host of related activities. As Congress chose to state the precept, an "activity does not lose identity as a trade or business merely because it is carried on within a larger aggregate of similar activities or within a larger complex of other endeavors which may, or may not, be related to the exempt purposes of the organization." This is known as the *fragmentation rule*, by which—as a matter of legal fiction—a nonprofit organization's disparate activities may be fragmented and each discrete fragment reviewed in isolation. For example, the activity of advertising in a nonprofit organization's exempt publication is severed from the publication activity and regarded as an unrelated activity, even though otherwise the publication activity is a related business.

The federal law also provides that, where an activity "carried on for profit constitutes an unrelated trade or business, no part of such trade or business shall be excluded from such classification merely because it does not result in profit." In other words, just because an activity results in a loss in a particular year, that is an insufficient basis for failing to treat the activity as an unrelated one. Conversely, the mere fact that an activity generates a profit is not alone supposed to lead to the conclusion that the activity is unrelated (although on occasion that is the conclusion).

An activity that consistently results in annual losses likely will not be regarded as a *business*. If that is the only unrelated activity, then it cannot be an *unrelated business*. Some nonprofit organizations, however, have more than one unrelated business. They can offset the losses generated by one business against the gains enjoyed by another business in calculating unrelated business taxable income. But, if the loss activity is not a business, its losses cannot be credited against unrelated gain.

Just as the element of *profits* is not built into the statutory definition of the term *trade or business*, so too is the factor of *unfair competition* missing from that definition. Yet, unfair competition was the force that animated enactment of the unrelated business rules; the IRS and the courts sometimes take the matter of competition into consideration in assessing whether an activity is related or unrelated to exempt purposes.

Another term absent from the statutory definition of *business* is *commerciality*. Nothing in that definition authorizes the IRS and the courts to conclude that an activity is an unrelated one solely because it is conducted in a commercial manner, which basically means it is undertaken the way a comparable activity is carried on by for-profit businesses (discussed ahead). Yet, they engage in the practice anyway.

REGULARLY CARRIED-ON BUSINESSES

To be considered an unrelated business, an activity must be *regularly carried on* by a nonprofit organization. That is, income from an activity is considered taxable only when (assuming the other criteria are satisfied) the activity is conducted more often than sporadically or infrequently. The factors that determine whether an activity is regularly carried on are the frequency and continuity of the activities, and the manner in which the activities are pursued.

These factors are to be evaluated in light of the purpose of the unrelated business rules, which is to place nonprofit organizations' business activities on the same tax law basis (what some are wont to call a level playing field) as those of their nonexempt competitors. Specific business activities of a tax-exempt organization will generally be deemed to be regularly carried on if they are, as noted, frequent and continuous, and pursued in a manner that is generally similar to comparable commercial activities of for-profit organizations.

Where a nonprofit organization duplicates income-producing activities performed by commercial organizations year-round, but conducts these activities for a period of only a few weeks a year, they do not constitute the regular carrying on of a business. Similarly, occasional or annual income-producing activities, such as fundraising events, do not amount to a business that is regularly carried on. The conduct of year-round business activities, such as the operation of a parking lot one day every week, however, constitutes the regular carrying on of a business. Where commercial entities normally undertake income-producing activities on a seasonal basis, the conduct of the activities by an exempt organization during a significant portion of the season is deemed the regular conduct of the activity. For this purpose, a season may be a portion of the year (such as the summer) or a holiday period.

Outsourcing has become a popular management technique for nonprofit organizations. They often attempt to outsource unrelated activities (and try to bring the profits in as nontaxable income, usually royalties (discussed ahead)). This arrangement entails a contract that sometimes casts the party with whom the nonprofit organization is contracting as the organization's *agent*. While this is meritorious from a management perspective (such as to ensure quality), it is a bad idea from the tax law viewpoint. Pursuant to the law of *principal* and *agent*, the activities of the agent are attributable to the principal. In this setting, the nonprofit organization is the principal. Attribution of the agent's activities to the exempt organization obliterates what would otherwise be the favorable tax law outcome from the outsourcing, by treating the exempt organization as if it directly is conducting the outsourced activity.

RELATED OR UNRELATED?

The term *unrelated trade or business* is defined to mean "any trade or business the conduct of which [by a tax-exempt organization] is not substantially related (aside from the need of such organization for income or funds or the use it makes of the profits derived) to the exercise or performance by such organization of its charitable, educational, or other purpose or function constituting the basis for its exemption." The parenthetical clause means that an activity is not related, for these purposes, simply because the organization uses the net revenue from the activity in furtherance of its exempt purposes.

The revenue from a regularly conducted trade or business is subject to tax, unless the activity is substantially related to the accomplishment of the organization's exempt purposes. The key to taxation or nontaxation in this area is the meaning of the words *substantially related.* Yet the law provides merely that, to be substantially related, the activity must have a *substantial causal relationship* to the accomplishment of an exempt purpose.

The fact that an asset is essential to the conduct of an organization's exempt activities does not shield from taxation the unrelated income produced by that asset. The income-producing activities must still meet the causal relationship test if the income is not to be subject to tax. This issue arises when a tax-exempt organization owns a facility or another asset that is put to a dual use. For example, the use of an exempt organization's auditorium as a motion picture theater for public entertainment in the evenings is an unrelated activity even though the theater is used exclusively for exempt functions during the daytime hours. The fragmentation rule (discussed previously) allows this type of use of a single asset or facility to be split into two businesses.

Activities should not be conducted on a scale larger than is reasonably necessary for the performance of exempt functions. Activities in excess of what is needed for the achievement of exempt purposes may be seen by the IRS or a court as unrelated businesses.

There is a host of court opinions and IRS rulings providing illustrations of related and unrelated activities. Colleges and universities operate dormitories and bookstores as related businesses but can be taxed on travel tours and the conduct of sports camps. Hospitals may operate gift shops, snack bars, and parking lots as related businesses but may be taxable on sales of pharmaceuticals to the public and on performance of routine laboratory tests for physicians. Museums may, without taxation, sell items reflective of their collections but are taxable on the sale of souvenirs and furniture. Trade associations may find themselves taxable on sales of items (such as uniforms, tools, and manuals) and particular services to members, while dues and subscription revenue are nontaxable. Fundraising events may be characterized as unrelated activities, particularly where the activity is regularly carried on or compensation is paid.

UNRELATED BUSINESS TAXABLE INCOME

As noted above, to be subject to the unrelated business income tax, the revenue involved must be derived from an activity that satisfies (or, depending on one's point of view, fails) three tests. Thus, *unrelated business taxable income* is gross income derived by a tax-exempt organization from an unrelated trade or business that is regularly carried on by it, less any allowable deductions which are directly connected with the carrying of the trade or business. (This definition does not incorporate the application of certain *modifications* (discussed ahead)).

Some tax-exempt organizations are members of partnerships. In computing its unrelated business taxable income, an exempt organization must (subject to the modifications) include its share (whether or not distributed) of the partnership's gross income from the unrelated business and its share of the partnership deductions directly connected with the gross income. (This is an application of what the tax law terms the *look-through rule*.) An exempt organization's share (whether it is distributed or not) of the gross income of a publicly traded partnership must be treated as gross income derived from an unrelated business, and its share of the partnership deductions is allowed in computing unrelated business taxable income (again, subject to the modifications).

EXCEPTED ACTIVITIES

The foregoing general rules notwithstanding, certain businesses conducted by tax-exempt organizations are exempted from unrelated business income taxation. One of the frequently used exemptions from this taxation is for a business in which substantially all the work is performed for the organization without compensation. Thus, if an exempt organization conducts an unrelated business using services provided substantially by volunteers, the net revenue from that business is spared taxation. For example, a religious organization that operated a farm was held not taxable on the income derived from the farming operations because the farm was maintained by the uncompensated labor of the members of the order. This exemption protects from taxation many ongoing fundraising activities for charitable organizations.

Caution should be exercised, however, because *compensation* is not confined to a salary, wage, or fee; the slightest amount of remuneration can nullify an individual's status as a *volunteer*. In one instance, a court held that this exception was not available, in the case of a tax-exempt organization that regularly carried on gambling activities to raise funds for charitable purposes, because the dealers and other individuals received tips from the patrons of the games. In another case, this court ruled that this exception was defeated because free alcoholic beverages provided to the collectors and cashiers in connection with the conduct of bingo games by an exempt organization amounted to "liquid compensation"; this holding was, however, rejected on appeal.

Also exempted is a business carried on by a tax-exempt organization primarily for the convenience of its members, students, patients, officers, or employees. This exception is available, however, only to organizations that are charitable, educational, and the like or are governmental colleges and universities. Read literally, this exception pertains only to the classes of individuals who have the requisite relationship directly with the exempt organization; for example, it applies, as noted, with respect to services carried on by an exempt hospital for the convenience of its patients. The IRS ruled, however, that the doctrine was available when an exempt organization's services were for the convenience of patients of another, albeit related, exempt entity. (The IRS will not go much farther in this regard; the agency refused to extend the convenience doctrine to embrace spouses and children of an exempt university's students.)

Exemption is accorded to a business that consists of the selling of merchandise by a tax-exempt organization, substantially all of which has been received by the organization as contributions. This exception was created to shelter the revenue of exempt thrift stores from unrelated income taxation. For this exception to be utilized, however, the exempt organization itself must be in the requisite business; it is not enough to have the business owned and operated by an independent contractor who merely uses an exempt organization's name and pays over certain receipts to the exempt organization.

Unrelated trade or business does not include qualified public entertainment activities. A *public entertainment activity* is any entertainment or recreational activity traditionally conducted at fairs or expositions promoting agricultural and educational purposes. Typically, these activities attract the public to fairs or expositions or promote the breeding of animals or the development of products or equipment.

To be *qualified,* a public entertainment activity must be conducted in (1) conjunction with an international, national, regional, state, or local fair or exposition; (2) accordance with the provisions of state law that permit the activity to be operated or conducted solely by a qualifying organization or by a governmental agency; or (3) accordance with the provisions of state law that permit a qualifying organization to be granted a license to conduct no more than 20 days of the activity, on payment to the state of a lower percentage of the revenue from the licensed activity than the state requires from nonqualifying organizations.

To warrant application of the public entertainment activities exception, a *qualifying organization* must be a tax-exempt charitable, social welfare, or labor organization that regularly conducts, as one of its substantial exempt purposes, an agricultural or educational fair or exposition.

The term *unrelated trade or business* also does not include *qualified convention and trade show activities*. Activities of this nature, traditionally conducted at conventions, annual meetings, or trade shows, are designed to attract attention from persons in an industry. There is no requirement for these persons to be members of the sponsoring organization. The purposes of these shows are to display industry products; to stimulate interest in, and demand for, industry products or services; or to educate persons within the industry in the development of new products and services or new rules and regulations affecting industry practices.

To be *qualified*, a convention and trade show activity must be carried out by a qualifying organization in conjunction with an international, national, regional, state, or local convention, annual meeting, or show that the organization is conducting. One of the purposes of the organization in sponsoring the activity must be the promotion and stimulation of interest in, and demand for, the products and services of that industry in general, or the education of attendees regarding new developments or products and services related to the exempt activities of the organization. The show must be designed to achieve its purpose through the character of the exhibits and the extent of the industry products displayed.

A *qualifying organization* is a charitable, social welfare, or labor organization, or a trade association, which regularly conducts such a show as one of its substantial exempt purposes.

For a charitable, veterans', or other organization, as to which contributions are deductible, the term *unrelated business* does not include activities relating to a distribution of low-cost articles that is incidental to the solicitation of charitable contributions. A *low-cost article* is an item that has a maximum cost of $5.00 (indexed for inflation; $9.50 for 2009) to the organization that distributes the article (directly or indirectly). A *distribution* qualifies under this rule if it is not made at the request of the recipients, if it is made without their express consent, and if the articles that are distributed are accompanied by a request for a charitable contribution to the organization and a statement that the recipients may retain the article whether or not a contribution is made.

For a charitable, veterans', or other organization to which deductible contributions may be made, the term *business* does not include exchanging with another like organization the names and addresses of donors to or members of the organization, or the renting of these lists to another like organization. Still other exceptions apply with respect to certain local organizations of employees, the conduct of certain games of chance, and the rental of poles by mutual or cooperative telephone or electric companies.

EXCEPTED INCOME

Certain types of passive and other income (principally research revenue) are exempt from the unrelated business income tax, pursuant to a statutory regime entailing a listing of *modifications*. Because the unrelated income tax applies to businesses actively conducted by tax-exempt organizations, most types of passive income are exempt from taxation. This exemption generally embraces dividends, interest, securities loans payments, annuities, royalties, rent, capital gains, and gains on the lapse or termination of options written by exempt organizations. Income in the form of rent, royalties, and the like from an active business undertaking is taxable; that is, merely labeling an item of income as rent, royalties, and so forth does not make it tax-free.

The following exemptions apply to the conduct of research: income derived from research (1) for the United States, or any of its agencies or instrumentalities, or any state or political subdivision of a state; (2) performed for any person at a tax-exempt college, university, or hospital; and (3) performed for any person at an exempt organization operated primarily for purposes of carrying on fundamental research, the results of which are freely available to the public.

Some organizations do not engage in *research*; rather, they merely test products for public use just prior to marketing or undertake certification tasks. Other organizations, principally universities and scientific research institutions, are engaging in research, but their discoveries are licensed or otherwise transferred to for-profit organizations for exploitation in the public marketplace. This closeness between businesses and nonprofit organizations—known as *technology transfer*—can raise questions as to how much commercial activity is being sheltered from tax by the research exception.

For the most part, the tax law is clear regarding what constitutes *dividends, interest,* an *annuity, rent,* and *capital gain*. There can be, however, considerable controversy concerning what constitutes a *royalty*. The term, not defined by statute or regulation, is being defined by the courts.

Generally, a *royalty* is a payment for the use of one or more valuable intangible property rights. In the tax-exempt organizations setting, this is likely to mean payment for the use of an organization's name and logo. The core issue usually is the extent to which the exempt organization receiving the (ostensible) royalty can provide services in an attempt to increase the amount of royalty income paid to it. This issue was the subject of extensive litigation spanning many years, principally involving revenue from the rental of mailing lists and revenue derived from affinity card programs. The resulting rule is that these services are permissible as long as they are insubstantial. Beyond that, the IRS may contend that the exempt organization is in a *joint venture*, which is an active business undertaking that defeats the exclusion.

A specific deduction of $1,000 is available. This means that the first $1,000 of unrelated business income is spared taxation.

EXCEPTIONS TO EXCEPTIONS

There are two exceptions to the foregoing exceptions, one involving unrelated debt-financed income, the other concerning income from subsidiaries.

A tax-exempt organization may own *debt-financed property*; the use of the property may be unrelated to the organization's exempt purposes. In a situation where both facts are present, when the exempt organization computes its unrelated business taxable income, income from the debt-financed property must be included as gross income derived from an unrelated business. The income is subject to tax in the same proportion that the property is financed by debt. The debt involved must be what the federal tax law terms *acquisition indebtedness*. This body of law applies even where the income is paid to an exempt organization in one of the otherwise protected forms, such as interest or rent.

Some tax-exempt organizations elect to spin off their unrelated activities to taxable subsidiaries. The tax on the net income of the unrelated business is then not borne directly by the exempt organization. The managers of an exempt organization may be averse to reporting any unrelated business income or the unrelated activity may be too large in relation to related activity.

If funds are transferred from a taxable subsidiary to an exempt parent, that income generally will be taxable as unrelated business income to the parent, even if it is interest, rent, royalties, or annuities. This is the outcome where the parent has, directly or indirectly, more than 50 percent control of the subsidiary.

EXCEPTIONS TO EXCEPTIONS TO EXCEPTIONS

As an exception to an exception to an exception, if the subsidiary pays dividends to the tax-exempt parent, the dividends are not taxable to the parent because they are not deductible by the subsidiary. Also, a unique, temporary (unless it is made permanent) carve-out rule protects interest, rent, royalties, and annuities from unrelated business income taxation where the amount involved is reasonable and paid during calendar years 2006–2009. Congress may extend this period.

FUNDRAISING AND UNRELATED BUSINESS RULES

It is a substantial understatement to say that charitable organizations do not normally regard their fundraising activities as unrelated business endeavors. Yet, unknown to many in the philanthropic community, fundraising practices and the unrelated business rules have been enduring a precarious relationship for years. Charitable fundraising and the unrelated business rules intersect in several ways.

Fundraising as Unrelated Business

Fundraising practices can possess the technical characteristics of an unrelated business. Reviewing the criteria for unrelated business income taxation (discussed previously), some fundraising activities are trades or businesses, regularly carried on, and not efforts that are substantially related to the performance of charitable functions. Further, some fundraising endeavors have a commercial counterpart and are being conducted in competition with that counterpart, and are being undertaken with the objective of realizing a profit. Treatment of a fundraising effort as an unrelated business (or worse, the basis for denial of tax exemption) may appear to be a rather strained result, but nonetheless can be a logical and accurate application of the rules.

The beginning of serious regard of fundraising activities as businesses can be traced to law changes in 1969, when Congress authorized the taxation of revenue from the acquisition and publication of advertising by tax-exempt organizations. To accomplish this result, Congress codified two rules previously contained only in the federal tax regulations. It enacted laws that state: (1) The term *trade or business* includes any activity carried on for the production of income from the sale of goods or the performance of services, and (2) an activity of producing or distributing goods or performing services from which gross income is derived does not lose identity as a trade or business merely because it is carried on within a larger aggregate of similar activities or within a larger complex of other endeavors that may or may not be related to the exempt purposes of the organization. As the result of creation of both of these rules, the fundraising practices of charitable organizations are exposed and thus more vulnerable to the charge that they are unrelated businesses.

In one case, at issue was the tax status of a membership organization for citizens' band radio operators that used insurance, travel, and discount plans to attract new members. The organization contended that it was only doing what many tax-exempt organizations do to raise contributions, analogizing these activities to fundraising events such as rallies and dinners. The court rejected this argument, defining a *fundraising event* as a "single occurrence that may occur on limited occasions during a given year and its purpose is to further the exempt purpose of the organization." These events were contrasted with endeavors that are "continuous or continual activities which are certainly more pervasive a part of the organization than a sporadic event and [that are] an end in themselves." (Many charitable institutions have major, ongoing fundraising and development programs that are permanent fixtures among the totality of the entities' activities, with the purpose of raising money but not otherwise furthering charitable ends (see Chapter 1).)

A court concluded that a novel "fundraising" scheme was an unrelated business. A nonprofit school consulted with a tax-shelter investments firm in search of fundraising methods, the result being a program in which individuals purchased various real properties from the school, which the school simultaneously purchased from third parties; both the sellers and the buyers were clients of this firm. There were about 22 of these transactions during the years at issue, from which the school received income reflecting the difference between the sales and purchase prices. Finding the "simultaneous purchase and sale of real estate not substantially related to the exercise or performance of the [school's] exempt function," the court held that the net income from the transactions was unrelated business taxable income.

A case concerned a tax-exempt school that solicited charitable contributions by means of mailing of packages of greeting cards as inducements to prospective donors. The IRS asserted that the school was actually involved in the unrelated business of selling the cards. The tax regulations, however, provide that an activity "does not possess the characteristics" of a business "when an organization sends out low cost articles incidental to the solicitation of charitable contributions." The government asserted that this rule was inapplicable in this case because the funds involved were not "gifts," but a court disagreed, writing that to read the law in that narrow manner would "completely emasculate the exception." The court held that the case turned on the fact that the unrelated business rules were designed to prevent exempt organizations from unfairly competing with for-profit entities (discussed previously) and that the school's fundraising program did not give it an "unfair competitive advantage over taxpaying greeting card businesses."

Greeting cards and similar items, when used in conjunction with the solicitation of charitable contributions, are termed *premiums*. This fundraising practice has spawned considerable litigation and IRS ruling activity. An unrelated business may be present where the value of the premium approximates the amount of the "gift." Also, if the premiums are mailed with the gift solicitation, the resulting payment to the charity probably is a charitable gift; if the premiums are made available to the ostensible donor following the "gifts," there may be commercial activity.

Thus, a court wrote, in a case involving a greeting card program of a national, tax-exempt veterans' organization, that "when premiums are advertised and offered only in exchange for prior contributions in stated amounts," the activity is commercial, but if the organization "had mailed the premiums with its solicitations and had informed the recipients that the premiums could be retained without any obligation arising to make a contribution," the activity is not a business because it is not a competitive practice. Also, in the latter instance, there is a bona fide gift. Another court ruled that the revenue derived by an exempt veterans' organization from the distribution of cards to its members constituted unrelated business income, concluding that the organization was acting with a profit motive and that the card program was the "sale of goods." IRS rulings reflect this approach as well. Yet, another court held, without referencing the other two decisions, that the revenue generated by an exempt veterans' organization from the dissemination of greeting cards was not income from an unrelated business but rather contributions resulting from a fundraising program.

Regularly Carried-On Test

In many instances, the only rationale that precludes taxation of the net income derived from a fundraising effort is the fact that the fundraising activity is not regularly carried on (discussed previously). The IRS's internal rules for its agents have long stated that "exempt organization business activities which are engaged in only discontinuously or periodically will not be considered regularly carried on if they are conducted without the competitive and promotional efforts typical of commercial endeavors." Thus, the IRS observed that an "annually recurrent dance or similar fundraising event for charity would not be regular since it occurs so infrequently." These "similar fundraising events" include dinners, theater outings, charity balls, golf and similar tournaments, car washes, and bake sales. A court concluded that the annual fundraising activity of a charitable organization, the presentation of a professional vaudeville show one weekend per year, was not regularly carried on, commenting that the "fact that an organization seeks to ensure the success of its fundraising venture by beginning to plan and prepare for it earlier should not adversely affect the tax treatment of the income derived from the venture."

Just as some fundraising practices are technically trades or businesses, however, so are many regularly carried-on activities. Inasmuch as other rationales for avoiding unrelated income taxation (such as the contention that the activity is substantially related to charitable purposes or that the income is passive in nature) are unlikely to apply in the fundraising context, it is quite possible for a fundraising activity to be deemed a business that is regularly carried on. An IRS ruling concerned a religious organization that conducted, as its principal fundraising activity, bingo games and related concessions; the games were held three nights a week and the resulting revenue was substantial. The IRS concluded that the bingo games "constitute a trade or business with the general public, the conduct of which is not substantially related to the exercise or the performance by the organization of the purpose for which it was organized other than the use it makes of the profits derived from the games."

In a well-known instance, a tax-exempt labor organization raised funds by sponsoring public concerts two weekends a year—every six months. The concert time alone (four days annually) did not cause this activity to be regularly carried on; the organization, however, devoted considerable time to *planning* for the concerts. This gave the IRS the opportunity to expand the rules as to what it means to regularly carry on a business, no longer confining its analysis to the period of time the event actually took place. The IRS now takes into account the amount of time the organization prepared for the activity (*preparatory time*) and the time following the activity that is associated with it (*winding-down time*). A fundraising activity may thus be found to be regularly carried on when preparatory and winding-down time are considered, but not when only the time of the event is evaluated. In this case, the labor organization was held to be regularly carrying on the concert business and thus was taxed on the net ticket receipts. Two courts, however, have rejected this preparatory time/winding-down time analytic approach; one of these courts noted that the time involved in purchasing alfalfa sprouts for sandwiches did not prevent the operation of a sandwich stand by a hospital auxiliary at a state fair from qualifying for nontaxation.

Private Benefit

It is common for charitable organizations to provide information to prospective donors about the financial and legal implications of proposed contributions. This is particularly likely where the matter entails a planned gift (see Chapter 6) or other type of gift that is integrated with estate planning. Yet, case law suggests that the provision of services of this nature rises to the level of impermissible private benefit, which causes the activity to be an unrelated business or even endanger the tax-exempt status of charitable organizations. (This case law, however, is diametrically contrary to common practices, engaged in on a daily basis, in the development offices of universities, hospitals, churches, and other charitable organizations.)

A fundamental precept of the federal tax law concerning charitable organizations is that they may not, without imperiling their tax-exempt status, be operated in a manner that causes persons to derive a private benefit as a consequence of their operations. The offering, by a charitable organization, of services that constitute personal financial and tax planning—an essential element in attracting large appreciated property contributions and planned gifts— may not be considered exempt activities or permissible forms of fundraising but rather the provision of private benefit. While it would seem inconceivable that, when a charitable organization works with a prospective donor to effect a major gift that will generate important financial support to the institution and significant tax savings for the donor by reason of a charitable contribution deduction and/or estate planning techniques, the organization is jeopardizing its exempt status because it is providing a private benefit, this conclusion is the import of a court decision.

This case concerned the tax status of an organization that engaged in financial counseling by providing income and estate tax planning services (including charitable giving considerations) to wealthy individuals referred to it by participating religious organizations. The IRS contended that this organization could not qualify for federal income tax exemption because it served the private interests of individuals by enabling them to reduce their tax burden. The organization's position was that it was merely engaging in activities that charitable organizations may themselves undertake without fear of loss of exemption. Siding with the government, the court wrote that this organization's "sole financial planning activity, albeit an exempt purpose furthering fundraising efforts, has a nonexempt purpose of offering advice to individuals on tax matters that reduces an individual's personal and estate tax liabilities." As the court dryly stated: "We do not find within the scope of the word charity that the financial planning for wealthy individuals described in this case is a charitable purpose."

Subsequently, this court held that an admittedly religious organization was not tax-exempt because it engaged in a substantial nonexempt purpose, which was the counseling of individuals on the purported tax benefits accruing to those who became ministers of the organization. The court found the organization, named The Ecclesiastical Order of the Ism of Am, to be akin to a "commercial tax service, albeit within a narrower field (i.e., tax benefits to ministers and churches) and a narrower class of customers (i.e., the ministers)," and thus said that it served private purposes. The many detailed discussions in the organization's literature of ways to maximize tax benefits led the court to observe that "although [this organization] may well advocate belief in the God of Am, it also advocates belief in the God of Tax Avoidance." Yet the court attempted to narrow the scope of its opinion by noting that "we are not holding today that any group which discusses the tax consequences of donations to and/or expenditures of its organization is in danger of losing or not acquiring tax-exempt status."

But the court revisited this topic a few months later, holding that an organization, the membership of which consists of religious missions, was not entitled to tax-exempt status as a religious organization because it engaged in the substantial nonexempt purpose of providing financial and tax advice. Once again, the court was heavily influenced by the recent rush of cases before it, concerning, in the words of the court, "efforts of taxpayers to hide behind the cover of purported tax-exempt religious organizations for significant tax avoidance purposes." As the court saw the facts of the case, each member "mission" was the result of individuals attempting to create churches involving only their families to "convert after-tax personal and family expenses into tax deductible charitable contributions"; the central organization provided sample incorporation documents, tax seminars, and other forms of tax advice and assistance to those creating the missions. Consequently, the court was persuaded that the "pattern of tax avoidance activities which appears to be present at the membership level, combined with [the organization's] admitted role as a tax adviser to its members," justified the conclusion that the organization was ineligible for tax exemption.

Fundraising and Program Activities

Part of the dilemma in this area—confusion as to what is fundraising—stems from *functional accounting*, a process adopted by the IRS several years ago and imposed on charitable organizations as part of the annual information return preparation and filing process (see Chapter 5). This method of accounting separates a charitable organization's functions into three categories: program, administration, and fundraising. The dilemma exists because many individuals—including some in law and fundraising—regard fundraising as part of program because its purpose is to promote the organization's activities in some fashion. This misunderstanding is in part fueled by the distinctions in law between exempt functions and nonexempt functions. Because it is inconceivable that fundraising is a nonexempt function, it must be an exempt function—or so the reasoning goes. From that position, it is an easy jump in logic to the conclusion that fundraising is the same as program, but such a conclusion is erroneous.

Thus, the IRS has the unrelated business rules as an approach for regulating charitable fundraising. The courts have trended toward a line of thinking that equates charitable giving and associated tax planning with private benefit, thereby causing denial or loss of tax exemption. Either way, the basic rules governing tax-exempt status and unrelated business activity are being applied in relation to fundraising endeavors. A court, in 1984, was the first court to squarely face and analyze the difference, for tax law purposes, between a fundraising activity and a business activity. The issue was whether income, received by a charitable organization as the result of assignments to it of dividends paid in connection with insurance coverages purchased by members of a related professional association at group rates, was to be taxed as unrelated business income. The court ruled that the program constituted fundraising, not a commercial venture. Although this holding was subsequently overturned, the opportunity was presented to develop a contrast between fundraising efforts and business undertakings.

At the outset, this court wrote that, where the tax-exempt organization involved in an unrelated business case is a charitable one, the court "must distinguish between those activities that constitute a trade or business and those that are merely fundraising." Admittedly, said the court, this distinction is not always readily apparent, as "charitable activities are sometimes so similar to commercial transactions that it becomes very difficult to determine whether the organization is raising money from the sale of goods or the performance of services [the statutory definition of a *business* activity (discussed previously)] or whether the goods or services are provided merely as an incident to a fundraising activity." Nonetheless, the court held that the test is whether the activity in question is "operated in a competitive, commercial manner," which is a "question of fact and turns upon the circumstances of each case." "At bottom," the court wrote, the inquiry is "whether the actions of the participants conform with normal assumptions about how people behave in a commercial context" and "if they do not, it may be because the participants are engaged in a charitable fundraising activity."

In this case and in application of these rules, the court stressed five elements: (1) the activity under examination was a pioneering idea at its inception, (2) the activity was originally devised as a fundraising effort and has been so presented since then, (3) the "staggering amount of money" and "astounding profitability" that were generated by the activity, (4) the degree of the organization's candor toward its members and the public concerning the operation and revenue of the program, and (5) the fact that the activity was operated with the consent and approval of the association's membership. Concerning this third element (unfortunately, the one that generally is the most improbable), substantial profits and consistently high profit margins are usually cited as reasons for determining that the activity involved is a business. In this case, however, the amounts of money generated by the dividends assignment arrangement were so great that they could not be rationalized (at least not by the court) in conventional business analysis terms; the only explanation of this phenomenon that was suitable to the court was that the funds were the result of successful fundraising. The U.S. Supreme Court subsequently held that the activity was an unrelated business and then the organization changed its methods of operation to the point that the IRS ruled that the activity was not an unrelated business, but the lower court's conceptual framework remains of utility.

Sales of Merchandise

Generally, the sale of merchandise to the public is a commercial enterprise and, thus from the standpoint of the law of tax-exempt organizations, usually is an unrelated business. On occasion, nonetheless, sales of merchandise can be nontaxable events, such as those protected by the convenience business rule (discussed previously). The facts and circumstances of each case will determine whether merchandise sales are a related or unrelated business.

In one instance, a public charity had as its tax-exempt purpose the eradication of breast cancer by funding research, educating the public, and sponsoring screening and treatment programs. This organization and its affiliates sell merchandise, almost all of which bears a symbol that is universally known as the image for breast cancer awareness, to the public. The charitable organization's toll-free number and website address accompany the merchandise, enabling purchasers to obtain information on the need for early detection of breast cancer and the practice of positive breast health. The IRS, reversing decades of policy about merchandise sales, ruled that the sale of this merchandise "reminds and encourages those who wear, display or see the images about breast cancer and encourages the organization's message that early detection of breast cancer and breast health practices save lives," and thus that this sales activity is substantially related to the organization's exempt purpose.

Principal–Agent Relationships

Some charitable organizations, in an attempt to minimize their exposure to the unrelated business income tax, contract with independent companies for services pertaining to fundraising that might be considered unrelated activities if the organizations were to conduct the activities themselves. Often, this approach is successful, yet it can backfire if the company is regarded as an agent of the charity. (The functions of an agent are regarded in the law as being those of the principal.) In this instance, the activities of the agent can be attributed to the charitable organization (as the principal) for the purpose of calculating the extent of the total activities to in turn determine whether the bundle of activities constitutes a business that has been regularly carried on. In a case, a court adopted this position (at the behest of the IRS), concluding that a publishing company operated as an agent of a charitable organization, so that the agent's advertising solicitation services were deemed to be activities of the charity.

Royalty Exception

In general, royalties received by tax-exempt organizations are not taxable as unrelated business income (discussed previously). Therefore, an option for charitable organizations is to structure an activity so that the income generated by it is a tax-free royalty. The meaning of the term *royalty*, as applied in the charitable context, has been the subject of considerable litigation. Employing the definition of the term as devised in court, a charitable organization must be certain that the payment meets the fundamental definition of a royalty (a payment for the right to use intangible property), then strive to minimize the services it provides in efforts to generate the income.

Volunteers Exception

Another exception from the unrelated business rules that can be quite helpful in the charitable fundraising setting is the one for businesses conducted by volunteers (discussed previously). This exception shelters nearly every activity from unrelated business income taxation—as long as the individuals involved in the operations are, in fact, volunteers (that is, are uncompensated).

Sales of Donated Items Exception

Still another unrelated business exception that can be useful in the fundraising context is the one for businesses that involved the sale of donated items. The principal use of this exception may be in connection with charitable auctions, although it may not be needed because these auctions are usually not regularly carried on (discussed previously). This exception is also useful for charities that raise funds by means of contributions of vehicles, such as automobiles, boats, and airplanes; the disposition of these gift items is nicely shielded by this exception.

Travel and Tour Activities

Travel tour activities, offered on a fee basis, that constitute a business that is not substantially related to a tax-exempt organization's purposes are forms of unrelated business. Whether travel tour activities conducted by an exempt organization are substantially related to an exempt purpose is determined by an analysis of all of the relevant facts and circumstances, including how a travel tour is developed, promoted, and operated.

This matter of travel opportunities as unrelated business started in the higher education context, in connection with tours offered by tax-exempt colleges, universities, as well as alumni and alumni associations. Also, some religious organizations sponsor foreign tours. The IRS, in 1977, ruled that an international travel tour program conducted by an exempt alumni association was an unrelated business; the agency cited the absence of any "formal educational program" and the lack of any plan for "contacting and meeting with alumni in the countries visited." The IRS determined that the activities of this association in working with commercial travel agencies in the planning of the tours, mailing announcements, and receiving reservations constituted an unrelated business that was regularly carried on; the tours were perceived by the IRS as being inherently recreational rather than educational. Tours that feature organized study, lectures, reports, library access, and reading lists may be considered educational in nature. Tours that are "not significantly different from commercially sponsored" tours are usually unrelated businesses, as are extensions (or add-on) tours.

An absence of, in the language of the tax regulations, "scheduled instruction or curriculum related to the destination being visited" can lead to a finding of an unrelated business. Thus, for example, it is not a related business for a tax-exempt university alumni association to operate a tour program for its members and guests, where a faculty member is a guest on the tour and participants are encouraged to continue their "lifelong learning" by joining a tour. Conversely, a tour conducted by teachers and directed to students enrolled in degree programs at educational institutions can be a related business, particularly where five or six hours per day are devoted to organized study, preparation of reports, lectures, instruction, and recitation by the students; a library of relevant material is available; examinations are conducted at the end of the tour; and academic credit is offered for participation in the tour.

A tax-exempt membership organization can exist to foster cultural unity and educate Americans about their country of origin. Tours of these organizations that are designed to "immerse participants in [the country's] history, culture and language" may be related businesses, particularly where "substantially all of the daily itinerary" is devoted to instruction and visits to places of historical significance. If the trips, however, consist of optional tours and destinations of principally recreational interest, and lack instruction or curriculum, they will likely be unrelated businesses.

A tour where the participants assist in data collection to facilitate scientific research can qualify as a related business. An archaeological expedition with a significant educational component can constitute a related business. A tour enabling participants to attend plays and concerts is an unrelated business, where the emphasis is on social and educational activities, rather than amounting to a "coordinated educational program."

Advocacy travel can entail related business. For example, travel tours that enable a tax-exempt organization's members to travel to Washington, D.C., where the participants spend substantially all of their time over several days attending meetings with legislators and government officials, and receiving briefings on policy developments related to the issue that is the organization's focus, are related businesses. This is the case even though the participants have some time in the evenings to engage in social and recreational activities.

DONOR RECOGNITION PROGRAMS

The IRS caused a substantial stir, in 1991, by determining that a payment received by a tax-exempt college bowl association from a for-profit corporation sponsoring a bowl football game was taxable as unrelated business income, on the ground that the payment was for a package of valuable services rather than being a gift. This IRS pronouncement provided the agency's view of the tax consequences of what is today known as a *corporate sponsorship*, where the corporate name of the sponsoring business is included in the name of the event. This association contended that the payment was a gift, but the IRS held that the company received a substantial quid pro quo (see Chapter 8) for the payment. This determination raised the larger question for charities generally: What is the tax consequence of a donor recognition program, where the "donor" is provided ample (and often valuable) recognition for the "gift"?

This donor recognition problem festers to this day. Initially, the IRS tried to quell the controversy by proposing, in early 1992, guidelines for its examining agents to use when conducting audits of charitable organizations. Before these guidelines could be finalized, Congress legislated on the subject later in the year; this legislation was, however, vetoed (for other reasons). In early 1993, the IRS proposed regulations on the point; the regulations never matured to final form. Congress legislated in this area in 1997.

This legislation added to the federal tax statutory law the concept of the qualified sponsorship payment. These payments received by tax-exempt organizations and state colleges as well as universities are exempt from the unrelated business income tax, in that the activity of soliciting and receiving the payments is not an unrelated business. From the standpoint of fundraising, these rules differentiate between a qualified sponsorship payment, which is essentially a deductible charitable contribution and as to which there is merely an acknowledgment, and a payment for services that are, or are in the nature of, advertising.

Technically, a *qualified sponsorship payment* is a payment made by a person engaged in a trade or business to a tax-exempt organization, with respect to which there is no arrangement or expectation that the person will receive any substantial return benefit other than the use or acknowledgment of the name or logo (or product lines) of the person's trade or business in connection with the organization's activities. It is irrelevant whether the sponsored activity is related to or unrelated to the organization's exempt purpose.

This use or acknowledgment does not include advertising of the person's products or services, including messages containing qualitative or comparative language, price information or other indications of savings or value, an endorsement, or an inducement to purchase, sell, or use the products or services. For example, if in return for receiving a sponsorship payment, a tax-exempt organization promises to use the sponsor's name or logo in acknowledging the sponsor's support for an educational or fundraising event conducted by the organization, the payment is not taxable. If an organization provides advertising of a sponsor's products, however, the payment made to the organization by the sponsor to receive the advertising is subject to the unrelated business income tax (assuming the other requirements for taxation are satisfied).

A qualified sponsorship payment does not include any payment where the amount of the payment is contingent on the level of attendance at one or more events, broadcast ratings, or other factors indicating the degree of public exposure to one or more events. The fact that a sponsorship payment is contingent on an event actually taking place or being broadcast, in and of itself, however, does not cause the payment to fail to qualify. Also, mere distribution or display of a sponsor's products by the sponsor or the exempt organization to the public at a sponsored event, whether for remuneration or not, is considered a *use* or *acknowledgment* of the sponsor's product lines—and not advertising.

This law does not apply to a payment that entitles the payor to the use or acknowledgment of the name or logo (or product line) of the payor's trade or business in a tax-exempt organization's periodical. A *periodical* is regularly scheduled and printed material published by or on behalf of the payor organization that is not related to and primarily distributed in connection with a specific event conducted by the payee organization. Thus, this exclusion does not apply to payments that lead to acknowledgments in a monthly journal but applies if a sponsor received an acknowledgment in a program or brochure distributed at a sponsored event. The term *qualified sponsorship payment* also does not include a payment made in connection with a qualified convention or trade show activity (discussed previously).

To the extent a portion of a payment would (if made as a separate payment) be a qualified sponsorship payment, that portion of the payment is treated as a separate payment; that is, a payment can be bifurcated as between an excludable amount and a nonexcludable amount. Therefore, if a sponsorship payment made to a tax-exempt organization entitles the sponsor to product advertising and use or acknowledgment of the sponsor's name or logo by the organization, the unrelated business income tax does not apply to the amount of the payment that exceeds the fair market value of the product advertising provided to the sponsor.

The provision of facilities, services, or other privileges by a tax-exempt organization to a sponsor or the sponsor's designees (such as complimentary tickets, Pro-Am playing spots in golf tournaments, or receptions for major donors) in connection with a sponsorship payment does not affect the determination as to whether the payment is a qualified one. Instead, the provision of the goods or services is evaluated as a separate transaction in determining whether the organization has unrelated business income from the event. In general, if the services or facilities do not constitute a substantial return benefit (or if the provision of the services or facilities is a related business), the payments attributable to them are not subject to the unrelated business income tax. Likewise, a sponsor's receipt of a license to use an intangible asset (such as a trademark, logo, or designation) of the exempt organization is treated as separate from the qualified sponsorship transaction in determining whether the organization has unrelated business taxable income.

Certain exclusivity arrangements do not qualify for this exclusion. A website link between a corporately sponsored tax-exempt organization and the corporate sponsor can cause at least part of a payment to not qualify under these rules. IRS ruling policy is that an exempt organization may provide a link to the Web site of a company that is a corporate sponsor of the organization in connection with the acknowledgment of the sponsorship payment, with the provision of the link itself constituting an acknowledgment and not advertising.

This statutory exemption from taxation for qualified sponsorship payments is in addition to the other exemptions from the unrelated business income tax. These exceptions include the one for activities substantially all the work for which is performed by volunteers (discussed previously), and for activities not regularly carried on (discussed previously). The exemption for qualified sponsorship payments is a *safe harbor* type of exemption, so that if the criteria for it are not met, the organization has the opportunity to utilize (if it can) one or more other exceptions.

COMMERCIALITY DOCTRINE

The commerciality doctrine is a body of law, as to which the fundraising community should be wary, that the courts have grafted onto the statutory and regulatory rules pertaining to tax-exempt organizations, principally public charities. Pursuant to this body of law, an exempt organization is engaged in a nonexempt function when the activity in question is conducted in a manner that is commercial in nature. An activity is a *commercial* one if it has a direct counterpart in, or is conducted in the same manner as is the case in, the realm of for-profit corporations. Crucial to application of this doctrine is the matter of *competition* (usually termed *unfair competition*) between nonprofit and for-profit entities. The doctrine frequently is applied to determine whether an organization is exempt; the doctrine recently is being used to ascertain the presence of unrelated business. Examples of the latter are the charity that sets up a bake sale on a sidewalk a few yards from a for-profit bakery or the charity that conducts a car wash on a lot across the street from a gas station that includes a car wash facility.

The commerciality doctrine was born in 1924, the result of loose language in a Supreme Court opinion. It was applied over the ensuing decades, principally in cases involving nonprofit publishing organizations. More recently, the doctrine has been used to deny or revoke exemption in cases involving entities such as nonprofit adoption agencies, conference centers, credit counseling entities, and prisoner rehabilitation groups. The most famous case in this area concerned a religious organization that operated, in advancement of a church's doctrine, a vegetarian restaurant and health food store; a court held that this organization could not be exempt because these operations were businesses that were in direct competition with for-profit restaurants and health food establishments. The reason that this case is so significant is that, when the decision was considered on appeal, the appellate court stated the factors that are to be relied on in assessing commerciality; they are quite striking.

The first of these elements sets up a presumption that an activity is commercial: the sale of goods or services to the public. (Application of this principle throughout the charitable sector would result in the loss of tens of thousands of tax exemptions, such as for schools, hospitals, museums, and theaters.) The other factors are whether the nonprofit organization (1) is in direct competition with for-profit counterparts, (2) sets its prices on the basis of formulas common in the for-profit retail context, (3) engages in marketing, (4) has hours of operation that are the same as those of comparable for-profit organizations, (5) has employees, (6) has employees that are trained, and (7) does not receive charitable contributions. The IRS has ruled that a listing of a nonprofit organization in the telephone yellow pages is evidence of commerciality. There is even an IRS ruling stating that maintenance of a Web site is an indication that an exempt organization is functioning in a commercial manner. Thus, often a huge gap looms between an assertion of commercial behavior by a charitable organization and reality.

PROVISION OF SERVICES

Fundraising, as the foregoing illustrates, is not confined to the raising of revenue in the form of gifts and grants. It can entail the sale of services (and goods). In general, net income from the provision of services by a tax-exempt organization to another organization (or, as just noted, to the public), including another exempt organization, is unrelated business taxable income. This is because it is not automatically an exempt function for one exempt organization to provide services to another exempt organization, even where both organizations have the same category of exempt status. For example, the IRS ruled that the provision of administrative services by an exempt association to an exempt employees' beneficiary association, where the latter entity provided a health and welfare benefit plan for the former entity's members' employees, was an unrelated business. Indeed, the provision of management services by an exempt charitable organization to unaffiliated charitable organizations led to the revocation of the organization's exemption.

Related Businesses

One of the exceptions to this general rule is that it can be a related business for a tax-exempt organization to provide services to another exempt entity. As an illustration, an exempt business association with an aggressive litigation strategy placed the litigation function in a separate exempt organization because of a substantial risk of counterclaims and other retaliatory actions against the association and its members; the IRS concluded that the provision by the association of management and administrative services to the other exempt organization was in furtherance of the association's exempt purposes. Also, the provision of professional, managerial, and administrative services among a group of interrelated health care organizations, directly or by means of a partnership, was ruled to be a bundle of related businesses. Further, the IRS ruled that an educational institution was engaged in a related business when it provided "central services" to a group of affiliated colleges (such as campus security, a central steam plant, accounting services, and a risk and property insurance program).

One of the biggest difficulties in this area is tax exemption, as a charitable entity, for an organization that wants to provide services to charitable organizations, usually the smaller ones that do not have the resources to acquire the needed services. Usually, the IRS takes the position that, as noted, the provision of these services is an unrelated business (or, if substantial, is a basis for denial or revocation of exemption). Nonetheless, the IRS, in an extraordinary ruling issued in late 2008, rewrote and considerably loosened the rules in this connection, altering its interpretation of the commerciality doctrine (discussed previously) as it did so.

This ruling concerned a community foundation that engages, in furtherance of its grantmaking, in various internal grant management and administrative functions, including undertaking research of potential grantees, designing and operating strategic grantmaking programs, exercising proper oversight over the grants made, and numerous routine administrative, accounting, and clerical tasks necessary for the daily operation of the organization. The sources of funding of the foundation's grants are component funds and certain affiliated noncomponent funds, the latter being supporting organizations, pooled income funds, and other split-interest trusts.

This community foundation proposed to sell its internal grant management and administrative services to other grantmaking charities, primarily private foundations, that operate independently in the community and who lack the staff, expertise, or resources to conduct their own internal grantmaking functions. The foundation's goal in providing these services is to educate and assist these entities to enable them to provide more efficient support to the citizens of the community and ultimately for them to establish cooperative relationships with the community foundation that will maximize the pool of charitable resources available for the strategic funding of community-based programs. The foundation advised the IRS that education will be a core component of all the services it intends to sell and that every participating entity will receive, on a continuing basis, instruction and educational materials from it on tactics for strategic and effective grantmaking in the community.

The foundation intended to charge a reasonable fee based on its staff's hourly rate in providing the services. Each participating charitable organization will be required to execute a sales contract with the community foundation, pursuant to which it becomes an "enrollee organization." This contract will include a menu of core organizational functions that the foundation agrees to perform for the enrollee organization. Although the community foundation will generally contract only with organizations located and operating in this community, it conceded that exceptions may be made where an organization is located elsewhere but retains it to administer funds to be distributed within the community.

The following nine services are to be sold to enrollees:

1. Assistance with establishment of a grantmaking program (such as development of guidelines and procedures for reviewing requests).

2. Review and evaluation of grant requests and preparation of written reports on findings; this may include the conduct of site visits and pre-grant inquiries to obtain information necessary to evaluate proposals (such as interviews).

3. Preparation of research in specific grantmaking areas of interest and/or identification of nonprofit organizations conducting programs in interest areas.

4. Design and/or maintenance of a system of monitoring funded programs.

5. Identification of opportunities for collaboration with other funders.

6. Handling day-to-day inquiries from potential grant recipients.

7. Printing checks for approved grants and expenses, and balancing an enrollee's checking account.

8. Organization and staffing of board and grant committee meetings.

9. Tracking of all grant applications and grants awarded, and generating related reports.

The IRS ruled that these proposed services will constitute the conduct of a variety of businesses that will be regularly carried on. The focus thus was on the question of whether these businesses will be substantially related to the community foundation's exempt purpose. The IRS's analysis began with a review of the primary objective of the unrelated business rules, which is to eliminate unfair competition by placing the unrelated business activities of tax-exempt organizations on the same tax basis as the nonexempt business endeavors with which they compete.

Review by the IRS of the "foundation management industry" as a whole revealed that there are "dozens of for-profit companies that provide services similar to those [the community foundation] intends to sell." These companies provide a "diverse array of services," which the IRS enumerated in great detail, ranging from grantmaking services to check writing and reconciliation services. The agency concluded that these services are "nearly identical to those you propose to sell and that you are in direct competition with the for-profit foundation management industry."

Nonetheless, wrote the IRS, the "fact that commercial entities may also provide similar services, in and of itself, is not determinative as to whether a particular service is or is not substantially related to exempt functions." The agency said that, if the provision of a service "contributes importantly to benefiting the charitable class served by an organization's activities, the commercial nature of the service should not be controlling." If, however, "commercial alternatives are available, the argument that a service is substantially related to an organization's exempt function because the organization is uniquely qualified to provide a particular service to help charitable organizations address unmet charitable needs in the community served by the organization would be difficult to sustain."

The IRS classified the proposed services as grantmaking, administrative, and clerical. The grantmaking services, said the IRS, are those referenced in items 1 through 5. These services were ruled to be those that contribute importantly to the accomplishment of the community foundation's exempt purpose. By providing this package of services, the foundation was said to be able to "uniquely coordinate" the enrollees' grantmaking activities for the benefit of the community, provide advice about unmet charitable needs in the community, and provide advice about how to effectively advance those needs. Noting that "similar services are available from the for-profit foundation management industry," the IRS wrote that the community foundation's grantmaking services are "uniquely tailored" to enable it to achieve its exempt purpose "effectively and efficiently." These services, then, ruled the IRS, are related businesses.

The administrative services, held the IRS, are those in item 4 (this class of service is classified twice and differently). The "skill set required to conduct these activities is not," said the IRS, "unique" to the charitable sector. These activities are "conducted throughout the business community on a daily basis by individuals such as office administrators, personnel managers, and executive assistants." The clerical services are said to be those in items 6 through 9. These activities are said to require office staff "trained in general office procedures, including word processing, data entry and bookkeeping entries." These are the functions of "secretaries, receptionists and bookkeepers." The IRS held that the administrative and clerical services do not contribute importantly to accomplishment of the community foundation's exempt purposes. Some of these services, which are "generic and routine commercial services," amount, it is said, to "back office administration."

Another element of the law that the IRS considered is the inquiry as to whether an activity is conducted on a scale larger than is reasonably necessary to achieve an organization's tax-exempt purpose. The IRS wrote that an organization's income will be subject to the unrelated business income tax where the activities generating the income are not "narrowly tailored" to accomplishment of exempt purposes. The community foundation's grant-making services were found to be so narrowly tailored; the administrative and clerical services were not. As to the latter, the proposed sales of these services are activities that "encompass a wide range of services and are too broadly conducted." This is a separate rationale for concluding that these activities are unrelated businesses.

The IRS reminded the community foundation that it must make a reasonable allocation of the fees it receives from the enrollee organizations, and of the expenses involved, as between the related and unrelated business activities (discussed previously).

Services to Related Organizations

The other exception to the general rule is available where the tax-exempt organizations are related entities, usually as parent and subsidiary. In the health care context, for example, the IRS has long had a ruling policy that the provision of services by and to related exempt entities is not an unrelated business. This policy was initially articulated in rulings concerning the tax consequences of creation of a health care delivery system by means of a joint operating agreement. The arrangement entails what the IRS terms the provision of *corporate services* by and among exempt organizations (in the case of this type of system, usually several hospitals and a parent supporting organization). The IRS stated that, if the participating exempt organizations are in a parent–subsidiary relationship, corporate services provided between or among them that are necessary for the accomplishment of their exempt purposes are treated as other than an unrelated business, and the financial arrangements between or among them are viewed as merely a *matter of accounting* (phraseology meaning that the transactions or arrangements are disregarded for tax purposes). Indeed, the IRS has extended the matter-of-accounting rationale to relationships that are analogous to parent–subsidiary arrangements.

This outcome obviously was welcome news for tax-exempt organizations that were (or were about to be) operating within the framework of joint operating agreements. But, from the larger perspective, the development was a transformative one for many other exempt organizations. Inasmuch as the tax law rationale underlying these agreements could not be confined to that context, it meant that, in any situation in which an exempt organization had a parent–subsidiary relationship with another exempt organization, the provision of corporate services could be protected from unrelated business income taxation pursuant to this rationale. It also meant that the matter-of-accounting reasoning could be extended to any arrangement where the relationship between two exempt organizations was comparable to that of parent and subsidiary.

The first time this parent–subsidiary rationale was used outside the health care setting was in connection with an arrangement that is well known in the fundraising community: where a tax-exempt social welfare organization or business association has a related foundation, to which it provided corporate services. Earlier, IRS rulings held that this provision of services was an unrelated business; now, the IRS reversed its view, holding that this type of arrangement does not generate unrelated business income because of the "close structural relationship" between the two organizations.

As to arrangements where the relationship is analogous to that of parent and subsidiary, the first illustration was provided in the case of vertically, horizontally, and geographically integrated charitable health care systems, utilizing supporting organizations, where the IRS ruled that the affiliation agreements involved relationships analogous to that of parent and subsidiary. A subsequent case concerned two charitable organizations that managed health care facilities; they entered into a management agreement with a third such organization. By reason of the agreement, where each of these entities was independent of the others, these two charitable organizations were found by the IRS to have ceded to the third organization "significant financial, managerial and operational authority over their affairs, including exclusive authority over capital and operating budgets, strategic plans, managed care contracting, the ability to allocate or reallocate services among the health care facilities [they] manage, and the ability to monitor and audit compliance with directives." The IRS ruled that these two organizations were "effectively under the common control" of the third organization. Therefore, the IRS held that these organizations were within a relationship analogous to that of a parent and subsidiary, so that the provision of these corporate services did not result in unrelated business income.

In recent years, the IRS has been going out of its way to avoid use of this related-party rationale, relying instead on other principles of law to effectuate the same result. In one of these instances, involving the leasing of facilities by a tax-exempt hospital, the IRS ruled that the rental arrangement was an exempt function (related business), because of the direct physical connection and close professional affiliation of the institutions. The lessor and lessee hospitals, however, were closely associated with an exempt medical school; thus, the IRS could have ruled that the two hospitals were in a relationship analogous to that of parent and subsidiary.

In another circumstance, a large number of tax-exempt colleges and universities devised an innovative arrangement enabling charitable remainder trusts (see Chapter 6), as to which they are trustees and remainder interest beneficiaries, to participate in the investment return generated by the institutions' endowment funds (an economic performance considerably greater than what the trusts were achieving on their own). The IRS ruled that these arrangements were not unrelated businesses because the colleges and universities were not receiving any economic return and thus were not engaged in a business. Even if these institutions of higher education charged a (reasonable) fee for these investment services, however, the income would not be unrelated business income because the services are being provided to affiliated entities.

SUMMARY

This chapter provided a summary of the unrelated business rules, including the concepts of related and unrelated businesses, the exceptions from the unrelated business rules, and an explanation as to how the unrelated business rules apply in the charitable fundraising setting. The chapter also discussed the federal tax law concerning donor recognition programs (particularly the corporate sponsorship rules), the commerciality doctrine, and the law concerning the sale of services as a form of fundraising.

8

OTHER FEDERAL TAX LAW REGULATION OF FUNDRAISING

As other chapters in this book attest, the federal government is highly involved in the regulation of fundraising by charitable organizations. This type of fundraising regulation includes new annual reporting requirements (see Chapter 5), charitable giving rules (Chapter 6), unrelated business rules (Chapter 7), emerging governance principles (Chapter 10), and the interrelationship between charitable fundraising and IRS audit policies (Chapter 11). Additional forms of federal regulation of fundraising (the subject of this chapter) exist, however. All of them are of critical importance to the professional fundraiser. Specifically, this chapter will:

- Summarize the federal tax law charitable gift substantiation requirements.

- Summarize the federal tax law concerning quid pro quo contributions.

- Summarize the federal tax law disclosure rules.

- Describe the relevant portions of the rules concerning application for recognition of tax-exempt status.

- Address the import of the federal law public charity classifications.

- Summarize the federal tax law appraisal rules.

- Summarize the federal tax law recordkeeping rules.

- Explain the import of Form 8283.

- Summarize various unique federal tax law reporting rules.

- Summarize the federal tax law applicable to fundraising by noncharitable tax-exempt organizations.

GIFT SUBSTANTIATION REQUIREMENTS

The federal tax law contains significant charitable gift substantiation rules. Under this body of law, a donor who makes a charitable contribution of $250 or more in a year, for which he, she, or it wishes to claim a federal income tax charitable contribution deduction, must obtain appropriate written substantiation from the donee charitable organization.

Specifically, this income tax charitable deduction is not allowed for a separate contribution of $250 or more unless the donor has sufficient written substantiation from the charitable donee of the contribution in the form of a contemporaneous written acknowledgment. Thus, donors cannot rely solely on a canceled check or similar documentation as substantiation for a gift of $250 or more. Recordkeeping rules apply in instances of gifts in amounts less than $250 (discussed ahead).

An acknowledgment meets this requirement if it includes the following information: (1) the amount of money and a description (but not a statement of the value) of any property other than money that was contributed; (2) whether the donee organization provided any goods or services in consideration, in whole or in part, for any money or property contributed; and (3) a description and good-faith estimate of the value of any goods or services involved or, if the goods or services consist solely of intangible religious benefits, a statement to that effect. The phrase *intangible religious benefit* is defined as "any intangible religious benefit which is provided by an organization organized exclusively for religious purposes and which generally is not sold in a commercial transaction outside the donative context." An acknowledgment is considered to be *contemporaneous* if the contributor obtains it on or before the earlier of (1) the date on which the donor filed a tax return for the tax year in which the contribution was made or (2) the due date (including extensions) for filing the return.

Other defined terms apply. The phrase *goods or services* encompass money, property, services, benefits, and privileges. Certain goods or services, however, are disregarded for these purposes: (1) those that have insubstantial value and (2) certain annual membership benefits offered to an individual in exchange for a payment of no more than $75 per year. A charitable organization provides goods or services *in consideration* for a donor's transfer if, at the time the donor makes the payment to the charity, the donor receives or expects to receive goods or services in exchange for the payment. Goods or services a charitable organization provides in consideration for a payment by a donor include goods or services provided in a year other than the year in which the payment was made. A *good-faith estimate* means a charitable organization's estimate of the fair market value of any goods or services, without regard to the manner in which the organization in fact made the estimate.

As noted, this substantiation rule applies with respect to separate payments. Separate payments are generally treated as separate contributions and are not aggregated for the purpose of applying the $250 threshold. In cases of contributions paid by withholdings from wages, the deduction from each paycheck is treated as a separate payment. The IRS has the statutory authority to issue anti-abuse rules in this area (addressing practices such as the writing of multiple checks to the same charity on the same date); the IRS, however, has yet to engage in this rulemaking.

The written acknowledgment of a separate gift need not take any particular form. Thus, acknowledgments may be made by letter, postcard, e-mail, or computer-generated form. A donee charitable organization may prepare a separate acknowledgment for each contribution or may provide donors with periodic (e.g., annual) acknowledgments that set forth the required information for each contribution of $250 or more made by the donor during the period.

The U.S. Tax Court has made the administration of this area of the law much more difficult than the statute indicates on its face. This is because it held that these rules apply with respect to verbal (unwritten) *expectations* or *understandings* a donor may have of the charitable recipient when making a contribution. This court thus equated, for this purpose, expectations with goods or services. It is not clear how representatives of charitable organizations are supposed to divine their donors' inner thoughts when they are giving. The value of these expectations is also difficult to discern. (See Chapter 12.)

It is the responsibility of a donor to obtain the required substantiation of a gift and maintain it in his or her tax records. (Again, the charitable contribution deduction is dependent on compliance with these rules.) Some charitable organizations have adopted the practice of providing this form of acknowledgment irrespective of the gift amount or value. A charitable organization that knowingly provides a false written substantiation to a donor may be subject to a penalty for aiding and abetting an understatement of tax liability.

These substantiation rules do not apply to transfers of money or property to charitable remainder trusts or to charitable lead trusts. The requirements are, however, applicable to transfers to pooled income funds. (See Chapter 6.) In the case of contributions to these funds, the contemporaneous written acknowledgment must state that the gift was made to the charitable organization's pooled fund and indicate whether any goods or services (in addition to the income interest) were provided in exchange for the transfer. The contemporaneous written acknowledgment, however, need not include a good-faith estimate of the value of the income interest.

QUID PRO QUO CONTRIBUTIONS RULES

Among the various forms of payments that are partially gifts and partially payments for goods or services (see Chapter 1) are those made in connection with special-event programs, where the patron receives something of value (such as a theater performance or a dinner, or the opportunity to play in a sports tournament), yet makes a payment in excess of that value amount. In these circumstances, the amount paid that is in excess of the value received by the patron is a deductible charitable gift. These payments are known as *quid pro quo contributions.*

Many years ago, the IRS held that payments by corporate sponsors of college and university bowl games were not charitable gifts to the bowl game associations, but must be treated by the associations as forms of unrelated business income (see Chapter 7) on the ground that the corporate sponsors received a valuable package of advertising and similar services. This controversial position led to IRS and congressional hearings, proposed regulations, and finally legislation. This legislation shields *qualified sponsorship payments* from taxation (see Chapter 7). A payment of this nature is one made by a person engaged in a trade or business, from which the person received no substantial return benefit other than the use or acknowledgment of the name or logo (or product lines) of the person's trade or business in connection with the organization's activities. This use or acknowledgment does not include advertising of the person's products or services. *Advertising* entails qualitative or comparative language, price information or other indications of savings or value, or an endorsement or other inducement to purchase, sell, or use the products or services.

A quid pro quo contribution is formally defined as a payment made partly as a contribution and partly in consideration for goods or services provided to the payor by the donee organization. This term does not, as noted, include a payment made to an organization, operated exclusively for religious purposes, in return for which the donor receives solely an intangible religious benefit that generally is not sold in a commercial transaction outside the donative context. The federal tax law imposes certain disclosure requirements on charitable organizations that receive forms of quid pro quo contributions.

Specifically, if a charitable organization (other than a state, a possession of the United States, a political subdivision of a state or possession, the United States, and the District of Columbia) receives a quid pro quo contribution in excess of $75, the organization must, in connection with the solicitation or receipt of the contribution, provide a written statement that (1) informs the donor that the amount of the contribution that is deductible for federal income tax purposes is limited to the excess of the amount of any money and the value of any property other than money contributed by the donor over the value of the goods or services provided by the organization, and (2) provides the donor with a good-faith estimate of the value of the goods or services.

In other words, this law is designed to cause a donor or patron to know that the only amount deductible in these circumstances as a charitable gift (if any) is the amount paid to a charity in excess of any benefits provided by the charity. A rather unhelpful rule states that a charitable organization may use any reasonable methodology in making this good-faith estimate as long as it applies the methodology in good faith. A good-faith estimate of the value of goods or services that are not generally available in a commercial transaction may be determined by reference to the fair market value of similar or comparable goods or services. Goods or services may be *similar or comparable* even though they do not have the unique qualities of the goods or services that are being valued. Of course, where the goods or services are available on a commercial basis, the commercial value of them is used for this purpose.

In determining this $75 threshold, separate payments made at different times of the year with respect to fundraising events generally will not be aggregated. The IRS, however, has the authority to issue anti-abuse rules in this area (addressing practices (as noted above) such as the writing of multiple checks for the same transaction).

These rules do not apply where only *de minimis* token goods or services (such as key chains and bumper stickers) are provided to the donor. In defining what is *de minimis*, long-standing IRS pronouncements are followed. Nor do these rules apply to transactions, involving charitable organizations, where a donative element is absent (such as the charging of tuition by a school, the charging of health care fees by a hospital, or the sale of gift shop items by a museum).

An aspect of this area that plagues the fundraising community is the matter of *celebrity presence.* Generally, the value of a performer at an event (such as a singer or comedian) must be taken into account for these purposes. If, however, a celebrity is present at an event and does nothing, or does something that is different from that for which he or she is celebrated, the value of the individual's presence is zero. (An example of the latter is a tour of a tax-exempt museum conducted by an artist whose works are on display.) If the celebrity performs as such, the charitable organization must utilize the commercial value of the performance in complying with these rules. Making these distinctions and calculating these values can be difficult.

No part of a payment can be considered a contribution unless the payor intended to make a payment in an amount that is in excess of the fair market value of the goods or services received. This requirement of *donative intent* has particular application in the instance of auctions conducted by charitable organizations. The procedure preferred by the IRS is that a charity holding an auction will publish a catalog that meets the requirements for a written disclosure statement, including the charity's good-faith estimate of the value of items that will be available for bidding. This, of course, places the burdens on the charitable organization of determining the values and publishing the catalog (although a nicely designed catalog can burnish the quality of an auction).

A penalty is imposed on charitable organizations that do not satisfy these disclosure requirements. For failure to make the required disclosure in connection with a quid pro quo contribution of more than $75, a penalty of

$10 per contribution applies, not to exceed $5,000 per fundraising event or mailing. An organization can avoid this penalty if it can show that the failure to comply was due to reasonable cause.

In general, a person can rely on a contemporaneous written acknowledgment provided in the substantiation context (discussed previously) or a written disclosure statement provided in the quid pro quo transaction setting. An individual may not, however, treat an estimate of the value of goods or services as their fair market value if he or she knows, or has reason to know, that the value is unreasonable (that is, excessive).

DISCLOSURE REQUIREMENTS

Several documents that a charitable (or other tax-exempt) organization has filed with the IRS are available to the public, including the application for recognition of exemption (discussed ahead) and certain annual information returns (see Chapter 5). The IRS, in its instructions accompanying the principal annual return (Form 990), cautions: "Some members of the public rely on Form 990, or Form 990-EZ, as the primary or sole source of information about a particular organization. How the public perceives an organization in such cases may be determined by the information presented on its returns."

A tax-exempt organization's completed Form 990 or Form 990-EZ is available for public inspection and disclosure. Schedule B that accompanies the return is generally not available for public inspection, although it is available in the case of political organizations that file either return (and private foundations). A Form 990-T filed by a charitable organization to report unrelated business income (see Chapter 7) is also available for public inspection and disclosure (even though this return is a tax return, rather than an information return).

Availability through IRS. These documents are available from the IRS (assuming the agency has them). Form 4506-A may be filed to request (1) a copy of a tax-exempt organization's return, report, notice, or application for recognition of exemption, and/or (2) an inspection of a return, report, notice, or application at an IRS office.

Availability through Exempt Organization. In general, a tax-exempt organization must:

- Make its application for recognition of exemption and its annual information returns available for public inspection without charge at its principal, regional, and district offices during regular business hours

- Make each annual information return available for a period of three years, beginning on the date the return is required to be filed or is actually filed, whichever is later

- Provide a copy without charge, other than a reasonable fee for reproduction and actual postage costs, of all or any part of any application or return required to be made available for public inspection to any individual who makes a request for such copy in person or in writing

- Provide copies of required documents in response to a request made in person at its principal, regional, and district offices during regular business hours

- Provide these copies to a requester on the day the request is made, except for unusual circumstances

In the case of an in-person request, where unusual circumstances exist so that fulfillment of the request on the same business day would create an unreasonable burden for the tax-exempt organization, the organization must provide the copies no later than the next business day following the day that the unusual circumstances cease to exist or the fifth business day after the date of the request, whichever occurs first. *Unusual circumstances* include requests received (1) that exceed the organization's daily capacity to make copies, (2) shortly before the end of regular business hours that require an extensive amount of copying, or (3) on a day when the organization's managerial staff capable of fulfilling the request is conducting special duties, such as student registration or attending an off-site meeting or convention.

A tax-exempt organization may charge a reasonable fee for providing copies. Before the organization provides the documents, it may require the individual requesting the copies to pay the fee. If the organization has provided an individual making the request with notice of the fee, and the individual does not pay the fee within 30 days, or if the individual pays the fee by check and the check does not clear, the organization may disregard the request.

A tax-exempt organization is not required to comply with a request for a copy of its application for recognition of exemption or an annual information return if the organization has made the requested document widely available. (It must nonetheless comply with the public inspection rules.) This *widely available* requirement is satisfied by posting the document on a Web site that the exempt organization maintains or on a Web site maintained by another organization where:

- The Web site clearly informs readers that the document is available and provides instructions for downloading it.

- The document is posted in a format that, when accessed, downloaded, viewed, and printed in hard copy, exactly reproduces the image of the application for recognition of exemption or annual information return as it was originally filed with the IRS (except for any information permitted by statute to be withheld from public disclosure).

- An individual with access to the Internet can access, download, view, and print the document without special computer hardware or software required for that format and without payment of a fee to the exempt organization or another entity maintaining the Web site.

If the Director, Exempt Organizations Examinations (or a designee) determines that a tax-exempt organization is being harassed, the organization is not required to comply with any request for copies that it reasonably believes is part of a harassment campaign. Whether a group of requests amounts to a harassment campaign depends on the relevant facts and circumstances, such as a sudden increase in requests, an extraordinary number of requests by form letters or similarly worded correspondence, hostile requests, evidence showing bad faith or deterrence of the organization's exempt purpose, and a demonstration that the organization routinely provides copies of its documents on request. An exempt organization may disregard any request for copies of all or part of any document beyond the first two received within a 30-day period or the first four received within a one-year period from the same individual or the same address, irrespective of whether the IRS has determined that the organization is a victim of a harassment campaign.

APPLICATION FOR RECOGNITION OF EXEMPTION

To be tax-exempt as charitable entities and to be charitable donees, organizations are required to secure a determination letter (or ruling) to that effect from the IRS. This application process (see Chapter 2) requires the organization to provide considerable detail about any fundraising program(s) it may have or be contemplating (Form 1023, Part VIII, question 4). The application identifies nine types of fundraising (it missed some), which, if engaged in, must be described: mail solicitations, email solicitations, personal solicitations, solicitations of vehicles, seeking of foundation grants, telephone solicitations, Web site–based solicitations (from the organization's own or from another organization's site), and seeking of government grants.

The application requires a description and disclosure of the organization's contracts (if any) entered into for fundraising purposes, including a recitation of the related revenue and expenses. If the organization performs fundraising for other organizations, that relationship requires discussion. The applicant must list all states and local jurisdictions in which it conducts fundraising—a tall order for an entity that solicits nationally (because it would technically have to list hundreds, maybe thousands, of counties, cities, towns, townships, boroughs, and the like). The organization is also asked whether it maintains "separate accounts for any contributor under which the contributor has the right to advise on the use or distribution of funds," which is a reference largely to the maintenance of donor-advised funds, and if so to describe the arrangement.

An applicant organization must additionally reference its fundraising costs in the financial statement or proposed budget submitted as part of the application.

PUBLIC CHARITY CLASSIFICATIONS

A charitable organization is classified as either a *public* or a *private* charity (see Chapter 4). One of the ways to avoid private foundation status is to be a publicly supported organization; one of the ways to be a publicly supported organization is to qualify as a *donative* charity. An organization can achieve that classification by meeting a *facts-and-circumstances* test, where the amount of public support normally received by the organization may be as low as 10 percent of its total support.

A variety of criteria may be utilized to demonstrate compliance with this test. One criterion is the extent to which the charitable organization is attracting public support: Can the organization demonstrate an active and ongoing fundraising program? The tax regulations state that an entity may satisfy this aspect of the test "if it maintains a continuous and bona fide program for solicitation of funds from the general public, community, or membership group involved, or if it carries on activities designed to attract support from governmental units or other [publicly supported] organizations."

The IRS may monitor the extent of a charitable organization's fundraising efforts, to ascertain whether the organization qualifies as an entity other than a private foundation.

APPRAISAL RULES

The law contains requirements relating to proof when an individual, a closely held corporation, a personal service corporation, a partnership, or an S corporation claims a charitable deduction for a contribution of certain property. These requirements, when applicable, must be complied with for the deduction to be allowed.

General Appraisal Requirements

The requirements apply to contributions of property (other than money and publicly traded securities) if the aggregate claimed or reported value of the property (and all similar items of property for which deductions for charitable contributions are claimed or reported by the same donor for the same tax year, whether contributions are donated to the same donee or not) is in excess of $5,000. The phrase *similar items of property* means property of the same generic category or type, including stamps, coins, lithographs, paintings, books, nonpublicly traded stock, land, or buildings.

For each gift of this type, the donor must obtain a *qualified appraisal* and attach an *appraisal summary* to the tax return on which the deduction is claimed (discussed ahead). For a gift of nonpublicly traded stock, the claimed value of which does not exceed $10,000 but is greater than $5,000, the donor is not required to have a qualified appraisal but must attach a partially completed appraisal summary form to the tax or information return on which the deduction is claimed.

These rules are *directory* rather than *mandatory*, meaning that the *doctrine of substantial compliance* applies. When applying this doctrine, the courts look at whether the government's administrative requirements relate to the substance of the statutory law. If they do, strict adherence to all statutory and regulatory requirements is necessary. If they do not, a looser standard is applicable, where the courts are more tolerant of innocent noncompliance. One court held that these appraisal substantiation requirements "do not relate to the substance or essence of whether or not a charitable contribution was actually made" and thus allowed a charitable deduction even though all of these technicalities were not followed.

Qualified Appraisal

A *qualified appraisal* is an appraisal made no more than 60 days prior to the date of the contribution of the appraised property. The appraisal must be prepared, signed, and dated by a *qualified appraiser* and cannot involve a prohibited type of appraisal fee (discussed ahead).

Certain information must be included in a qualified appraisal:

- A sufficiently detailed description of the contributed property

- The physical condition of the property (in the case of tangible property)

- The date (or expected date) of the contribution

- The terms of any agreement or understanding the use, sale, or other disposition of the property

- The name, address, and Social Security number of the qualified appraiser

- The qualifications of the qualified appraiser

- A statement that the appraisal was prepared for income tax purposes

- The date or dates on which the property was valued

- The appraised fair market value of the property on the date (or expected date) of the contribution

- The method of valuation used to determine the fair market value

- The specific basis for the valuation

- A description of the fee arrangement between the donor and the appraiser

A qualified appraisal must be signed and dated by the qualified appraiser no earlier than 60 days before the date of the contribution and no later than (1) the due date (including extensions) of the return on which the charitable deduction is first claimed, (2) the due date (including extensions) of the return on which the charitable deduction is first reported (where the donor is a partnership or S corporation), or (3) if the deduction is first claimed on an amended return, the date on which the amended return is filed.

An appraisal is not a qualified appraisal for a contribution, even if these requirements are satisfied, if a reasonable person would conclude that the donor failed to disclose or misrepresented facts that would cause the appraiser to overstate the value of the contributed property. The fee for a qualified appraisal cannot be based on the appraised value of the property. The donor must retain the qualified appraisal "for so long as it may be relevant in the administration of any internal revenue law." If the contributed property is a partial interest (see Chapter 6), the appraisal must be of that interest.

One qualified appraisal for a group of similar items of property contributed in the same tax year is acceptable, as long as the appraisal includes all of the required information for each item. If a group of items has an aggregate value appraised at $100 or less, the appraiser may select these items for a group description rather than a specific description of each item.

A *qualified appraisal* must be prepared by a qualified appraiser in accordance with generally accepted appraisal standards. Under a rule being considered by the IRS, these standards are the substance and principles of the Uniform Standards of Professional Appraisal Practice as developed by the Appraisal Standards Board of the Appraisal Foundation.

Appraisal Summary

The appraisal summary must be on Form 8283 (discussed ahead), signed and dated by an appropriate representative of the donee and qualified appraiser (or appraisers), and attached to the tax return on which the donor is first claiming or reporting the deduction for the appraised property. The signature on behalf of the donee does not mean that the charity is concurring in the appraised value of the contributed property.

Certain information must be included in the appraisal summary:

- The name and taxpayer identification number of the donor
- A sufficient description of the property
- A summary of the physical condition of the property (in the case of a tangible property)
- The manner and date of acquisition of the property
- The basis in the property
- The name, address, and taxpayer identification number of the donee

- The date the donee received the property

- The name, address, and taxpayer identification number of the qualified appraiser (or appraisers)

- The appraised fair market value of the property on the date of the contribution

- A declaration by the qualified appraiser

The rules pertaining to separate versus group appraisals also apply to appraisal summaries. A donor who contributes similar items of property to more than one charitable donee must attach a separate appraisal summary for each donee.

If the donor is a partnership or an S corporation, it must provide a copy of the appraisal summary to every partner or shareholder who is allocated a share in the deduction for a charitable contribution of property described in the appraisal summary. The partner or shareholder must attach the appraisal summary to his or her tax return.

Qualified Appraiser

A *qualified appraiser* is an individual with verifiable education and experience in valuing the type of property for which the appraisal is performed. An individual is treated as having the requisite education and experience if, as of the date of signing the appraisal, the individual has (1) successfully completed professional or college level course work in valuing the type of property and has two or more years of experience in valuing the type of property or (2) earned a recognized appraisal designation for the type of property involved.

The course work must be obtained from a professional or college level educational institution, a generally recognized professional appraisal organization that regularly offers educational programs in the principles of valuation, or an employer as part of an employee apprenticeship or educational program that is substantially similar to the preceding types of programs. A *recognized appraisal designation* is a designation awarded by a recognized professional appraiser organization on the basis of demonstrated competency. Education and experience in valuing the relevant type of property are *verifiable* if the appraiser specifies in the appraisal the appraiser's education and experience in valuing the type of property involved and the appraiser makes a declaration in the appraisal that, because of the appraiser's education and experience, the appraiser is qualified to make appraisals of the relevant type of property being valued.

An individual is not a qualified appraiser if the donor had knowledge of facts that would cause a reasonable person to expect the appraiser to falsely overstate the value of the donated property. The donor, donee, or certain other related persons cannot be a qualified appraiser of the property involved in the transaction. More than one appraiser may appraise donated property, as long as each appraiser complies with the requirements.

The qualified appraiser must declare on the appraisal summary that he or she holds himself or herself out to the public as an appraiser and declare that, because of the competencies described in the appraisal, he or she is qualified to make appraisals of the type of property being valued. The appraiser also must state that he or she understands that a false or fraudulent overstatement of the value of the property described in the qualified appraisal or appraisal summary may subject the appraiser to a civil penalty for aiding and abetting an understatement of tax liability, and consequently the appraiser may have appraisals disregarded.

Generally, no part of the fee arrangement for a qualified appraisal can be based on a percentage (or set of percentages) of the appraised value of the property. If a fee arrangement is based in any way on the amount of the appraised value of the property that is allowed as a charitable deduction, it is treated as a fee based on a percentage of the appraised value of the property. (In certain circumstances, this rule does not apply to appraisal fees paid to a generally recognized association that regulates appraisers.)

The following individuals cannot be qualified appraisers:

- An individual who receives a prohibited fee (discussed previously)

- The donor of the property

- A party to the transaction in which the donor acquired the property, unless the property is contributed within two months of the date of its acquisition and the appraised value is not in excess of the acquisition price

- The donee of the property

- An individual who is (1) related to or an employee of any of the foregoing three categories of individuals or married to an individual who has a defined relationship with any of these individuals or (2) an independent contractor who is regularly used as an appraiser by any of the foregoing three categories of individuals and who does not perform a majority of his or her appraisals for others during the tax year

- An individual who is prohibited from practicing before the IRS at any time during the three-year period ending on the date the appraisal is signed by the individual

Clothing and Household Items

Generally, a federal income tax charitable contribution deduction is not allowed for a contribution of clothing or a household item unless the item is in good used condition or better at the time of the contribution and the noncash substantiation requirements (discussed previously) are satisfied.

The rule requiring that the property be in good used condition or better is inapplicable to a contribution of a single item of clothing or a household item for which a charitable deduction of more than $500 is claimed, if the donor submits with the tax return on which the deduction is claimed a copy of a qualified appraisal (discussed previously) of the property prepared by a qualified appraiser and a completed Form 8283, Section B (discussed ahead).

RECORDKEEPING RULES

The fundraising community should be aware that the recordkeeping requirements that need to be followed by a donor to sustain a federal income tax charitable contribution deduction were significantly revised by statutory law changes enacted in 2004 and 2006, and reflected in substantial regulations that are currently under development at the IRS. (These rules are the responsibility of the donor, not the charitable donee; nonetheless, the professional fundraiser needs to cultivate a happy donor base, accomplished in part by being able to explain these rules when necessary.)

Cash Contributions Requirements

The income tax charitable contribution deduction is not allowed for any contribution of a monetary gift unless the donor maintains, as a record of the contribution, a bank record or written communication from the donee. The substantiation document must show the name of the donee, and the date and amount of the contribution.

A *monetary gift* includes, in addition to gifts of cash or by check, a payment made by credit card, a transfer of a gift card redeemable for cash, a gift by electronic fund transfer, use of an online payment service, or contribution by payroll deduction. A *bank record* includes a statement from a financial institution, an electronic fund transfer receipt, a canceled check, a scanned image of both sides of a canceled check obtained from a bank Web site, or a credit card statement. A *written communication* includes email correspondence.

In the case of a charitable contribution made by payroll deduction, a donor is considered to have satisfied this substantiation requirement if the donor obtains (1) a pay stub, Form W-2, or other employer-furnished document that sets forth the amount withheld during the tax year for payment to a charitable donee, and (2) a pledge card or other document prepared by or at the direction of the donee that shows the name of the donee.

This substantiation must be received by the donor on or before the earlier of (1) the date the donor files the original income tax return for the tax year in which the contribution was made or (2) the due date (including extensions) for filing the donor's original return for that year. Certain organizations are treated as donees for this purpose, even if the organization, pursuant to the donor's instructions or otherwise, distributes the amount received to one or more charitable organizations. These entities are all charitable entities and principal combined fund organizations for purposes of the Combined Federal Campaign.

This general gift substantiation requirement does not apply to a donor who incurs unreimbursed expenses of less than $250 incident to the rendition of services. If a partnership or an S corporation makes a charitable contribution, the entity is treated as the donor for these substantiation purposes. These rules do not apply to a monetary gift to a charitable remainder trust or an income interest trust; they apply, however, to transfers to pooled income funds (see Chapter 6).

An income tax charitable contribution deduction is not allowed for a contribution of $250 or more unless the donor substantiates the contribution with a contemporaneous written acknowledgment from the donee (discussed previously). The substantiation rules for gifts less than $250 or those of $250 or more can be satisfied by use of a single document as long as that document contains the required information and is obtained by the donor no later than the substantiation receipt deadline (discussed previously).

Noncash Contributions Requirements

In general, a donor who claims an income tax charitable contribution deduction for a noncash charitable gift of less than $250 is required to obtain a receipt from the donee or keep reliable records. For such a gift by an individual, partnership, S corporation, or C corporation that is a personal service corporation or closely held corporation, there is no charitable deduction unless the donor maintains for each contribution a receipt from the charitable donee showing the following elements: the name and address of the donee, the date of the contribution, a description of the property in sufficient detail, and, if the gift is of securities, the name of the issuer, the type of security, and whether the securities are publicly traded.

If, however, it is impractical to obtain a receipt from the donee (such as when a donor deposits canned food at a charity's unattended drop site), the donor may satisfy the recordkeeping rules by maintaining reliable written records for the contributed property. The reliability of a written record is to be determined on the basis of all of the facts and circumstances of a particular case, including the contemporaneous nature of the writing evidencing the gift. Nonetheless, a *reliable written record* must include the above elements, the fair market value of the property on the contribution date, the method used to determine the value, and, in the case of a contribution of clothing or a household item (discussed previously), the condition of the item.

An income tax charitable contribution deduction is not allowed for a noncash charitable contribution of $250 or more, but not more than $500, unless the donor substantiates the gift with a contemporaneous written acknowledgment (discussed previously). This deduction is not allowed for a noncash charitable contribution of more than $500, but less than $5,000, unless the donor substantiates the contribution with a contemporaneous written acknowledgment and meets the Form 8283, Section A, completion and filing requirements (discussed ahead). This latter rule is applicable to individuals, partnerships, S corporations, and C corporations that are personal service corporations or closely held corporations.

Generally, there is no federal income tax charitable contribution deduction for a noncash charitable gift of more than $5,000 unless the donor substantiates the contribution with a contemporaneous written acknowledgment, obtains a qualified appraisal prepared by a qualified appraiser (discussed previously), and completes and files Form 8283, Section B. Nonetheless, a qualified appraisal is not required and a completed Form 8283, Section A, substitutes for a completed Form 8283, Section B, for contributions of publicly traded securities, inventory, vehicles, and intellectual property (see Chapter 6).

Generally, a federal income tax charitable contribution deduction is not allowed for a noncash charitable contribution of more than $500,000 unless the donor substantiates the contribution with a contemporaneous written acknowledgment, obtains a qualified appraisal prepared by a qualified appraiser, completes and files Section B of the Form 8283, and attaches a copy of the qualified appraisal of the property to the return on which the deduction is claimed. Again, a qualified appraisal is not required and a completed Form 8283, Section A, substitutes for a completed Form 8283, Section B, for contributions of publicly traded securities, intellectual property, vehicles, and inventory. These rules as to substantiation documents that must be submitted with a tax return also apply to a return reflecting a carryover of the deduction (see Chapter 6).

FORM 8283

A completed Form 8283, Section A, includes the donor's name and taxpayer identification number, the name and address of the donee, the date of the contribution, and certain information about the contributed property. That information consists of (1) a description of the property in sufficient detail; (2) a statement as to the condition of the property; (3) in the case of securities, the name of the issuer, the type of security, and whether the securities are publicly traded; (4) the fair market value of the property on the contribution date; and (5) the method used in determining the property's value. This schedule also is to include information about the manner the property was acquired by the donor and the approximate date of acquisition (or substantial completion) of the property, the donor's basis in the property, and, in the case of tangible personal property, whether the donee has certified it for a use that is related to the donee's exempt purpose. In the case of a contribution of a vehicle, the donor must attach a copy of the acknowledgment to the Schedule A for the return on which the deduction is claimed.

A completed Form 8283, Schedule B, includes the donor's name and taxpayer identification number; the donee's name, address, taxpayer identification number, and signature; the date signed by the donee, and the date the donee received the property; the appraiser's name, address, taxpayer identification number, an appraiser declaration, signature, and the date signed by the appraiser; the fair market value of the contributed property, a description of the property and its condition; the manner of acquisition and the approximate date of acquisition (or substantial completion) of the property by the donor; the donor's basis in the property; and a statement explaining whether the charitable contribution was made by means of a bargain sale and, if so, the amount of consideration received by the donor for the transfer.

UNIQUE REPORTING RULES

Certain types of charitable contributions give rise to unique reporting and like obligations, including those involving contributions of intellectual property; automobiles, airplanes, and boats; and gifts of certain fractional interests.

Intellectual Property Gifts

A donee charitable organization, other than most private foundations, that receives or accrues net income during a year from an item of qualified intellectual property contributed to it must file an information return with the IRS (Form 8899). This return is required for any year of the donee that includes a portion of the ten-year period beginning on the date of the contribution (discussed ahead) but not for any years beginning after the expiration of the legal life of the property.

This information return must include the following:

- The name, address, tax year, and employer identification number of the donee filing the return

- The name, address, and taxpayer identification number of the donor

- A description of the qualified intellectual property in sufficient detail as to identify the property received by the donee

- The date of the contribution

- The amount of net income of the donee for the tax year that is properly allocable to the intellectual property

A donee filing this return is required to furnish a copy of it to the donor of the property, on or before the date the donee is required to file the return with the IRS. The donee is required to file this return on or before the last day of the first full month following the close of the donee's tax year as to which net income from the property is properly allocable.

Automobiles, Airplanes, Boats

Federal tax law rules entail deductibility and substantiation requirements in connection with contributions to charity of motor vehicles, boats, and airplanes—collectively termed *qualified vehicles*. These requirements supplant the general gift substantiation rules (discussed previously) where the claimed value of the gifted property contributed exceeds $500.

Statutory Regime. Pursuant to these rules, a federal income tax charitable contribution deduction is not allowed unless the donor substantiates the contribution by a contemporaneous written acknowledgment of the contribution by the donee organization and includes the acknowledgment with the donor's income tax return reflecting the deduction. This acknowledgment must contain the name and taxpayer identification number of the donor and the vehicle identification number or similar number. If the gift is of a qualified vehicle that was sold by the donee charitable organization without any "significant intervening use or material improvement," the acknowledgment must also contain a certification that the vehicle was sold in an arm's-length transaction between unrelated parties, a statement as to the gross proceeds derived from the sale, and a statement that the deductible amount may not exceed the amount of the gross proceeds. If there is such use or improvement, the acknowledgment must include a certification as to the intended use or material improvement of the vehicle and the intended duration of the use and a certification that the vehicle will not be transferred in exchange for money, other property, or services before completion of the use or improvement. An acknowledgment is *contemporaneous* if the donee organization provides it within 30 days of the sale of the qualified vehicle or, in an instance of an acknowledgment including the foregoing certifications, of the contribution of the vehicle.

The amount of the charitable deduction for a gift of a qualified vehicle is dependent on the nature of the use of the vehicle by the donee organization. If the charitable organization sells the vehicle without any significant intervening use or material improvement of the vehicle by the organization, the amount of the charitable deduction may not exceed the gross proceeds received from the sale. Where there is such a use or improvement, the charitable deduction is based on the fair market value of the vehicle.

The legislature history accompanying this law states that these two exceptions are to be strictly construed. To meet this *significant use* test, the organization must actually use the vehicle to substantially further the organization's regularly conducted activities and the use must be significant. The test is not satisfied if the use is incidental or not intended at the time of the contribution. Whether a use is *significant* also depends on the frequency and duration of use.

The legislative history of this legislation provided an example of a charitable organization that, as part of its regularly conducted activities, delivers meals to needy individuals. The use requirement would be satisfied if the organization used a donated vehicle to deliver food to the needy. Use of the vehicle to deliver meals substantially furthers a regularly conducted activity of the organization. The use also must be significant, which depends on the nature, extent, and frequency of the use. If the organization used the vehicle "only once or a few times" to deliver meals, the use would not be considered significant. If the organization used the vehicle to deliver meals every day for one year, the use would be considered significant. If the organization drove the vehicle 10,000 miles while delivering meals, such use likely would be considered significant. Use of a vehicle in such an activity for one week or for several hundreds of miles generally would not be considered a significant use.

This legislative history provides a second example concerning use by a charitable organization of a donated vehicle to transport its volunteers. The use would not be significant merely because a volunteer used the vehicle over a "brief period of time" to drive to or from the organization's premises. Conversely, if at the time the organization accepts the contribution of a qualified vehicle, the organization intends to use the vehicle as a "regular and ongoing" means of transport for volunteers of the organization, and the vehicle is so used, the significant use test would be met.

The legislative history provides a third example, concerning an individual who makes a charitable contribution of a used automobile in good running condition and that needs no immediate repairs to a charitable organization that operates an elder care facility. The organization provides the donor with a written acknowledgment that includes a certification that the donee intends to retain the vehicle for a year or longer to transport the facility's residents to community and social events and to deliver meals to the needy. A few days after receiving the vehicle, the donee organization commences to use the vehicle three times a week to transport some of its residents to various community events and twice a week to deliver food to needy individuals. The organization continues to regularly use the vehicle for these purposes for approximately one year and then sells the vehicle. The donee's use of this vehicle constitutes a significant intervening use prior to the sale by the organization.

A *material improvement* includes major repairs to a vehicle or other improvements to the vehicle that improve its condition in a manner that significantly increases the vehicle's value. Cleaning the vehicle, minor repairs, and routine maintenance do not constitute a material improvement. This legislative history does not provide any examples pertaining to this exception. Presumably this exception is available only when the donee charitable organization expresses its intent at the outset (at least in part by means of the certification) that the donee plans to materially improve the vehicle.

A donee organization that is required to provide an acknowledgment under these rules must also provide that information to the IRS. A penalty is imposed for the furnishing of a false or fraudulent acknowledgment, or an untimely or incomplete acknowledgment, by a charitable organization to a donor of a qualified vehicle.

Regulatory Gloss. The IRS issued guidance concerning these rules for deductible charitable contributions of qualified vehicles. This guidance added another exception to these rules, which is for circumstances where the charity gives or sells the vehicle at a significantly below-market price to a needy individual, as long as the transfer furthers the charitable purpose of helping a poor or distressed individual who is in need of a means of transportation. The guidance also explains how the fair market value of a vehicle is determined.

The IRS issued a form (Form 1098-C) to be used by donee charitable organizations to report to the IRS contributions of qualified vehicles and to provide the donor with a contemporaneous written acknowledgment of the contribution.

The items on this form include:

- *Box 4a*—This is checked by the charitable donee to certify that the donated vehicle was sold to an unrelated party in an arm's-length transaction.

- *Box 4c*—Here the charity enters the gross proceeds it received from the sale of the donated vehicle. If box 4a is checked, the donor generally may take a deduction in an amount equal to the lesser of the amount in box 4c or the vehicle's fair market value on the date of the contribution.

- *Box 5a*—This is checked by the charity to certify that the donated vehicle will not be sold before completion of a significant intervening use or material improvement by the charity. If this box is checked, the donor generally may take a deduction equal to the vehicle's fair market value.

- *Box 5b*—This box is checked by the charity to certify that the donated vehicle is to be transferred to a needy individual in direct furtherance of the donee's charitable purpose of relieving the poor or distressed or underprivileged who are in need of a means of transportation. If this box is checked, the donor generally may take a deduction equal to the vehicle's fair market value.

A donor of a qualified vehicle must attach Copy B of this form to the donor's income tax return in order to take a deduction for the contribution of the vehicle where the claimed value is in excess of $500. Generally, the donee must furnish Copies B and C of the form to the donor no later than 30 days after the date of sale if box 4a is checked or 30 days after the date of the contribution if box 5a or 5b is checked.

Copy A of this form is to be filed with the IRS, Copy C is for the donor's records, and Copy D is retained by the charitable donee.

Other issues may arise in this context.

Appraisal. If the value of the contributed vehicle is in excess of $5,000, the donor is obligated to obtain an independent appraisal of the value of the vehicle (discussed previously).

Penalties. Both parties are potentially liable for penalties for aiding and abetting understatements of tax liability, for preparation of false tax returns, and for promoting abusive tax shelters. Indeed, the IRS imposed these penalties in the context of a charitable organization's used vehicle contribution program when the organization had a practice of providing donors with documentation supporting the full fair market value of contributed vehicles in each instance, even when some of the vehicles were in poor condition and could be sold only for salvage or scrap.

Unrelated Business Considerations. When vehicles are contributed to a charitable organization and the organization disposes of them, the charity may be perceived as being in the business of acquiring and selling the vehicles. Nonetheless, this activity is not considered an unrelated business, because of the *donated goods exception.* In some instances, payments to a charitable organization in the context of these programs may be characterized as tax-excludable royalties. (See Chapter 7.)

Contributions "to" Charity. To be deductible, a contribution must be to (or for the use of) a qualified charitable organization. To be *to* a charity, the gift must be made under circumstances where the donee has full control of the donated money or other property and full discretion as to its use. When a charitable organization utilizes the services of a for-profit company to receive and process donated vehicles, the gift may be deemed to be to the company, rather than the charity, in which case there is no charitable contribution deduction. This situation can be resolved, however, by denominating the company as the agent of the charity for this purpose.

Private Benefit Doctrine. The IRS raised the issue of applicability of the private benefit doctrine (see Chapter 2) in this setting. The agency posits situations in which an automobile dealer or some other third party is the true beneficiary of a transaction. If the private benefit is more than insubstantial, the charitable organization's tax-exempt status could be jeopardized.

Private Inurement Doctrine. The IRS has also raised the possibility of application, in this setting, of the private inurement doctrine (*id.*). When such a third party is an insider with respect to the charitable organization, that doctrine could be implicated, thereby endangering the organization's exempt status.

Intermediate Sanctions. The intermediate sanctions rules (id.) are applicable when a transaction constitutes an *excess benefit transaction* and the charitable organization's dealings are with a *disqualified person* with respect to it. The IRS has applied the intermediate sanctions rules in connection with used vehicle donation programs. The IRS may also assess a penalty for willful and flagrant violation of these standards.

Fractional Interests in Art

The value of a donor's charitable contribution deduction for the initial contribution of a fractional interest in an item of tangible personal property (or collection of such items) is determined, in part, on the fair market value of the property at the time of the contribution of the fractional interest, and whether the use of the property will be related to the charitable donee's exempt purposes.

Additional rules apply, however, in instances of gifts of fractional interests to charitable organizations after August 17, 2006. For example, for purposes of determining the deductible amount of each additional contribution of an interest (whether it is a fractional interest or not) in the same item of property, the fair market value of the item is the lesser of (1) the value used for purposes of determining the charitable deduction for the initial fractional contribution or (2) the fair market value of the item at the time of the subsequent contribution.

Recapture of this income tax charitable deduction can occur in two circumstances. First, if a donor makes an initial fractional contribution and thereafter fails to contribute all of the donor's remaining interest in the property to the same charitable donee before the earlier of ten years from the initial fractional contribution or the donor's death, the donor's charitable deduction(s) for all previous contribution(s) of interests in the item must be recaptured, plus interest. If the donee of the initial contribution is no longer in existence as of that time, the donor's remaining interest may be contributed to another charitable entity.

Second, if the charitable donee of a fractional interest in an item of tangible personal property fails to take substantial physical possession of the item during the above-described period or fails to use the property for an exempt use during the above-described period, the donor's charitable income tax deduction(s) for all previous contribution(s) of interests in the item must be recaptured, plus interest. In either of these circumstances, where there is a recapture, an additional tax is imposed in an amount equal to 10 percent of the amount recaptured.

An income tax charitable contribution deduction is not allowed for a contribution of a fractional interest in an item of tangible personal property unless, immediately before the contribution, all interests in the item are owned by the donor or by the donor and the donee charitable organization. The IRS is authorized to make exceptions to this rule in cases where all persons who hold an interest in an item make proportional contributions of undivided interests in their respective shares of each item to the donee organization.

As an illustration of these rules, A owns an undivided 40 percent interest in a painting; B owns an undivided 60 percent interest in the same painting. The IRS may determine that A may take a deduction for a charitable contribution of less than the entire interest in the painting held by A, if both A and B make proportional contributions of undivided fractional interests in their respective shares of the painting to the same donee organization. For example, A contributes 50 percent of A's interest and B contributes 50 percent of B's interest.

NONCHARITABLE FUNDRAISING RULES

Certain fundraising disclosure rules are applicable to all types of tax-exempt organizations, principally social welfare organizations, other than charitable ones. These requirements are designed to prevent noncharitable organizations from engaging in fundraising activities under circumstances in which donors will assume that the contributions are tax-deductible, when in fact they are not. These rules do not, however, apply to an organization that has annual gross receipts that are normally no more than $100,000. Also, where all of the parties being solicited are exempt organizations, the solicitation need not include the disclosure statement (inasmuch as these grantors have no need for a charitable deduction).

Technically, in general, this law applies to any organization to which contributions are not deductible as charitable gifts and that (1) is tax-exempt, (2) is a political organization, (3) was either type of organization at any time during the five-year period ending on the date of the fundraising solicitation, or (4) is a successor to one of these organizations at any time during this five-year period. The IRS is accorded the authority to treat any group of two or more organizations as one organization for these purposes where "necessary or appropriate" to prevent the avoidance of these rules through the use of multiple organizations.

Under these rules, each fundraising solicitation by or on behalf of a tax-exempt noncharitable organization must contain an express statement, in a "conspicuous and easily recognizable format," that gifts to it are not deductible as charitable contributions for federal income tax purposes. The term *fundraising solicitation* is defined in this setting as any solicitation of gifts made in written or printed form, by television, radio, or telephone (although an exclusion is available for letters or calls that are not part of a coordinated fundraising campaign soliciting no more than ten persons during a calendar year). Despite the reference in the statute to "contributions and gifts," the IRS interprets this rule to mandate the disclosure when any exempt organization (other than a charity) seeks funds, such as dues from members.

Failure to satisfy this disclosure requirement can result in imposition of penalties. The penalty is $1,000 per day (maximum of $10,000 per year), albeit with a reasonable cause exception. In an instance of an intentional disregard of these rules, however, the penalty for the day on which the offense occurred is the greater of $1,000 or 50 percent of the aggregate cost of the solicitations that took place on that day, and the $10,000 limitation is inapplicable. For these purposes, the days involved are those on which the solicitation was telecast, broadcast, mailed, otherwise distributed, or telephoned.

The IRS promulgated rules in amplification of this law, particularly the requirement of a disclosure statement. The rules, which include guidance in the form of "safe-harbor" provisions, address the format of the disclosure statement in instances of use of print media, telephone, television, and radio. They provide examples of acceptable disclosure language and methods (that, when followed, amount to the safe-harbor guidelines), and of included and excluded solicitations. They also contain guidelines for determining the $10,000 threshold.

The safe-harbor guideline for print media (including solicitations by mail and in newspapers) is fourfold: (1) the solicitation includes language such as the following: "Contributions or gifts to [name of organization] are not deductible as charitable contributions for federal income tax purposes"; (2) the statement is in at least the same typesize as the primary message stated in the body of the letter, leaflet, or advertisement; (3) the statement is included on the message side of any card or tear-off section that the contributor returns with the contribution; and (4) the statement is either the first sentence in a paragraph or itself constitutes a paragraph.

The safe-harbor guideline for telephone solicitations includes the first of the above elements. In addition, the guideline requires that (1) the statement be made in close proximity to the request for contributions, during the same telephone call, by the telephone solicitor, and (2) any written confirmation or billing sent to a person pledging to contribute during the telephone solicitation be in compliance with the requirements for print media solicitations.

Solicitation by television must, to conform to this guideline, include a solicitation statement that complies with the first of the print medium requirements. Also, if the statement is spoken, it must be in close proximity to the request for a contribution. If the statement appears on the television screen, it must be in large, easily readable type appearing on the screen for at least five seconds.

In the case of a solicitation by radio, the statement must, to meet this safe-harbor test, comply with the first of the print medium requirements. Also, the statement must be made in close proximity to the request for contributions during the same radio solicitation announcement.

Where the soliciting organization is a membership entity, classified as a trade or business association or other form of business league, or a labor or agricultural organization, the following statement conforms to the safe-harbor guideline: "Contributions or gifts to [name of organization] are not tax-deductible as charitable contributions. They may be tax-deductible, however, as ordinary and necessary business expenses."

If an organization makes a solicitation to which these rules apply and the solicitation does not comply with the applicable safe-harbor guideline, the IRS is authorized to evaluate all of the facts and circumstances to determine whether the solicitation meets the disclosure rule. A "good faith effort" to comply with these requirements is an important factor in this evaluation of the facts and circumstances. Nonetheless, disclosures made in "fine print" do not comply with the statutory requirement.

This disclosure requirement applies to solicitations for contributions as well as solicitations for attendance at testimonials and similar fundraising events. The disclosure must be made in the case of solicitations for contributions to political action committees.

Exempt from this disclosure rule are the following:

- Billing of those who advertise in a tax-exempt organization's publications
- Billing by social clubs for food and beverages
- Billing of attendees of a conference
- Billing for insurance premiums of an insurance program operated or sponsored by an organization
- Billing of members of a community association for mandatory payments for police and fire (and similar) protection
- Billing for payments to a voluntary employees' beneficiary association as well as similar payments to a trust for pension and/or health benefits

General material discussing the benefits of membership in a tax-exempt organization, such as a trade association or labor union, does not have to include the required disclosure statement. The statement is required, however, where the material both requests payment and specifies the amount requested as membership dues. If a person responds to the general material discussing the benefits of membership, the follow-up material requesting the payment of a specific amount in membership dues (such as a union checkoff card or a trade association billing statement for new member) must include the disclosure statement. General material discussing a political candidacy and requesting persons to vote for the candidate or "support" the candidate need not include the disclosure statement, unless the material specifically requests either a financial contribution or a contribution of volunteer services in support of the candidate.

SUMMARY

This chapter provided summaries of the federal tax law charitable gift substantiation requirements, quid pro quo contributions, disclosure rules, appraisal rules, and various unique reporting rules. It described the relevant portions of the rules concerning application for recognition of tax-exempt status and addresses the import of the federal public charity classifications. The import of the Form 8283 was explained. The chapter ended with a summary of the federal tax law applicable to fundraising by noncharitable exempt organizations.

9

FUNDRAISING AND CONSTITUTIONAL LAW

The purpose of this chapter is to summarize the constitutional law principles that pertain to charitable fundraising. Foremost among these principles is the right of free speech, found principally in the First Amendment to the U.S. Constitution. Fundraising for charitable purposes is one of the highest forms of free speech and thus is entitled to considerable protection. Other constitutional law principles at play in this context are the rights of due process and equal protection, as well as delegation of legislative authority. Specifically, this chapter will:

- Summarize the basics of free speech constitutional law.

- Articulate the difference between commercial speech and protected speech.

- Explain the concept of governments' police power.

- Summarize fundraising free speech principles.

- Summarize the principal U.S. Supreme Court opinions on free speech principles and charitable fundraising.

- Identify some of the significant subsequent court decisions on free speech principles and charitable fundraising.

- Summarize free speech law pertaining to airport terminal solicitations.

- Summarize free speech law in the context of door-to-door advocacy.

- Explain the law concerning free speech principles and registration fees.

- Explore the outer boundaries of free speech rights.

- Discuss the law concerning charitable fundraising and fraud.

- Summarize the basics of due process rights and charitable fundraising.

- Summarize the basics of equal protection rights and charitable fundraising.

- Discuss the law concerning delegation of legislative authority.

- Discuss the law concerning treatment of religious organizations.

- Summarize other pertinent constitutional law issues.

FREE SPEECH BASICS

The First Amendment to the Constitution states that Congress "shall make no law...abridging the freedom of speech." This prohibition of denial of free speech rights is applicable to the states by application of the Fourteenth Amendment, which provides that a state may not "deprive any person of life, liberty, or property, without due process of law; nor deny to any person within its jurisdiction the equal protection of the laws."

The word *liberty*, as used in the Fourteenth Amendment, includes the liberties of freedom of speech and of the press, as well as the general right of liberty or action, as guaranteed by the First Amendment and similar state constitution provisions. Freedom of speech is a limitation on *governmental* regulation; it does not extend to matters such as enforcement of codes of ethics (unless the organization involved is deemed as a matter of law to be an arm of a government) or promulgation of watchdog agency requirements (see Chapters 2 and 10).

TYPES OF SPEECH

Constitutional law differentiates between *protected* speech (sometimes referred to as *pure* speech) and *commercial* speech. The latter form of speech is treated, from a law standpoint, as the subject of economic regulation, the scope of which must be tested only for rationality. Laws regulating protected speech, by contrast, must be narrowly tailored (or confined) to an appropriate governmental interest. Fundraising for charitable purposes is an exercise of the right of protected free speech, under both federal and state law principles. This application of free speech rights stands as the single most important bar to more stringent governmental regulation of the process of soliciting charitable contributions.

As discussed below, three significant Supreme Court cases hold that fundraising for charity is one of the highest forms of free speech, that is, it is protected speech. Each of these decisions was decided on a 5–4 basis; the dissenters asserted that the fundraising regulation statutes were limiting only commercial speech and did so in a reasonable manner.

As also discussed below, governments have the power—the police power—to regulate, for the protection of their citizens, the process of soliciting contributions for charitable purposes. They cannot exercise this power, however, in a manner that unduly intrudes on the rights of free speech of the soliciting charities—and their consultants and solicitors. There is, not surprisingly, considerable tension between free speech rights and application of the police power; the litigation in this area involves a collision of these two precepts.

The most significant clash between a government's police power to regulate for the benefit of its citizens and the free speech rights associated with charitable solicitations involves the application of percentage limitations on fundraising costs as a basis for determining whether a charity may lawfully solicit contributions in a jurisdiction. These percentage restrictions are, by application of Supreme Court pronouncements, blatantly violative of charities' free speech rights or, more elegantly stated, are unconstitutionally overbroad in violation of the First and Fourteenth Amendments to the U.S. Constitution.

POLICE POWER

Each state and municipality inherently possesses the *police power*. This power enables a state or one of its political subdivisions to regulate—within the bounds of constitutional and other law principles—the conduct of its citizens and others, so as to protect the safety, health, and welfare of its people. At the same time, there is stress in this area of the law, in that the states may not unduly burden or discriminate in the context of interstate commerce.

Generally, it is clear that a state can enact and enforce, in the exercise of its police power, a charitable solicitation act (see Chapter 3) that requires a charity that is planning on fundraising in the jurisdiction to first register with (or secure a license or permit from) the appropriate regulatory authorities and subsequently to submit periodic reports about the results of the solicitations. There is nothing innately unlawful about such a law that also requires professional fundraisers and professional solicitors to likewise register and report. This empowers the regulatory authorities to investigate the activities of these organizations and persons in the presence of reasonable cause to do so, and that imposes injunctive remedies, fines, and imprisonment for violation of the statute. A state can regulate charitable fundraising notwithstanding the fact that the solicitation occurs in interstate commerce, utilizes the federal postal system, or does both. As a state court put the matter, compliance with a state charitable solicitation act "may burden interstate commerce to some degree, that burden is outweighed by this State's interest in protecting its citizens from the fraud and deceit of unscrupulous 'charitable' organizations."

Consequently, the laws that regulate charitable solicitations are by no means constitutionally deficient per se. They are, instead, legitimate utilizations of the states' police power. At the same time, these laws must, like all legislation, conform to certain basic legal standards or be challenged in court. As a court observed, while the government "may regulate [charitable] solicitation in order to protect the community from fraud . . . [a]ny action impinging upon the freedom of expression and discussion . . . must be minimal, and ultimately related to an articulated, substantial governmental interest." Another court put the matter this way, writing that "since every person has the right to solicit contributions for charity if he acts in good faith and makes an honest application of the funds so obtained, regulations of this character [that is, those regulating charitable fundraising] which are arbitrary and which assume to say what person or what institution may or may not engage in charitable work are objectionable, as a denial of a common right." The Supreme Court summed this matter, stating that, although government has "legitimate interests" in this field, it must serve those interests by "narrowly drawn regulations" that do not unnecessarily interfere with First Amendment freedoms.

The lawsuits against enforcement of charitable fundraising statutes and ordinances that prevail are not those that attack the laws broadside but those that focus on one or more aspects of specific applicability, such as those laws' impact on the practice of religious beliefs, violation of free speech rights caused by refusals to allow solicitations by organizations with fundraising costs in excess of a set percentage, or contraventions of equal protection rights stemming from exemptions or preferences accorded certain organizations.

FUNDRAISING FREE SPEECH PRINCIPLES

Supreme Court opinions on the subject of charitable fundraising have laid down these fundamental constitutional law precepts:

- The solicitation of charitable contributions is protected speech, not merely commercial speech.

- Any restrictions on charitable fundraising must be narrowly tailored to advance a legitimate governmental interest.

- Where the issue is the constitutionality of the use of percentages to assess the legality or other consequences in law of fundraising expenses and the state's interest is the prevention of fraud, the use of percentage limitations will be voided because such a use is unconstitutionally overbroad.

- Where a state has a sufficient interest in regulating charitable fundraising, the nexus between the mode of regulation and the furtherance of that interest must be substantial.

- A fundraising regulation law cannot constitutionally burden a charitable speaker or a speaker for a charity with unwanted speech during the course of a solicitation.

- A state can constitutionally regulate charitable fundraising by means of antifraud laws, antitrespass laws, and disclosure laws.

- Overregulation of charitable solicitations leads to the chilling of speech in direct contravention of free speech principles.

SUPREME COURT OPINIONS

Three opinions authored by the U.S. Supreme Court articulated the pertinent legal principles, forcefully applying them to void fundraising regulation laws, predicated on fundraising cost percentages, as being unconstitutionally overbroad in transgression of free speech principles.

Absolute Percentage Limitation

The first of these Supreme Court opinions emanated from its consideration of a municipal ordinance that prohibited door-to-door or on-street solicitations by charitable organizations that expend more than 25 percent of their receipts for fundraising and administration. Thus, that law forced the requirement that, for a lawful charitable solicitation to occur, the fundraising charity devote at least 75 percent of receipts for charitable program purposes. This percentage limitation was absolute, in that it did not permit a charitable organization to demonstrate the reasonableness of its nonprogram expenses, notwithstanding the fact that the costs exceed the limitation.

The municipality denied a fundraising permit to a charitable organization, because the entity could not demonstrate that 75 percent of its receipts would be used for charitable purposes. The organization was an environmental protection entity, characterized by the Supreme Court as one of a category of organizations that was "advocacy-oriented." It employed canvassers who traveled door to door distributing literature and answering questions on environmental topics, soliciting contributions, and receiving complaints about environmental matters for which the organization might afford assistance.

Unable to secure a permit to solicit in the municipality, the organization sued, alleging that the ordinance violated free speech principles. It prevailed in the federal trial court, in the court of appeals, and in the Supreme Court, with all three courts finding the ordinance to be constitutionally overbroad as an unwarranted transgression of free speech rights.

The municipality claimed that it was merely exercising its police power (discussed previously) in an attempt to prevent fraud and protect public safety and residential privacy. The Supreme Court agreed that the town had a substantial governmental interest in so protecting the public but concluded that this interest was "only peripherally promoted by the 75-percent requirement and could be sufficiently served by measures less destructive of First Amendment interests." Thus, in this conflict between the police power and free speech rights, the latter predominated. As the Court stated the matter, the municipality may "serve its legitimate interests, but it must do so by narrowly drawn regulations designed to serve those interests without unnecessarily interfering with First Amendment freedoms."

The Supreme Court wrote that "charitable appeals for funds, on the street or door to door, involve a variety of speech interests—communication of information, the dissemination and propagation of views and ideas, and the advocacy of causes—that are within the protection of the First Amendment." Thus, the Court in this opinion did not expressly hold that all types of charitable solicitations are forms of protected speech; rather, this constitutional law shelter was provided only for the form of solicitation that is "characteristically intertwined with informative and perhaps persuasive speech seeking support for particular causes or for particular views on economic, political, or social issues." Consequently, this opinion left open the question as to whether protected solicitations are only those that are intermixed with program functions, as opposed to fundraising efforts, such as annual giving appeals and planned gift solicitations, where little or no advocacy is present.

Also, just as there was lack of clarity as to whether every charitable solicitation is an act involving free speech, the Court's opinion could have been interpreted to mean that its holding was not applicable to every type of charitable organization. The Court cited, but did not discuss, the appellate court's observation that the 75-percent limitation might be enforceable against the "more traditional charitable organizations" or "where solicitors represent themselves as mere conduits for contributions." Rather, the Court said that the 75-percent rule cannot constitutionally be applied to "advocacy" groups, defined as "organizations whose primary purpose is not to provide money or services for the poor, the needy or other worthy objects of charity, but to gather and disseminate information about and advocate positions on matters of public concern." Quoting from the appellate court's discussion of this point, the Court added that these groups characteristically use paid solicitors who "necessarily combine" the solicitation of financial support with the "functions of information dissemination, discussion, and advocacy of public issues."

Having defined this class of charities, the Court recognized that, even though the salaries they pay were reasonable, they would necessarily expend more than 25 percent of their receipts on salaries and administrative expenses. Then, as observed, the Court proceeded to conclude that a ban on charitable solicitations, applied to these types of charitable organizations by means of the 75-percent limitation, is an unjustified infringement of the First and Fourteenth Amendments to the U.S. Constitution.

One of the principal consequences of this case was the Court's rejection of the absolute percentage limitation on fundraising and administrative costs as a basis for prohibiting charitable solicitations. The Court observed that the "submission [by the municipality] is that any organization using more than 25 percent of its receipts on fundraising, salaries and overhead is not a charitable, but a commercial, for-profit enterprise and that to permit it to represent itself as a charity is fraudulent." The Court wrote that this is not the proper conclusion to be drawn and that "this cannot be true of those organizations that are primarily engaged in research, advocacy or public education and that use their own paid staff to carry out these functions as well as to solicit financial support." Likewise, the Court could not find a substantial relationship between the 75-percent limitation and the protection of public safety or of residential privacy.

This opinion clearly stated that an *absolute* percentage limitation on fundraising costs as applied to *advocacy* organizations that solicit *door to door* is unconstitutional. The opinion, however, left open these significant questions: (1) Is a *rebuttable* percentage limitation on fundraising costs likewise a violation of free speech rights? (2) Are these protections available to charitable organizations *other than* advocacy groups? (3) Are these protections available to types of fundraising *other than* door-to-door or on-street appeals? And (4) what is the validity of percentage limitations that apply, not directly to a charity, but to the compensation of a professional fundraiser or professional solicitor? As discussed next, these questions and others were resolved in subsequent Supreme Court pronouncements.

Rebuttable Percentage Limitation

The Supreme Court later considered a charitable solicitation law—a state statute. This law generally prohibited, within the state, the solicitation of contributions for a charitable organization that has paid or will pay as expenses more than 25 percent of the amount raised. This law, however, unlike the rigid ordinance of the above municipality, authorized a waiver, pursuant to rules to be developed by the secretary of state, of the percentage limitation "in those instances where the 25 percent limitation would effectively prevent a charitable organization from raising contributions." Because of the challenge of this law by a professional fundraising company, this was the first time the Court considered the so-called *rebuttable* percentage limitation in the fundraising context.

Before reviewing this statute, the Court revisited its rationale for striking down the municipality's ordinance. The Court noted its earlier pronouncement that the absolute percentage limitation was a "direct and substantial" limitation on protected activity that could not be upheld because it was not a "precisely tailored means of accommodating" the legitimate interests of the town in protecting the public from fraud, crime, and undue annoyance. The Court again noted that the fundamental flaw underlying the municipal ordinance was the assumption that a charity with fundraising expenses in excess of a fixed percentage was operating in a commercial manner; the Court observed that "there is no necessary connection between fraud and high solicitation and administrative costs."

In answer to the question as to "whether the constitutional deficiencies in a percentage limitation on funds expended in [charitable] solicitation are remedied by the possibility of an administrative waiver of the limitation for a charity that can demonstrate financial necessity," the Court concluded that the "waiver provision does not save the statute." Once again, the law deploying a percentage limitation was found to be inherently defective because "it operates on a fundamentally mistaken premise that high solicitation costs are an accurate measure of fraud."

The Court seemed to concede that this state statute may be somewhat more effective at repelling fraud than the municipality's ordinance, due to the waiver provision. But it added that the fact that the statute "in some of its applications actually prevents the misdirection of funds from the organization's purported charitable goal is little more than fortuitous." The Court posited these examples: The statute may well restrict free speech that "results in high costs but is itself a part of the charity's goal or that is simply attributable to the fact that the charity's cause proves to be unpopular," yet if an organization "indulges in fraud, there is nothing in the percentage limitation that prevents it from misdirecting funds." "In either event," the Court concluded, the percentage limitation, "though restricting solicitation costs, will have done nothing to prevent fraud." "In all its applications," wrote the Court, this statute "creates an unnecessary risk of chilling free speech." The Court reasserted its theme in these contexts: "The possibility of a waiver may decrease the number of impermissible applications of the statute, but it does nothing to remedy the statute's fundamental defect."

The state offered reasons in the nature of characteristics of its law, other than the waiver provision, as to why its statute should be salvaged in contradistinction with the municipal ordinance. The Court was unmoved by these features: (1) a charity's ability to solicit funds without having to first prove compliance with the percentage limitation, (2) the limitation applied only to fundraising expenses and not to a variety of other noncharitable expenditures (such as postage), (3) a charity's ability to elect to apply the percentage limitation on a campaign-by-campaign basis, and (4) the applicability of the statute to all forms of fundraising for charitable purposes, not just door-to-door solicitation.

As to the first of these propositions, the Court found elements of a "before-the-fact" prohibition on solicitation, such as the requirement that a contract between a charity and a professional fundraiser must be filed with the state in advance of a solicitation and the fact the registration of a professional fundraiser will be approved by the state only where the application is in conformity with the statute. But more importantly, the Court decided that this distinction about restraint before or after the commencement of fundraising makes little difference, in that "whether the charity is prevented from engaging in First Amendment activity by the lack of a solicitation permit or by the knowledge that its fundraising activity is illegal if it cannot satisfy the percentage limitation, the chill on the protected activity is the same."

As to the second and third points, the Court dismissed the distinctions as meaning "only that the statute will not apply to as many charities as did the [municipal] ordinance" and added that they "do nothing to alter the fact that significant fundraising activity protected by the First Amendment is barred by the percentage limitation." The fourth point was rejected on the ground that the broader scope of the statute "does not remedy the fact that the statute promotes the State's interest only peripherally." Dryly, the Court wrote that the "statute's aim [in attempting to attack fraud] is not improved by the fact that it fires at a number of targets." Thus, the percentage limitation enacted by the state was voided by the Court on the same ground as that of the ordinance: It was unconstitutionally overbroad in transgression of free speech rights.

Regarding the four questions left unanswered by the Supreme Court when considering the municipal ordinance, the Court in the state statute case clearly answered the first question in the affirmative: A rebuttable percentage limitation is just as constitutionally deficient as an absolute one.

The second and third questions basically went unaddressed in this second opinion. Yet there is nothing in that opinion that suggests that free speech rights, in connection with fundraising, are extended only to advocacy groups. Indeed, throughout most of the opinion, reference is only to charities, with the Court observing that advocacy groups are the "organizations that were of primary concern to the Court" in its prior opinion. The only instance of an attempt by the Court in the second opinion to bifurcate the charitable world in these regards came when it made reference to "organizations that have high fundraising costs not due to protected First Amendment activity"; this distinction was dismissed with the observation that "this statute cannot distinguish those organizations from charities that have high costs due to protected First Amendment activities." Consequently, there should be little doubt that free speech rights in this setting are extended to all charities, either because the law treats all charitable organizations as protected when fundraising or because the law has yet to contemplate a statute that can constitutionally differentiate between the two categories of charitable entities.

Moreover, there is nothing in this opinion that suggests that free speech protections are available only for fundraising that occurs door to door. Indeed, the opinion specifically notes, without comment as to the distinction, that the statute "regulates all charitable fundraising, and not just door-to-door solicitation." Again, there should be little doubt that free speech rights in these regards are extended to all forms of fundraising for charitable purposes.

The fourth question was not fully answered in the opinion concerning the state statute. Yet the ultimate outcome was subtly hinted at in this opinion. In the case construing the statute, the plaintiff was not a charitable organization but a professional fundraiser. This generated a number of legal problems, principally the question of standing to sue, but the merits of the opinion implicitly stated that free speech rights in the charitable fundraising context extend beyond rights asserted directly by charitable organizations.

Fundraisers' and Solicitors' Fees

Four years later, the U.S. Supreme Court rendered still another opinion addressing the constitutionality of a charitable fundraising regulation law. At issue in this instance were provisions of another state's charitable solicitation act. Just as the statute in the previous case attempted to sidestep constitutional law infirmities by being more sophisticated than the municipal ordinance, the authors of the statute in this case tried to be constitutional by being more sophisticated than their counterparts in the first statute case. Part of the problem with the statute in this case was that it was worded as a near parody of the previous Supreme Court rulings and was a too-obvious attempt to stay within the boundaries of fundraising regulation circumscribed by the law of free speech rights.

The state charitable solicitation act in this third case did not place a limitation on fundraising expenses by charitable organizations. Rather, it endeavored to constitutionally place a limitation on the amount or extent of fees paid by a charitable organization to professional fundraisers or professional solicitors. The general rule as articulated by this law was that a professional fundraiser or solicitor could not lawfully charge a charitable organization an "excessive and unreasonable" fee. This law established a three-tiered schedule, using percentage-based mechanical presumptions, for determining whether a particular fee was in fact excessive and unreasonable.

Under this statute, a fee that was not in excess of 20 percent of the gross receipts collected was deemed "reasonable and nonexcessive." Where a fee was between 20 and 35 percent of gross receipts collected, the law deemed the fee to be excessive and unreasonable on a showing that the solicitation at issue "did not involve the dissemination of information, discussion, or advocacy relating to public issues as directed by the [charitable organization] which is to benefit from the solicitation." A fee in excess of 35 percent was presumed to be excessive and unreasonable, although the fundraiser or solicitor could rebut the presumption by showing that the amount of the fee was necessary because (1) the solicitation involved the dissemination of information or advocacy on public issues directed by the charity or (2) otherwise the ability of the charity to raise money or communicate its ideas and positions to the public would be seriously diminished. The Court described an additional feature of the statute, in that "even where a prima facie showing of unreasonableness has been rebutted, the fact-finder must still make an ultimate determination, on a case-by-case basis, as to whether the fee was reasonable—a showing that the solicitation involved the advocacy or dissemination of information does not alone establish that the total fee was reasonable."

The Supreme Court concluded that this three-tiered, percentage-based definition of a "reasonable" fundraising fee failed to pass constitutional law muster, as being unduly burdensome on free speech. It rejected the rationale that the statute is constitutional because it was designed to ensure that the maximum amount of funds reaches the charity on the ground that the law is overbroad and in violation of the First Amendment's "command that government regulation of speech must be measured in minimums, not maximums." The Court likewise dismissed the thought that the state's law's flexibility more narrowly tailored it to the state's asserted interests than was the case with the other statute or the ordinance, noting that "permitting rebuttal cannot supply the missing nexus between the percentages and the State's interest."

The Court considered other justifications offered by this state for regulating the reasonableness of fundraisers' fees, portraying them as resting on one or both of two premises: "(1) that charitable organizations are economically unable to negotiate fair or reasonable contracts without governmental assistance; or (2) that charities are incapable of deciding for themselves the most effective way to exercise their First Amendment rights." Rejecting both premises, the Court wrote that there is no constitutional law basis for the claim by the state of the "power to establish a single transcendent criterion by which it can bind the charities' speaking decisions," finding the state's position "paternalistic."

The Court observed that the First Amendment "mandates that we presume that speakers, not the government, know best both what they want to say and how to say it." "To this end," continued the Court, the "government, even with the purest of motives, may not substitute its judgment as to how best to speak for that of speakers and listeners; free and robust debate cannot thrive if directed by the government." On this point, the Court then administered this coup de grace: "We perceive no reason to engraft [sic] an exception to this settled rule for charities."

The Court in this case also attacked the general concept of forcing fundraising charities to prove reasonableness of fees on the basis of the size of the fundraiser's fee. That fee, wrote the Court, may be one of many factors affecting fundraising expenses; others include the type of fundraising involved and the integration of a non-fundraising event with a fundraising event. Moreover, added the Court, the contested law is "impermissibly insensitive to the realities faced by small or unpopular charities, which must often pay more than 35 percent of the gross receipts collected to the fundraiser due to the difficulty of attracting donors" and thus its "scheme must necessarily chill speech in direct contravention of the First Amendment's dictates."

In this case invalidating this aspect of the statute, the Court returned to a theme articulated in its opinion concerning the other statute: the ability of the states to combat fundraising fraud by means of antifraud statutes and general disclosure requirements. The Court acknowledged that these laws may not be the most efficient methods of preventing fraud in this setting, but added that the First Amendment "does not permit the State to sacrifice speech for efficiency."

Having dispensed with this aspect of the state's charitable solicitation act, the Court turned to a somewhat comparable feature: another provision requiring that professional fundraisers disclose to potential donors, before commencing an appeal for funds, the percentage of charitable contributions collected during the previous 12 months that were expended for charitable purposes. While the state contended that this was a limitation only on commercial speech (discussed previously), in that it relates merely to the fundraiser's profits from a solicitation, the Court wrote that, even if that is true, "we do not believe that the speech retains its commercial character when it is inextricably intertwined with otherwise fully protected speech." Declaiming that "we cannot parcel out the speech, applying one test to one phrase and another test to another phrase," the Court held that this "prophylactic, imprecise, and unduly burdensome rule" is also unconstitutional.

SUBSEQUENT COURT OPINIONS

The foregoing three U.S. Supreme Court decisions set the stage for more litigation over the permissible reach of state charitable solicitation laws. Aside from the specific rules to be gleaned from these three opinions, one of the basic principles of law that is important is that these fundraising regulation laws may, in the words of the Court in the third of these opinions, "not burden a speaker [be it a charity or a fundraising professional] with unwanted speech during the course of a solicitation." A sampling of subsequent court opinions follows.

A state statute required professional solicitors to submit the script of an oral solicitation of charitable gifts to the state at least ten days before the commencement of the solicitation. The state argued that this requirement promoted the state's interest in the prevention of fraud and misrepresentation in charitable solicitations, and that it was the only effective regulation of fundraising by telephone. A federal court concluded that this law was an unconstitutional prior restraint on speech. It held that there "is a thin line between reviewing a script for misrepresentations and reviewing it for content." The court wrote that state officials were able to "recast solicitation scripts so as to reflect their judgment as to how a solicitation can be made." The state attempted to convince the court that its officials properly utilized this law, but the court held that none of the state's assurances persuaded it that "bureaucratic review of solicitation scripts is not rife with potential for abuse."

The Supreme Court upheld a regulation prohibiting solicitations on property of the U.S. Postal Service. The appellate court below held that the sidewalk in front of the post office involved was a public forum (discussed ahead). The Court, however, found that the sidewalk was a nonpublic forum, being intended "solely to assist postal patrons" to obtain access to postal services, leading to the conclusion that an in-person solicitation of money on the post office sidewalk could be prohibited without violation of free speech rights. This solicitation of funds was held to be "inherently disruptive of the postal service's business" in that it "impedes the normal flow of traffic." The Court applied a reasonableness test, which permits restrictions on speech in nonpublic forums as long as they are viewpoint-neutral.

A state supreme court found unconstitutional a provision in the state's charitable solicitation act forbidding telemarketing for charitable purposes and thus voided the provision. The court held that an outright ban on telephone solicitations is impermissible as being violative of charities' rights of free speech. It noted that the state must use the least restrictive means to protect its citizens from charitable fundraising fraud and observed that the state failed to show that the ban on telephone fundraising provides any deterrence to fraud.

A federal court concluded that, although a law requiring disclosure to prospective donors of a person's status as a solicitor was constitutional, requirements of disclosure of the percentage of contributions to be received by a charity that will be devoted to charitable purposes and sending of confirmation containing this percentage amount were unconstitutional, as violations of the doctrine of free speech.

A state court held constitutional a statute requiring professional solicitors for charitable organizations to register, report, pay an annual fee, and post a bond. This statute was characterized as "designed to protect a charitably minded public from being improperly solicited, abused and even defrauded." The court wrote that this law "bears a rationale relationship to the valid state objective," which is the protection and advancement of the "public's health, safety, morals, and general welfare."

A state court held unconstitutional a statute requiring an organization that plans, promotes, and operates fundraising events for charitable organizations to disclose to prospective donors the amount to be expended for fundraising, management, and program, where the program amount is less than 70 percent of the total received. The court said that implicit in this percentage "triggering device" for the disclosures "is an assumption, on the part of the Legislature, that when less than 70 percent of a charitable contribution is allocated to the 'program services' of a recipient charitable organization, the organization's 'efficiency' and its purported charitable purpose are both suspect, and it should therefore be required to disclose its financial inner-workings to prospective contributors." The court concluded that these premises are "untenable" and thus that the statute has "fundamental flaws in [its] design and operation."

A state court held unconstitutional a charitable solicitation act provision that compelled a fundraiser who charged a fee in excess of 50 percent of the adjusted gross proceeds to disclose to the person solicited that the charity received less than one-half of the proceeds. The court wrote that "more narrowly tailored means of preventing fraud are available than compelling the fundraiser to disclose to the person solicited the percentage of funds that the charity receives." The court suggested that the fundraiser can be compelled to file financial information with the state for public dissemination or the state can vigorously enforce its antifraud laws.

Another aspect of the interrelationship between the principles of free speech and charitable fundraising involves burgeoning disclosure requirements. A court stated that the "potential chilling effect [of certain disclosure requirements] on the exercise of First Amendment rights . . . is manifest, together with the invasion of privacy." Two provisions of a city ordinance were struck down on this basis: one that required a "detailed financial statement" for the most recent year and one that required disclosure of the name, address, and telephone number of each trustee, director, and officer. These disclosures were said to "directly expose the applicant's internal operations to public scrutiny and are unrelated to any legitimate governmental interest, including the City's stated interest in preventing fraudulent solicitations."

On this basis, a court struck down two provisions of a county ordinance. One, part of a registration requirement, mandated that applicants file a "specific statement of all contributions collected or received" within the year preceding the filing, including the "expenditures or use made of such contributions, together with the names and addresses of all persons or associations receiving . . . compensation . . . from such contributions and the respective amounts thereof." This law was deemed facially invalid because it was "unduly burdensome, unnecessarily compels applicants to disclose their internal operations, and fails to materially advance the County's substantial and legitimate interest in preventing fraudulent solicitations." The other required disclosure of the names and addresses of an applicant's directors and officers, as well as submission of a copy of the applicant's board resolution authorizing the solicitation. The court said: "These requirements similarly chill the exercise of free speech rights by compelling publication of the applicant's private and internal operations and are not intimately related to the County's legitimate interest in preventing fraud."

It is nonetheless clear that the basic features of a state's charitable solicitation act will pass constitutional law muster. This fact was illustrated by a federal court decision upholding one of these laws—principally against a free speech challenge. The features of this law that were found to be lawful are the registration and disclosure requirements, the registration fee, a bond or letter of credit requirement, and the authority in the state to deny or revoke a fundraising license in certain circumstances.

AIRPORT TERMINAL SOLICITATIONS

The courts have devoted considerable attention to the constitutionality of regulations governing the raising of funds (and the distribution of literature) for charitable purposes in government-owned and -operated airport terminals. These terminals are considered *public forums*, with the result that restrictions on charitable fundraising in these facilities are subject to the restrictions under the free speech doctrine, which void laws that are overbroad in relation to the furtherance of legitimate governmental interests (discussed previously).

The law in this area classifies government-owned property as being one of three types: the traditional public forum, the public forum created by government designation, and the nonpublic forum. Examples of traditional public forums are public streets, sidewalks, and parks. A speaker (including a solicitor of charitable gifts) may be excluded from a traditional public forum only when the exclusion is necessary to serve a compelling state interest and is narrowly drawn to achieve that interest.

Designated public forums are areas that are not traditionally open to assembly and debate but have been intentionally opened, by government authorities, for public discourse. The test for exclusion is the same with respect to traditional public forums; that is, the government may impose only reasonable time, place, and manner restrictions, unless there is a compelling state interest. In contrast, restrictions on speech are permissible in nonpublic forums as long as they are reasonable and viewpoint-neutral.

The U.S. Supreme Court held that an airport terminal operated by a public authority is a nonpublic forum. A ban on charitable fundraising in such an airport was ruled to be reasonable. The solicitation was held to have a disruptive effect on business, with "targets" likely to be on tight schedules, and perhaps entail fraud. The purpose of these airports, wrote the Court, is the "facilitation of passenger air travel, not the promotion of expression." The Court approved of the decision by the airport authority to confine solicitation to the sidewalk areas outside the terminal. A concurring opinion, however, reflected the view that the airport authority's argument about congestion in the terminal was not particularly convincing; there it was stated that "inconvenience does not absolve the government of its obligation to tolerate speech."

DOOR-TO-DOOR ADVOCACY

Somewhat comparable to free speech considerations in the realm of charitable fundraising is the matter of free speech considerations pertaining to door-to-door advocacy. This type of activity includes religious proselytizing, political campaigning, and distribution of publications. Implicated in this context are laws, often ordinances, requiring individuals who wish to engage in these activities to first register with a government and obtain a permit.

For decades, the U.S. Supreme Court has invalidated restrictions on door-to-door canvassing and pamphleteering. Most of these cases involved First Amendment challenges brought by Jehovah's Witnesses organizations because door-to-door canvassing is mandated by their religious principles. Moreover, because they lack significant financial resources, the ability of these organizations to proselytize is seriously diminished by laws that burden their efforts to canvass door to door.

These cases involved petty offenses that raised constitutional law questions of serious magnitude – questions that invoked the doctrines of the free exercise of religion (discussed previously) and freedom of the press as well as the freedom of speech. The cases emphasize the value of the speech involved, and canvassing in addition to pamphleteering as vehicles for the dissemination of ideas. Overall, the Court is of the view that a "requirement that one must register before he undertakes to make a public speech to enlist support for a lawful movement is quite incompatible with the requirements of the First Amendment." These cases, however, also recognized the interests a town (or other government) may have in some form of regulation—particularly when the solicitation of contributions is involved.

The Supreme Court, in the most recent of these cases, considered the issue as to whether a town ordinance that required an individual to obtain a permit prior to engaging in the door-to-door advocacy of a political cause and to display on demand the permit, which contains the individual's name, violates the First Amendment protection accorded to anonymous pamphleteering or discourse. The Court found that this law contravened First Amendment principles. The very breadth of the speech covered by the ordinance raised constitutional law concerns, with the Court finding it "offensive—not only to the values protected by the First Amendment, but to the very notion of a free society—that in the context of everyday public discourse a citizen must inform the government of her desire to speak to her neighbors and then obtain a permit to do so."

The ordinance involved prohibited canvassers from going on private property for the purpose of explaining or promoting any cause, unless they received a permit and the residents visited had not posted a "no solicitation" sign. The town contended that the ordinance served the purposes of prevention of fraud and crime, as well as protection of the privacy of residents. The Court stated that these are "important interests" that the town "may seek to safeguard through some form of regulation of solicitation activity." It essentially was the extent of the speech covered by the ordinance that led the Court to nonetheless strike it down. The Court mused that, "had this provision been construed to apply to commercial activities and the solicitation of funds, arguably the ordinance would have been tailored to the [town's] interest in protecting the privacy of its residents and preventing fraud" (discussed ahead).

REGISTRATION FEES

It is a common practice for a state's charitable solicitation law to embody a registration fee. These fees must be tested against principles protecting free speech, in that freedom of expression must be, in the words of the U.S. Supreme Court, "available to all, not merely to those who can pay their own way." Courts have held that, as one put the matter, a "licensing fee to be used in defraying administrative costs is permissible, but only to the extent that the fees are necessary."

One of the more interesting cases in this context involved the legality of a sliding scale registration fee. This fee regime requires a charitable organization soliciting in the state involved to pay a fee based on its nationwide level of contributions in the prior year. The rationale for the fee was that it yielded funds approximate to the costs of administering and enforcing this charitable solicitation act. A federal court concluded that this fee is a form of *user fee* that is "constitutionally sound." This court stated that "larger charities generally generate more registration and renewal documents to review, require more research relating to administrative, management, and membership activities, and give rise to more public inquiries, more paperwork requiring data entry, and more investigative effort." The charitable organization involved contended that this registration fee cannot be a user fee, in that the state does not provide it with the requisite *service.* The court, however, ascertained that charities seeking to solicit contributions in the state "use the state's apparatus for regulating charities," which amounts to a "benefit" in the form of the "privilege of soliciting in [the state] where donor confidence is enhanced owing to the state's regulation of charities." (See Chapter 12.)

Another case involved a challenge to the constitutionality of a state statute that imposes an $80 registration fee on professional solicitors. At issue was whether the costs to the attorney general's office of enforcing this law could be considered in setting the fee. The court involved wrote that "fees that serve not as revenue taxes, but rather as a means to meet the expenses incident to the administration of a regulation and to the maintenance of public order in the matter regulated are constitutionally permissible." The court ruled that costs associated with fraud and misappropriation of funds are necessary in the supervision of charitable organizations and thus may be taken into account in establishing the fee. At the same time, the court said that enforcement costs may not be so included "*simply because* they are in some manner related to the enforcement of" the statute, but that the "propriety of inclusion of particular enforcement costs should be determined case-by-case" (emphasis by the court). Then, the court found that both sets of costs may be included in this case, making the fee a "legitimate" one that merely defrays them, in that there is a "sufficient link" between the attorney general's enforcement activities with respect to the law and the revenues collected pursuant to it.

OUTER BOUNDARIES OF SPEECH RIGHTS

During the course of nearly 30 years, there has been an impressive array of opinions holding that a charitable organization, when fundraising, is engaging in one of the highest forms of free speech. There is a limit, however, to the expanse of a constitutional right; this is the case in the realm of charitable fundraising regulation. An illustration of this boundary pertains to gambling events.

The law in a state was amended to add restrictions on the conduct of bingo games by charitable organizations. A charitable entity, having violated several of these restrictions and directed by the state to cease conducting the games, refused to comply; the dispute ended up in court. The charity's principal argument was that the state acted in violation of free speech rights in attempting to curtail this bingo operation, inasmuch as it was one of the charity's ways of espousing its program and soliciting contributions. That contention was rejected by the court, which held that wagering is an activity that can be regulated without transgressing free speech principles. The bingo games law was found to be constitutional because it is neutral with respect to the content and viewpoint of expression.

In this case, the playing of bingo was found to not be speech. The court noted that, while the game-playing entails shouts of "BINGO!" and thus "employs vocal chords," the event is not "expression." Thus, this court held, in effect, that simply terming an activity *fundraising* is insufficient to automatically bring into play constitutional law protections. The court opined that a law that "serves purposes unrelated to the content of expression is deemed neutral, even if it has an incidental effect on some speakers or messages but not others." The statute was found to be "indifferent" to the content and viewpoint of expression by charitable organizations.

This emphasis on *neutral* legislation, then, marks the (or an) outer boundary of the ambit of protected charitable fundraising speech. Expression may not be easily regulated; events may be.

FUNDRAISING AND FRAUD

The most recent charitable fundraising case considered by the Supreme Court involved a charity that paid to a telemarketing firm, pursuant to a contract, an amount equal to 85 percent of the gifts made to it. The telemarketing company did not disclose to prospective donors that 15 percent of their gifts are distributed to the charity. On these facts, a state asserted that the telemarketing firm engaged in common-law and statutory fraud; the charitable solicitations were characterized as being "knowingly deceptive and materially false."

The Supreme Court held that fundraisers for charitable organizations may be prosecuted for fraudulent solicitations without the prosecuting state running afoul of free speech principles. The Court wrote that the First Amendment "does not shield fraud" and that "fraudulent charitable solicitation is unprotected speech." It stated that its prior decisions "took care to leave a corridor open for fraud actions to guard the public against false or misleading charitable solicitations."

The Court stated that a basis for fraud may not be found in the "percentage of donations the fundraisers would retain" or "their failure to alert potential donors to their fee arrangements at the start of each telephone call." It observed that a state attorney general "surely cannot," just by alleging fraud, "gain case-by-case ground this Court has declared off limits to legislators" (discussed previously). Rather, there is fraud when there are "particular representations made with intent to mislead." (See Chapter 12.)

DUE PROCESS RIGHTS

Laws regulating the fundraising activities of charitable organizations and those who assist them in this regard must afford those persons their due process rights as prescribed by the Fifth Amendment to the U.S. Constitution. That amendment provides that a person may not be "deprived of life, liberty, or property, without due process of law." This principle is made applicable to the states by means of the Fifth Amendment.

In the context of the state charitable solicitation acts, the principal due process arguments arose with respect to limitations on fundraising due to percentages of fundraising costs. These limitations are unconstitutional, as violations of the right of free speech (discussed previously). The free speech transgressions occurred irrespective of whether the percentage limitation was *absolute* (that is, where a charitable organization was not afforded the opportunity to demonstrate to the regulators that its fundraising costs were reasonable, notwithstanding the fact that the percentage ceiling was exceeded) or *rebuttable* (where there was no flexible standard but instead a presumption that expenses in excess of a percentage were unreasonable).

Nonetheless, in the due process setting, the absolute percentage limitation probably amounted to a violation of due process rights. The rebuttable percentage limitation may well have been in compliance with due process requirements because charities were afforded the opportunity to demonstrate the reasonableness of their fundraising costs—and thus become or remain registered in the jurisdiction—notwithstanding the fact that their fundraising costs exceeded the rebuttable percentage limitation.

Still, these laws contain ample opportunities for due process rights to be recognized or violated. For example, some states laws provide for review of contracts between charitable organizations and professional fundraisers and/or professional solicitors. Thus, an attorney general or secretary of state may be empowered to undertake this review of contracts between charities and consultants. Some laws state that, if the government official is not satisfied that the agreement does not "involve an excessively high fundraising cost," he or she can "disapprove" the contract. Yet these laws do not state guidelines or procedures to be followed by the government agency in making that determination.

Other statutory provisions that are potential due process violations are these: a rule that a charitable organization cannot expend an "unreasonable" amount for management expenses, that a registration can be suspended or revoked where the applicant has engaged in a "dishonest" practice, and that a license can be revoked where the contributions solicited are not being applied for the purpose stated in the application for the license. Any time a fundraising regulation statute contains requirements that are buttressed by subjective findings by the regulators, the potential for a due process abuse exists.

EQUAL PROTECTION RIGHTS

A charitable solicitation act must conform with the guarantee of equal protection of the laws as provided by the Fourteenth Amendment to the U.S. Constitution. This means that this type of a law may not contain a discriminatory classification of organizations. An equal protection argument is most frequently raised in connection with the exceptions from coverage provided for in many of the charitable solicitation acts.

Conventional wisdom has been that there is nothing unreasonable or arbitrary in exempting from fundraising law requirements those organizations that solicit only from their members, in that the considerations in such solicitations, compared to solicitations from the public, are different. This approach has been seen to be in conformity with the general rule that states have the authority, as part of the police power (discussed previously), to exercise wide discretion in classifying organizations in the adoption of laws, as long as the basis for doing so is not arbitrary. Recent court opinions, however, raise questions as to the constitutionality of these exemptions. Nonetheless, organizations already accountable to governments (such as colleges, universities, and hospitals) or to their memberships may validly be granted exemption from fundraising regulation, if only as a matter of administrative convenience because a state may lack the resources to monitor solicitations by every charitable entity.

Another equal protection argument stems from the fact that some state and other charitable solicitation acts provide one or more forms of exemption from them for organizations that are identified by name. While this is a relatively common practice, it technically is repugnant to equal protection principles. In one case, a city ordinance prohibited charitable solicitations unless the charity first obtained the consent of the city council. A charitable organization, identified by name, was, however, exempted from this requirement. During a review of the ordinance for constitutional law qualification, a court held that "it is obvious that the exemption of the [named charity] constitutes a deprivation of the equal protection of the laws."

An application of equal protection principles as applied in the fundraising context was seen in a case challenging the constitutionality of imposition of a registration fee on professional solicitors in the employ of professional fundraisers. The issue in the case was whether the levying of this fee, while excluding officers, volunteers, employees of charitable organizations, and fundraising counsel from the payment of it, violated the equal protection clause of the Fourteenth Amendment. The court ruled that there was no constitutional law impairment with respect to this distinction.

DELEGATION OF LEGISLATIVE AUTHORITY

A cardinal principle of administrative law is that an administrative agency may find facts and issue regulations but must do so in the context of a policy established by a legislative body, which has fixed standards for the guidance of the agency in the performance of its functions. Administrative enforcement of charitable solicitation acts is, therefore, subject to this principle.

Thus, the U.S. Supreme Court observed that a "narrowly drawn ordinance, that does not vest in [government] officials the undefined power to determine what messages residents will hear may serve [the government's] important interests without running afoul of the First Amendment." The Court, however, continued, "in the area of free expression, a licensing statute placing unbridled discretion in the hands of a government official or agency constitutes a prior restraint and may result in censorship."

This principle of law was employed by a state supreme court to void a charitable solicitation ordinance adopted by a city. This ordinance empowered a board with the authority to deny to a charity the right to solicit funds in that city on a finding that the charity's objective is "adequately covered" by the programs of another charity previously issued a solicitation permit. Pursuant to this ordinance, the board rejected an application to solicit funds in the city that was submitted by a cancer society chapter, on the ground that a charitable hospital with a permit and the local community chest were adequately covering the objectives of the chapter's proposed solicitation, which was a campaign to generate funds to combat cancer. In invalidating this ordinance, the court wrote that a "legislative body cannot vest powers in a commission which restrict persons or organizations unless in the legislation there is set up some standards of action which relate to legitimate objects for the exercise of the police power and which operate equally upon all persons and organizations."

In the charitable solicitation act (or ordinance) context, then, the regulators do not have unfettered authority to ascertain which charities may solicit funds within the jurisdiction. The flaw in this city's ordinance was the arbitrary power vested in the enforcement authorities to make judgments as to whether an applicant for a permit proposes to serve an object, purpose, or movement in a field not "adequately covered." Even where it is permissible for the regulators to make a determination involving an appraisal of facts, an exercise of judgment, and the formulation of an opinion, the process must occur with reference to legislatively derived standards that are properly within the police power.

A court upheld a city ordinance in the face of an assertion that the regulatory official involved was delegated an "arbitrary power to determine what constitutes a charitable, religious, etc., organization and purpose and to grant or withhold permits or licenses for charitable organizations without prescribing any guidelines for the exercise of the officer's discretion." The court concluded that this ordinance contained "sufficient guidelines" and "detailed provisions," so that the regulatory official was not bestowed "unbridled discretion to make broad determinations without guide-lines."

Some state charitable solicitation statutes, despite this constitutional law principle, authorized or authorize the regulators to act with a breadth of discretion that raises questions about the arbitrariness of their actions and whether legislative power has been unconstitutionally delegated. For example, a charitable solicitation act granted "full discretion" to a secretary of state in allowing a solicitation, and the secretary had the authority to decide whether a charitable organization was "reputable" and whether the purposes involved were "legitimate or worthy." Another act continues to authorize state officials to permit charitable solicitations by "bona fide" groups.

Sometimes, the *retention* of legislative authority is a constitutional law violation, such as where the legislative body is able to withhold or grant a permit for charitable fundraising in the absence of objective standards. For example, this type of law was voided, as being a violation of due process requirements (discussed previously), where the fundraising permit could be issued in the "uncontrolled discretion" of the legislative branch of a government. This can be another form of prior restraint on First Amendment freedoms (discussed previously) that the law will not tolerate.

TREATMENT OF RELIGIOUS ORGANIZATIONS

The First Amendment provides, in the religion clauses, that "Congress shall make no law respecting an establishment of religion, or prohibiting the free exercise thereof." While most First Amendment religion cases involve either the establishment clause or the free exercise clause, both of these religion clauses are directed toward the same goal: the maintenance of government neutrality with regard to religious beliefs and activities. Thus, the U.S. Supreme Court observed that the First Amendment "rests upon the premise that both religion and government can best work to achieve their lofty aims if each is left free from the other within its respective sphere."

This dichotomy is amply reflected in the matter of tax exemption for religious organizations. The Supreme Court held, in a case concerning an attack on exemption for religious properties as being violative of the establishment clause, that government may become involved in matters relating to religious organizations so as to "mark boundaries to avoid excessive entanglement" and to adhere to the "policy of neutrality that derives from an accommodation of the Establishment and Free Exercise Clauses that has prevented the kind of involvement that would tip the balance toward government control of Church or government restraint on religious practice." Thus, tax exemption for religious organizations does not violate the religion clauses inasmuch as it promotes neutrality; the alternative (taxation) would necessarily lead to prohibited excessive entanglements (such as valuation of property, imposition of tax liens, and foreclosures).

The Supreme Court has summed up its approach to establishment clause and free exercise clause cases: "In short, when we are presented with a state law granting a denominational preference, our precedents demand that we treat the law as suspect and that we apply strict scrutiny in adjudging its constitutionality." It is against this constitutional law backdrop that the approach of governments to regulation of the fundraising practices of churches and other religious entities may be viewed.

Many of the state charitable solicitation acts provide some form of exemption for religious organizations (see Chapter 3). This traditional exemption derives from the belief that the First and Fourteenth Amendments to the U.S. Constitution (and comparable provisions of state constitutions) prohibit this type of regulation of religious groups. Nonetheless, in the face of fundraising abuses committed in the name of religion, some states have attempted to expand applicability of their charitable solicitation acts to religious organizations. In response, organizations are challenging these new requirements, contending they are laws respecting an establishment of religion and a prohibition on the free exercise of religion.

The current state of the law on this subject is that the courts first ascertain whether the purpose of a solicitation pursued by a religious organization is primarily religious. If it is, regulation of the activity must pass a test of strict scrutiny, showing that (1) the state has a compelling interest in undertaking the regulation, (2) the statute has a secular purpose, (3) the primary effect of the law neither advances nor inhibits religion, and (4) the law does not foster excessive government entanglement with religion. Second, if the state's interest is sufficiently compelling, then, although the law inhibits religion to some degree, it may validly outweigh the religious interest. Third—and this is the element that is the most difficult of certainty—it *may* be that, where the funds solicited are to be used for a secular purpose, the state can regulate—in exercise of its police power (previously discussed)—the fundraising of a religious group to the same degree as a secular group.

OTHER CONSTITUTIONAL LAW ISSUES

Other principles of constitutional law can operate to void a charitable fundraising statute. These are usually variations of free speech considerations (previously discussed) yet warrant special emphasis.

A statute can be unconstitutionally vague. Laws of this nature are found to be contrary to constitutional law precepts when they are so vague that, in Supreme Court parlance, individuals of "common intelligence must necessarily guess at [their] meaning and differ as to [their] application." The Court stated: "The general test of vagueness applies with particular force in review of laws dealing with speech. 'Stricter standards of permissible statutory vagueness may be applied to a statute having a potentially inhibiting effect on speech; a man may the less be required to act at his peril here, because the free dissemination of ideas may be the loser.'" One court struck down a registration requirement because the law, in addition to specifying certain information that had to be provided, also allowed the government involved to require, in its discretion, additional information (a common provision). Inasmuch as, "from reading the statute, it is impossible to discern with precision what information must be provided" as part of the registration process, the vagueness caused the law to be pronounced invalid on its face.

A government cannot lawfully mandate or regulate the content of protected speech. This point has particular relevance to the increasing tendency of states to require a soliciting charitable organization to make certain statements to prospective donors. In one instance, city and county ordinances that required the use of an "information card" were held unconstitutional because the ordinances mandated the inclusion of information, which the city and county viewed as being of "assistance to the public in determining the nature and worthiness of the solicitation."

SUMMARY

This chapter opened with a summary of the basics of the constitutional law principles concerning free speech. It articulated the fundamental difference between commercial speech and protected speech (which includes charitable fundraising). The chapter explained the concept of governments' police power and summarized free speech principles. It summarized the principal U.S. Supreme Court opinions, and the subsequent significant court decisions, on free speech principles and fundraising. The chapter summarized free speech law pertaining to airport terminal solicitations, door-to-door advocacy, and registration fees. It explored the outer boundaries of free speech rights and discussed the law concerning charitable fundraising and fraud. The chapter then turned to the other relevant constitutional law areas of due process, equal protection, delegation of legislative authority, and treatment of religious organizations. The chapter concluded with a summary of other pertinent constitutional law issues.

10

FUNDRAISING AND GOVERNANCE

Today, more than ever, the professional fundraising community is, usually involuntarily, enmeshed in the matter of governance of charitable organizations. For decades, the law concerning governance of nonprofit organizations was almost solely confined to state (and, to some extent, local) law. This state of affairs is rapidly changing, with the subject of nonprofit organizations' governance becoming a province of federal (mostly tax) law. Also to be taken into account, in this context, are the principles of the watchdog agencies as they relate to fundraising. Specifically, this chapter will:

- Address contemporary nonprofit governance philosophy in general.

- Summarize emerging principles as to nonprofit governing boards' fundraising responsibilities.

- Inventory the various watchdog agency standards as they pertain to fundraising.

- Describe the current emphasis on organization and board effectiveness.

- Look at law compliance and public disclosures as governance standards.

- Explore the matter of allocation of expenditures, including those for fundraising.

- Consider the importance of mission statements.

- Characterize the new approach of the IRS to governance.

- Discuss officer and employee tax liability.
- Provide a perspective on nonprofit governance.

GOVERNANCE PHILOSOPHY IN GENERAL

In some quarters, the philosophy underlying the concept of governance of nonprofit organizations is changing. The traditional roles of the nonprofit board have been oversight of the organization's operations and policy determination; historically, the implementation of policy and management has been the responsibilities of the officers and key employees. An emerging view, sometimes referred to as *best practices*, imposes on the nonprofit board greater responsibilities and functions (and thus potentially greater liability), intended to immerse the board more deeply in management. This new view is nicely reflected in the characterization of the nonprofit board in the American National Red Cross Governance Modernization Act (see Chapter 2): the "governance and strategic oversight board."

The origins of this shift of view regarding the appropriate role of the governing board of a nonprofit organization are difficult to find. There has been the occasional scandal in the nonprofit management context, such as that involving the United Way of America; these scandals in the nonprofit realm have increased somewhat in recent years, due in large part to greater focus by the media on charitable organizations and the various investigations conducted by the staff of the Senate Finance Committee. These incidents alone, however, do not account for the contemporary magnitude of interest in nonprofit organization governance. Certainly, a major factor contributing to this phenomenon is the raft of recent scandals in the for-profit sector and the resulting enactment of the Sarbanes-Oxley Act, which has had an enormous impact on the evolution, over the past few years, of nonprofit organization governance principles and practices.

BOARD FUNDRAISING RESPONSIBILITIES

Inasmuch as emerging good governance principles (summarized ahead) are directed principally at public charities, there is considerable emphasis on fundraising practices and procedures. Boards of directors of these charitable organizations are thus importuned to, as the Philanthropic Advisory Service standards stated, "establish and exercise controls" over the fundraising process as undertaken by officers, employees, volunteers, consultants, and other contractors. This includes the type or types of fundraising engaged in by the organization, the records kept, compliance with federal and state fundraising law, and the like.

Many of these standards address the quality of the solicitation materials; organizations may not always regard this as the province of the board. For example, the BBB (Better Business Bureau) Wise Giving Alliance standards require that an organization's solicitation and other informational materials be "accurate, truthful, and not misleading." Likewise, the Evangelical Council for Financial Accountability standards state that representations of fact, description of the organization's financial condition, or narrative about events must be "current, complete, and accurate"; "material omissions or exaggerations of fact" are not permitted. Similarly, the Standards for Excellence Institute standards provide that solicitation materials "should be accurate and truthful and should correctly identify the organization, its mission, and the intended use of the solicited funds."

The draft of the IRS's good governance principles stated that "[s]uccess at fundraising requires care and honesty." The board of directors of a charitable organization "should adopt and monitor policies to ensure that fundraising solicitations meet federal and state law requirements and [that] solicitation materials are accurate, truthful, and candid." The American National Red Cross Governance Modernization Act principles (discussed previously) call for the members of the board to assist with fundraising on behalf of the organization.

The good governance principles formulated by the Panel on the Nonprofit Sector state that solicitation materials and other communications addressed to prospective donors "must clearly identify the organization and be accurate and truthful." The Panel stated that a prospective donor "has the right to know the name of anyone soliciting contributions, the name and location of the organization that will receive the contribution, a clear description of its activities, the intended use of the funds to be raised, a contact for obtaining additional information, and whether the individual requesting the contribution is acting as a volunteer, employee of the organization, or hired solicitor."

Thus, to satisfy this panoply of standards, a board of a fundraising charitable organization should endeavor to be certain that the solicitation materials involved are accurate, candid, current, complete, honest, and truthful, and that they are not exaggerative, do not have material omissions, and are not misleading.

WATCHDOG AGENCIES AND FUNDRAISING

Charitable organizations, particularly those that are engaged in fundraising, often become subject to standards set and enforced by a watchdog agency. Watchdog agencies, while not promulgators of law, can have a powerful impact on the public perception of a charitable organization and its ability to successfully generate gifts and grants. Indeed, watchdog agencies have long been in the forefront of standards-setting for nonprofit organizations.

Charitable organizations that are caught up in watchdog agencies' standards enforcement and public rankings often believe they are powerless to offset the reviews and ratings of these agencies; yet in fact they have certain rights with respect to the standards themselves and the manner in which they are applied.

Watchdog Standards and Charities' Rights

For the most part, however, these rights cannot rise to the level of constitutional law protections, such as those accorded pursuant to the principles of due process enunciated in the Fifth and Fourteenth Amendments to the U.S. Constitution and in comparable provisions in the constitutions of the states. This is because due process rights are generally granted only with respect to actions by a government. The *state action doctrine*, however, can mandate adherence to due process requirements by a nongovernmental organization when there is sufficient entanglement between government and the nongovernmental group, such as in the form of support or activities in tandem.

Nonetheless, where a nongovernmental organization promulgates and enforces standards, there are two situations where the law requires that the standards and the application of them be *fair*.

The first of these situations is the presence of a significant economic factor. That is, where the power of the standards enforcement agency becomes so great as to cause adverse economic consequences to the charity that is ranked as not meeting standards, the courts can intervene to rectify the application of unfair standards or the unfair application of standards. The test in either circumstance is whether the standards and/or the administration of them are *fair* or *reasonable*. There is no question that the ratings of and reports on charitable organizations by watchdog agencies have economic consequences to the affected charities: Individual and corporate donors rely on the listings to determine which organizations are to receive their gifts; private foundations and other grantors similarly rely on these listings in determining their grantees; state governmental agencies take the status of charities in relation to the independent agencies' standards into account in determining the status of charities under the states' charitable solicitation acts; and the IRS from time to time relies on the rankings of these agencies. Moreover, the watchdog agencies readily provide information to the media, and the resulting publicity can cause one or more of the same three results to occur.

The second of these situations is when the agency's ratings power is in an area of public concern. Again, there is little doubt that these agencies envision themselves as operating in the public interest, forcing disclosure of information to the public and otherwise acting for the benefit of prospective donors. Public reliance on the watchdog agencies' pronouncements has become so great that they have the power to make a national organization's fundraising success significantly dependent on a favorable rating, or to divert gifts from a national organization that receives a negative rating. A positive rating accorded a charity by a watchdog agency may well confer on the charity a significant "competitive" advantage in relation to one or more organizations that receive an adverse rating.

The foregoing two principles have been succinctly stated in a book on antitrust law: "Self-regulation programs should be based on clearly defined standards that plainly indicate what is considered proper and improper. Vague standards invite arbitrary action," and "[s]tandards once set also should be administered in a reasonable manner."

The setting and application of standards by the watchdog agencies are squarely subject to both of these threshold tests, and fundamental fairness dictates that their enforcement of standards be on the basis of processes that are reasonable.

Philanthropic Advisory Service Standards

The Philanthropic Advisory Service (PAS) was the division of the Council of Better Business Bureaus (CBBB) that monitored and reported on charitable organizations that solicit nationwide contributions and grants. The primary goal of the division, which began substantive operations in 1971, was to promote ethical standards of business practices and protect consumers through self-regulation and monitoring activities. The PAS standards, which have been superseded by the Wise Giving Alliance standards (discussed ahead), are recounted here because of their historical significance as being one of the first efforts to disseminate and enforce a set of nonprofit governance principles.

PAS evaluated charitable organizations according to the "CBBB Standards for Charitable Solicitations." These standards covered five basic areas: public accountability, use of funds, solicitations and informational materials, fundraising practices, and governance.

Public Accountability. PAS required that a charity provide, on request, an annual report that included various items of information about the charity's purposes, current activities, governance, and finances. Additionally, a charity was required to provide on request a complete annual financial statement, including an accounting of all income and fundraising costs of controlled or affiliated entities.

A charity also was required to "present adequate information [in financial statements] to serve as a basis for informed decisions." According to the PAS, information needed as a basis for informed decisions included items such as:

- Significant categories of contributions or other income

- Expenses reported in categories corresponding to major programs and activities

- A detailed description of expenses by "natural classification" (e.g., salaries, employee benefits, and postage)

- Accurate presentation of fundraising and administrative costs

- The total cost of multipurpose activities
- The method used for allocating costs among the activities

Organizations that receive a substantial portion of their income as the result of fundraising activities of controlled or affiliated entities were required to provide, on request, an accounting of all income received by and fundraising costs incurred by these entities.

Use of Funds. PAS required that a charity spend a "reasonable percentage" of total income on programs, as well as a "reasonable percentage" of contributions on activities that are in accordance with donor expectations. In this context, PAS defined a "reasonable percentage" to mean "at least" 50 percent. Charities were also expected to ensure that their fundraising costs were "reasonable." In this context, fundraising costs were reasonable if those costs did "not exceed" 35 percent of related contributions. In the area of total fundraising and administrative costs, PAS standards also provided that these costs be "reasonable." In this latter context, these costs were reasonable if they did "not exceed" 50 percent of total income. A charity was expected to establish and exercise "adequate controls" over its disbursements.

Soliciting organizations were to substantiate, on request, their application of funds, in accordance with donor expectations, to the programs and other activities described in solicitations.

Solicitations and Informational Materials. PAS standards required that solicitation and informational materials be "accurate, truthful and not misleading, both in whole or in part." These terms were not defined. Solicitation materials also were required to include a "clear description" of the program and other activities for which funds were requested. Solicitations that described an issue, problem, need, or event but did not clearly describe the programs or other activities for which funds are requested did not meet the standard for accuracy and truthfulness.

Direct contact solicitations (including telephone appeals) were required to identify the solicitor and his or her relationship to the benefiting organization or cause, and the programs or other activities for which funds were requested. Solicitations in conjunction with the sale of goods, services, or admissions had to identify, among other things, the "actual or anticipated portion" of the sales or admission price that would benefit the charitable organization or cause.

Fundraising Practices. PAS standards provided that soliciting organizations must "establish and exercise controls" over fundraising activities by their officers, employees, volunteers, consultants, and contractors, including the use of written contracts and agreements. Organizations were required to establish and exercise "adequate controls" over the contributions they receive. Donor requests for confidentiality were to be honored, including requests that a donor's name not be exchanged, rented, or sold. Fundraising was to be conducted "without excessive pressure"; examples of this type of

pressure included solicitations in the guise of invoices, harassment, intimi-
dation, coercion, threats of public disclosure or economic retaliation, and
"strongly emotional appeals which distort the organization's activities or
beneficiaries."

BBB Wise Giving Alliance Standards

The BBB Wise Giving Alliance (Alliance) was formed in 2001, the product of
the merger of the National Charities Information Bureau (another of the early
watchdog agencies) into the CBBB Foundation and the PAS. The Alliance is
affiliated with the CBBB.

According to its Web site, the Alliance "collects and distributes information on hundreds of nonprofit organizations that solicit [contributions]
nationally or have national or international program services." It "routinely
asks such organizations for information about their programs, governance,
fund raising practices, and finances when the charities have been the subject
of inquiries." The Alliance "selects charities for evaluation based on the volume
of donor inquiries about individual organizations." The organization serves
"donors' information needs" and helps donors "make their own decisions
regarding charitable giving."

The Alliance developed its "Standards for Charity Accountability," to
"assist donors in making sound giving decisions and to foster public confidence
in charitable organizations." One of the purposes of these standards is to
"promote ethical conduct" by charitable organizations. The BBB states that
these standards are "voluntary."

Measuring Effectiveness. The standards provide that an organization
"should regularly assess its effectiveness in achieving its mission." An organization should have "defined, measurable goals and objectives in place and a
defined process in place to evaluate the success and impact of its program(s)
in fulfilling the goals and objectives of the organization" and a process that
"identifies ways to address any deficiencies."

An organization should "[h]ave a board policy of assessing, no less than
every two years, the organization's performance and effectiveness and of determining future actions required to achieve the mission." There should be a
submission to the board, "for its approval, a written report that outlines the
results of the aforementioned performance and effectiveness assessment and
recommendations for future actions."

Finances. These standards require that an organization "[s]pend at least
65 percent of its total expenses on program activities," "[s]pend no more than
35% of related contributions on fund raising," avoid unwarranted accumu-
lation of funds, disclose the organization's annual financial statements, and
have a board-approved annual budget.

Fundraising and Informational Materials. The standards require that an
organization's solicitation and other informational materials be "accurate,
truthful, and not misleading"; that an organization prepare an annual report

that is available to the public; that an organization posts its annual information returns on its Web site; that the charity disclose how it benefits from a cause-related marketing campaign; and that an organization promptly responds to an inquiry from the BBB.

Evangelical Council for Financial Accountability Standards

Religious organizations have established watchdog agencies that focus only on religious entities. Among them is the Evangelical Council for Financial Accountability (ECFA), which states that it is an "accreditation agency dedicated to helping Christian ministries earn the public's trust through adherence to seven Standards of Responsible Stewardship." The ECFA states that these standards, "drawn from Scripture, are fundamental to operating with integrity." In addition to these standards, the ECFA has developed a series of best practices that are intended to "encourage [its] members to strive for the highest levels of excellence." Founded in 1979, the ECFA states that its constituency comprises more than 2,000 evangelical Christian organizations. An organization that cannot comply with one or more of the standards is ineligible for membership in the ECFA.

Use of Resources. Every member of the ECFA must "exercise the management and financial controls necessary to provide reasonable assurance that all resources are used (nationally and internationally) in conformity with applicable federal and state laws and regulations to accomplish the exempt purposes for which they are intended." According to one of the best practices, a member organization should ensure, "by collaborating with the board and the CEO, Executive Director, or President (or similar position), that the organization has a clear financial plan that is aligned with strategic, operating, and development plans."

Financial Statements. Every organization that is an accredited member of the ECFA must obtain an annual audit performed by an independent certified public accounting firm, including a financial statement prepared in accordance with generally accepted accounting principles. The ECFA may provide for an alternative category of membership that does not require audited financial statements, in which case the organization must have financial statements that are compiled or reviewed by an independent certified public accounting firm. An ECFA best practice has the organization ensuring that "all material related-party transactions are disclosed in the financial statements."

Financial Disclosure. Every member must provide a copy of its current financial statements (including audited financial statements if required) on written request and provide other disclosures "as the law may require." A member "must provide a report, on written request, including financial information, on any specific project for which it is soliciting gifts." One of the ECFA best practices recommendations is that the organization posts its most recent annual financial statement and annual information return (Form 990) (if the organization files such a return) on its Web site.

Fundraising. The ECFA has several requirements in the area of fundraising. Representations of fact, description of the organization's financial condition, or narrative about events must be "current, complete, and accurate"; "material omissions or exaggerations of fact" are not permitted. Member organizations "must not create unrealistic donor expectations of what a donor's gift will actually accomplish within the limits of the organization's ministry." Organizations are asked to make every effort to "avoid accepting a gift from or entering into a contract with a prospective donor which would knowingly place a hardship on the donor, or place the donor's future wellbeing in jeopardy." When dealing with donors regarding commitments on "major estate assets," organizations must "seek to guide and advise donors so they have adequately considered the broad interests of the family and the various ministries they are currently supporting before they make final decisions."

These standards state that compensation of outside fundraising consultants or a member's employees based directly or indirectly on a percentage of charitable contributions raised is prohibited. ECFA standards also state that officers and directors may not receive any royalties for any product that is used for fundraising or promotional purposes by the organization. The ECFA member must honor all statements made by it in its fundraising appeals about the use of the gift.

The ECFA best practices state that an organization should "[g]enerate compensation arrangements for development personnel (internal and external) based on merit." These practices add: "Pay-for-performance plans may be structured if it [sic] avoids compensation based on [a] percentage of gift amounts."

Other Practices. The ECFA's best practices state that an organization should spend a "reasonable percentage" of its annual expenditures "on programs in pursuance of the organization's mission." An organization should "[p]rovide sufficient resources for effective administration and, if the organization solicits contributions, for appropriate fundraising activities."

Standards for Excellence Institute Standards

The Standards for Excellence Institute (Institute) is a membership organization of charitable entities that claims, in its marketing material, to uphold standards that are higher "than the minimal requirements imposed by local, state and federal laws and regulations." This program was launched to "strengthen nonprofit governance and management, while also enhancing the public's trust in the nonprofit sector." This organization "promotes widespread application of a comprehensive system of self-regulation in the nonprofit sector." These standards are based on "fundamental values" such as "honesty, integrity, fairness, respect, trust, compassion, responsibility and accountability," and provide guidelines for how nonprofit organizations should act to be "ethical and accountable in their programs operations, governance, human resources, financial management and fundraising."

Mission and Program. The Institute's standards provide that an organization's "purpose, as defined and approved by the board of directors, should be formally and specifically stated." The organization's "activities should be consistent with its stated purpose."

A nonprofit organization "should periodically revisit its mission (e.g., every three to five years) to determine if the need for its programs continues to exist." An organization "should evaluate whether the mission needs to be modified to reflect societal changes, its current programs should be revised or discontinued, or new programs need to be developed."

A nonprofit organization "should have defined, cost-effective procedures for evaluating, both qualitatively and quantitatively, its programs and projects in relation to its mission." These procedures "should address programmatic efficiency and effectiveness, the relationship of these impacts to the cost of achieving them, and the outcomes for program participants." Evaluations, which "should include input from program participants," should be "candid, be used to strengthen the effectiveness of the organization and, when necessary, be used to make programmatic changes."

Legal Compliance and Accountability. Organizations must be "aware of and comply with all applicable Federal, state, and local laws." These laws include those pertaining to fundraising, licensing, financial accountability, document retention and destruction, human resources, lobbying and political advocacy, and taxation.

Organizations "should periodically assess the need for insurance coverage in light of the nature and extent of the organization's activities and its financial capacity." A decision to forgo general liability or directors' and officers' liability insurance coverage "shall only be made by the board of directors and shall be reflected in" the appropriate board minutes. An organization "should periodically conduct an internal review" of its compliance with "legal, regulatory and financial reporting requirements"; a summary of the results of this review should be provided to the organization's governing board.

Openness. The Institute's standards require an organization to "prepare, and make available annually to the public, information about the organization's mission, program activities, and basic audited (if applicable) financial data." This report should also "identify the names of the organization's board of directors and management staff."

An organization "should provide members of the public who express an interest in the affairs of the organization with a meaningful opportunity to communicate with an appropriate representative of the organization." An organization "should have at least one staff member who is responsible to assure that the organization is complying with both the letter and the spirit of Federal and state laws that require disclosure of information to members of the public."

Public Education and Advocacy. The Institute's standards state that a nonprofit organization "should assure that any educational information provided to the media or distributed to the public is factually accurate and provides sufficient contextual information to be understood." An organization "should have a written policy on advocacy defining the process by which the organization determines positions on specific issues." The standards add that nonprofit organizations "engaged in promoting public participation in community affairs shall be diligent in assuring that the activities of the organization are strictly nonpartisan."

Fundraising. The Institute's standards as to fundraising state that an organization's fundraising costs "should be reasonable over time." That is, on average, over a five-year period, a charity should realize revenue from development activities that is "at least three times the amount spent on conducting them." Organizations with a fundraising ratio of less than 3:1 "should demonstrate that they are making steady progress toward achieving this goal, or should be able to justify why a 3:1 ratio is not appropriate for the individual organization."

Solicitation and program materials "should be accurate and truthful and should correctly identify the organization, its mission, and the intended use of the solicited funds." All statements made by a charitable organization in its fundraising appeals "about the use of a contribution should be honored." A charitable organization "must honor the known intentions of a donor regarding the use of donated funds."

Charitable organizations should respect the privacy of donors and "safeguard the confidentiality of information that a donor reasonably would expect to be private." Charities should provide donors with an opportunity to make anonymous gifts. They should provide donors the opportunity to have their names removed from any mailing lists that are sold, rented, or exchanged. Charities should honor requests by a donor to curtail repeated mailings or telephone solicitations from in-house lists. Solicitations should be "free from undue influence or excessive pressure," and be "respectful of the needs and interests of the donor or potential donor."

A charitable organization should have policies governing the acceptance and disposition of charitable gifts, including procedures to determine any limits on individuals or entities from which the organization will accept a gift, the purposes for which donations will be accepted, the type of property that will be accepted, and whether an "unusual or unanticipated" gift will be accepted in view of the organization's "mission and organizational capacity."

Fundraising personnel, whether they are employees or consultants, should not be compensated on the basis of a "percentage of the amount raised or other commission formula." When using the services of a paid professional fundraising counsel or professional solicitor, a charitable organization should contract only with those persons who are "properly registered with applicable regulatory authorities." Organizations should exercise control over any staff, volunteers, consultants, other contractors, businesses, or other organizations that solicit contributions on their behalf.

American Institute of Philanthropy Standards

The American Institute of Philanthropy (AIP) is, according to its Web site, a "nationally prominent charity watchdog service whose purpose is to help donors make informed giving decisions." It provides ratings of charities, using letter grades A–F.

Fundraising Expenses. Like all of the watchdog agencies, the AIP believes fundraising costs should be reasonable. In this organization's view, this means that a charity should expend at least 60 percent of its outlays for charitable purposes. The balance, of course, is to be allocated to fundraising and administration. Fundraising expenses should not exceed 35 percent. These percentages are based on related contributions, not total income (thereby usually making the fundraising cost ratio higher). The AIP sometimes takes it on itself to adjust an organization's fundraising expense ratio, such as where it is allocating a portion of its expenses to program in the context of direct mail fundraising.

Asset Reserves. In the view of the AIP, a reserve of assets to enable an organization to function without fundraising for less than three years is reasonable. Organizations with "years of available assets" of more than five years are considered the "least needy." (This fact earns an organization the grade of "F" irrespective of other considerations.)

Other Watchdog Agencies

Other charity watchdog organizations have come into being. One observer concluded that the number of them has "proliferated" and that each of them has its "own approach and mission." These recent entrants into the field include Charity Navigator and Ministry Watch. Another organization, the Philanthropy Group, provides customized research about charitable organizations for a fee.

These groups do not focus on governance issues; their emphasis is on program and fundraising. For example, Charity Navigator rates public charities on the basis of their *organizational efficiency* and *organizational capacity.* As to organizational efficiency, this rating process analyzes four categories of performance: program expenses, administrative expenses, fundraising expenses, and fundraising efficiency. (A charity that spends less than one-third of its annual revenue on program is automatically given an organizational efficiency score of zero.) Organizational capacity is rated on the basis of primary revenue growth, program expenses growth, and working capital ratio. Charities that are rated by Charity Navigator receive zero (exceptionally poor) to four (exceptional) stars.

ORGANIZATION EFFECTIVENESS

Increasing emphasis is being placed on the effectiveness of nonprofit organizations and on ways for organizations to evaluate their performance. The BBB

Wise Giving Alliance standards provide that an organization "should regularly assess its effectiveness in achieving its mission." An organization should have, according to these standards, "defined, measurable goals and objectives in place and a defined process in place to evaluate the success and impact of its program(s) in fulfilling the goals and objectives of the organization" and a process that "identifies ways to address any deficiencies." The board should have a policy of "assessing, no less than every two years, the organization's performance and effectiveness and of determining future actions required to achieve the mission." There should be a submission to the board, "for its approval, a written report that outlines the results of the aforementioned performance and effectiveness assessment and recommendations for future actions."

The Standards for Excellence Institute standards recommend that an organization "periodically revisit its mission," and evaluate whether the mission "needs to be modified to reflect societal changes, its current programs should be revised or discontinued, or new programs need to be developed." The Institute adds that a nonprofit organization should have "defined, cost-effective procedures for evaluating, both qualitatively and quantitatively, its programs and projects in relation to its mission." The Panel on the Nonprofit Sector added that the board "should establish and review regularly the organization's mission and goals and . . . evaluate, no less frequently than every five years, the organization's programs, goals, and [other] activities to be sure they advance its mission and make prudent use of its resources." Every board should set "strategic goals and review them annually." At a minimum, "interim benchmarks can be identified to assess whether the work is moving in the right direction."

BOARD EFFECTIVENESS

More recently, emphasis is being placed on the effectiveness of the boards of nonprofit organizations and on ways for boards to evaluate their performance. The standards of the ECFA state that board members should "annually pledge to carry out in a trustworthy and diligent manner their duties and obligations as a board member." There should be an annual monitoring of "individual board performance against the board members' service commitments." Board member participation should be evaluated "before extending terms"; board member evaluation and/or term limits should be used to "ensure that the organization is only served by effective members." There should be a process for "[p]roperly orient[ing] new board members for their board service and provid[ing] ongoing education to ensure that the board carries out its oversight functions and that individual members are aware of their legal and ethical responsibilities." The board should use "routine and periodic board self-evaluations to improve meetings, restructure committees, and address individual board member performance."

The Standards for Excellence Institute standards state that the nonprofit board is responsible for its operations, including the education, training, and development of its members, and recommends periodic evaluation of the board's performance. The Panel on the Nonprofit Sector's principles expands on these points, stating that board members "should evaluate their performance as a group and as individuals no less frequently than every three years." The Panel noted that a "regular process of evaluating the board's performance can help to identify strengths and weaknesses of its processes and procedures and to provide insights for strengthening orientation and educational programs, the conduct of board and committee meetings, and interactions with board and staff leadership."

LAW COMPLIANCE

Some of the good governance or best practices principles insist that an organization comply with applicable law. This is somewhat ironic, inasmuch as these principles are often seen as being more stringent than the mandates of law and frequently are inconsistent with what the law requires. Also, this principle is overly simplistic (notwithstanding the adage that "ignorance of the law is no excuse").

Summary of Standards

According to the standards of the Standards for Excellence Institute, organizations must be "aware of and comply with all applicable Federal, state, and local laws." These laws include those pertaining to fundraising, licensing, financial accountability, document retention and destruction, human resources, lobbying and political advocacy, and taxation. Likewise, the Treasury Department's voluntary best practices state that the board of a charitable organization is responsible for the organization's compliance with relevant laws. The Senate Finance Committee staff paper advised that the board of a charitable organization should "establish and oversee a compliance program to address regulatory and liability concerns."

The Committee for Purchase From People Who Are Blind or Disable proposal provides that nonprofit organizations should periodically conduct an internal review of the organization's compliance with existing statutory, regulatory, and financial reporting requirements, and prepare a summary of the results of this review to the board. The Treasury Department's voluntary guidelines state that a charity must comply with all applicable federal, state, and local law. The IRS believes that an active and engaged board is important to a charity's compliance with applicable tax law requirements.

The Panel on the Nonprofit Sector's first principle is that an organization "must comply with all applicable federal laws and regulations, as well as applicable laws and regulations of the states and the local jurisdictions in which it is based or operates." If the organization conducts programs outside the United States, it must abide by applicable international laws and conventions that are legally binding on the United States. The Panel observed that an organization's governing board is "ultimately responsible for overseeing and ensuring that the organization complies with all its legal obligations and for detecting and remedying wrongdoing by management." The Panel added that, "[w]hile board members are not required to have specialized legal knowledge, they should be familiar with the basic rules and requirements with which their organization must comply and should secure the necessary legal advice and assistance to structure appropriate monitoring and oversight mechanisms."

Conclusion

Certainly, a nonprofit organization, like any person, should be in compliance with all applicable law. It is possible, of course, for a board of directors of a nonprofit organization (and its officers and staff), acting in good faith, to be unaware of an applicable law. That may turn out to be not much of a defense (inasmuch as ignorance of the law is no excuse).

Still, adherence to this standard is not as easy as it may first appear. As an illustration, nearly all of the states have a charitable solicitation act that regulates fundraising for charitable purposes (see Chapter 3); there are thousands of similar county, city, town, and like ordinances. Suppose a charity posts a gift solicitation on its Web site. Is that solicitation a form of fundraising in every state and other jurisdiction (including internationally)? The answer to this question, technically, is yes. Yet no state regulator has yet come forward to assert that Web site fundraising triggers registration and reporting in every state, in accordance with every charitable solicitation act; that would, as a practical matter, be a wholly untenuous position, with disastrous ramifications for charities. Still, a charity engaging in this form of fundraising can be said to not be in compliance with all applicable state and local law.

CATEGORIES OF EXPENDITURES

From the beginning, good governance principles have fretted about the appropriate relationships among an organization's spending for program, management, and fundraising. This has gotten to the point where some of these guidelines deteriorate into specific percentages—an approach that has repeatedly been found unconstitutional when undertaken by state law (see Chapter 9).

Summary of Standards

The PAS started all of this when it stipulated that a charitable organization spend a "reasonable percentage" of its total income on programs, as well as a "reasonable percentage" of contributions on activities that are in accordance with donor expectations. In this context, the PAS defined a "reasonable percentage" to mean "at least" 50 percent. Charities were also expected to ensure that their fundraising costs are "reasonable." In this context, fundraising costs are reasonable if those costs do "not exceed" 35 percent of related contributions. In the area of total fundraising and administrative costs, the PAS standards also provided that these costs be "reasonable." In this latter context, these costs are reasonable if they do "not exceed" 50 percent of total income. A charity was expected to establish and exercise "adequate controls" over its disbursements. This concept was carried over to the BBB Wise Giving Alliance standards, which require that an organization "[s]pend at least 65 percent of its total expenses on program activities" and "[s]pend no more than 35 percent of related contributions on fund raising."

The ECFA's best practices sidestep percentages and state that an organization should spend a "reasonable percentage" of its annual expenditures "on programs in pursuance of the organization's mission." An organization should "[p]rovide sufficient resources for effective administration and, if the organization solicits contributions, for appropriate fundraising activities." The Standards for Excellence Institute standards state that a board should annually "review the percentages of the organization's resources spent on program, administration, and fundraising." These standards inch back to a percentage approach but not quite, providing that an organization's fundraising costs "should be reasonable over time." That is, on average, over a five-year period, a charity should realize revenue from development activities that is "at least three times the amount spent on conducting them." Organizations with a fundraising ratio of less than 3:1 "should demonstrate that they are making steady progress toward achieving this goal, or should be able to justify why a 3:1 ratio is not appropriate for the individual organization."

The AIP standards are rabid on the subject of fundraising costs. Like all of the watchdog agencies, AIP believes fundraising costs should be reasonable. In this organization's view, this means that a charity should expend at least 60 percent of its outlays for charitable purposes. The balance, of course, is to be allocated to fundraising and administration. Fundraising expenses should not exceed 35 percent. These percentages are based on related contributions, not total income (thereby usually making the fundraising cost ratio higher). AIP sometimes takes it on itself to adjust an organization's fundraising expense ratio (by making it higher), such as where the organization is, in accordance with generally accepted accounting principles, allocating a portion of expenses to program in the context of direct mail fundraising. A charity that violates these standards will be assigned, by the AIP, an overall "F."

The Panel on the Nonprofit Sector asserts that an organization "should spend a significant percentage of its annual budget on programs that pursue its mission." The budget "should also provide sufficient resources for effective administration of the organization, and, if it solicits contributions, for appropriate fundraising activities." The Panel, noting that some watchdog groups assert that public charities should (or must) spend at least 65 percent of their funds on program activities, found that standard to be "reasonable for most organizations," yet also noted that "there can be extenuating circumstances that require an organization to devote more resources to administrative and fundraising activities."

Conclusion

As a matter of law, government regulation of fundraising by charitable organizations, on the basis of the percentage of revenue devoted to the gift solicitation process, is illegal because it is blatantly unconstitutional (*id.*). The reason for this is that the rationale for this type of discrimination against charities is arbitrary, capricious, irrational, and unfair. It is, thus, imperious and irrational to have this percentage approach, in the fundraising setting, embedded in "good governance" standards. (Much irony may be found in the fact that the standards-setters insist that covered entities be in full compliance with the law (discussed previously), yet they ignore the law when it is inconsistent with their objectives.)

These standards need to get past the puerile insistence on application of percentages in the fundraising context. To be eliminated are these tiresome requirements that at least a certain percentage (such as 65 percent) of expenditures be for program and no more than another percentage (such as 35 percent) of related contributions be expended for fundraising. Amounts expended for program, fundraising, and management will vary (and vary year-to-year), depending on the organization's purpose, size, period of existence, nature of its donor base, and type(s) of fundraising.

DISCLOSURES TO PUBLIC

Good governance principles have always stressed dissemination of information about the organization to the public. The federal tax law requires disclosure of certain information (see Chapter 8); these principles usually go beyond the requirements of law.

Summary of Standards

The Philanthropic Advisory Service cast the topic of disclosure of information to the public as a matter of *public accountability*. The PAS required that a charity provide, on request, an annual report that includes various items of information about the charity's purposes, current activities, governance, and finances. A charity also was required to provide on request a complete annual financial statement, including an accounting of all income and fundraising costs of controlled or affiliated entities. Additionally, a charity was required to "present adequate information [in financial statements] to serve as a basis for informed decisions." According to the PAS, information needed as a basis for informed decisions included items such as:

- Significant categories of contributions or other income
- Expenses reported in categories corresponding to major programs and activities
- A detailed description of expenses by "natural classification" (e.g., salaries, employee benefits, and postage)
- Accurate presentation of fundraising and administrative costs, the total cost of multipurpose activities
- The method used for allocating costs among the activities

Organizations that receive a substantial portion of their income as the result of fundraising activities of controlled or affiliated entities were required to provide, on request, an accounting of all income received by and fundraising costs incurred by these entities.

The BBB Wise Giving Alliance requires that an organization prepares an annual report that is available to the public and that it posts its annual information returns on its Web site. Every member of the Evangelical Council for Financial Accountability is required to provide a copy of its current financial statements (including audited financial statements if required) on written request and provide other disclosures "as the law may require." An ECFA member "must provide a report, on written request, including financial information, on any specific project for which it is soliciting gifts." One of the ECFA best practices recommendations is that the member organization posts its most recent annual financial statement and annual information return (Form 990) (if the organization files such a return) on its Web site.

The Standards for Excellence Institute's standards require an organization to "prepare, and make available annually to the public, information about the organization's mission, program activities, and basic audited (if applicable) financial data." This report should also "identify the names of the organization's board of directors and management staff." An organization "should provide members of the public who express an interest in the affairs of the organization with a meaningful opportunity to communicate with an appropriate representative of the organization." An organization "should have at least one staff member who is responsible to assure that the organization is complying with both the letter and the spirit of Federal and state laws that require disclosure of information to members of the public." The Committee for Purchase's proposed best practices require an organization to prepare and make available annually to the public information about the organization's mission, program activities, and basic audit (if applicable) financial data.

The Treasury Department's voluntary best practices call on organizations to set forth their requirements as to financial reporting and accountability, and make their audited financial statements available for public inspection. Moreover, pursuant to these guidelines, charitable organizations should

(1) maintain and make publicly available a current list of any branches, subsidiaries, and/or affiliates that receive resources and services from them; (2) make publicly available or provide to any member of the public, on request, an annual report, that describes the charity's purposes, programs, activities, tax-exempt status, structure and responsibility of the governing body, and financial information; and (3) make publicly available or provide to any member of the public, on request, complete annual financial statements, including a summary of the results of the most recent audit, which present the overall financial condition of the organization and its financial activities in accordance with generally accepted accounting principles and reporting practices.

The IRS, in its draft of good governance principles, stated that by making "full and accurate information about its mission, activities, and finances publicly available, a charity demonstrates transparency." The board of directors of a charitable organization "should adopt and monitor procedures to ensure that the charity's Form 990, annual reports, and financial statements are complete and accurate, are posted on the organization's public Web site, and are made available to the public upon request." The agency stated, in its LifeCycle Educational Tool principles, that by making full and accurate information about its mission, activities, finances, and governance publicly available, a charity encourages transparency and accountability to its constituents. The IRS encourages every charity to adopt and monitor procedures to ensure that its Form 1023, Form 990, Form 990-T, annual reports, and financial statements are complete and accurate, are posted on its public Web site, and are made available to the public on request.

The Panel on the Nonprofit Sector wrote that an organization "should make information about its operations, including its governance, finances, programs and activities, widely available to the public." Charitable organizations "also should consider making information available on the methods they use to evaluate the outcomes of their work and sharing the results of those evaluations." The theme underlying this principle is that charities should "demonstrate their commitment to accountability and transparency" by offering additional information about their finances and operations to the public, such as by means of annual reports and Web sites, with the latter containing mission statements, codes of ethics, conflict-of-interest policies, whistleblower policies, and the like.

The redesigned annual information return includes a question as to whether the filing organization makes certain documents available to the public, including documents that are not required, as a matter of law, to be disclosed (such as audited financial statements) (see Chapter 5).

Conclusion

Thus, there are certain documents that a tax-exempt organization must, by requirement of the federal tax law, disclose to the public. There are other documents that the good governance standards suggest or require be made available to the public. Boards of nonprofit organizations must decide which (if any) of the latter category of documents will be disclosed. Of greatest controversy is disclosure of financial statements, which, of course, usually contain significant information about an organization's fundraising practices and outcomes.

MISSION STATEMENTS

As a matter of law, as part of its formation, an organization has a statement of its purposes, as part of compliance with the federal tax law organizational test (see Chapter 2). Some organizations, however, have developed a separate mission statement. This matter has increased in importance because of the emphasis placed by the IRS on mission statements as part of the redesign of the annual information return (see Chapter 5).

Summary of Standards

The standards of the Evangelical Council for Financial Accountability started things out in this area by providing that its members should develop a mission statement, "putting into words why the organization exists and what it hopes to accomplish." This statement should be "[r]egularly reference[d]" to assure that it is being "faithfully followed." The organization should "[h]ave the courage to refocus the mission statement, if appropriate."

The Standards for Excellence Institute's standards provide that an organization's "purpose, as defined and approved by the board of directors, should be formally and specifically stated." A nonprofit organization "should periodically revisit its mission (e.g., every three to five years) to determine if the need for its programs continues to exist." An organization "should evaluate whether the mission needs to be modified to reflect societal changes, its current programs should be revised or discontinued, or new programs need to be developed." The Treasury Department's voluntary best practices state simply that a charitable organization's governing instruments should delineate the organization's basic goal(s) and purpose(s).

The IRS, in its draft of good governance principles, stated that the board of directors of a charitable organization should adopt a "clearly articulated mission statement." This statement should "explain and popularize the charity's purpose and serve as a guide to the organization's work." A "well-written mission statement shows why the charity exists, what it hopes to accomplish, and what activities it will undertake, where, and for whom."

The Panel on the Nonprofit Sector wrote that the board "should establish and review regularly the organization's mission and goals and should evaluate, no less frequently than every five years, the organization's programs, goals and [other] activities to be sure they advance its mission and make prudent use of its resources." The IRS encourages every charity to establish and regularly review its mission. A clearly articulated mission, adopted by the board of directors, serves to explain and popularize the charity's purpose and guide its work. It also addresses why the charity exists, what it hopes to accomplish, and what activities it will undertake, where, and for whom. The redesigned annual information return, in two instances, makes reference to recitation of a filing organization's mission statement (*id.*).

Conclusion

A nonprofit organization, preferably at the board level, needs to decide whether it will have a mission statement. It may want one as a matter of good governance and/or to use in connection with preparation of the Form 990. As noted, if the reason for the statement is to repeat it on the Form 990, the board must approve the mission statement. Mission statements are not required by law and should be consistent with the organization's statement of purposes.

FUNDRAISING PRACTICES

Fundraising practices by charitable organizations have been at the forefront of watchdog agencies' and other entities' best practices standards from the beginning. Thus, the Philanthropic Advisory Service standards addressed the topic of the contents of solicitation and informational materials, as well as a variety of fundraising practices, including controls over fundraising activities, confidentiality of information, and avoidance of undue pressure. Some of these aspects of the standards are reflected in the BBB Wise Giving Alliance standards.

Other issues that may be addressed in these standards include the nature of compensation of outside fundraising consultants and of development personnel on a percentage basis, and adherence to donor intent. This is the case, for example, with the Evangelical Council for Financial Accountability standards and those of the Standards for Excellence Institute. The focus of the IRS in this area is more on fundraising policies, which tend to focus on the content of gift solicitation materials; the reasonableness of fundraisers' compensation; and compliance with applicable federal, state, and local law (discussed previously).

The elements of law that tend to arise in this context are nicely summarized in the principles of the Panel on the Nonprofit Sector. There, it is stated that solicitation materials and other communications addressed to prospective donors and the public "must clearly identify the organization and be accurate and truthful." The Panel stated that a prospective donor "has the right to know the name of anyone soliciting contributions, the name and location of the organization that will receive the contribution, a clear description of its activities, the intended use of the funds to be raised, a contact for obtaining additional information, and whether the individual requesting the contribution is acting as a volunteer, employee of the organization, or hired solicitor."

Contributions "must be used for purposes consistent with the donor's intent, whether as described in the relevant solicitation materials or as specifically directed by the donor." The Panel stated that solicitations should "indicate whether the funds they generate will be used to further the general programs and operations of the organization or to support specific programs or types of programs." The Panel advised charitable organizations to "carefully review the terms of any contract or grant agreement before accepting a donation."

An organization "must provide donors with specific acknowledgments of charitable contributions, in accordance with [federal tax law] requirements, as well as information to facilitate the donor's compliance with tax law requirements." The Panel noted that, not only is this type of acknowledgment generally required by law, "it also helps in building donors' confidence in and support for the activities they help to fund."

An organization should adopt "clear policies, based on its specific exempt purpose, to determine whether accepting a gift would compromise its ethics, financial circumstances, program focus or other interests." The Panel warned that "[s]ome charitable contributions have the potential to create significant problems for an organization or a donor," noting that funds may be disbursed for "illegal or unethical" purposes, may subject the donee organization to legal liability (e.g., under environmental protection laws), or result in unrelated business income.

An organization "should provide appropriate training and supervision of the people soliciting funds on its behalf to ensure that they understand their responsibilities and applicable federal, state and local laws, and do not employ techniques that are coercive, intimidating, or intended to harass potential donors." The Panel amplified this principle by recommending that a charitable organization should ensure that its fundraisers "are respectful of a donor's concerns and do not use coercive or abusive language or strategies to secure contributions, misuse personal information about potential donors, pursue personal relationships that are subject to misinterpretation by potential donors, or mislead potential donors in other ways."

An organization "should not compensate internal or external fundraisers based on a commission or a percentage of the amount raised." Compensation on this basis "can encourage fundraisers to put their own interests ahead of those of the organization or the donor and may lead to inappropriate techniques that jeopardize the organization's values and reputation and the donor's trust in the organization," and can lead to or be perceived as "excessive compensation."

An organization "should respect the privacy of individual donors and, except where disclosure is required by law, should not sell or otherwise make available the names and contact information of its donors without providing them an opportunity at least once a year to opt out of the use of their names." The Panel observed that "[p]reserving the trust and support of donors requires that donor information be handled with respect and confidentiality to the maximum extent permitted by law."

IRS AND GOVERNANCE

The IRS is taking an increasing interest in the matter of governance of tax-exempt organizations, particularly charitable entities. This interest is being manifested in a variety of forms ranging from promulgation (then abandonment) of a draft of good governance principles to making governance a centerpiece of the redesigned Form 990 (*id.*) to issuance of private letter rulings about board composition based on application of the private benefit doctrine (discussed ahead). The best indicators of the evolution of IRS thinking and policymaking in this area, including the IRS's role in promoting good governance practices by charitable organizations, are reflected in three speeches presented by Steven T. Miller, during the period he was Commissioner, Tax Exempt and Government Entities (TE/GE).

TE/GE Commissioner April 2007 Speech

Commissioner Miller, on April 26, 2007, opened the Georgetown University Law Center's annual conference on representing and managing tax-exempt organizations with an intriguing speech focusing on various "powerful and persistent forces" that are shaping today's nonprofit sector and could potentially cause the IRS to "significantly change or modify" the agency's approach to the sector. Commissioner Miller identified five of these forces.

One force is the rise of the Internet. He spoke of Web-based fundraising and the "possibility of virtual stateless charities." He said that the Internet "blurs what now seems like the quaint concept of state and national borders, with all that means for local jurisdiction over the charity."

Another force is the "continued concentration of wealth and the forthcoming transfer of that wealth to the next generation." Large parts of this wealth will be contributed to charity, driving the "creation and marketing of a variety of new giving techniques, both good and bad." This phenomenon caused the Commissioner to muse whether there should be concern with the level of annual charitable expenditures by charitable organizations, whether organizations created by single donors should exist in perpetuity, and the nature of the efficiency and effectiveness of exempt organizations.

The third force is the rise of the large nonprofit organization—what the Commissioner termed the "nation-sized nonprofits that are global in scope and scale." The "vast wealth" of these organizations is changing the nature of public policy debates, "especially to the degree these organizations may be able to implement programs with significant social impact on their own say-so, without meaningful public input or debate."

The fourth force is the "increasingly blurred line between the tax-exempt and the commercial sectors." This is raising the specter of an increase in the tax expenditure for exempt organizations, the matter of unfair competition, and the potential for undermining the "precious good will" possessed by most charitable entities. There are issues, the Commissioner said, as to whether "there has been drift in the nonprofit sector toward the commercial sector, and if so, how much."

The final (and most relevant) force is the "presence of abuse in the charitable sector." In this context, the Commissioner spoke of the "three main pillars" of the IRS's compliance program for the tax-exempt sector: customer education and outreach, determinations, and examinations. The third of these pillars, he lamented, "still leaves much to chance." Some of the problems in the sector are "insufficient transparency, lax management and a lack of meaningful ways to measure the effectiveness of an organization."

The Commissioner suggested two new pillars for the IRS's exempt organizations division program. One is use of the resources of the agency to gather "significant and reliable information about the sector, and to make it broadly available to the public, in a timely user-friendly fashion." Two obvious elements of this are the wholesale revamping of the Form 990 and electronic filing.

The second of these new pillars is promotion of "standards of good governance, management and accountability." The Commissioner observed that "[w]hat precisely the Service should do with governance practice is an intriguing concept, in part because it's neither self-evident that we should get involved, nor obviously something we should avoid." He made probably the best case that can be asserted for the intertwining of the matter of governance and tax-exempt organizations' compliance with the law: A "well-governed organization is more likely to be compliant, while poor governance can easily lead an exempt organization into trouble." He spoke, for example, of an "engaged, informed, and independent board of directors accountable to the community [the exempt organization] serves."

The Commissioner revealed that he was pondering this question: "whether it would benefit the public and the tax-exempt sector to require organizations to adopt and follow recognized principles of good governance." He was, of course, thinking about whether the IRS can make a "meaningful contribution" in this area by "going beyond its traditional spheres of activity" by asking the exempt community to meet "accepted standards of good governance." The Commissioner concluded these remarks by asserting that there is a "vacuum" that needs to be filled in the realm of education on "basic standards and practices of good governance and accountability." The Commissioner stated: "Someone needs to lead the sector on this issue. If not the IRS, then whom?"

TE/GE Commissioner November 2007 Speech

Commissioner Miller, on November 10, 2007, spoke at the Philanthropy Roundtable, revisiting many of the themes evoked at the Georgetown presentation earlier in that year. On this occasion, however, he referenced a trend not addressed in the Georgetown University presentation: the "constant increase in the number of tax-exempt organizations." Seventy thousand or more (gross, not net) exempt organizations are added to the sector annually, raising the question: "Whether we now have, or will get to the point where we will have, too many exempt organizations?" He noted this entails the addition of over 175 new exempt entities every day (Saturdays, Sundays, and holidays included)—one exempt organization for every 228 Americans. The Commissioner stated that the presence of a "very large number of tax-exempt organizations" presents the question as to whether "Americans are spending too much on duplicative infrastructure."

Returning to the matter of governance, the Commissioner expressed his view that the IRS "contributes to a compliant, healthy charitable sector by expecting the tax-exempt community to adhere to commonly accepted standards of good governance." He said that IRS involvement in this area is "not new"; the agency has been "quietly but steadily promoting good governance for a long time." He noted that "[o]ur determination agents ask governance-related questions" and "our agents assess an organization's internal controls as the agents decide how to pursue an examination." He continued: "We are comfortable that we are well within our authority to act in these areas." And: "To more clearly put our weight behind good governance may represent a small step beyond our traditional sphere of influence, but we believe the subject is well within our core responsibilities."

TE/GE Commissioner 2008 Speeches

On April 23 and 24, 2008, Commissioner Miller spoke at the Georgetown University Law Center annual conference on tax-exempt organizations. His remarks were a continuation of his thinking on governance issues and charitable organizations reflected in his speech at the conference the previous year and at the Philanthropy Roundtable 2007 meeting.

Mr. Miller, in his remarks on April 23, 2008, made three points clear: (1) the IRS is of the view that it has a "robust role" to play in the realm of charitable governance, (2) the IRS does not even entertain the thought that involvement in governance matters is beyond the sphere of the agency's jurisdiction, and (3) he cannot be convinced that, "outside of very very small organizations and perhaps family foundations, the gold standard should not be to have an active, independent and engaged board of directors overseeing the organization." Thus, the "question is no longer whether the IRS has a role to play in this area, but rather, what that role will be." That role will be primarily dictated by the governance section of the new Form 990, what he termed the "crown jewel" of the return.

One of the areas of discussion in the April 24, 2008, speech was the application process that obviously forces the IRS to struggle with "competing goals": "good customer service," which requires the agency to be "expeditious in processing and approving an application for [recognition of] tax exemption" and also for it to "take sufficient care to identify those who are trying to game the system, so that we can properly deny their applications."

As Mr. Miller noted, "organizations come to us inchoate." These entities are "just getting started, and we are asked to grant them [recognition of] exemption based on suppositions, intentions and guesstimates." This process, he said, "is not really built to ferret out all questionable organizations; it is built to get applicants to a favorable result within a reasonable period of time."

Commissioner of Internal Revenue Speech

The Commissioner of Internal Revenue, Douglas Shulman, spoke at the annual meeting of Independent Sector on November 10, 2008, with much to say about nonprofit governance. He said that he "admires" the tax-exempt sector: "Its diversity, its creativity and its risk-taking." This diversity "means many points of view are expressed, many problems are attacked in many ways, many solutions are found, and many benefits are created for the nation." He continued: "I firmly believe that the IRS must recognize and allow for this diversity—and not become a barrier to it." He added: "We shouldn't supplant the business judgment of organizational leaders, and certainly shouldn't determine how a nonprofit fulfills its individual mission. That's not our role."

But then, he noted, the sector "has had its encounters with abuse and misuse." He stated that the IRS "will continue to insist that the sector be squeaky clean, and that the high ideal of public benefit that underlies tax exemption is honored." He said that he "clearly see[s] our role as working with you and others to promote good governance, beginning with the proposition that an active, engaged and independent board of directors helps assure that an organization is carrying out a tax-exempt purpose and acts as its best defense against abuse." He said that "all of us must follow best practices in organizational leadership and management." There must be, he added, "clearly articulated values, mission, goals and accountability."

The Commissioner concluded his remarks with this: "We want to arm you with information and guidance you need to help you comply. We want to pay especially close attention to the largest segments of the exempt sector. And lastly, we want to protect the tax-exempt sector and the public by identifying and stopping those bad actors who misuse tax-exempt organizations or the privilege of tax-exempt status."

IRS Fiscal Year 2009 Annual Report

The IRS, late in 2008, issued an Exempt Organizations annual report, which included the agency's exempt organization's work plan for the government's fiscal year 2009. This report revealed that the IRS's Exempt Organizations Division is developing a checklist to be used by agents in examinations of tax-exempt organizations to determine whether an organization's governance practices "impacted the tax compliance issues identified in the examination" and to educate organizations "about possible governance considerations."

The Division will commence a training program to educate employees about "nonprofit governance implications" in the determinations, rulings and agreements, and education and outreach areas. The IRS is to begin identifying Form 990 governance questions that could be used in conjunction with other Form 990 information in possible compliance initiatives, such as those involving executive compensation, transactions with interested persons, solicitation of noncash contributions, or diversion or misuse of exempt assets.

Commentary

There is, thus, this question: Should the IRS be as deeply involved as it is in the matter of nonprofit governance, particularly in the absence of any law in support of the agency's involvement? This is, in some respects, a moot question, inasmuch as the IRS is quite active in nonprofit governance and can be expected to intensify its efforts as the redesigned Form 990 is filed, data collected, and audits commence. Still, it is a legitimate question, one that may eventually be resolved in court.

Answer: Yes. A well-governed organization, that is, one that is adhering to good governance principles, is likely to be one that is compliant with the law. That rationale is being seen as sufficient justification for IRS regulation of nonprofit, particularly charitable, governance. As Commissioner Miller saw the point, the IRS's role in nonprofit good governance may be a "small step beyond our traditional sphere of influence, but we believe the subject is well within our core responsibilities."

Answer: No. Throughout the course of the Charles Dickens novel, *A Tale of Two Cities*, Madame De Farge knits; she indefatigably knits. It can be said with confidence that she sticks to her knitting. According to the *Dictionary of American Slang*, the phrase *stick to one's knitting* means to "attend strictly to one's own affairs; not interfere with others; be singleminded." The mission of the IRS, as articulated on the agency's Web site, is to "provide America's taxpayers with top quality service by helping them understand and meet their *tax* responsibilities and by applying the *tax law* with integrity and fairness to all." The mission of the Tax Exempt and Government Entities Division is, again according to the Web site, the "uniform interpretation and application of the *Federal tax laws* on matters pertaining to the Division's customer base." The mission of the IRS and this Division is not to make pronouncements on good governance principles applicable (ostensibly or otherwise) to nonprofit organizations. The agency should attend strictly to its own affairs and not interfere with others. The IRS should stick to its knitting.

Here is a government agency that is way behind in the processing of applications for recognition of exemption, lacks the resources to respond in a timely fashion to ruling requests, is overwhelmed by the need to issue guidance in connection with recently enacted statutory law, and is lagging in the provision of other needed guidance. So, what does it do? Rather than devote time and energy to these important tasks, it wanders off into an area over which it has little or no jurisdiction or expertise.

According to the TE/GE Commissioner, the IRS expects the tax-exempt community to adhere to "commonly accepted standards of good governance." The difficulty with this is that such standards do not exist. There are at least 14 of these standards, some in draft form (discussed previously). Many of these standards are inconsistent. The standard setters cannot even agree on what size a nonprofit board should be, let alone how it should comport itself.

The IRS is sending the nonprofit community a mixed message on the topic of nonprofit governance. The TE/GE Commissioner is now quite adamant that the IRS is going to be playing a "robust role" in nonprofit governance and that the "gold standard" is an "active, independent and engaged board of directors." The Commissioner of Internal Revenue echoed these words, yet also said that the IRS should not "supplant the business judgment of [nonprofit] organizational leaders"; he added that the IRS wants to "arm" the charitable sector "with information and guidance you need to help you comply," suggesting an emphasis on education rather than dictation of governance modes and practices. The IRS fiscal year 2009 annual report recognizes the huge gap between its agents' rulings and examinations practices and applicable law, announcing a training program to educate its employees about "nonprofit governance implications."

In a speech on June 19, 2008, the Director of the Exempt Organizations Division acknowledged that, in connection with the processing of applications for recognition of exemption, "not all IRS agents have gotten the message" that the IRS focus, as to governance, is (or should be) on education.

In a nation that prides itself on government based on "rules of law," it is arbitrary and unfair for the IRS to be promoting good governance for nonprofit organizations in the absence of any law or even articulated informal standards that the agency may be using. The most we have are IRS-prepared forms and instructions. This hide-the-ball approach is a strange way for an administrative agency to be functioning.

Application of Private Benefit Doctrine

IRS agents (at least some of them) are blindly adhering to the IRS's views as to what constitutes good governance, with particular emphasis on adoption of a conflict-of-interest policy and structuring of a charitable organization's board so that a majority of it is independent. These agents are refusing to grant recognition of exemption to an organization that refuses to capitulate on these points.

Private letter rulings are surfacing, reflecting the IRS's stance. In the first of these rulings, the IRS held that, on the grounds of lack of serving a public interest and of the presence of private benefit (see Chapter 2), an organization could not qualify as a tax-exempt charitable organization inasmuch as it has only two directors, who are related. Thereafter, the agency ruled that an organization cannot qualify as an exempt charitable entity, in part because it was not "operated by a community based board of directors" (or because the board "lacks members who are representative of the community"). Subsequently, the agency ruled that an entity was not an exempt charity inasmuch as it did not adopt a conflict-of-interest policy and lacks an independent board. In this third instance, the agency wrote that the control by a family over the organization "could be used" for private ends and that the "structure of your organization indicates that it can be used to benefit private individuals." The IRS also ruled that a religious organization did not qualify for exemption in part because its pastor exercises "excessive control" over the entity.

Commentary

These private letter rulings, from the standpoint of tax law analysis, border on the absurd; there is no justification for them. No other agency of the federal government can get away with this sort of behavior—application of nonexistent rules and decisions based on pure speculation. The IRS is supposed to be bound by rules of law.

The organizations that are the subject of these rulings were denied recognition of tax-exempt status, in part because they are engaging in two practices that are not required by the federal tax law as a condition for tax exemption: failure to adopt a conflict-of-interest policy and lack of an independent board. How can a government agency action be lawfully based on an insinuation of requirements that are not mandated by the law's criteria?

This attempt to invoke the private benefit doctrine is plain error. That doctrine is to be applied when there is actual private benefit—it is a sanction (see Chapter 2). (The case law is clear that, when there is a small and/or related board, the fact-finder is to give the matter greater scrutiny; no case holds that tax exemption is to be automatically denied.) Private benefit is not to be invoked on the basis of wild speculation, such as the possibility that the organization's assets "could" be used to benefit one or more board members. If that was the standard, there would be few tax-exempt charitable organizations.

OFFICER AND EMPLOYEE TAX LIABILITY

Under the federal tax statutory law, a person "required to collect, truthfully account for, and pay over any tax" who willfully fails to collect or pay over the tax is liable for a "penalty," with the penalty being an amount equal to the amount of the tax involved, plus interest. A person includes an officer or employee of a corporation, including charitable entities, who has the duty to attend to these tax matters. These persons are known as responsible persons.

A federal district court in 2008, affirmed in 2009, held that the chair of the board of a tax-exempt hospital was personally liable for the hospital's unpaid payroll taxes. This decision is causing considerable alarm and confusion throughout the nonprofit sector. In this matter, a volunteer chair of the hospital's board (along with two employees) was held liable for $408,919 in taxes and interest. The board chair, who frequented the hospital, was held to have failed to take "responsible steps" to ascertain whether the taxes were paid (such as by demanding to see canceled checks). Pursuant to the hospital's bylaws, the board has final responsibility for the institution's administration, the board can hire and fire employees, and the board chair has the authority to sign hospital checks.

This is, indeed, a serious "penalty" for officers and employees of tax-exempt organizations. Yet, this penalty is confined to federal tax matters. It does not signal or authorize an increase in IRS involvement in the operations of exempt organizations.

The confusion being sowed by this decision is reflected in the following headline that appeared in a newspaper following the court of appeals decision: "Nonprofits' board members now held accountable by IRS." The article stated that the following is the issue: "When you volunteer on a nonprofit board, you could be on the hook if something goes wrong with the business operations." The article added that "nonprofits must create audit committees and conflict-of-interest policies that pass muster with the IRS." The first sentence is a grand overstatement (although the writer is somewhat protected by the word *could*). The second of these quoted statements is certainly not true (although some in the IRS think otherwise).

This penalty may not be imposed on an unpaid, volunteer member of a board of trustees or directors of a tax-exempt organization where the member is solely serving in an honorary capacity, does not participate in the day-to-day or financial operations of the organization, and does not have actual knowledge of the failure on which the penalty is imposed. (The district court, in the above case, held that this exception was not available.)

PERSPECTIVES ON NONPROFIT GOVERNANCE

Much of the subject of governance of nonprofit organizations is, for most normal people (including fundraisers and lawyers), rather monotonous. One really has to be a governance geek to enjoy wallowing around in this morass of management issues (particularly when one realizes that what constitutes proper governance policy and structure is often unique to an organization). For example, what sane person can really get excited about the topic of the number of individuals who should sit on a nonprofit board? Who can honestly say that he or she likes to read (let alone write) bylaws? Who can long pontificate on the nature of the executive authority as between the chair of the board and the president of the organization? Should there be one vice president or two? Should there be an audit committee or a finance committee? What does it mean to say that fundraising practices must be in compliance with all federal, state, and local law? (As to the latter, there is not a charity in the land that is in compliance with every local ordinance.) Some of these issues and documents are interesting but a huge chunk of what has to be dealt with here is grossly tedious—and, as discussed next, perhaps somewhat pointless.

Second, in reality, how far can policies and procedures take a nonprofit organization in assuring its good governance? At bottom, what counts are the personalities, morals, and leadership capabilities (or lack thereof) of the individuals at the organization's helm. If someone is intent on manipulating a nonprofit organization so as to cause mischief (or, worse, some form of evil), articles of organization, bylaws, policies, and procedures are not likely to throw up sufficient boundaries and barriers to thwart the wrongdoing. Independent Sector's Panel on the Nonprofit Sector noted that it has served up, in 2005 and 2006, "more than 100 recommendations for improving government oversight, including new rules to prevent unscrupulous individuals from abusing charitable organizations for personal gain." It is unlikely that "rules" will hinder, let alone deter, those who are unscrupulous from the pursuit of abuse.

Policies and the like may slow the evildoer down and force more cleverness on the part of the bad-intentioned than would otherwise be the case, but the bad stuff is still going to happen (if malevolence is the intent). An analogy may be made to political science (which is not a science): One can study political institutions without end but in the long run the political outcomes (elections, policy determinations, and the like) are not going to be dictated by documents and structures but by the individuals involved, undoubtedly augmented by good fortune, good timing, and similar fates. The political institutions are obviously necessary (even in some instances critical) but it is what individuals do with (and within) them that ultimately counts. The same is true with the management of a nonprofit organization: policies and procedures galore will make the entity look attractive (and help in producing an attractive annual information return (see Chapter 5)) but if the governance of it is indeed *good*, the directors, officers, and employees at the controls should be thanked, not a pile of documents. There should be, these days, greater emphasis on shaping effective programs and the funding of them, and less emphasis on the crafting of a pretty infrastructure.

Third, some of this good governance business should be—yet rarely is—evaluated in the far larger and more significant context of political philosophy. Government in America is touted as a democracy. It is a fundamental principle of the meaning of a democratic state that there be a strong nonprofit sector. Another obvious corollary of democratic government is that the people live—within bounds necessary to forge a civil society—in freedom. When these two precepts are combined, it becomes perfectly clear that, in the United States, if a group of individuals wants to start a charity it should be free—indeed, encouraged—to do so. There should be minimal (if any) fretting about laws that dictate governing board size, composition, independence, and the like.

The Nonprofit Panel observed that "[a]ny approach to preserving the soundness and integrity of the nonprofit community must strike a careful balance between the two essential forms of regulation—that is, between prudent legal mandates to ensure that organizations do not abuse the privilege of their exempt status, and, for all other aspects of sound operations, well-informed self-governance and mutual awareness among nonprofit organizations." For the most part, this statement is true but the balance today is out of whack; the former is more dominant than it should be in relation to the latter. The nonprofit sector is currently overwhelmed with demands for many policies and procedures, and assertions as to which governance principles to apply.

For the most part, nonprofit governance practices will take care of themselves; there is plenty of law to apply should matters go amiss. Examples are the operational test, the primary purpose test, the commensurate test, the private inurement doctrine, the private benefit doctrine, and the intermediate sanctions rules (see Chapter 2). Revocation of tax-exempt status is a sanction; the IRS routinely revokes the exemption of organizations when they fail to operate primarily for an exempt purpose, become inactive, do not file annual information returns, do not keep adequate records, and/or do not respond to requests from the IRS for information. The many issues surrounding the matter of governance of nonprofit organizations should be evaluated from the foregoing perspectives.

SUMMARY

This chapter summarized contemporaneous governance philosophy in general, then focused on emerging principles as to governing board fundraising responsibilities. The various watchdog agency standards, as they apply in the fundraising context, were inventoried. Other subjects described were organization and board effectiveness, law compliance and public disclosures as governance standards, allocation of expenditures (including those for fundraising), and the importance of mission statements. The new approach of the IRS to governance matters was characterized. There is a brief discussion of personal liability for a nonprofit organization's federal taxes. The chapter concluded with a perspective on nonprofit governance.

11

FUNDRAISING AND IRS AUDITS

The IRS, of course, has the authority to examine—audit—tax-exempt charitable (and other) organizations. Until recently, this has not been a priority for the IRS. With more appropriations from Congress, considerable prodding from members of Congress, and an energetic Commissioner of Internal Revenue, IRS audits of exempt organizations have been steadily increasing. Today, IRS audit activity involving exempt organizations is at an all-time high. Thus, fundraisers (on staff or consultants) serving charitable organizations should be on notice that the chance of their organization getting audited, while inherently slight, is statistically greater than ever. Some of the current audit issues directly relate to charitable fundraising. Specifically, this chapter will:

- Summarize the structure of the IRS from an audit perspective.

- Review the reasons for IRS audits of charitable organizations.

- Inventory IRS audit issues.

- Describe the types of IRS audits.

- Describe the IRS compliance check programs.

- Detail the elements of the college and university compliance check questionnaire.

- Describe the IRS audit process, including how to prepare for and cope with it.

- Summarize the IRS appeals process.

- Describe the IRS fast-track settlement process.

- Focus on the possibility of retroactive revocation of tax-exempt status.

- Look at the church audit rules.

- Note the possibility of the need to resolve audit issues by means of litigation.

ORGANIZATION OF IRS

The leadership of nonprofit organizations, and those who represent these entities, should understand the organizational structure of the IRS. Among the many reasons for this is to gain a perspective on the IRS audit function. Generally, an IRS audit is less traumatic if the overall process is understood. It helps with the coping.

The IRS is an agency (bureau) of the Department of the Treasury. One of the functions of the Treasury Department is assessment and collection of federal income and other taxes. Congress has authorized the Secretary of the Treasury to, in the language of the Internal Revenue Code, undertake what is necessary for "detecting and bringing to trial and punishment persons guilty of violating the internal revenue laws or conniving at the same." This tax assessment and collection function has largely been assigned to the IRS.

The IRS Web site proclaims that the agency's mission is to "provide America's taxpayers with top quality service by helping them understand and meet their tax responsibilities and by applying the tax law with integrity and fairness to all." (A commentator wrote: "The specific role of the Internal Revenue Service in the [federal tax] system is to both collect and protect the revenue without incidentally frustrating or terrorizing the taxpayer population.") The function of the IRS, according to its site, is to "help the large majority of compliant taxpayers with the tax law, while ensuring that the minority who are unwilling to comply pay their fair share."

The IRS is headquartered in Washington, D.C.; its operations there are housed principally in its National Office. An Internal Revenue Service Oversight Board is responsible for overseeing the agency in its administration and supervision of the execution of the nation's internal revenue laws. The chief executive of the IRS is the Commissioner of Internal Revenue. The National Office is organized into four operating divisions; the pertinent one is the Tax Exempt and Government Entities (TE/GE) Division, headed by a Commissioner. Within the TE/GE Division is the Exempt Organizations Division, which develops policy concerning and administers the law of tax-exempt organizations. The components of this Division are Rulings and Agreements, Customer Education and Outreach, Exempt Organizations Electronic Initiatives, and Examinations.

The Examinations Office, based in Dallas, Texas, focuses on tax-exempt organizations' examination programs and review projects. This office develops the overall exempt organizations enforcement strategy and goals to enhance compliance consistent with overall TE/GE strategy, as well as implements and evaluates exempt organizations examination policies and procedures. Two important elements of the Examinations function are the Exempt Organizations Compliance Unit (discussed ahead) and the Data Analysis Unit.

REASONS FOR IRS AUDITS

The reasons for an IRS examination of a tax-exempt charitable organization are manifold. Traditionally, the agency has focused on particular categories of major exempt entities, such as health care institutions, colleges and universities, political organizations, community foundations, and private foundations. Recent years have brought more targeted examinations, such as those involving credit counseling entities and down payment assistance organizations.

An examination of a tax-exempt organization may be initiated on the basis of the size of the organization or the length of time that has elapsed since a prior audit. An examination may be undertaken following the filing of an annual information return (see Chapter 5) or a tax return, inasmuch as one of the functions of the IRS is to ascertain the correctness of returns. An examination may be based on a discrete issue, such as compensation practices or political campaign activity (see Chapter 2). Other reasons for the development of an examination include media reports, a state attorney general's inquiry, or other third-party reports of alleged wrongdoing. The IRS has a form that can be used to file a complaint about an exempt organization (Form 13909).

IRS AUDIT ISSUES

The audit of a tax-exempt charitable organization is likely to entail one or more of the following issues:

- The organization's ongoing eligibility for exempt status (see Chapter 2)
- Public charity/private foundation classification (see Chapter 4)
- Unrelated business activity (see Chapter 7)
- Compliance with charitable giving, fundraising, and/or gaming law requirements (see Chapters 6 and 8)
- Extensive advocacy undertakings (see Chapter 2)

- One or more excise tax issues

- Whether the organization filed accurate and complete required returns and reports (see Chapter 5)

- Payment (or nonpayment) of employment taxes

- Involvement in a form of joint venture

TYPES OF IRS AUDITS

There are four basic types of IRS audits (examinations) of nonprofit, tax-exempt organizations. As discussed below, a compliance check is not technically an audit. Also, there are special procedures for inquiries and examinations of churches.

Field Examinations

Common among the types of IRS examinations of tax-exempt organizations are *field examinations*, in which one or more revenue agents (typically, however, only one) review the books, records, and other documents and information of the exempt organization under examination, on the premises of the organization or at the office of its representative. IRS procedures require the examiner to establish the scope of the examination, state the documentation requirements, and summarize the examination techniques (including interviews and tours of facilities).

Office and Correspondence Examinations

The IRS's office/correspondence examination program entails examinations of tax-exempt organizations by means of office interviews and/or correspondence. An *office interview* case is one where the examiner requests an exempt organization's records and reviews them in an IRS office; this may include a conference with a representative of the organization. This type of examination is likely to be of a smaller exempt organization, where the records are not extensive and the issues not particularly complex. A *correspondence examination* involves an IRS request for information from an exempt organization by letter, fax, or e-mail communication.

Office or correspondence examinations generally are limited in scope, usually focusing on no more than three issues, conducted by lower grade examiners. The import of these examinations should not be minimized, however. A correspondence examination can be converted to an office examination. Worse, an office examination can be upgraded to a field examination.

Team Examinations

For years, one of the mainstays of the IRS tax-exempt organizations examination effort was the *coordinated examination program* (CEP), which focused not only on exempt organizations but also on affiliated entities and arrangements (such as subsidiaries, partnerships, and other joint ventures) and collateral areas of the law (such as employment tax compliance and tax-exempt bond financing). The CEP approach (which was much dreaded), involving relatively sizeable teams of revenue agents, was concentrated on large, complex exempt organizations, such as colleges, universities, and health care institutions. Exempt organizations management could expect the CEP exercise to span about three years, with the IRS agents decamping in offices at the exempt organization, to which they would daily directly commute.

The CEP approach was abandoned in 2003 and replaced by the *team examination program* (TEP). Both the CEP and TEP initiatives nonetheless share the same objective, which is to avoid a fragmenting of the exempt organization examination process by using multiple agents. The essential characteristics of the TEP approach that differentiates it from the CEP approach are that the team examinations are being utilized in connection with a wider array of exempt organizations, the number of revenue agents involved in an examination is somewhat smaller, and the revenue agents are less likely to semi-permanently carve out office space in which to live at the exempt organization undergoing the examination. The TEP agents, however, are still likely to want an office for occasional visits and storage of computers and documents.

A TEP case generally is one where the annual information return (see Chapter 5) of the tax-exempt organization involved reflects either total revenue or assets greater than $100 million (or, in the case of a private foundation (see Chapter 4), $500 million). Nonetheless, the IRS may initiate a team examination where the case would benefit (from the government's perspective) from the TEP approach or where there is no annual information return filing requirement. IRS examination procedures include a presumption that the team examination approach will be utilized in all cases satisfying the TEP criteria.

In a TEP case, the examination will proceed under the direction of a case manager. One or more tax-exempt organizations revenue agents will be accompanied by others, such as employee plans specialists, actuarial examiners, engineers, excise tax agents, international examiners, computer audit specialists, income tax revenue agents, and/or economists. These examinations may last about two years; a post-examination critique may lead to a cycling of the examination into subsequent years. The IRS examination procedures stipulate the planning that case managers, assisted by team coordinators, should engage in when launching a team examination; these procedures also provide for the exempt organization's involvement in this planning process.

It is all quite an event. Long-standing friendships (even marriages) and sustained battles can emerge.

Criminal Investigations

The foregoing types of IRS audits are those normally used to examine non-profit, tax-exempt organizations. The IRS, however, has within it a Criminal Investigation Division (CID), the agents of which occasionally are involved in exempt organizations examinations. The management of an exempt organization under audit is free to decide whether to involve legal counsel in the process. Some organizations elect (foolishly) to save the costs of lawyers and weather examinations on their own. Other organizations are content to have an accountant provide the representation. When the IRS agent or agents arrive, management of the exempt organization should be quick to read their badges or business cards. If the initials *CID* appear, the decision as to whether to involve a lawyer has been made for the organization.

COMPLIANCE CHECKS

An overlay to the IRS program of examinations of tax-exempt organizations is the agency's *compliance check projects*, which focus on specific compliance issues. These projects, orchestrated by the Exempt Organizations Compliance Unit, are a recent invention of the IRS; they are designed to maximize the agency's return (gaining data and assessing compliance) on its investigation efforts. In a pronouncement issued in early 2008, the IRS stated that its exempt organizations examination and compliance-check processes are among the "variety of tools at [the agency's] disposal to make certain that tax-exempt organizations comply with federal tax law designed to ensure they are entitled to any tax exemption they may claim."

Usually, in the commencement of these projects, the IRS contacts exempt organizations only by mail to obtain information pertaining to the particular issue. An exempt organization has a greater chance of being a compliance check target than the subject of a conventional audit. A compliance check, however, can blossom into an examination.

At the present, nine compliance check projects are in play, with varying levels of intensity.

Executive Compensation

The IRS announced, in 2004, an Executive Compensation Compliance Initiative. The agency then stated that it was going to "identify and halt" the practice of some tax-exempt organizations of paying excessive compensation and other benefits to insiders (see Chapter 2). This program entailed contact (compliance check letters) with 1,223 public charities and private foundations. More than 100 of these organizations became the target of formal examinations.

As it turned out, the IRS found less wrongdoing (unreasonable compensation) than initially contemplated. Thus, in a preliminary report on its findings (2007), the agency wrote that "examinations to date do not evidence widespread concerns other than reporting." (Over 30 percent of these compliance check recipients were required to amend their annual information returns.) Cryptically, the IRS concluded that, "although high compensation amounts were found in many cases, generally they were substantiated based on appropriate comparability data." (Translation: *High* compensation is not necessarily *excessive* compensation.) Twenty-five examinations resulted in proposed excise tax assessments pursuant to the intermediate sanctions rules (over $ 4 million) and the self-dealing rules (over $16 million).

These compliance checks continue. Inquiries into compensation levels are part of other compliance checks and usually are embedded in every examination of a tax-exempt organization.

Political Campaign Activities

The IRS began a Political Activities Compliance Initiative, starting with the 2004 election campaign, in response to various allegations of participation by charities, including churches, in political campaigns in violation of the tax law (see Chapter 2). This initiative continued with the 2006 and 2008 election cycles, and may be anticipated to remain in place.

The effort with respect to the 2004 elections caused the IRS to review 166 cases. For the most part, either no violations were found or the IRS helped organizations correct their activities by issuing *written advisories*. Revocation of exemption was proposed in three instances. There were 237 cases in connection with the 2006 elections. No exemption revocations have been reported as a result of these cases, although the IRS uncovered about $300,000 in inappropriate campaign contributions (about one-half of which have been refunded). As of mid-2009, the IRS had not issued a report on the involvement of public charities in the 2008 elections.

Hospitals

The IRS, in 2006, initiated a Hospital Compliance Project, the purpose of which is to study tax-exempt hospitals and assess how these institutions believe they are providing a community benefit, as well as to determine how exempt hospitals establish and report executive compensation. This massive effort, involving 487 hospitals, was commenced with the mailing of a nine-page questionnaire containing 81 questions. Information was requested regarding the type of hospital and patient demographics, governance, medical staff privileges, billing and collection practices, and categories of programs that might constitute community benefit, such as uncompensated care, medical education and training, medical research, and other community programs conducted by hospitals.

After preliminarily processing the data gathered from these questionnaires, the IRS issued a preliminary report (2007), observing that "there is variation in the level of expenditures hospitals report in furtherance of community benefit." (The report did not address the point that the law does not include a uniform definition of *community benefit*.) This report also noted that "there is considerable variation in how hospitals report uncompensated care." (The term *uncompensated care* was deliberately not defined in the questionnaire because the IRS wanted to learn how the exempt hospital community is applying it.) Hospitals, according to the report, also "vary in how they measure and incorporate bad debt expense and shortfalls between actual costs and Medicare or Medicaid reimbursements into their measures, and whether they use charges or costs in their measures." The IRS formally published the results of this study in early 2009. The agency reported that the average and median total compensation amounts paid to the top management executives at exempt hospitals were $490,000 and $377,000, respectively. The IRS concluded that the amounts of compensation reported "appear high but also appear supported under current law."

Excess Benefit Reporting

Another of the ongoing IRS compliance initiatives, one that is relatively low key these days, is a project concerning compliance with the intermediate sanctions reporting rules (see Chapter 2). The annual information return asks questions about exempt organizations' participation in excess benefit transactions. When one of these returns, lacking answers to these questions, is received by the IRS, an exempt organizations law specialist in the National Office may contact the organization, seeking the response(s).

Fundraising Costs Reporting

Another low-key ongoing IRS compliance initiative is a project concerning the reporting of fundraising costs. From time to time, IRS reviewers of annual information returns will come across a return that reflects a considerable amount of gifts and grants, and little or no fundraising expense. This anomaly is likely to perplex the reviewer, who may contact the organization for an explanation. The IRS may also advise the organization that its subsequent annual information returns may be reviewed, from this perspective, by personnel in the Exempt Organizations Compliance Unit.

Tax Exempt Bonds Recordkeeping

The IRS, in 2007, undertook a compliance check initiative, this one targeting charitable organizations that are engaged in tax-exempt bond financing. The agency has concluded (based on about 40 audits in fiscal year 2006) that there is a lack of compliance with certain record retention rules. The IRS is currently surveying about 500 charitable organizations in this regard.

Charitable Giving Scam

The IRS has embarked on a project inquiring as to charitable contributions of interests in limited liability companies, involving questionable transactions concerning successor member interests in these companies. This program is unique in that, instead of a mailing of letters or questionnaires, the IRS developed and is sending (starting in late 2007) a prototype information document request (IDR) (discussed ahead). This IDR (11 single-spaced pages) includes some pointed questions. (Management of charitable organizations, even if not involved in this successor member interest scheme, should ponder these questions in the context of considering whether to accept an unconventional charitable gift.)

Community Foundations

The IRS has launched a compliance check project, by the mailing of questionnaires to the nation's community foundations. Concerned that these foundations may be wandering outside of their legal bounds, the IRS is asking detailed questions about these foundations' "area of service" (in that they are, after all, *community* foundations), revenues, assets, investments, grantmaking, business relationships, fees paid, and staff.

Colleges and Universities

One of the most significant of the IRS's compliance initiatives is the one targeting tax-exempt colleges and universities. Because of the general importance of this compliance check program, it needs to be reviewed in some detail. The compliance check questionnaire designed for this program (elevated to a formal IRS form, number 14018), which weighs in at 33 pages with 94 questions (many with subquestions), is nearly of as great consequence to the general charitable community as the redesigned annual information return (see Chapter 5).

COLLEGE AND UNIVERSITY COMPLIANCE CHECK PROJECT

This college and university questionnaire focuses on unrelated business, endowment funds, and executive compensation. The questionnaire has been sent to a cross-section of small, midsized, and large private and public four-year colleges and universities (about 400 institutions).

The IRS said it expects to receive most of the responses to this questionnaire within the next several months. It plans on analyzing the results of the questionnaire and conducting sample examinations. A report on this project may be expected in 2009.

Basic Information

This questionnaire's questions include the following:

- How many students (full-time equivalents) were enrolled at the institution in the fall of 2006?

- What was the size of the faculty in the fall of 2006?

- What was the number of employees as of the first quarter of 2006?

- What was the student/faculty ratio in the fall of 2006?

- If the institution is a private one, does it currently have a conflict-of-interest policy that governs members of the institution's "ruling body" and its "top management" officials?

- If the institution is a private one, does it currently have a conflict-of-interest policy that governs full-time faculty?

- Does the institution make its audited financial statements available to the public?

- What was the annual published full-time tuition rate for undergraduate students in the fall of 2006?

- What was the annual average tuition discount rate used to calculate the net average tuition after discounts for the fall of 2006?

- For the year ending in 2006, what were the institution's gross assets, net assets, gross revenue, and total expenses?

- Does the institution conduct distance-learning activities?

- Does the institution conduct educational programs internationally?

- Identify the institution's five highest paid employees for 2006, and their positions, compensation (from the institution and related organizations), and their NCAA athletically related income.

- Identify (and provide additional information as to) the five highest gross revenue-generating organizations that are related to the institution, by category of disregarded entities, tax-exempt organizations, partnerships, and taxable entities.

- In the case of a private institution, identify policies as to transactions with noncharitable organizations concerning provision of goods or services, lending of money, rental of property, transfers of assets, cost-sharing and expense reimbursement arrangements, licensing arrangements, shared employees, and other transfers of assets, liabilities, or funds.

- In the case of a private institution, identify items of income as to which the institution has a policy that "establishes arm's-length assurances" when the amounts are paid from a controlled organization.

- Describe how the institution determines pricing in its dealings with related organizations.

Activities

- Provide information concerning advertising, corporate sponsorships, rental activities, Internet sales, travel tours, broadcasting, affinity card programs, royalty arrangements, commercial research, hotel and restaurant operations, conference center operations, parking lot operations, operation of bookstores, and operation of golf courses. (See Chapter 7.)

- Identify which activities generate entirely unrelated business income (UBI), some UBI, or no UBI, and whether there was any debt-financing.

- Indicate whether another party managed an activity.

- Indicate whether there were losses from each activity in three out of five years (2001–2005).

- Identify similar information concerning activities conducted in a partnership, S corporation, or controlled entity in which the institution has an ownership share.

- Identify other activities that generated more than $50,000 in gross revenue.

- Identify the five largest activities, by gross revenue, that were not treated as unrelated businesses, both conducted directly and by means of joint ventures.

- Did the institution file a Form 990-T?

- Identify the bases for allocation of expenses in connection with unrelated businesses.

- For all activities reported on Form 990-T, provide a percentage breakdown of direct and indirect expenses (or do so on the questionnaire).

- Identify the five unrelated businesses that resulted in the largest losses.

- For all activities reported on Form 900-T, provide a percentage breakdown of "inter-company" expenses and other expenses (or do so on the questionnaire).

- Did the institution rely on one or more independent accountants or legal counsel for advice as to whether its activities were related or unrelated, allocation of expenses between unrelated and exempt activities, and/or pricing between the institution and its related organizations for expenses incurred in unrelated activities?

Endowment Funds

- Did the institution have one or more endowment funds?

- Does another organization hold or maintain one or more endowment funds on the institution's behalf?

- Does the organization have an investment policy for its endowment funds?

- Who manages the investments in the endowment funds?

- Does the institution have an investment committee that oversees investment of endowment fund assets (and, if so, how many individuals serve on the committee)?

- Did the institution engage an independent consultant for investment guidance?

- How did the institution compensate internal and external investment managers?

- Were compensation arrangements for internal and/or external investment managers approved by a board committee or the full board?

- What was the average amount of the investment assets per full-time student?

- What was the total year-end fair market value (FMV) of the endowment's assets?

- What was the year-end FMV of *quasi-endowments* (defined as endowment pool investments of which the principal can be spent at the discretion of the institution's trustees)?

- What was the year-end FMV of *term endowments* (defined as endowment pool investments of which the principal can be spent after a defined term has expired)?

- What was the year-end FMV of *true endowments* (defined as an endowment pool consisting of gifts of which only the return on principal investment can be spent)?

- Does the institution or a related entity have any *life income funds* (even if not in connection with an endowment fund) (defined as assets contributed to the institution on the condition that the institution pays a specified amount of income to the donor or specified individuals, after which the institution has complete ownership of the assets (see the following three questions))?

- What percent of the endowment was comprised of charitable gift annuities?

- What percent of the endowment was comprised of charitable remainder trusts?

- What percent of the endowment was comprised of pooled income funds?

- Did the institution make foreign investments of endowment funds through an investment entity?

- As of the last day of the fiscal year ending in 2006, what percent of endowment assets was invested in areas such as fixed income funds, equity funds, real estate, international funds, cash, and alternative investments (e.g., hedge and venture capital funds)?

- What is the primary investment objective for the institution's portfolio for the next five years?

- Did the board or committee members place restrictions on the purchase or sale of certain securities because of particular donor restrictions or special requests?

- Provide information on distributions from endowment funds, such as for scholarships, research, general education support, general university operations, and/or chairs or professorships.

- List the top five restrictions (e.g., fellowships or student aid) placed on endowments by donors or board/committee members.

- Did the institution monitor endowment distributions to ensure that they were used for the donors' intended purposes?

Executive Compensation

- Provide information for the six highest-paid officers, directors, trustees, and key employees, including the individuals' name, title, and amount of compensation from the institution and related organizations.

- Identify the type of remuneration paid to these individuals; 34 types are listed, including base salary, bonus, plan contributions, use of vehicle, value of institution-provided housing, personal services provided, and forms of deferred compensation.

- Did the institution provide loans or other extensions of credit to these individuals or their family members?

- If the institution is a private one (all of the remaining questions pertain only to private colleges and universities), did it have a formal written compensation policy that governed compensation of at least some of the officers, directors, trustees, or key employees?

- Did the institution hire an outside executive compensation consultant to provide comparable compensation data to determine the compensation of these individuals?

- If the answer to the previous question is yes, did the consultant provide other services? If so, describe them.

- Who in the institution sets the compensation amounts (e.g., board of directors or compensation committee)?

- As to these six individuals, was there an employment or independent contractor agreement?

- Did the institution use a process intended to satisfy the intermediate sanctions' rebuttable presumption of reasonableness procedure in determining compensation for these persons?

- Were payments made to these individuals pursuant to the intermediate sanctions' initial contract exception?

- Did the institution document the basis for setting these persons' compensation before the compensation was paid?

- Was the person a disqualified person immediately prior to entering into the employment or independent contractor arrangement?

- Did the board of directors or other governing body that did not have a conflict of interest approve the person's compensation?

- Did the individual recuse himself or herself from discussions about, and/or voting on, his or her compensation?

- Did the institution obtain an independent compensation comparability survey that was used in setting these individuals' compensation?

- If the answer to the foregoing question is yes, was the person's compensation set within the range of the comparability survey data?

- If the answer to the foregoing question is yes, what percentage from the comparability survey data was used to determine the person's compensation?

- Identify the factors that were included in the comparability data and used by the institution, and/or a compensation consultant, in setting each of these individuals' compensation, such as compensation levels paid by similar organizations (tax-exempt and taxable), the level of the individual's education and experience, the specific responsibilities of the position, the individual's previous salary or compensation package, similar services in the same geographical or metropolitan area, similar number of employees or students, and the organizations' annual budget and/or gross revenue/assets.

- Indicate the sources used to obtain comparability data for each of these individuals' compensation, such as published surveys of compensation at similar institutions, Internet research on compensation at similar institutions, telephone surveys of compensation at similar institutions, an outside expert hired to provide comparable compensation data and a report, a report prepared by a compensation analyst employed by the institution, written offers of employment from similar institutions, annual information returns filed by other colleges and universities, and the annual budget or gross revenue/assets.

Commentary

Inasmuch as it is the contemporary practice of IRS agents—in the application for recognition of tax exemption, annual information return review, and audit processes—to quickly extrapolate from and apply the contents of IRS documents such as this far beyond their original sphere, it behooves nearly every exempt organization to contemplate this questionnaire and muse as to how the entity would answer these questions if (and perhaps when) they were propounded to it. The questionnaire, much like the new Form 990, will soon be the basis for many policies, procedures, and protocols (and new law) that the IRS will be expecting of public charities and other exempt organizations in general.

Here is a mere sampling of these across-the-board issues. Agents will continue to insist on conflict-of-interest policies (see Chapter 10). Pressure for public distribution of audited financial statements will intensify. Agents will look closely at related revenue-generating organizations. Now that the special rule for nontaxation of certain payments from controlled organizations has been extended (see Chapter 7), agents will be examining whether the payments are reasonable in amount.

The IRS has clearly signaled the areas in the unrelated business setting that it will be examining. Activities that are being treated as unrelated businesses and that consistently generate losses will be reviewed, with the losses likely prevented from being used to offset income from other unrelated businesses. Much greater attention will be given to the calculation and allocation of expenses associated with unrelated businesses.

As to endowment funds, the IRS will be looking at (or for) investment policies, and examining the process used to oversee fund management and investments, including compensation of fund managers. The interest of the IRS in so-called life income funds, even if not associated with an endowment fund, is remarkable. Agents are likely to pay particular attention to alternative and foreign investments. Of course, there will be continued pressure for distributions from endowment funds, particularly in the education context, with emphasis on student assistance.

Concerning executive compensation, with this questionnaire, the IRS has spelled out rather obviously the issues it will be concentrating on, all with private inurement and excess benefit transactions backdrops. The IRS is focusing on types of compensation and loans, the use of independent compensation consultants, the presence of a compensation policy, and use of the rebuttable presumption of reasonableness. The IRS has laid out the elements of comparability data it expects to be considered, as well as the sources of this data.

IRS involvement in governance matters pertaining to public charities is once again evidenced. Throughout this questionnaire are references to conflict-of-interest policies, investment policies and committees, compensation policies, and public dissemination of audited financial statements (see Chapter 10).

HARDENING THE TARGET

There are 13 steps a tax-exempt organization can take to improve and maximally enhance its "public face" in advance of any IRS examination that may reduce the chances of an examination or, failing that, move the examination to its conclusion quickly, efficiently, and with minimal costs.

Review Governing Instruments

A nonprofit organization should, from time to time, review its governing instruments. These are the *articles of organization* (articles of incorporation, constitution, declaration of trust, and the like) and *bylaws*. The purpose of this exercise is to ensure that these documents accurately describe the organization's purposes and do not contain words or phrases that are inconsistent with its tax-exempt status. The IRS examiner will definitely review these instruments.

Review Operations

The IRS will certainly inquire into the tax-exempt organization's programs and other activities. The organization should have sufficient documentation about each of its programs (including annual reports, grant requests, and fundraising literature), and the relationship between them and achievement of its exempt purposes. Documentation of this nature that is in the organization's files when the IRS arrives is far more potent than materials assembled after the agency has initiated contact.

Review Books and Records

The organization should attend to its financial, operational (e.g., grant files), and governance (e.g., minutes) records. Of all of the types of documents that will be read by an IRS examiner, only board and committee minutes have the ability to be created specifically in anticipation of (and in an attempt to influence the outcome of) an IRS (or other government agency) review of the organization's operations. The organization should be certain that it knows where these records are located and that they contain what is required. A document retention policy will impress the IRS revenue agent.

Review Publications

The organization should review its publications that are disseminated to the public. Examples of these are charitable gift solicitation materials, magazines, journals, newsletters, mission statements, and federal or state lobbying disclosure reports. These materials should be reviewed to identify any statements that may be harmful in relation to the organization's tax-exempt status. (Recently, a nonprofit organization claiming to promote safety in flying, principally through publication of a magazine, was audited. Perusing issues of the magazine, the IRS agent found little material about flying safety but came upon this disclaimer in each issue: "This publication is strictly for your entertainment value." The IRS revoked the organization's exempt status.) Usually, this text cannot be amended but at least the organization and its professional representatives can become aware of any problematic language and prepare accordingly.

Review Correspondence

Reviewing correspondence (including email) is a tedious exercise but it must be done because an IRS examiner is likely to do so. There may be documents that adversely (at least potentially) impact public charity status or the merits of a tax-exempt activity (such as a scholarship or fellowship program).

Review Federal Returns

The principal returns that will be examined are the annual information return (see Chapter 5) and any unrelated business income tax return (see Chapter 7). In addition to endeavoring to properly prepare and timely file these returns, they should be reviewed from time to time with a prospective audit perspective. The IRS examination procedures instruct agents to look for "gaps or incongruities" and "entries [not] credible on their face."

Review Contracts

In anticipation of the IRS doing so, a nonprofit organization should review its contracts (including letter agreements and perhaps signed informal memoranda). Of particular interest to the IRS are employment contracts, severance agreements, management agreements, fundraising contracts, and leases.

Other Documents

Documents that please IRS revenue agents are properly prepared codes of ethics, conflict-of-interest policies, document retention and destruction policies (as noted), whistleblower policies, insurance policies (usually), consultants' reports (particularly as to compensation), and appraisals (see Chapters 2 and 8). If the organization is a member of a partnership or other joint venture, the appropriate documentation will be reviewed. An examiner may review reports concerning an exempt organization issued by or filed with a federal, state, or local government agency.

Review Web Site

A nonprofit organization should periodically review its Web site with the federal tax law perspective in mind. It goes without saying that this is the easiest of text to revise. If an organization is selected for an audit, it may be assumed that the IRS has visited (or certainly will visit) the site. This matter impacts program, unrelated business, and fundraising.

Employment Taxes

Nonprofit organizations with employees are exposed to examination by IRS employment tax agents, in addition to exempt organizations agents. These organizations should stay current with the withholding and reporting requirements, periodically review the employee/independent contractor classification of their workers, and be certain that their files contain adequate justification for any independent contractor status.

Media Coverage

Not every nonprofit organization should have, or can afford, a media consultant. Nonetheless, an organization should do what it can to get its programs and accomplishments publicized. Also, an organization should maintain a file of newspaper articles and other forms of media coverage about it (particularly if the reports are favorable).

Testaments

Some nonprofit organizations operate programs that generate letters and other forms of comment about their activities from program beneficiaries and perhaps others. A file of these documents should be maintained (again, particularly if they are favorable).

Legal Audit

The foregoing pre-audit precautions are the minimum. The nonprofit organization that wants to do all it can to avoid an IRS audit or smooth the process once enmeshed in one should engage the services of a competent nonprofit lawyer to conduct a comprehensive legal audit.

WINNING AUDIT LOTTERY

The following steps should be expected by a nonprofit organization, once it has become the subject of an IRS audits, reviewing them should help it get through the examination process as painlessly as possible.

Telephone Call

The practice of the IRS, in connection with a typical examination of a non-profit organization, is to commence the process with a telephone call—what the IRS terms the *initial contact*. (Many executives of nonprofit organizations find this approach unduly startling and rather unnerving, and prefer to get the bad news by letter.) The caller will, of course, announce that the organization has been selected (somewhat of a euphemism) for an IRS examination. This IRS representative will also advise the organization of the year or years that will be covered by the examination and attempt to set the date for the pre-examination conference.

Notice of Examination

This telephone call will be followed up with a letter from the IRS serving as formal notice of the examination, which is likely to be based on the filing of one or more annual information returns. This letter, which will undoubtedly bear the same date as the above telephone call, will propose an initial conference about the examination. This notice will contain this bit of empathy from the IRS: "We realize some organizations may be concerned about an examination of their returns."

Documents Requested

The initial information document request, which will almost certainly accompany the notice of examination, will ask for organizational documents, operational documents, and certain books and records.

This IDR will undoubtedly request copies of the tax-exempt organization's organizing document, its bylaws, the application for recognition of exemption, the determination letter recognizing its exempt status, and the minutes of the meetings of the organization's governing body for the year preceding the first year of the audit period, for the year(s) of the audit period, and for the year immediately succeeding the audit period.

The IDR will undoubtedly request copies of the exempt organization's annual information return for the year preceding the first year of the audit period, for the year(s) of the audit period, and for the year immediately succeeding the audit period; printed materials used to promote the organization's activities; and contracts to which the organization was a party during the audit period.

This IDR will probably request copies of bank statements for all accounts (checking, savings, investments), canceled checks and deposit slips, check registers, the general ledger, and documentation in support of expenses claimed.

Get Organized

Having received the initial telephone call from the IRS, and the initial contact letter and IDR, the nonprofit organization should select a team that will be charged with overseeing (from the organization's standpoint) the examination. With this group, the organization will want to try to maintain as much control over the situation, and get through the examination process as quickly, as possible. These goals, however, may prove elusive.

Contact Person

The nonprofit organization facing an IRS audit should designate an individual to be the single point of contact for the examination; the examiner will be expecting selection of this individual. All requests for documents and interviews should be to this individual, who should be responsible for timely responses. This individual should also maintain a log of IDRs from and documents provided to the IRS.

Communications Strategy

The IRS may contact third parties, such as the nonprofit organization's bank, contractors, and others with whom it does business. This can lead to media attention. The organization should be ready with a thoughtful statement for the media.

Know the Cast

It is important that the nonprofit organization know who from the IRS is involved in the audit. The appropriate representative(s) of the organization should meet, greet, and record the names of the revenue agents involved, as well as of the case manager (or, at least, procure the manager's name and contact information). The organization should determine if the office of the IRS Chief Counsel will be assisting the revenue agents. Likewise, the organization should ascertain whether one or more specialists, such as engineers, computer audit specialists, or financial analysts, are being assigned to the case.

Office Facilities

The IRS may expect workspace on the nonprofit organization's premises, in the form of a workroom with locking door, desks and chairs, telephones, file cabinet (with lock), and space and power supply for a desktop computer, printer, and fax machine. The agents will want access to a photocopier. Careful consideration should be given as to the location of this workspace. The organization should endeavor to place this office as far away as possible from a dining area or kitchen where (talkative) employees congregate.

Initial and Other Interviews

The initial interview is likely to be a crucial step—for both parties—in the examination process. If all goes in accordance with IRS procedures, the examiner will have carefully prepared for the meeting. Needless to say, the nonprofit organization should be prepared as well; this entails at least three elements:

(1) appropriate preparation, by the lawyer or other individual who is guiding the organization through the audit, of the individuals who are to be interviewed by the examiner; (2) availability of all of the documents requested by the IRS or an explanation as to why one or more of these documents will not or cannot be provided; and (3) suitable tidying and "spiffing up" of the office premises and the interviewees.

The nonprofit organization's representative should not hesitate to ask questions up front (although they may not be answered). One question is the reason for the examination, such as an event or issue. Another is whether the agent has any special areas of interest to explore. The agent may be asked whether there is an examination plan and a tentative schedule that can be shared with the organization.

Thereafter, the IRS may conduct additional interviews with the same individuals and/or interview others. All of this is likely to be done in conjunction with document reviews, more IDRs, tours, and other examination techniques. First impressions are important; everyone should endeavor to be polite. The organization should make every effort to convey the substance of the organization's governance, law compliance, programs, and other good works.

COPING WITH EXAMINERS

When an IRS examination of a nonprofit organization begins, one of the first orders of business (from the organization's standpoint) is to assess the personality of the examiner or examiners. Initially (and thus superficially), this exercise can produce great variations, such as from nice to rude, quiet to assertive. As this minuet gets underway, those representing the organization should not lose sight of the fact that the agent (1) is also positioning himself or herself, assaying the personalities of these representatives, trying to determine if these people are going to be cooperative or disingenuous, and (2) is backed up by one of the most powerful components of the federal government.

Most often, an IRS examiner will commence the process with politeness, burnished with an air of cool assurance. This demeanor can change, of course, for better or worse, as the examiner interacts with the nonprofit organization (trustees, directors, officers, employees, maybe volunteers), its representatives (such as lawyer or accountant), and perhaps third parties (such as a bank or other provider of goods or services). Sometimes it's bonding; sometimes it's combat. This element of the facts interrelates with the factor of the level of knowledge of the law of tax-exempt organizations the examiner brings to the skirmish; not surprisingly, some have more than others. The less the understanding of the law accumulated by the examiner, the greater the likelihood of bluster. Usually, the examiner will work, in a cooperative and courteous manner, with the nonprofit organization in developing and analyzing the applicable law. But, there is always the possibility of the type of examiner who, having (1) taken a nonsensical position, (2) asked for authority on a point of law, and (3) been told that there is nothing specific to cite (other than common sense), retorts—and this is not being made up: "If you can't provide me with some precedent, then I am the authority." (Next step: the call to the case manager.)

This is, then, a matter of group dynamics, including at least three types of interactions involving the IRS examiner: contact with other IRS personnel, the individual(s) comprising the nonprofit organization, and the individual(s) representing the nonprofit organization. It is infrequent but disagreement, animosity, and other forms of friction can be displayed by IRS personnel in the presence of those representing, in one capacity or another, the nonprofit organization. (On one memorable occasion, a lawyer, having appeared at an audit conference where the IRS representatives were confused over the schedule and thus unprepared for the meeting, watched, with equal doses of bemusement and incredulity, a tetrad of IRS employees quarrel with one another over who was at fault. Four sets of lawyers had flown in for the conference from different cities; the conference had to be rescheduled.)

The greatest amount of apprehension (from the standpoint of the nonprofit organization under examination) and tension is likely to develop between the IRS examiner and an employee, officer, or similar proxy for the nonprofit organization. The IRS makes most individuals nervous, so there is no surprise in concluding that an IRS audit is a prescription for much angst for the auditee. Moreover, most executives of nonprofit organizations are passionate about their organization and its programs, and tend to get exercised (or upset or angry) when challenged on these fronts. Thus, when it comes to interactions between an IRS examiner and this type of representative of a nonprofit organization, the lawyer representing the organization (if there is one) generally will work assiduously with this individual in preparing him or her for the IRS interview or other exchange with the examiner and keep the communication between these individuals to a minimum. Conversely, there are some nonprofit organizations executives, officers, and directors whose personality is sufficiently infectious that the lawyer wants them to spend as much time with the examiner(s) as reasonably possible. Admittedly, this is a rare phenomenon but it can happen.

If there is to be an altercation, it probably will occur between an IRS examiner and a lawyer representing the nonprofit organization under audit. Some of these dustups may be pure personality clashes (or posturing) but far more likely is the belief, on the part of the lawyer, that the examiner either is misconstruing one or more aspects of the law of exempt organizations or is in some fashion being unreasonable. As noted, some agents are more schooled in this area than others. Disagreement over the state of the law does not always lead to a donnybrook but it can generate frustration and tempers can flare. The lawyer in this circumstance should always strive to act civilly, but there are occasions, sometimes dictated by the exigencies of advocacy, when legal counsel needs to stand up to the examiner on matters of substantive and/or procedural law.

TOURS

A particularly vexing (from the nonprofit organization's standpoint) aspect of these IRS examinations is the tour. The IRS examiner(s) quite likely will want, relatively early in the process, to tour the organization's facilities. In some instances, of course, there will not be any facilities to tour or the facilities will consist of a few offices that are not conducive to touring. The IRS representatives, by contrast, will almost certainly seek a tour of a tax-exempt organization's facilities where they house program and/or fundraising activities, such as those of a school, college, university, hospital, association, or large public charity.

These tours pose problems for nonprofit organizations; the larger the organization, the greater the headache. Management of an organization usually prefers to confine the fact of an IRS audit to as few employees as possible; a tour by the IRS widely spreads the news. These tours can depress employees' morale (or scare them); they will assume the worst when they see the IRS prowling the premises. A bigger dilemma is that one or more employees will say something to an IRS examiner that is detrimental to the cause.

The lawyer representing an audited nonprofit organization certainly should not permit one of these tours to unfold at random. The best practice is a dress rehearsal, preferably the day before the tour so that the employees involved will have the lawyer's instructions fresh in their minds and they will have minimum time to become anxious. The route of the tour should be mapped out; this needs to be carefully done, because if the tour path is obviously short, the examiner will want to explore other areas that are in plain sight. The employees whose offices are located along the tour route should be carefully counseled as to what to say and what not to say. Ideally, these individuals will be well dressed (at least on tour day) and polite (same), will answer questions put to them by the examiner (assuming they know the answer), and will confine their responses to the scope of the questions and volunteer nothing. In short, these employees should be given a quick course in how to function as a witness. Much can go wrong on the tour; good preparation includes making the premises (and the employees) as attractive and looking as well organized and operated as possible.

Tour participants should include, in addition to the IRS examiner(s), one executive of the nonprofit organization and one lawyer representing the organization. The executive should choreograph the tour, leading the agents, pointing out the significant physical features of the premises (such as departments), and stopping at the desks of the most important (and trustworthy) of the employees. The lawyer should be poised to intervene should an employee start imparting information that is inconsistent with a favorable audit outcome. Here is where a blurt or a blunder is most likely; all involved on behalf of the organization should be cautious and on high alert (without appearing so). The plan (and hope) should be to conclude the tour as soon as reasonably possible, without providing information (if any) to the IRS that is deleterious to the organization's tax-exempt status or other tax liability, and with minimal disruption to the operation of the organization and the mood of the staff.

IRS AUDIT PROCESS

Following the fact-gathering phase (responses to IDRs, interviews, tours, conferences, and the like), the revenue agents will analyze the information and begin to discuss tentative findings, concerns, or issues that require resolution. If matters are not resolved, at some point the examination will move into a process of formal notification of issues (with attendant tax consequences), typically in the form of a *notice of proposed adjustment.*

Examination activity may uncover issues for which there is a lack of clear precedent to guide the revenue agent(s). A technical advice process is available by which the headquarters function (National Office) of the Exempt Organizations Division will become involved to establish the government's position. This procedure includes a pre-submission process pursuant to which a consultation occurs between the agents conducting the examination, the nonprofit organization involved, and headquarters personnel.

Should matters still not be resolved, the revenue agent(s) will issue a report. This is known formally as the Revenue Agent's Report (RAR) and informally as the *30-day letter.* This is because, if the nonprofit organization wishes to challenge one or more findings in the RAR, it has 30 days to do so. The challenge is in the form of a written *protest,* followed by at least one conference. At this point, failing a resolution, the organization battles on, either to an administrative appeal (discussed ahead) or by receiving a *90-day letter,* which is the first formal step on the way to litigation (discussed ahead).

CLOSING AGREEMENTS

An examination of a nonprofit organization may be settled. The formal way to do this is by means of a *closing agreement.* These agreements are being used with increasing frequency to resolve a variety of exempt organizations matters. This is particularly the case as utilization of the technical advice procedure declines (due to the length of its time and the nonprofit organization's costs involved). As two IRS officials nicely wrote, a closing agreement in the exempt organizations context is a "remedy for ambivalent conditions."

While not the solution for every disagreement with the IRS, a closing agreement can be, in the words of these officials, a "pragmatic method to resolve sensitive matters in which there are mitigating circumstances." From the standpoint of the IRS, closing agreements "promote compliance" while conserving the IRS's "scarce resources." The agency is able to resolve a compliance problem that otherwise would "consume time and resources (through the revocation or assessment process) and obtains a commitment to future compliance." The nonprofit organization "obtains both certainty that the matter is concluded once and for all and guidance on how to comply in the future."

APPEALS PROCESS

The appeals process in the IRS may take some getting used to. When one thinks of an *appeal* in the contexts of courts, it is a transfer of the dispute from one discrete court to another. With the IRS, the appeal stays in the agency; the decision of the Examination Division of the IRS is appealed to the office of Appeals within the IRS. Nonetheless, the Appeals function in practice amounts to an independent agency; it is detached from the rest of the IRS.

The mission of the Appeals component of the IRS is, in the words of IRS procedures, to "resolve tax controversies, without litigation, on a fair and impartial basis" from the standpoint of the federal government and the taxpayer, and in a manner that will enhance voluntary compliance and public confidence in the integrity and efficiency of the IRS. The Appeals office strives to be independent, and develops as well as implements measures that balance "customer satisfaction" and "business results." The Chief of Appeals, who reports to the Commissioner of Internal Revenue, is responsible for planning, managing, and executing nationwide activities for the Appeals function.

Arriving at Appeals is often a good development for a nonprofit organization. The difference in approach between that of an examining revenue agent and an appeals officer can be breathtakingly dramatic. An IRS appeals officer is likely to view a tax-exempt organization's circumstances far more sympathetically than did the examining agent(s). The typical pattern is that the examiner will take a hard-line position in the case, proposing revocation of exemption or imposition of a substantial penalty, with the appeals officer willing to work with the organization in preserving its exemption or reducing the penalty. An appeals officer usually will interpret the law more favorably (from the exempt organization's standpoint) and be more flexible in allowing an exempt organization to alter one or more aspects of its operations to retain (or obtain) exemption.

IRS appeals officers in general like to resolve tax law disputes by compromising on amounts due, such as taxes or penalties. Often the amount at issue will be halved, simply to close the case. In the tax-exempt organizations context, this mindset works when the issue is a penalty for failure to timely file an annual information return, assessment of unrelated business income tax, and the like. This approach cannot be taken, of course, when the issue is exempt status. As one appeals officer was heard to say, an organization cannot be "partially exempt."

A nonprofit organization with an appeals case involving eligibility for tax exemption may find that the appeals officer will uphold exempt status if the organization pays a certain amount of money to the IRS. This sum (which usually is negotiable) may be rather arbitrary, being the officer's determination as to what is fair recompense to the government for processing the case. This sum may be roughly equivalent to the amount of income tax the organization would have had to pay were it a taxable entity during the examination period.

One problem with Appeals is the length of time it takes to plod through the process; an appeal can easily consume three years. (There are only 12 appeals officers handling tax-exempt organizations matters.) Also, considerable time can pass before the matter is taken up by an appeals officer. While practitioners do not want to dip into this well too often, a technique for getting some attention in Appeals is to write a letter complaining about the plight to the Taxpayer Advocate Service, with a copy to the appeals officer.

FAST-TRACK SETTLEMENT PROGRAM

The IRS initiated a program enabling organizations with issues under examination by the TE/GE Division to use a fast-track settlement (FTS) process to expedite resolution of their cases. This program allows tax-exempt organizations that have unagreed issues in at least one open period under examination to work with the Division and the Office of Appeals to resolve outstanding disputed issues while the case is still in TE/GE jurisdiction. The Division and Appeals jointly administer this FTS process.

The procedures for using this FTS program are based on those the IRS developed to implement the Large and Mid-Size Business Division FTS dispute resolution program and the Small Business/Self-Employed Taxpayer Division FTS dispute resolution program. FTS is available for exemption, public charity/private foundation status, and certain other issues where the exempt organization has a written statement of its position and there is a "limited number" of factual and/or law issues. FTS is not available for a list of matters, including issues designated for litigation, correspondence examination cases, frivolous issues, and cases involving civil or criminal fraud.

An organization that is interested in participating in this FTS process, or that has questions about the program and its suitability for a particular case, may contact the TE/GE group manager of the agent conducting the audit for the period(s) under examination. The organization, examining agent, or group manager may initiate an application (Form 14017) to the FTS process. A notice of proposed adjustment (Form 5701) or a revenue agent report will be prepared by the examining agent. If a case is not accepted for inclusion in the program, the IRS will discuss other dispute resolution opportunities with the organization.

FTS employs various alternative dispute resolution techniques to promote agreement. An FTS Appeals official will serve as a neutral party. This official thus will not perform in a traditional Appeals role but rather will use dispute resolution techniques to facilitate settlement. An FTS session report will be developed to assist in planning, and reporting on developments during the FTS session. This report will include a description of the issues, the amounts in dispute, conference dates, and a plan of action for the session. If the parties resolve any of the issues at the session, the parties and the Appeals official will sign the session report acknowledging acceptance of the terms of settlement for purposes of preparing computations. The TE/GE FTS process is confidential.

FTS may be initiated at any time after an issue has been fully developed but before issuance of a 30-day letter (or its equivalent). This is a pilot program, available for two years. Thereafter, the Division and Appeals will evaluate the program, consider making adjustments, and decide whether to make it permanent.

RETROACTIVE REVOCATIONS

An outcome of an IRS audit of a nonprofit organization can be revocation of its tax-exempt status. A worse outcome is *retroactive* revocation of exempt status. An exemption ruling may be retroactively revoked if the organization omitted or misstated a material fact (such as in an application for recognition of exemption or an annual information return), operated in a manner materially different from that originally represented, or engaged in a prohibited transaction. A *prohibited transaction* is a transaction entered into for the purpose of diverting a substantial part of an organization's corpus or income from its exempt purpose.

The IRS has the discretion as to whether to revoke an organization's tax-exempt status prospectively or retroactively. This discretion is broad, reviewable by the courts only for its abuse. The IRS is rarely thwarted in this regard. The agency has been known to grant recognition of exemption to an organization, then years later change its mind, and revoke the exemption back to the date the organization was formed, setting the organization up for a huge tax liability. (Most government agencies cannot get away with behavior like this, due to a principle called *fairness.*) Sometimes, a law change triggers retroactive revocation. For example, the IRS introduced rules in 1970 prohibiting exempt schools from maintaining racially discriminatory policies; a school formed in 1959 lost its exemption in 1976 for this reason; the IRS tried to revoke the school's exemption all the way back to 1959 but a court allowed retroactivity only to 1970.

Two court opinions are against the IRS on this point. In one case (1956), the facts did not change during the period involved, the organization adequately disclosed on its annual information returns the facts that prompted the attempted revocation of exemption, there were no misrepresentations of fact, and the proposed assessment of tax was, in the words of the court, "so large as to wipe [the organization] out of existence." The court acknowledged that the IRS can change its policies but wrote that "it is quite a different matter to say that having once changed his mind the Commissioner may arbitrarily and without limit have the effect of that change go back over previous years during which the taxpayer operated under the previous ruling." The court refused to condone this "harsh result." In the second case (2008), the organization's originally stated purpose and operations did not change over the years. A court ruled that the IRS was bound by its initial determination because the organization had been operating in the manner originally represented and that the agency "abused its discretion by retroactively revoking the exempt status it originally granted" to the organization.

CHURCH AUDIT RULES

Special statutory rules apply to IRS inquiries and examinations of churches and conventions and associations of churches. A *church tax inquiry* is any inquiry by the IRS to a church (other than certain requests and a church tax examination) that serves as a basis for determining whether the church qualifies for tax exemption, is carrying any unrelated business, or otherwise is engaged in activities that may be subject to federal taxation. The term *church tax examination* means any examination, for purposes of making one or more of those three determinations, of church records at the request of the IRS or the religious activities of any church.

The IRS may commence a church tax inquiry only when the agency has satisfied certain *reasonable belief* requirements and certain *notice* requirements. A church tax examination may be undertaken only where certain notice and conference opportunity requirements are met; even then, the examination may proceed only (1) in the case of church records, to the extent necessary to determine the liability for and the amount of any federal tax, and (2) in the case of religious activities, to the extent necessary to determine whether an organization claiming to be a church is a church for any period.

In general, the IRS must complete a church tax inquiry or examination (and make a final determination as to either or both) within a two-year period beginning on the date the examination notice was issued. Also, in general, in the case of a church tax inquiry as to which there is no examination notice, the IRS must complete the inquiry (and make a final determination with respect to it) within the 90-day period beginning on the date the inquiry notice was issued. The running of these two periods may be suspended under certain circumstances.

There are limitations on the ability of the IRS to revoke the tax-exempt status of a church and on the agency's ability to send a notice of deficiency of a tax involved in a church tax examination or otherwise assess a tax underpayment in connection with an examination. Statutes of limitation apply in connection with exempt status revocations and unrelated business income tax assessments and collections. A proceeding to compel compliance with a summons issued in connection with a church tax inquiry or examination may be stayed under certain circumstances. Limitations are imposed on the ability of the IRS to conduct subsequent inquiries and/or examinations of a church.

One of the requirements for properly launching a church tax inquiry is that an "appropriate high-level Treasury official" must commence it by making a "reasonable belief" determination as to its appropriateness. The Internal Revenue Code defines that official as the Secretary of the Treasury or "any delegate of the Secretary whose rank is no lower than that of a principal Internal Revenue officer for an internal revenue region." Prior to a major reorganization of the IRS (1998–1999), the designated official was the appropriate regional commissioner. That position, however, was abolished as part of the reorganization; the statutory definition (enacted in 1984) has not been amended. The IRS delegated the authority to begin church tax inquiries to the Exempt Organizations Director, Examinations (discussed previously). A federal court, in early 2009, ruled that a church tax inquiry was not properly undertaken because this individual is not sufficiently elevated in rank.

LITIGATION

When there is a federal tax issue involving a nonprofit organization that cannot be resolved administratively (that is, within the IRS), the matter may be taken to court. Again, the issue may be tax-exempt status, public charity status, unrelated business, and the like. There are two basic pathways to the courthouse.

An organization facing loss of tax-exempt status or similar adverse treatment at the hands of the IRS may, once all administrative remedies have been exhausted, petition the U.S. Tax Court for relief following the issuance of a notice of tax deficiency or may pay a tax and sue for a refund in the appropriate federal district court or the U.S. Court of Federal Claims, following expiration of a statutory six-month waiting period.

A special declaratory judgment procedure is available by which to litigate the tax status of charitable organizations (exempt and/or public charity status) and farmers' cooperatives. Again, appropriate administrative remedies must be exhausted or time periods must have run. There is no need to pay any tax to come within the jurisdiction of the court. This declaratory judgment jurisdiction is vested in the U.S. District Court for the District of Columbia, the U.S. Court of Federal Claims, and the U.S. Tax Court.

There are many practical considerations facing a tax-exempt organization that is a prospective litigant. One of them is the cost. The process can be quite expensive. Preparation of the complaint or petition entails relatively minimal time (and thus relatively minimal cost). Legal fees can quickly mount during the discovery process and other preparations for trial. The trial as well will trigger considerable fees. An organization should obviously engage in a cost-benefit analysis before launching a lawsuit. In nearly all instances, the decision to sue the federal government should be made by the organization's governing board.

Another consideration is the court in which the case will be filed and the litigation will take place. Forum-shopping is usually inevitable. One of the considerations in this context is whether, as noted, a tax needs to be paid to gain access to the court. Another consideration is the precedents that comprise each court's jurisprudence; the exempt organization obviously will want to avoid a court where there are one or more decisions adverse to the organization's position. Some organizations want to litigate in their home district court, rather than in Washington, D.C. On some occasions, a jury trial will be requested.

SUMMARY

This chapter summarized the organization of the IRS, reviewed the reasons for IRS audits of charitable organizations, inventoried the IRS audit issues, and described the types of IRS audits. The IRS compliance check programs were discussed, with emphasis on the all-important college and university compliance check questionnaire. The IRS audit and appeals processes were analyzed (including the new fast-track settlement process). The matter of retroactive revocations of tax exemption was reviewed, as were the church audit rules. The chapter concluded with a quick look at the possibility of the need to resolve audit issues by litigation.

12

PERSPECTIVES AND COMMENTARIES

The previous chapters summarize the federal and state laws that combine to form the law of fundraising as it relates to charitable solicitations. Because these bodies of law are so complex and sometimes strange, this chapter offers some perspectives and commentaries on the subject of charitable fundraising law. Specifically, this chapter will:

- Offer a perspective on charitable fundraising and the law.

- Comment on the distinctions between fundraisers and solicitors.

- Explore the scope of state law.

- Discuss the elements of the fundraiser's contract.

- Summarize the ways these laws apply in connection with charitable auctions.

- Discuss a court opinion that sees this regulation as a benefit to fundraising charities.

- Explore the interaction of charitable fundraising and the private inurement doctrine.

- Explore the matter of charitable solicitations and fraud.

- Explore the matter of charitable solicitations and the substantiation rules.

- Inventory some proposals for relief.

CHARITABLE FUNDRAISING AND THE LAW

The law of fundraising for charitable purposes is based on federal, state, and local statutes and ordinances, which are accompanied, interpreted, and expanded by myriad regulations, rules, forms, instructions to forms, and court opinions. The resulting total mass of law comprises an extensive set of requirements that the managers of a charitable organization, those who advise them, and those who raise funds for them, should generally understand. Lawyers and accountants who advise soliciting charities should, of course, comprehend this law in some detail; knowledge of generalities (the subject of this book), coupled with specific advice from these advisors from time to time, should suffice for managers.

A sizable majority of this statutory and other law is enacted and promulgated at the state level. There, the process of raising funds for charitable purposes is heavily regulated. Thus, the amount of this law that will be encountered by a charitable organization engaged in fundraising will depend substantially on the number of states in which solicitations for charitable gifts take place. A charitable organization that is raising funds in every state and wants to comply with all applicable laws has before it a monumental task.

Consequently, the greatest problem created by the law for the charitable fundraising community is the barrage of registration, reporting, disclosure, and other requirements demanded by the various state charitable solicitation acts—what one court termed the "apparatus" of each of the states for regulating charities. As a result, one of the chief governmental relations challenges for the field as the 21st century is underway to arrest expansion of this form of regulation. It is antithetical to the legitimate fundraising process, if only because of the extraordinary expenses and other burdens it imposes on philanthropy.

Commentators have described this regulatory burden quite colorfully. In one instance, the charitable solicitation regulatory process in the states was portrayed as a half-centipede with 51 feet, with 47 [the number of state solicitation acts] of them outfitted with "shoes of different styles, shapes, materials, and construction." In another instance, the situation was analogized to state law requiring drivers' licenses: "Imagine how difficult it would be [for someone living on the East Coast] to visit one's family on the West Coast if one had to obtain a driver's license in every state along the way"; because of the states' unwillingness to cooperate with each other in this regard, "charities often spend large sums of money on administrative expenses just to satisfy the patchwork of laws and regulations" throughout the nation.

An article in a major newspaper in early 2009 reported of conflict between federal and state laws pertaining to the tracking of sexual offenders. Federal law requires the states to adopt strict standards for registering these offenders. Apparently, state officials are complaining about the cost of compliance; some are asserting that these rules may be unconstitutional. Some states are "leaning toward ignoring major requirements." One state attorney general observed that "some of the provisions didn't make sense." This article refers to a "patchwork of differing state laws." Not a single state has been deemed to be in compliance with the federal law. An advocate of the federal law said that the "single most important thing about it was creating a more consistent, uniform process across the country." When this multistate law situation is juxtaposed with the patchwork of state charitable solicitation acts, it is striking how state officials can sound like charity executives when the proverbial shoe is on the other foot.

Despite some major and impressive successes by the philanthropic world in the courts (see Chapter 9), states are continuing their interventionist policies in this arena, creating new laws and otherwise expanding the scope of their involvement in the charitable fundraising process.

Reasonable people agree that some form of regulation in this area is quite appropriate. Instances of fraudulent and other bogus fundraisers and fundraising occur. Donors, like consumers, deserve some guidance and protection against misleading fundraising. Wrongdoers should be aggressively prosecuted and punished. The integrity of the charitable dollar is vital to a strong philanthropic sector. Fundraising scandals taint the process for everyone.

At the same time, balance is required. The subject is, after all, charitable giving—an act of generosity that is voluntary. Moreover, fundraising is constitutionally protected, principally through the doctrine of free speech (id.). Charitable contributions are the lifeblood of the sector. It is wonderful—and sometimes quite a marvel—for a state to occasionally nab a solicitor engaged in fraud, but these accomplishments bear a price tag of enormous expense to and administrative burdens on all others in the fundraising world. Many ask: Are all of these requirements for paperwork, disclosure, recordkeeping, bonding, and the like necessary? Are they doing much good?

During a conference, a respected professional fundraiser lamented that he could not find any empirical evidence to back up the immense depth of the charitable solicitation "problem" as depicted by state regulators and watchdog groups. (That is because there is no such evidence.) His imagery deserves a verbatim quote: "Does all of this activity amount to hunting flies with an elephant gun or chasing elephants with a flyswatter?" (The former is the case.)

This commentator believed that the states are taking a shotgun approach to regulation in this field. He advocated a more focused, "surgical" strategy and advised against expending inordinate amounts of money and time on what he called "low-risk" problems. There was much wisdom there; as is so often the case, the trick is in the implementation.

In fact, the states' approach to charitable fundraising regulation does little to deter wrongdoing and substantially frustrates legitimate charitable solicitations. Do these laws, as one federal court of appeals pretended, rid the country of "illegitimate charities," enhance public confidence in the charitable sector, and generate higher levels of giving to the charities that remain? Of course not. Instead, they are nonproductive overkill, another administrative burden imposed on charities, a justification to bloat a bureaucracy, a rationalization to hunt flies with an elephant gun. These laws are actually counterproductive in that they sap charitable resources and send the message to the public that the charitable sector, which is so important to the nation, is merely a pack of cheats and scoundrels, and only massive regulation by the states can protect citizens against them.

State regulation in this area is out of control. It is expanding for the sake of expansion; the very process of law-writing has become little more than a contest among the state legislatures to determine which can come up with the most grandiose charitable solicitation act. The laws just get lengthier, more intricate; there is constant revision of them. The states are trying to micromanage charitable solicitations in ways that are patronizing to the charitable organizations involved, such as by dictating the contents of their contracts with fundraisers and solicitors. Substantial law revision in this field is an ongoing and escalating phenomenon. Compliance with any one of these laws—assuming one can keep up with the changes—is often difficult; compliance with the batch of them can be impossible.

There has to be a better system. Present law needs to be reformed to accommodate the legitimate fundraising process and allow it to prosper—for the benefit of society—while protecting the public and restraining the few outlaws. Charitable fundraising is among the highest acts of free speech. When constitutional law rights are in play, government regulation is supposed to be minimal, even if some wrongdoing has to be tolerated. Today's philosophy underlying state-law regulation of fundraising is infected with a regulatory mindset that follows precisely the opposite approach: maximum regulation even if it is harmful to the innocent.

Some years ago, a governor of a state was contemplating signing a new charitable solicitation statute, one that employed percentage limitations to regulate charitable fundraising. The state's attorney general advised the governor to veto the legislation on the ground that, "under federal case law, the bill is unconstitutional." The attorney general wrote that the U.S. Supreme Court has repeatedly held that "using percentages to determine the legality of the fundraiser's fee [which was not what the Court addressed] is an unwarranted limitation on protected speech as reflected in charitable fundraising activities, and is not narrowly tailored to the state's interest in preventing fraud" (id.). In his letter, this attorney general observed that the proposed unconstitutional statute was nonetheless "laudable as public policy," raising the obvious question as to how an attorney general (or any other lawyer) can assert that laws, which the courts have repeatedly held to be flagrantly unconstitutional, be somehow nonetheless "laudable as public policy."

FUNDRAISERS AND SOLICITORS: THE DIFFERENCES

A major problem with the state charitable solicitation acts is the failure of the legislators and regulators to divine an adequate definition of the terms *professional fundraiser* and *professional solicitor* (or equivalent terminology) (see Chapter 3). In the past, the definitions and distinctions written into the various state acts sufficed; today, they are so out-of-date, unrealistic, and inconsistent as to be nearly worthless.

In earlier, simpler times, the law viewed the fundraising professional as a consultant, one who assisted charitable organizations in planning a solicitation program or campaign, although the charity was the actual solicitor of the gifts. The professional solicitor, by contrast, was a person who, in lieu of but on behalf of a charity, solicited gifts. At best, the latter had a poor reputation as one who begged door-to-door or on a street corner, or—worse—solicited by telephone during dinnertime or on weekends from the proverbial boiler room.

Those distinctions have been blurred and sometimes erased by the advent of developments such as direct mail solicitations, telemarketing, and Internet communications. The bright line of demarcation between consultants and solicitors has disappeared. This dichotomy started to fade with the massive use of direct mail fundraising, where those who consulted on the design of the literature also physically introduced it into the mails, thereby arguably becoming part of the solicitation process. Soliciting by telephone in recent years has come out of hiding and into respectability, with the callers regarded as solicitors. Some of those who previously were solely solicitors began adding fundraising planning to their package of services. The distinction was irreversibly eliminated when telemarketing came into vogue as a fundraising medium, causing the easy dissimilarity between fundraising executives and solicitors to be lost forever.

Under contemporary legal precepts, many of those who are, generically, professional fundraising consultants are considered professional solicitors. This results in two problems. First, despite recent changes in practice, professional solicitors still suffer from the stigma of the past—the image of being the underbelly of philanthropy. Consequently, professional fundraising executives are loath to be viewed—by charities, their colleagues, or the regulators—as professional solicitors.

Second, the state charitable solicitation acts nearly uniformly treat professional solicitors more harshly than is the case with professional fundraisers. Registration fees and bond requirements are higher, and more disclosure and reporting are required. Fundraisers are forced to go through great legalistic contortions and acrobatics to avoid being classified under the law as solicitors, even though their services often partake of the functions of both. But the law does not accommodate this hybrid form, except to treat consultants and solicitors the same—as solicitors—which only compounds the problem and magnifies inherent unfairness. Indeed, some state charitable solicitation acts have essentially abandoned the distinction, regarding just about everyone who assists charities in the fundraising process as solicitors.

Even if the assumption is granted that the professional solicitor is the bane of the field, reasonable individuals should somehow be able to conjure up a workable definition of the two categories. The distinction between those who have some role in the solicitation process and those who do not is, for the most part, obsolete. It makes little or no sense to regard a consultant as a solicitor simply because among the bundle of services performed is the function of helping to place fundraising literature in the mail. A more appropriate differentiation would be between those who first receive the donated funds and remit a net amount (if any) to the charities, and those whose services are paid for by charitable organizations that received the contributions directly. What is needed is a definitional distinction that allows the states to monitor and prosecute the weekend bandits without unduly and unnecessarily regulating the legitimate fundraising executives and consultants.

SCOPE OF STATE LAW

Every statutory law has its boundaries; a statute can reach only so far. What are the outer limits of a charitable solicitation act? Oddly, there is almost no law on the point. Given that the applicability of these acts almost always arises in the context of *fundraising*, which commonly entails the request for *contributions*, and inasmuch as the other principal terms employed are *charitable* and *solicitation*, it would not be unreasonable to assume that the state charitable solicitation acts do not extend beyond the realm of the solicitation of gifts (and perhaps grants). Yet, at least in some states, that assumption is erroneous.

In one of the most extreme of these circumstances, a state's attorney general asserted, the state's fundraising law also embraces the *sale* of goods or services by or on behalf of charitable organizations where it is advertised that some or all of the proceeds of the sale will be paid over for charitable purposes. This position is manifested in an attorney general opinion, holding that a person who solicits funds for a charitable organization, representing that a portion of the proceeds will be used for charitable purposes, must be licensed as a professional fundraiser, even though the transaction embodying the "solicitation" is wholly a sale. In the case, an individual solicited advertisements for a book, to be published by a charitable organization, representing to prospective advertisers that part of the funds so earned would be used for charitable purposes.

In the analysis underlying this opinion, there is considerable discussion about circumstances in which a transaction is partly a gift and partly a purchase; there should be no question that transactions of this nature (see Chapter 6) invoke the statute. Yet, the opinion extends to transactions in which there is no element of a gift (nor solicitation of a gift in the context of a purchase).

The state's statutory definition of a contribution excludes most dues; the attorney general read that exclusion to mean that all other forms of purchases of services (or goods) are to be treated as contributions! Despite this opinion, it is hard to believe that a state's charitable solicitation act applies to sales transactions simply because some proceeds of the transactions will be devoted to charitable ends. This would mean that a charitable organization that generates revenue only through the sale of goods or services (such as a theater or home for the elderly or a charity raising money by means of a car wash or bake sale) would have to comply with one or more charitable solicitation acts.

Regarding the matter of the boundary, this attorney general opinion also asserted that, if "simply because the donor [note the term] was provided some benefit, such a payment could not be deemed a charitable contribution, then all of the safeguards established in [the act] could easily be circumscribed by an organization or fundraiser." In fact, the matter is precisely the opposite: If a payment is not a charitable contribution, the transaction would fall outside the reach of the statute. The "safeguards" of these laws would be "circumscribed," but only because they simply do not apply.

What this matter comes down to is that a purchase is not a contribution; only a contribution is a contribution. A court sagely observed: "But at the end of the day, even if you put a calico dress on it and call it Florence, a pig is still a pig." An attorney general or other state official can try to dress up a purchase and call it a gift, but the objective analysis remains that a purchase is not a gift.

In one instance, an attorney general's office attempted to apply the state's charitable solicitation act to the solicitation of corporate sponsors for a marathon conducted to generate proceeds for a charitable organization. The matter found its way into court, where it was held that the statute was inapplicable. The court concluded that the transaction was a "commercial" one and that it did not involve "gifts." As the court succinctly stated, the solicitation had "nothing to do with philanthropy." That is the correct statement of the law generally: These statutes do not apply where the charitable "fundraising" does not entail the soliciting or making of any contributions or grants.

Thus, notwithstanding the state of the "law" in this one jurisdiction, the better view is that the state charitable solicitation acts apply only where the transaction involved entails, in whole or in part, a contribution. If a state legislature wanted to expand its charitable solicitation act to encompass all sales of goods and services by and for charities, presumably it could do so; such an expansion of the law, however, might prove impolitic.

THE FUNDRAISER'S CONTRACT

The term *professional fundraiser* is defined under the charitable solicitation statutes of many states (see Chapter 3). A one-word generic definition of a professional fundraiser, however, is *consultant*—or, in more formal legal parlance, *independent contractor.* The latter term is used in law to differentiate someone from an *employee.* But, a key word in the term is *contractor.*

Almost all consultants have a written agreement with their clients. It is axiomatic, then, that a professional fundraiser should have a written contract with each charitable client. In fact, several state laws require that the relationship between a charitable organization and a professional fundraiser (and/or professional solicitor) be the subject of a written contract.

The reasons for a written agreement are obvious. The principal one is to avoid disagreements later about what each party to the arrangement is expected or required to do. At the other extreme, a written memorialization gives the substantive basis for litigation, should that prove necessary.

Basic Elements

What are the basic elements that should be in a contract between a charitable organization and a professional fundraiser? The place to begin in answering that question is to enumerate the nine elements that any contract of this nature should contain. They are:

1. A description of the services to be provided by the party designated as the provider of the services

2. A statement of the fees to be paid by the party designated to receive the services

3. A provision indicating legal ownership of any property that may be utilized or created in the contractual relationship

4. A provision stating the duration of the agreement

5. A provision stating the parties' ability to terminate the agreement

6. A provision stating the state's law that governs interpretation of the agreement

7. An indemnification clause, whereby one party agrees to absorb the costs of certain liabilities found against the other party

8. A provision stating that the contract memorializes the entire agreement between the parties and cannot be amended except in writing by the parties

9. A statement of the effective dates of the agreement

These items, then, should be reflected in any contract between a charitable organization and a professional fundraiser. Many of the specific clauses will vary, of course, depending on the type of fundraising involved. But, irrespective of whether the fundraising will utilize direct mail, special events, annual campaign, planned giving, or whatever, or whether the fundraising is in the context of a capital campaign, the advice is the same: The professional fundraiser and the charitable organization are best served by a reasonably detailed statement of services to be provided, and of amounts and schedules of fees to be paid.

Specific Elements

A clear statement about the amount and timing of payment of fees to the professional fundraiser will minimize, if not eliminate, the likelihood of fee disputes. If the fees are to be paid in phases, and the charitable organization is to make payment following the close of a phase, the professional fundraiser should be certain that the charity's payment obligations along the way are clearly stated. If the fundraiser desires timely payment, some monitoring and prodding of the charitable client may be necessary.

A full statement of services to be performed is the trick to avoiding breach-of-contract litigation. The professional fundraiser must thread a way between two extremes: not promise to do more than should or can be done, yet not make the statement of services so skimpy as to cause the charitable client to wonder what it is paying for.

The professional fundraiser should be cautious about verbal statements that may heighten expectations of the client. This type of statement may later arguably become part of the contractual relationship. Because of the potential validity of oral agreements, a clause confining the agreement to its written form is essential.

As noted earlier, it is important to state in a contract of this nature who owns each particular property that is to be used in connection with, or may be created as the result of, the provision of services. In the context of the professional fundraiser's contract, the ownership of these properties should be addressed: mailing lists, intellectual property, artwork, and photographs. Additional properties may also be the subject of an ownership clause.

It is rarely a good idea for a professional fundraiser to guarantee results to a charitable organization client. If this is done, however, the fundraiser should be certain that the guarantee—and any accompanying conditions—is well stated.

A charity's contract for professional fundraising assistance is a contract for what the law terms *specific performance*. This is particularly true where the charity is contracting with one or more individuals. The charitable organization involved should insist that the contract be nontransferable. These conditions are generally present when the professional fundraiser is a company. The charity is contracting with the particular firm and presumably has no interest in having the obligation to perform services transferred to another company (or to an individual). Indeed, the charity may insist that the contract specify the provision of services by one or more named fundraising professionals who are employed by or otherwise affiliated with the company.

When the fundraising professional is an individual, the contract should state that he or she is rendering services as an independent contractor, rather than as an employee (assuming that is the case).

If the agreement states that the charitable organization client is to provide an approval (e.g., of the text of a letter or the graphics of a brochure), the agreement should also state that the approval must be in writing. The professional fundraiser should subsequently be certain that the approval is obtained on a timely basis, in writing. Also, it is appropriate to stipulate that these needed approvals will not be "unreasonably withheld."

Fee Arrangements

Caution should be exercised by the fundraising professional in describing the fee arrangement. It is considered, in many quarters, to be unprofessional or even unethical for a fundraiser to be compensated on a contingent, percentage, commission, or similar fee basis. Antitrust laws, however, may preclude enforcement of this type of prohibition, which usually is in a code of ethics. In general, a fee arrangement under these terms is by no means illegal, although in extreme instances a contingent fee arrangement may jeopardize the tax-exempt status of the client charity.

Contingent fee arrangements exist in many ways in addition to a stated percentage of contributions received. For example, compensation tied to the number of solicitation letters mailed, where the fundraiser controls the timing and extent of the mailing, is a form of contingent compensation.

A percentage limitation, in state law, on the amount of compensation that can be paid by a charitable organization to a professional fundraiser is unconstitutional (see Chapter 9).

Solicitor Status

Some state laws preclude a fundraiser from treatment as a professional fundraiser where the compensation is other than a "flat fixed fee" arrangement. If the compensation is otherwise, the professional may be classified as a professional solicitor (discussed previously). This adverse result can in turn lead to more stringent government regulation. A trend in charitable lawmaking is to stringently monitor and restrict the activities of solicitors. This is being done by means of strenuous pre-campaign contract reviews, greater disclosure and reporting requirements, and more.

The description of services in the contract should be reviewed from this definitional standpoint. One of the essential elements of the definition of a professional solicitor is an active participation in the solicitation process. A professional fundraiser can all too easily fall into this trap by agreeing to, for example, mail the solicitation letters or place the solicitation telephone calls.

Another characteristic of a professional solicitor often is that this type of a person receives the gifts directly from the donors and remits the net amount to the charity. A professional fundraiser should be paid a fee by the charity, with the charity having received the gross amount of the gifts directly; the contract should make that feature clear, or at least avoid any language contemplating the receipt of gift funds by the professional fundraiser.

State Laws

It goes without saying that parties to a contract are expected to obey all applicable laws. It is not necessary, however, for the contract to contain language expressly reflecting that general obligation.

Nonetheless, among the laws that directly relate to both the professional fundraiser and the charitable organization client are the various charitable solicitation acts. These laws impose registration, reporting, bonding, and other requirements on both professional fundraisers and their charitable clients (see Chapter 3). Because the registration and reporting forms for both parties cross-refer, the professional fundraiser should at least contemplate a clause in the contract that requires both parties to notify each other of the states in which they are registered and of any adverse regulatory developments that may arise.

Many states mandate that certain elements be in the contract that a charitable organization has with a professional fundraiser and/or with a professional solicitor. These laws usually also require retention of the contract in the records of the parties for a stated period of time (usually three years after the conclusion of the solicitation) and often require filing of the contract with the state. (It must be reiterated that a charitable organization, professional fundraiser, and/or professional solicitor involved in a solicitation in one or more of these states is expected to comply with the requirements of each of them. Thus, for example, a contract with respect to a solicitation intended to take place in all of these states should contain all of the provisions mandated by each of these laws.)

This contract content requirement is typically more extensive with respect to a contract involving a professional solicitor. For example, in one state, the rule involving a charitable organization's contract with a professional fundraiser is that the contract must "contain such information as will enable [the regulatory office] to identify the services the [professional fundraiser] is to provide and the manner of his [or her or its] compensation." By contrast, under the law of this state, the contract between a charitable organization and a professional solicitor must "clearly state the respective obligations" of the parties, and "state the minimum amount which the charitable organization shall receive as a result of the solicitation campaign, which minimum amount shall be stated as a percentage of gross revenue."

One of the most extensive contract content requirements applicable to agreements between charitable organizations and professional solicitors is that of the state in which the contract must contain provisions as to (1) an "estimated reasonable budget disclosing the target amount of funds to be raised over the contract period"; (2) the type and amount of projected expenses for the period; (3) the amount projected to be remitted to the charitable organization; (4) the duration of the agreement; (5) the "geographic scope" of the fundraising; (6) a description of the methods of fundraising to be employed; (7) a clause assuring "record keeping and accountability"; (8) if the contract provides that the fundraiser will retain or be paid a stated percentage of the gross amount raised, an estimate of the "target gross amount" to be raised and to be remitted to the charitable organization; (9) if the contract provides for payment at an hourly rate for fundraising, the total estimated hourly amount and the estimated number of hours to be spent in fundraising; (10) the amounts of all commissions, salaries, and fees charged by the fundraiser, and its agents and employees; (11) the method used for computing these commissions, salaries, and fees; (12) if the fundraiser, its agents and employees, or members of the families of these persons own an interest in, manage, or are a supplier or vendor of fundraising goods or services, disclosure of that relationship; (13) if the foregoing rule is applicable, the method of determining the related supplier's or vendor's charges; and (14) the fact that the contract was approved and accepted by a majority of the directors of the charitable organization and by the president of the organization.

One state has a law prohibiting the appearance of two provisions in a contract between a charitable organization and a professional fundraiser or professional solicitor: (1) the charitable organization may not use contributions from a solicitation for its charitable purposes until some or all fundraising expenses have been paid; and (2) the fundraiser or solicitor may engage in a direct mail or other solicitation in the name of the charitable organization for the purpose of "paying or offsetting preexisting fundraising expenses."

In one state, the contract between a charitable organization and a professional fundraiser or professional solicitor (or commercial co-venturer) may be canceled by the charitable organization within 15 days after the date the contract is filed with the state; this right of cancellation must be stated in the agreement. In another state, if this type of contract involves a "possibility" that the charitable organization "might ultimately receive" less than 50 percent of the gross receipts of the solicitation involved, that fact must be "specifically and prominently" disclosed in the contract (and orally, before execution of the contract).

Conclusion

As is the case with all laws, everyone involved is presumed to know them. In the fundraising context, both the contracting charity and the professional fundraiser are expected to know and conform to the state charitable solicitation acts. Some of these laws, as noted, mandate the contents of contracts between charities, fundraisers, and solicitors. These are independent obligations, bearing potential liabilities (e.g., civil penalties and/or injunctive relief) for both parties. Neither party should assume that the other is in compliance with these laws.

A professional fundraiser should have a solid, comprehensive, and professional-looking prototype agreement to present to prospective charitable clients. With a suitable agreement, a professional fundraiser can concentrate on development work without fear of the adverse consequences of a defective contract.

CHARITY AUCTIONS AND FUNDRAISING LAW

Considerable confusion and misunderstanding surround the federal tax law applicable to the conduct of charity auctions, particularly regarding application of the charitable gift substantiation and quid pro quo contribution rules (see Chapter 8). This uncertainty was manifested in two articles in a personal finance magazine, where it was written that a "special circle of tax hell has been carved out for you if you're involved in one of today's hottest fundraising activities: charity auctions."

This body of law has seven elements:

1. The tax treatment, with respect to the charitable organization, of the funds expended by the patrons at the auction

2. The charitable contribution deduction available to those who contribute something to be auctioned

3. The charitable contribution deduction that may be available to those who acquire an item at a charity auction

4. The substantiation rules

5. The quid pro quo contribution rules

6. The state sales tax rules

7. The federal tax rules for reporting the event to the IRS

(There can be different and additional complexities when the fundraising event is a lottery, raffle, or other game of chance.)

Charity Auctions as Businesses

The federal tax law envisions a tax-exempt organization as being a bundle of *businesses*. For this purpose, a *business* is any activity that entails the production of income from the sale of goods or the performance of services. An activity does not lose its identity as a business merely because it is carried on within a larger aggregate of similar activities or within a larger complex of other endeavors of the organization.

Some businesses are *related* ones, in that the conduct of them helps advance the organization's exempt purposes (other than simply through the generation of funds). Other businesses are *unrelated*, because the conduct of them does not relate to achievement of a charitable, educational, or similar purpose; this type of business usually is carried on solely for the purpose of generating income. (See Chapter 7.)

Thus, a charity auction is a business; it is the performance of a service (the sale of items). These auctions are not inherently exempt functions; in the case of private schools, for example, the conduct of an auction (a common occurrence) is not an educational undertaking. Consequently, the conduct of a charity auction is the conduct of an unrelated business by the charitable organization.

The net revenue of a charity auction would, therefore, be taxable as unrelated business income, were it not for one or more exceptions. The principal exception relates to the fact that, for an unrelated business to create taxable income, it must be *regularly carried on*. An annual auction held by a charitable organization is not an activity that is regularly carried on; thus, the net income is not taxable as unrelated business income. (If a charity were to hold an auction every weekend, however, this exception would not be available.)

Another important exception is the one for businesses that constitute the sale of merchandise, substantially all of which has been donated to the exempt organization. This exception was written for nonprofit thrift shops, but is available in the case of auctions, irrespective of their frequency.

The third exception is for businesses in which substantially all the work in carrying it on is performed by volunteers. If a charity auction is conducted entirely by volunteers, the net income from it is not taxed as unrelated business income. (Some charity auctions are able to rely on all three exceptions.)

Thus, it is almost inconceivable that the "net income" realized as the result of a charity auction would be subject to unrelated business income taxation, but only because of one or more statutory exceptions.

Charitable Contribution Deductions—Donors of Items to Be Auctioned

In general, the contribution of an item to a charitable organization, for the purpose of being auctioned creates a charitable contribution deduction. The usual rule is that the deduction is equal to the fair market value of the contributed property. (This analysis is based on the assumption that the charity holding the auction is a public charity and not a private foundation.)

There are, however, some wrinkles here. If the item donated is tangible personal property that has appreciated in value, the charitable deduction is confined to the donor's basis in the property. This is because the gift was made for an unrelated purpose—sale by the charitable donee.

If the item donated has a value in excess of $5,000, the deduction depends on a bona fide appraisal (see Chapter 8). An appraisal summary must be included with the donor's tax return. The charitable organization must report the sale to the IRS (assuming the auction took place within three years of the gift).

There is no charitable deduction for a gift of the right to the use of property. Thus, for example, if someone contributes the opportunity to use his or her vacation property for two weeks, there is no charitable deduction equal to the fair rental value of the property. (Moreover, the period of time the property is used by the winning bidder must be considered by the donating individual(s) as personal time for purpose of the rules regarding the deductibility of business expenses in connection with the property.)

There is no charitable deduction for a gift of services. Thus, for example, if a lawyer donates his or her will-drafting services, there is no charitable deduction equal to the hourly rate the lawyer would charge for his or her time in preparing the will. Notwithstanding this rule (found in the tax regulations, there would be no deduction in any event because, by statute, a charitable deduction is not available for gifts of property created by the donor.

Further, special rules apply when a business makes a charitable contribution of items from its inventory, a charitable contribution of scientific property used for research, and a charitable contribution of computer technology and equipment for elementary and secondary school purposes.

Substantiation rules apply with respect to gifts of items that have a value of $250 or more and are donated to, then auctioned by a charitable organization (discussed ahead). Other substantiation rules apply irrespective of the value of the contributed property (*id.*).

Charitable Contribution Deductions—Acquirers of Items at an Auction

The law in the area of charitable giving in general once was that, for a payment to a charitable organization to be deductible as a gift, the payor had to have a *donative intent*. The law, however, has shifted to a more mechanical computation: In general, deductible payments to a charity are those that exceed the fair market value of anything that the "donor" may receive in return, other than items of insignificant value. Nonetheless, in the auction and comparable contexts, the *donative intent* rule still applies: No part of a payment to a charitable organization that is in consideration for goods or services can be a contribution unless the person intended to, and did, make a payment in an amount that exceeds the fair market value of the goods or services.

Whether one who acquires an item at a charity auction is entitled to a charitable contribution deduction is another matter. Thus, the above-referenced article in the personal finance magazine correctly observed that, in explanation of enactment of the substantiation and quid pro quo rules (discussed ahead): "It was widely assumed that Congress was after folks who buy stuff at auctions and then deduct most or even all of the price as a charitable contribution."

There are two schools of thought here; both are valid on their face. One is that the auction is the marketplace, so that whatever is paid for an item at an auction is its fair market value at that time. Pursuant to this view, the transaction is always a purchase in its entirety; there is no gift element and thus no charitable contribution deduction.

The other school of thought is that an item auctioned at a charity auction has a fair market value, irrespective of the amount expended for it at the auction. This approach allows a charitable deduction for an amount paid at a charity auction for an item of property that is in excess of the value of the property. The likelihood of a charitable deduction in this setting is enhanced if the charity publishes a catalog of the items to be auctioned, including estimates of the value of the items.

In actual practice, most items disposed of at a charity auction are acquired for a value that does not involve any gift element (because the amount paid is roughly equal to the value of the item or perhaps is less), and thus there is no charitable contribution deduction. If an individual wants to validly claim a charitable deduction, the burden of proof is on the putative donor, who must prove that the amount paid was in excess of the property's fair value.

This burden of proof can probably be met when it is relatively easy to prove the fair market value of the item, such as an appliance or automobile. Where the value of an item is difficult to discern, however, it will be arduous for a patron of the auction to convince the IRS that a portion of the amount paid was a deductible gift.

The determination of the fair market value of an item is the work of appraisers; essentially, they look at comparables. If a house sold for $200,000, all other factors being equal, that is the value at the time of sale of neighboring houses. Thus, the critical factor is the determination of the *market*. This involves geographical, economical, and timing elements.

Some disparage the idea that the value of an item sold at a charity auction is set at the time of that purchase. There cannot be any dispute, however, that an auction constitutes a market. Thus, one must logically assume that the price paid for an item at a charity auction is its fair market value. This is particularly the case where the value is difficult to ascertain commercially. For example, if a charitable organization auctioned an automobile with a sticker price of $30,000, and received $35,000 for the vehicle, it is reasonable to assume that the individual who acquired the vehicle is entitled to a charitable deduction of $5,000. If, however, a charitable organization auctioned a football, signed by members of the team, which the organization valued at $500 and which sold for $2,000, who is to say what the value of that item was at the time of the auction? An ardent fan may believe the ball is priceless. The organization may have made a good-faith estimate of $500 of value, but that may not necessarily be the true value of the item under the circumstances of its sale. If the auction is regarded as the marketplace and that is the sole consideration, the fair market value of the football was $2,000, not $500.

Substantiation rules apply with respect to gifts made in the context of acquiring an item auctioned by a charitable organization, assuming the gift element is $250 or more.

Substantiation Rules

The position of the IRS on charity auctions can be found in rulings as far back as 1967. There is little question, however, that charitable organizations and their donors have not, over the ensuing years, understood the IRS's stance, which, frankly, has been quite clear and sensible. Consequently, Congress believed it had to enact legislation in this area and, in 1993, it did.

At this point, it is necessary to place this subject in a real-life context. Can it honestly be said that an individual who attends an auction sponsored by a charitable organization is there to make a gift? Someone who wants to contribute to the charitable organization can obviously do so at any time; certainly there is no need to attend the charity's auction. Individuals participate in the auction to help support the charitable organization *and* to purchase items. Also, frequent visits to the bar (a charity auction should never be without at least one) or peer pressure often is the reason underlying high bids, not donative intent.

A statutory substantiation rule is this: A donor who makes a separate charitable contribution of $250 or more in a year must, to be able to deduct the gift, obtain the requisite written substantiation from the donee charitable organization. This substantiation must be an acknowledgment of the gift and must contain the following information: (1) the amount of money and a description (but not the value) of any property other than money that was contributed; (2) whether the donee organization provided any goods or services in consideration, in whole or in part, for any money or property contributed; and (3) a description and good-faith estimate of the value of any goods or services so provided.

These rules are applicable with respect to gifts of items to be auctioned (assuming a charitable contribution deduction is available or desired). Also, as far as acquisition of an item at a charity auction is concerned, if there is no gift element, it is clear that the rules do not apply.

Where, however, (1) the patron at a charity auction believes that he or she had made a charitable contribution in the course of acquiring an item, (2) the ostensible gift element is $250 or more, and (3) a charitable deduction is desired, these rules come into play. The "donor" must notify the charitable organization that he or she believes that a gift was made at the auction, with the intent of receiving the necessary acknowledgment. If the charity agreed that a gift was made, it would issue a written substantiation showing the amount that was "contributed" (here, the full amount of the winning bid) and a description and good-faith estimate of the value of the item acquired. The difference, then, would be the amount deductible as a charitable gift.

The process would not function so smoothly if the charitable organization believed that no part of the payment is a charitable gift. It might refuse to issue the acknowledgment or refuse to commit itself to a good-faith estimate of the value of the item auctioned. As a practical matter, however, relations with donors and patrons are such that a charity usually cannot be that cavalier.

These rules place considerable pressure on charitable organizations. To return to the previous example, is the organization willing to issue a substantiation acknowledgment that the auctioned football has a value of $2,000, so that the winning bidder can claim a charitable deduction of $1,500? A charitable organization that knowingly provides a false written substantiation to a donor may be subject to the penalty for aiding and abetting an understatement of tax liability.

Quid Pro Quo Rules

Congress has required this: When a person makes a gift to a charitable organization in excess of $75 and receives something of material value in return, the charitable donee is to make a good-faith estimate of the value of the item and notify the donor that only the difference between the fair market value of the item and the amount paid for it (if any) is deductible as a charitable contribution.

Here, the application of the tax rules in the charity auction context becomes less clear. Superficially, the quid pro quo contribution rules would seem to apply in the charity auction setting where the amount transferred exceeds $75 and there is a gift element.

A *quid pro quo contribution* is a payment "made partly as a contribution and partly in consideration for goods or services provided to the payor by the donee organization." Thus, it can be argued that the purchase of an item at a charity auction, at a price known to be in excess of the fair market value of the item, is both a contribution and a payment made in consideration of something (a purchase).

Nonetheless, if the donor and the donee are in harmony, and if the amount paid at a charity auction exceeds $75, the charitable organization can make the necessary disclosure, notifying the donor that the deductible amount is confined to the payment less the value of the item. It is important that the charitable organization be correct in this regard, because of the penalties imposed.

Sales Tax Rules

As discussed, every transaction at an auction (for the benefit of a charity or otherwise) is, in whole or substantial part, a *purchase*. Thus, a charity conducting an auction is engaging in *sales*, which can trigger application of the state's sales tax. This is a state-by-state matter; thus it is difficult to generalize on the point, other than to say that the law of the applicable state should be reviewed.

A state is likely to exempt charitable organizations from having to pay the state's sales tax. This exemption, however, does not mean that the entity is exempt from the requirement of collecting the sales tax.

FUNDRAISING REGULATION BENEFITS

A federal court of appeals ruled that, where a state charitable solicitation act requires a sliding-scale registration fee based on a charitable organization's nationwide level of public contributions in the prior year, the requirement is lawful. The underlying justification for this fee structure was the tremendous benefit charitable organizations derive from state regulation. This appellate court definitely misconstrued the fundraising regulatory milieu.

First, the court cast the ability of a charitable organization to solicit funds in a state as a "privilege." That is not true; charitable fundraising is the exercise of a "right" and that right is protected by constitutional law principles (see Chapter 9). The court's overall analysis was flawed because of this faulty lens through which it viewed the facts.

The court found that the registration fee ($200 annually in the case) amounted to a "constitutionally sound" user fee, representing a "fair, if imperfect, approximation of the cost of using [the state's] facilities and services for the charity's benefit." The facts were said to show that the state's costs of "monitoring charities increase with larger charities." This cost increase, the court observed, "arises because larger charities generally generate more registration and renewal documents to review, require more research relating to administrative, management, and membership activities, and give rise to more public inquiries, more paperwork requiring data entry, and more investigative effort." Thus, "because a charity's fee is directly related to the workload the charity is expected to create for the [state], the sliding-scale fee is a fair, if imperfect, approximation of [the state's] costs."

This lame rationalization for the sliding-scale fee does not make sense. Why did the court passively accept the assertion that larger charitable organizations generate more paperwork for the bureaucracy than smaller ones? The opinion is silent as to any facts in support of this conclusion (there probably weren't any); indeed, the conclusion seems counterintuitive. It stands to reason just as soundly that the larger charitable organizations will be better known, better organized and staffed, and better advised.

Might not the "facts" relied on by the court be precisely the opposite? The larger, more recognizable and sophisticated charities may elicit fewer inquiries from the public and thus require less investigative effort. The larger charities are likely to entail less "research." Their registration and renewal documents are likely to be more properly prepared and complete, causing infrequent review and follow-up problems. How can larger amounts reflected in numbers cause more "data entry" time? It takes as much time to enter into a database "$100,000" as it does "$900,000." There will always be exceptions, of course, but these generalities are at least as valid as those placidly accepted by the court.

The court did not address the point of what would happen to soliciting charities if all states were to adopt this fee approach. Fifty-one jurisdictions (including the District of Columbia) charging $200 a year is an annual cost of $10,200.

The court's treatment of the user fee rationale is the most questionable. Conceding that the state's fee, "although not the typical user fee, nonetheless fits comfortably within the user fee category," the court held that "charities seeking to solicit in [the state] use the state's apparatus for regulating charities." This, the court ascertained, is a "benefit," in the form of the "privilege of soliciting in [the state] where donor confidence is enhanced owing to the state's regulation of charities."

Where does one begin to assess these conclusions? How about the thought that charities soliciting in the state "use" the state's "apparatus for regulating charities"? Forced on them while they kick and scream is the reality; "use" is not. The regulation is compulsive and burdening; it is not a "benefit."

The amorphous definition of *user fee* wrought by the court is illogical. The law is that this type of fee is one collected by a government as reimbursement for use of government-owned or government-provided facilities or services. The court wrote that the registration fee structure is a user fee because it represents a "fair, if imperfect, approximation of the cost of using [the state's] facilities and services for the charity's benefit." If these "benefits" combine to warrant a user fee, then every tax is a user fee. In contorting this registration fee into a user fee, the court basically nullified any meaningful distinction between user fees and general revenue taxes.

How about the precept that the state's regulation of charities "enhances donor confidence," so that the "apparatus" is a "benefit"? Oh, were that the case! The fact is that the state's statute and the rest of the charitable solicitation acts do no such thing. If "donor confidence" is so great, why the need for higher registration fees to pay for responses to public inquiries, investigations, and research? There is no evidence whatsoever that these laws enhance donor confidence. If anything, they undercut donor confidence by fooling the citizenry into thinking something meaningful is being done; they enhance donor cynicism.

A footnote in this opinion states that the state law provides charities with another benefit: "eliminating illegitimate charities." Come again? Then why is there all this need for the state administration, monitoring, investigations, and enforcement? In a separate (and wholly inconsistent) footnote, the court observed that the "largest single activity in the Office of the Secretary of State is the administration and enforcement of [the state's] laws governing charitable solicitations." With all these illegitimate charities gone, thanks to the fundraising law, who is the state regulating?

Courts are supposed to rule based on facts, not suppositions. The irrationality continued as the court wrote about still another putative "benefit" to charitable organizations from this "apparatus": This law is causing the level of charitable giving to increase, "as citizens are likely to donate to charities that have been investigated and found to be reputable." There is absolutely no factual basis for this conclusion. Is a charitable organization considered "reputable" and thus more entitled to gift support if it has weathered an investigation by a state agency?

The court offered one more appalling assertion—another "benefit" derived from regulation. The charities soliciting in the state "may" find that their "share of available funds" will increase. Why? Because, "as illegitimate charities are weeded out, the amount of available funds will be spread among a smaller pool of charities." This type of factless analysis and writing is essentially pure speculation.

As charitable organizations around the country struggle under the annual registration, reporting, disclosure, and other burdens that many state charitable solicitation acts impose, they will draw no comfort from the thought that they are in fact being "benefited."

FUNDRAISING AND PRIVATE INUREMENT

Another federal court of appeals concluded that a fundraising company was not an insider, for private inurement purposes (see Chapter 2), with respect to the public charity known as the United Cancer Council (UCC).

Basically, the UCC was (it has since become bankrupt) a public charity, so recognized by the IRS. The UCC entered into a five-year direct mail fundraising contract with the company. While the UCC received about $2.25 million as the result of the fundraising, the company received more than $4 million in fees. The parties had co-ownership rights in the UCC's mailing list.

The lower court held that the UCC paid the fundraising company excessive compensation, that the company exploited its rights over the list for its private gain, that the company was an insider with respect to the UCC, and that this relationship created private inurement. The court upheld the IRS's retroactive revocation of the UCC's exempt status, to the date when the contract began.

The court of appeals grounded its findings on the premise that the lower court's "classification of [the fundraising company] as an insider of UCC was based on the fundraising contract." That is, the focus was on the contract's terms. The lower court and the IRS were characterized as contending that the "contract was so advantageous to [the fundraising company] and so disadvantageous to UCC that the charity must be deemed to have surrendered the control of its operations and earnings to the noncharitable enterprise that it had hired to raise money for it."

The appellate court wrote that "[f]undraising has become a specialized professional activity and many charities hire specialists in it." It continued: "If the charity's contract with the fundraiser makes the latter an insider, triggering

342 Perspectives and Commentaries

the inurement clause of section 501(c)(3) and so destroying the charity's tax exemption, the charitable sector of the economy is in trouble."

The UCC's "sound judgment" in entering into the contract with the fundraising firm was questioned by the appellate court. The court wrote that the UCC "drove (so far as the record shows) the best bargain that it could, but it was not a good bargain." Nonetheless, the court continued, the private inurement proscription "is designed to prevent the siphoning of charitable receipts to insiders of the charity, not to empower the IRS to monitor the terms of arm's-length contracts made by charitable organizations with the firms that supply them with essential inputs, whether premises, paper, computers, legal advice, or fundraising services." The lower court and the IRS's position, wrote the court, "threatens to unsettle the charitable sector by empowering the IRS to yank a charity's tax exemption simply because the Service thinks its contract with its major fundraiser is too one-sided in favor of the fundraiser, even though the charity has not been found to have violated any duty of faithful and careful management that the law of nonprofit corporations may have laid upon it."

The court said it could not find anything in the facts to support the "theory that [the fundraising company] seized control of UCC and by doing so became an insider." The Court stated: "There is nothing that corporate or agency law would recognize as control." It wrote that the trial court used the word *control* "in a special sense not used elsewhere, so far as we can determine, in the law, including the federal tax law." (The lower court defined an *insider* as a person who has "significant control over the [charitable] organization's activities.") The appellate court concluded that "[t]here was no division of charitable revenues to an insider here, nothing that smacks of self-dealing, disloyalty, breach of fiduciary obligation or other misconduct of the type aimed at by a provision of law that forbids a charity to divert its earnings to members of the board or other insiders."

This court of appeals remanded this case to the trial court for consideration in light of the doctrine of private benefit (*id.*). Regarding this remand, the court wrote that the "board of a charity has a duty of care . . . and a violation of that duty which involved the dissipation of the charity's assets might (we need not decide whether it would—we leave that issue to the [lower court] in the first instance) support a finding that the charity was conferring a private benefit, even if the contracting party did not control, or exercise undue influence over, the charity. This, for all we know, may be such a case." The case was ultimately settled, so the private benefit doctrine was never applied to its facts.

This opinion, as these things go, is extraordinary; it is wrong in so many ways, both procedurally and substantively. Regarding procedure, it is common for a federal appellate court opinion to begin by discussing the appropriate standard for the court's review. It is noteworthy that the court of appeal skipped this step in its UCC opinion.

Yet here is what this same court had to say on the subject in another case: "The [lower court's] holding [that an organization was not entitled to exemption] must be sustained on appeal unless clearly erroneous." The UCC case should also have been reviewed under the "clearly erroneous" standard.

The court of appeals is not alone in adhering to this standard. Here is another appellate court: "A finding that a corporation is not operated exclusively for charitable purposes cannot be disturbed unless clearly erroneous." Another one: "We review the [lower court] decision [finding an organization not entitled to exemption] for clear error." Another: "[The] factual finding [that an organization is operated for a substantial nonexempt purpose] [is] reviewable under the clearly erroneous standard." One more: "[O]ur review [of a denial of tax exemption] is on a clearly erroneous basis."

It thus was outside the province of this court of appeals to decide whether the lower court was right or wrong. The most it should have done was determine if the trial court was clearly erroneous in its UCC decision. Certainly, right or wrong, the lower court's judgment in this case was not clearly erroneous.

Regarding substance, many in the nonprofit sector were cheered by this finding that a fundraising company was not functioning as an insider with respect to a charitable organization, for purposes of the private inurement proscription. Those who supported this outcome did so because they applauded what the court said. Unfortunately, the court lacked the authority to say what it said, and what it said does not have much to do with the facts of this case, which admittedly are extreme. Radical facts often elicit radical decisions (which probably is one reason why the IRS litigated this one).

Everyone likes to win; no one likes to lose. This is certainly true in litigation. Here, the nonprofit sector won (at least in the short run) and the government lost. Yet there are wins and there are wins. Some wins rest on reason; they are correct outcomes. Indeed, most wins are in this category. Other wins, however, are flukes, oddball results that are not deserved. This appellate court opinion is in the oddball category. The court, in trying to help the nonprofit sector, distorted or strayed widely from the facts of the case and the applicable law.

This appellate court, obviously, was concerned with the IRS. It saw the agency poised to run amok in this area, out to revoke the tax-exempt status of every charity that gets entangled in what in hindsight is a bad business deal. The IRS was viewed as "yanking" charitable exemptions for those who enter into "one-sided" contracts. The court mused that if the "charity's contract with the fundraiser makes the latter an insider . . . the charitable sector of the economy is in trouble."

An argument does not get any more disingenuous than that. The lower court never made any such statement. In fact, this court wrote: "We are not holding that an arm's-length arrangement that produces a poor result for an organization necessarily would cause the organization to lose its tax-exempt status."

The fact is that the appellate court's position rested on an incorrect premise. It was inappropriate for it to write that the trial court's "classification of [the fundraiser] as an insider of UCC was based on the fundraising contract." Rather, the conclusion about insider status was based on the actual relationship between the parties that arose as the *consequence* of the contract. The facts are crystal clear that the fundraising company had the UCC in its clutches and exploited the charity for its private ends. It is nothing short of unbelievable for this appellate court to sweepingly assert that this contract was an arm's-length one and regard it as typical of fundraising contracts.

In its anti-IRS diatribe, the court of appeals faulted the IRS for being "ignorant" of contract law. The reverse is true: The court was ignorant of the law of tax-exempt organizations. How else to explain the astoundingly erroneous statement that the lower court's use of the word *control* is "not used elsewhere, so far as we can determine, in the law, including federal tax law"? To what extent did the court make this determination? It could have looked in the Internal Revenue Code, where the term *disqualified person*, as applied as part of the excess benefit transactions rules (*id.*) with respect to public charities like the UCC, is defined as any person who was "in a position to exercise substantial influence over the affairs of the organization." That definition is almost identical to the lower court's definition.

How about the assertion that "nothing [here] smacks of self-dealing"? Again, a mere glance at the Code would have been enlightening to the court. Although the self-dealing rules do not apply in this case, the appellate court brought them up. Self-dealing includes furnishing of services between a charity and a disqualified person, payment of compensation by a charity to a disqualified person, and use of assets of a charity by or for the benefit of a disqualified person. Contrary to the appellate court's belief, the facts in this case reflected rampant self-dealing (in the generic sense).

This case was to have been resolved by application of the private benefit doctrine. This could have amounted to quite a mess. The court of appeals never really addressed the question of whether there was private inurement in this case; it essentially focused on the question of whether the fundraising company was an insider in relation to the UCC. If there was private inurement (and there was) and that inurement was not insubstantial (and it was not), how could there not be private benefit? All forms of private inurement are also forms of private benefit; apparently the appellate court did not know that.

This appellate court had the opportunity to nicely solidify the law in this area, and interlace the private inurement doctrine with the excess benefit transaction rules. The court, by mischaracterizing the facts and misstating or overlooking law, wasted this opportunity and unnecessarily injected considerable confusion with respect to the matter of vendors, including fundraisers, as insiders.

FUNDRAISING AND FRAUD

In 2003, the U.S. Supreme Court decided a major fundraising regulation case. The case concerned regulation based on the percentage of contributions devoted to fundraising and other nonprogram expenses (see Chapter 9). This time, however, the state involved was alleging common-law and statutory fraud, committed by a for-profit fundraising company (Telemarketing). By contract with the charity, the company was paid 85 percent of the contributions collected. The state asserted that this arrangement, coupled with nondisclosure of the percentage compensation element to prospective donors, constituted fraud.

In this case, Telemarketing clearly had the more compelling position. The Supreme Court has thrice ruled that states cannot regulate charitable fundraising on the basis of fundraising expense percentages (*id.*). States have been repeatedly rebuffed in their attempts to equate the merits of a charity with its fundraising expense ratio (see Chapter 9). These percentages simply cannot be used by a government (or legitimately by any other entity) to assess worthiness or efficiency of charitable organizations.

This state was nonetheless trying to perpetuate this myopic approach to fundraising regulation merely by slapping another label on charitable fundraising: *fraudulent.* The attorney general's thought was that fundraising on behalf of a charitable organization, where the fundraising expense ratio is "high," is per se fraudulent. That approach should not be allowed. The Supreme Court has said that states can proceed against fraud in the charitable fundraising setting, but that does not mean that ostensibly high fundraising costs automatically constitute fraud.

One of the weaknesses of the position of the state lay in the matter of percentages themselves. There is nothing magic about the number 85. If fundraising costs of 85 percent mean fraud, then what about 75 percent? 55 percent? 25 percent? This approach would give states unwarranted latitude in selecting charities and fundraisers for prosecution. The state pulled a bit of a cheap trick by attaching to its complaint affidavits from donors who said they would not have given had they known of the relationship with Telemarketing. There are individuals who are unhappy when fundraising expenses are 10 or 15 percent. Some donors naively believe there ought not to be *any* fundraising costs. The several states that filed amicus briefs on behalf of the position of the principal state went so far as to assert that a fundraising solicitation includes a "representation" that "at least a substantial portion" of the gift will be used for charitable purposes, so apparently, in the view of the states, a 55 percent fundraising ratio amounts to fraud.

Also, the amount that Telemarketing received was hardly all profit. (The state was misleading in framing the issue when it wrote that the professional fundraiser "keeps almost all the funds donated.") It had operational expenses and financial obligations to third parties. The record did not reflect what Telemarketing's profit margin was; that is none of the government's business in any event. The guess here is that the amount of profit that Telemarketing had been earning in providing services to the charitable organization involved was far less than 85 percent and was certainly smaller than the amount of public funds wasted by the state in litigating this case (and losing) for more than 11 years. (The states had the audacity to whine before the Supreme Court about their "limited resources.")

Further, the state was arguing that, by soliciting contributions and not revealing the fundraising cost percentage, the fundraiser was "misleading" and being "deceptive" with respect to prospective donors. Engaging in that type of speech was cast as fostering "deceptive implications and half-truths." That is nonsense; charities routinely engage in fundraising without disclosing that information. Moreover, the Supreme Court has repeatedly held that that type of forced speech at the point of solicitation is contrary to free speech principles. Indeed, the state went so far as to assert that this form of speech can amount to fraud even where there are "legitimate reasons" for "high" solicitation costs.

Mischaracterization of the law and what this case was about was not confined to the words from the state. The *amici* states wrote that the issue before the Court was "whether the First Amendment protects fraudulent misrepresentations regarding the intended uses for charitable donations." That, of course, was not the issue at all; the issue was whether "high" fundraising costs and a refusal to voluntarily disclose those costs amount to fraud.

It was by no means clear why the Supreme Court accepted this case. The state supreme court did a fine job in explicating the law on the point; the High Court could have let that decision stand. The hope in some quarters was that the Court decided to take the case to make it obvious to the states one more time—inasmuch as they apparently have yet to get the message—that percentage-based fundraising charitable regulation is unconstitutional. Blithely terming expensive fundraising *fraud* does not change that. Essentially, that is how matters turned out.

The charitable fundraising community dodged the proverbial bullet in this case. There was fear that the Court might curtail free speech rights in this context. No one ever asserted that fraud in fundraising for charitable organizations was protected by free speech principles. Obviously, fraud by or on behalf of a charitable organization can be prosecuted. Thus, the (unanimous) opinion in this case was, literally, no news.

What the states set out to do in this case was to create in the law the principle that high fundraising costs are tantamount to per se fraud. In this they failed. The Supreme Court wrote that "[h]igh fundraising costs, without more, do not establish fraud." Also, "mere failure to volunteer the fundraiser's fee when contacting a potential donee, without more, is insufficient to state a claim for fraud."

Those two elements were the sum and substance of the states' case. The briefs are nearly silent on the matter of actual misleading affirmative representations. The court below ignored the affidavits on which the Court based its opinion. Indeed, the state supreme court wrote that "there is no alle-gation that [Telemarketing] made affirmative statements to potential donors." There is ongoing debate as to why the Court took this case; it is clear, however, that once into it the Court elected to decide it on the affirmative fraud basis, seizing on the statements in two affidavits.

The states tried to do exactly what the Court said they could not do: "gain case-by-case ground this Court has declared off limits to legislators." Their effort was a flop; the states obtained nothing with this opinion. The attorney general of the state can claim victory, but it is a classic hollow one. Indeed, the states were lucky. If the Supreme Court had not seized on and made much of two affidavits, the states would have lost in form what they lost in substance.

FUNDRAISING AND SUBSTANTIATION RULES

The U.S. Tax Court ruled that payments made to a charitable organization were not deductible as charitable gifts, because certain substantiation require-ments (see Chapter 8) were not met, in that there was an undisclosed return benefit. The amounts received by the charity were used to acquire a charitable split-dollar life insurance policy. The court held that there was a reasonable expectation that the charity would purchase the policy, which included a death benefit to one of the donors. The deduction was denied because this expec-tation was not disclosed and made the subject of a good-faith estimate in the substantiation documents.

Summary of the Facts

A married couple (H and W) claimed charitable contribution deductions for their payments (in 1997 and 1998) to a public charity of money, which the charity used to pay premiums on a life insurance policy for the life of W. The policy was a charitable split-dollar life insurance contract. Under this contract, the public charity was entitled to receive 56 percent of the death benefit and the couple's family trust was entitled to receive 44 percent of the benefit.

Eleven years before the first of these payments, the couple formed a fam-ily trust. They are the trustors, first designee trustees, and initial beneficiaries of this trust. Their children and W's parents or siblings become beneficiaries of the trust on the death of the couple.

In October 1997, H and W established a "foundation" (a donor-advised fund) within the public charity. On the same day, H wrote to the public charity stating that the family trust intended to purchase an insurance policy on the life of W and would grant the charity an option to acquire an interest in that policy. The policy was issued. The couple owned the policy through the trust.

H, as trustee of the trust, and the public charity entered into a death benefit option agreement, relating to the policy. H agreed to pay $4,000 of the $40,000 annual premium on the life insurance policy. H and the public charity agreed that, if the charity paid $36,000 of the annual premium, the charity would be entitled to its share of the death benefit. The agreement provided that the family trust and the public charity each own a separate interest in this life insurance policy.

Later in 1997, H and W sent money ($36,000) to the public charity for deposit into their foundation. An accompanying letter from H stated that the charity was not required to use the payment to pay the premium on the life insurance policy but that H "expected" the charity to use the payment to pay the premium. The next day, the couple paid the $4,000 of the premium.

The public charity credited $36,000 to the foundation account. It simultaneously debited the foundation account $36,000 to pay the charity's portion of the life insurance policy premium. Also, on the same day, the charity paid its $36,000 portion of the premium to the insurance company. The same series of transactions occurred the next year. As to both years, the public charity provided the couple with a document that stated that it did not provide any goods or services to the donors in return for the contribution.

The couple stopped making payments to the public charity after 1998. A statute that was designed to shut down these programs took effect for transfers after February 8, 1999. The IRS disallowed the charitable contribution deductions claimed by the couple for the transfers in 1997 and 1998 to the public charity.

Law

A person may not deduct a contribution of $250 or more unless the person substantiates the contribution with a contemporaneous written acknowledgment of the contribution by the charitable donee. This acknowledgment must include a statement as to whether the donee organization provided any goods or services in consideration for the contribution and provide a good-faith estimate of the value of any goods or services provided. A donee organization provides goods or services in consideration for a person's payment if, at the time the donor makes the payment to the donee, the payor receives or expects to receive goods or services in exchange for that payment.

The U.S. Supreme Court wrote that a charitable contribution is one for which the donor has "no expectation of any quid pro quo." The Court also wrote that the *"sine qua non* of a charitable contribution is a transfer of money or property without adequate consideration."

The federal tax law that effectively eliminated use of charitable split-dollar insurance plans makes reference to situations where there is an "understanding or expectation" that a person (such as a charitable organization) will directly or indirectly pay a premium in conjunction with one of these plans.

Analysis

The couple argued, of course, that the public charity was not required, and did not promise, to use the contributions to pay the premiums on the insurance policy on the life of W. The court held, however, that the public charity "provided consideration" for the payments because, at the time the payments were made to the charity, the couple "expected" to receive a share of the death benefit under the policy. Also, the court held, they "expected" the charity to use the funds they provided to pay the charity's portion of the premiums on the policy in 1997 and 1998.

This "expectation" on the part of the couple was deemed "reasonable" by the court because it was in the charity's financial interest to pay premiums on the couple's life insurance policy in return for a guaranteed death benefit.

The public charity did not state in its substantiation documents that it paid premiums for the insurance policy on the life of W under which the couple would receive a portion of the death benefit. Also, the charity failed to make a good-faith estimate of the value of these benefits. The court characterized this arrangement as a "scheme," including a "pot sweetened by charitable contribution deductions." The court held that the charitable contribution deduction was not available to this couple because the substantiation provided by the charitable donee was deficient.

Commentary

This is the type of decision that gives courts a bad name—for being simply unrealistic. Beating up on charitable split-dollar life insurance programs is easy in the aftermath of the frenzied and unprincipled reaction in Congress that resulted in the statute that essentially outlawed these programs, but one would think the court would give some thought to the real-world consequences of its holding.

The substantiation rules are designed to cause disclosure of, and reduction of a charitable contribution deduction by the amount of, the provision of a *good* or a *service* by the recipient charitable organization. The Tax Court, in this case, blithely slid around, equating the provision of *goods and services* with *consideration* and *benefits* with *expectations*. This was a careless reading of the law.

Individuals and other persons make charitable contributions with expectations all the time. A person donates a parcel of land to a charity, expecting that the charity will improve the property, thereby enhancing the value of a neighboring piece of property that the person owns. An individual makes a charitable contribution to a donor-advised fund, with the expectation that the charity will always follow the advice of the donor. Parents make contributions to a university with the expectation that one or more of their children will be admitted to the institution. These expectations are not goods or services; it has not been thought that these types of situations trigger a good-faith estimate by the charity of the "value" of these expectations.

It would have been perfectly acceptable (not to mention correct) for the court to rule that the public charity was not under any legally binding mandate to pay the premiums and that the charity independently *elected* to *invest* the money, in an opportunity provided by the couple, in a manner to generate a reasonable rate of return.

Now, instead, if the court is correct, an *expectation* is consideration defeating the concept of a charitable gift. Search in vain for authority for this conclusion in the opinion—it is not there. As noted, donors make (deductible) charitable gifts with expectations all the time.

This is one court opinion where the court simply lost its perspective. It was not sufficiently careful in its writing; the least it could have done was narrowly tailor its conclusions to the facts of the case. For example, the court sloppily wrote that the public charity's "receipts [more correctly, substantiation documents] do not comply with the substantiation requirements ... because [the public charity] incorrectly stated in the receipts that [H and W] received no consideration for their payments." Well, the substantiation requirements do not call for disclosure of *consideration*; they call for disclosure of and an estimate of the value of *goods or services* provided.

It may well be that, as the court wrote, H and W "received substantial benefits from [the public charity] under the life insurance policy." But that is just how matters turned out. In any event, it is not these benefits that the substantiation requirements, according to the court, intended to be disclosed. Rather, the ostensible good or service provided was the expectation of receiving these benefits.

The error inherent in this opinion is reflected in the applicable federal tax statutes. The body of law pertaining to these substantiation requirements makes reference to the provision of *goods or services*. The body of law concerning the charitable split-dollar insurance rules refers to *understandings or expectations*. If Congress wanted the substantiation rules to apply in connection with *expectations*, it would have written that statute to say as much. The Tax Court blithely lifted the language of one statute and dumped it onto another one, thereby substantially expanding the reach of the latter.

This is not so much an anticharitable split-dollar insurance holding as an expansive charitable gift substantiation requirement holding. Charities and fundraisers must be ever so cautious in preparing the substantiation documents, for now—if the Tax Court was correct—charities must not only value what they *provided* in exchange for a gift, they must peer into the misty reaches of donor motivation and intent to discern what donors *expect to be provided* and value that.

This is the great fault with this opinion. It is one of the first court opinions construing the substantiation requirements. It has placed donors and donees in a precarious position. Mere expectations can—according to this decision—defeat, in whole or in part, charitable contributions. The lack of a substantiation alone can preclude a charitable deduction. And just how is an expectation valued?

Unnecessarily, this court opinion injected great confusion into the realm of substantiation that, obviously, was not needed. Had the insurance benefit been provided in exchange for the transfer of the money, that clearly, would have to be valued and made the subject of a good-faith estimate. But the expectation that the investment would be made in the insurance should not have to be valued and made part of the substantiation documentation. This is a most unfortunate decision—one that is greatly lacking in common sense and applicability in real life.

SOME PROPOSALS FOR RELIEF

One of the purposes of this book is to summarize the vast amount of government regulation of the process of raising funds for charitable objectives. With most forms of government regulation, a balance is struck between the scope of the regulating and the ongoing health and welfare of the regulated. That is, usually the regulating is not so strenuous that it severely retards the growth and viability of the process that is being regulated.

When it comes to state regulation of philanthropic fundraising, however, the law has pushed to the point where matters are out of balance: The regulatory process is impeding the fundraising process. Lack of compliance with and of enforcement of these laws is one of the principal factors keeping government regulation from consuming, frustrating, and/or discouraging fundraising for charity. This is not a proper state of affairs, for the regulated or the regulators, and it should be remedied.

Model Law

But, what to do? One solution that has been touted over the years is a model charitable solicitation statute. The thought underlying this proposal is that charitable organizations could more easily comply with the laws in all of the states if these laws were generally the same. There is some truth to this, although many of the compliance burdens would not change and could even increase. As to the latter, a lobbying effort to enact a model law could result in the substitution of a more strenuous statute for a weaker one in some states, or the adoption of a rigorous statute in a state where previously there was none.

This proposal simply has too many flaws, which is probably why it is still only a proposal. To date, charitable organizations have not been able to agree on the contents of a model charitable solicitations act because the issue is too divisive (starting with the question of exemptions (see Chapter 3)). Furthermore, the state regulators cannot agree on a uniform statute in this area. Thus, there is little likelihood that both the regulated and the regulators will agree on a model law in this context.

Also, the lobbying effort involved would be prodigious and enormously costly. It would probably take millions of dollars to formulate a law and then see it through to enactment in every state. Who would coordinate that effort? Where would the funds come from? Would simplicity really result from uniformity, or would it lead to more regulation in more states? These and other questions and dilemmas make the enactment of a uniform charitable solicitation act in every state unrealistic.

Reciprocal Agreements

As discussed, several of these state laws contain reciprocal agreement provisions (*id*). These provisions are considerably underutilized.

Here is an opportunity to breathe some uniformity into these laws and reduce the regulatory burdens, while simultaneously inducing more compliance in this area of law. This approach does not require amendment of the statute, only application of it. Pursuant to these provisions, a state regulator can allow a charitable organization to file, as its registration and/or annual report, a copy of the documents as filed in the home state. Many of these provisions also enable regulators to grant exemptions from compliance where the exemptions are part of the law in the home state.

Therefore, it is not so much uniformity of law that is required as it is unification of the process of complying with the law. How much easier it would be on charities that want to comply, but are overwhelmed by the complexity, if they could prepare documents in their home states and file copies of them in other states. The process would also be advanced and enhanced if there were greater uniformity regarding exemptions.

Uniform Annual Report

Another proposal is a uniform annual report. This proposal is likewise grounded on the thought that it is not the laws that need changing so much as the process of complying with them. It truly would be simpler for all concerned if a charity required to file annually in several states could file the same document.

Once again, however, reality intrudes and spoils the potential. The fact is that the state regulators, until recently, have not been able to agree on the contents of an annual report. (An effort was undertaken to create a uniform annual report that reflected the requirements of every state; the resulting document was so large and unwieldy that the project collapsed, literally of its own weight.)

A task force of the National Association of State Charity Officials has developed a uniform registration form, and several states and the District of Columbia have agreed to accept it. The task force prepared an information chart stating the addresses of state regulators, the fees to be paid, whether a state supplemental form will be required, and who must sign the form. There are additional instructions for completion of the form for different states. It is not clear how the forms and state supplements will be distributed or how the information chart will be kept up to date.

This, then, is the most promising of the simplification approaches. Even here, however, the forces of division and complexity have quickly intervened, with some states not being able to avoid the temptation—or, in some instances, statutory mandate—to require additional information by means of supplemental forms.

Other Forms of Uniformity

Still other forms of uniformity are possible. The states could strive for uniform rules and regulations by introducing some commonalities into such subjects as definitions and cost allocations, but the regulators cannot agree.

Even uniformity of enforcement would help. Some states are known to be strict in their enforcement of these laws; others have a reputation for being lackadaisical. This state of affairs creates an atmosphere of cynicism and lawbreaking, where some charities register only in the "tough" states, waiting to register in the others when and if they "get caught."

Another possibility lies with the Internet. The process of registering in and reporting to many states could obviously be alleviated by means of this medium. Yet, to date, there has been no effort—by a for-profit or nonprofit organization—to implement such a program.

Preemption

The most radical proposal is federal preemption of state law. With this approach, a federal charitable solicitation act would supplant all of these state laws. Although Congress enacts preemptive statutes from time to time, there has never been much interest in doing so in the charitable fundraising context. State officials would ferociously fight any attempt to supersede their fundraising laws. This approach also gets caught up in arguments about what regulatory functions are best left at the state level and the appropriateness of expansion of the scope and reach of the federal government.

A modified approach of this nature would be to have a federal charitable solicitation act applicable to multistate charitable solicitations, leaving the states to regulate intrastate solicitations. (This is the manner in which the securities and antitrust laws are constructed.) But state officials may be expected to battle this methodology as well.

SUMMARY

This chapter opened with a perspective on charitable fundraising and the law. The distinctions between fundraisers and solicitors were the subject of comment, as was the scope of state law. The elements of the fundraiser's contract were discussed. The ways fundraising laws apply in connection with charitable auctions were summarized. A court opinion that sees fundraising regulation as a benefit to charities was the subject of comment, as were court opinions concerning fundraising fraud and the substantiation rules. The interaction between charitable fundraising and the private inurement doctrine was explored. The chapter closed with an inventory of some proposals for relief.

Index

Action organizations, 48,
   52
Advertising, 212
Airport terminal solicitations,
   248–249
American Institute of Certified
   Public Accountants, 17
American National Red Cross
   Governance Modernization Act
   of 2007, 38, 260, 261
Annual reporting requirements,
   federal:
   disclosure rules, 214–216
   due dates, 123
   exceptions, 122–123
   and fundraising, 129, 135–138,
      141–151
   and gaming, 132–135, 138–141
   in general, 122–124
   and noncash contributions, 131,
      141–148
   penalties, 123–124
Application for recognition of
   exemption, 216–217
Appraisal rules, 217–222
Appraisal summary, 219–220
Art, fractional interests in,
   229–230

Articles of organization, 306
Associations of churches, as public
   charities, 97
Attorneys general, powers of,
   82
Auctions, charity. See Charity
   auctions.
Audits, IRS:
   appeals process, 315–316
   of churches, 318–319
   closing agreements, 314–315
   coping with, 311–313
   fast-track settlement program,
      316–317
   issues, 293–294
   and litigation, 319–320
   preparation for, 306–308
   process of, 308, 314
   reasons for, 293
   tours, 313–314
   types of, 294–296

Boards of directors:
   duties of, 260
   effectiveness of, 271–272
   fundraising responsibilities of,
      260–261
Bylaws, 306

Charitable, definition of, 38–39,
    67–68
Charitable contribution deduction:
  basic concepts, 154–155
  and contribution base, 161
  deduction reduction rules, 163
  partial interest gifts, 169
  percentage limitations on,
      160–163
  qualified appreciated stock,
      163–165
  twice basis deductions, 165–166
Charitable donees, qualified, 156
Charitable fundraising, defined, 2–4
Charitable gift:
  definition of, 4–5, 155–156
  substantiation rules, 210–211,
      347–351
Charitable gift annuities, 176–177
Charitable lead trusts, 175–176
Charitable pledges, 29–30
Charitable purposes, 38–39
Charitable remainder trusts,
    172–174
Charitable sales, concept of, 4
Charitable sales promotion,
    definition of, 72–73
Charitable solicitation acts:
  attorneys general, powers of, 82
  charitable, definition of, 67–68
  charitable organizations,
      regulation of, 69–70
  commercial co-ventures,
      regulation of, 72–73
  contracts, requirements of, 74–75
  definitions, other, 69
  exemptions from, 76–82
  fiduciary relationships, 75
  membership, definition of, 69
  paid solicitors, regulation of,
      71–72
  professional fundraisers,
      regulation of, 70–71
  prohibited acts, 74
  and reciprocal agreements, 75

  records, availability of, 75
  registration fees, 250–251
  sanctions, 83
  scope of, 66
  solicitation, definition of, 68–69
  solicitation notice requirements,
      73–74
Charity auctions:
  as businesses, 333–334
  and contribution deduction for
      items donated, 334–335
  and contribution deduction for
      items acquired, 335–337
  and quid pro quo contribution
      rules, 338
  sales tax rules, 338–339
  and substantiation rules, 337–338
Charleston Principles, 86–89
Churches:
  audits of, 318–319
  and charitable solicitation acts, 77
  as public charities, 96–97
Closing agreements, IRS, 314–315
Clothing, gifts of, 168, 221–222
Commensurate test, 19–20
Commercial co-venture, definition
    of, 72–73
Commerciality doctrine, 201–202
Community foundations, 106,
    203–206
Compensation:
  fundraising, 20–24
  in general, 127–128, 130, 303–305
Compliance checks, IRS:
  charitable giving scam, 299
  colleges and universities, 299–306
  community foundations, 299
  compensation, 296–297
  excess benefit reporting, 298
  fundraising costs reporting, 298
  hospitals, 297–298
  political campaign activities,
      297
  tax-exempt bonds recordkeeping,
      298

Conditional gifts, 157–159
Conduit foundations, 94
Consideration, 4, 155, 210–211
Contracts, fundraising:
  basic elements, 328–329
  fee arrangements, 330
  solicitor status, 330–331
  specific elements, 329–330
  state laws, 331–332
Contribution base, 161
Contribution holding period,
  147
Contributions. See Gifts.
Conventions of churches, as public
  charity, 97
Corporate sponsorships, 199–201

Dickens, Charles, 285
Disclosure on demand, 9–10
Disclosure rules, 214–216, 275–278
Disqualified persons, fundraisers as,
  21
Dissolution clause, 35
Donative intent, 155
Donor recognition programs,
  199–201
Door-to-door advocacy, 249–250
Due process rights, 253–254

Educational institutions:
  and charitable solicitation acts,
    77–78
  as public charities, 97–98
Endowment funds, 128, 301–303
Equal protection rights, 254
Events, fundraising, 137–138
Exempt operating foundations, 94
Exemptions from solicitation acts:
  churches, 77
  educational institutions, 77–78
  health care institutions, 78–79
  libraries, 78
  membership organizations, 79
  museums, 78
  named organizations, 80–81

other categories of organizations,
  81–82
political organizations, 80
religious organizations, 77
small solicitations, 79–80
specified individuals, 80
Expenditures, categories of, 273–275

Facts-and-circumstances test,
  104–105
Fast track settlement program, IRS,
  316–317
Fiduciary responsibility, principles
  of, 36–38
Flow-through entities, 162, 222
For the use of gifts, 156–157
Form 990, redesigned (2008):
  import of, 124
  parts of, 124–128, 150–151
  Schedule B, 128, 148–150, 214
  Schedule G, 129, 135–141
  Schedule M, 131, 141–148
  schedules, other, 128–131
Forms:
  990, 55–56, Chapter 5, 214,
    276–277, 279
  990-EZ, 122, 148, 214
  990-PF, 122, 148
  990-N, 122
  990-T, 122, 125, 127, 214, 277, 301
  1023, 39, 216–217, 277
  1040, 134
  1096, 127
  1098-C, 114, 127, 229
  1120, 134
  4506-A, 214
  5701, 316
  8282, 127, 150
  8283, 131, 147, 150, 219, 222,
    223–225
  8886-T, 127
  8899, 144, 225
  13909, 293
  14017, 316
  14018, 299

Forms:(*Continued*)
  W-2, 222
  W-2G, 127, 134
  W-3, 127
Fractional interests in art, gifts of,
    229–230
Fraud, fundraising, 252–253,
    345–347
Free speech principles:
  absolute percentage limitation,
    239–241
  airport terminal solicitations,
    248–249
  door-to-door advocacy, 249–250
  fundraisers' fees, 244–246
  in general, 236–237, 238–239,
    246–248
  outer boundaries, 251–252
  rebuttable percentage limitation,
    241–243
  solicitors' fees, 244–246
Fundraising, charitable, defined, 2–4
Fundraising expenses:
  allocations, 17–18
  average gift size factor, 14–15
  cost percentages, 10–11
  disclosure dilemma, 9–10
  floating average approach, 12–13
  line item approach, 11–12
  percentage limitations on,
    239–243
  pluralization approach, 13–14
  reasonableness of, 15–17
Fundraising methods:
  annual giving programs, 6–7
  events, 137–138
  gaming, 132–135, 138–141
  in general, 5
  planned gift programs, 8
  special-purpose programs, 7–8
  Web site solicitations, 84–89
Fundraising practices, 279–281
Fundraising regulation:
  benefits of, 339–341
  local, 326–327

  federal, Chapters 5–8
  scope of, 66, 322–324
  state, Chapters 3, 9

Gaming:
  regulation of, 132–135
  reporting of, 138–141
Gift acceptance policies, 58,
    147
Gifts:
  of airplanes, 144, 166, 226–229
  of archaeological artifacts,146–147
  of art, 143
  of automobiles, 144, 166,
    226–229
  of boats, 144, 166, 226–229
  of books, 143–144
  of cash, 222–223
  of clothing,144, 168, 221–222
  of collectibles, 145
  conditional, 157–159
  of drugs, 146
  of food inventory, 146
  for the use of charity, 156–157
  of fractional interests in art,
    229–230
  of historical artifacts, 146
  of household items, 144, 168,
    221–222
  of insurance, 170
  of intellectual property, 144,
    166–168, 225
  medical supplies, 146
  noncash, 223–224
  noncharitable, 231–233
  of partial interests, 169
  of property in general, 159–160
  of publications, 143–144
  of qualified conservation
    contributions, 145
  of real estate, 145
  of scientific specimens, 146
  of securities, 144–145
  of taxidermy, 146, 168–169
  of vehicles, 144, 166

Gift substantiation rules:
    and charity auctions, 337–338
    in general, 210–211, 347–351
Governance:
    and categories of expenditures,
        273–275
    disclosures to public, 275–276
    and fundraising practices, 279–281
    and IRS, 281–287
    law compliance, 272–273
    mission statements, 278–279
    perspectives on, 288–290
    philosophy of, 260
    policies, 55–64
Governmental units, as public
    charities, 99–100

Harassment campaigns, 216
Hospitals:
    and charitable solicitation acts,
        78–79
    as public charities, 98

Insiders, 40–41
Institutions:
    associations of churches, 97
    churches, 96–97
    conventions of churches, 97
    educational institutions, 97–98
    governmental units, 99–100
    hospitals, 98
    medical research organizations,
        98–99
    other entities, 100
    public college support
        foundations, 99
Insurance:
    gifts of, 170
    gifts using, 170
Intellectual property, gifts of,
    166–168, 225
Intermediate sanctions, 21, 22–24,
    46–47, 229
Internal Revenue Service:
    audits, Chapter 11

compliance checks, 296–306
    fast-track settlement program,
        316–317
    fiscal year 2009 work plan,
        284–285
    fundraising, definition of, 3–4
    and gaming, 132–135, 138–141
    good-governance principles, draft
        of, 57, 60, 61, 261, 277, 278
    and governance, 281–287
    organization of, 292–293
Internet, fundraising by means of,
    84–89

Joint ventures, 43–44

Law compliance, 272–273
Legislative activities rules, 2–3, 47–51
Legislative authority, delegation of,
    255–256
Litigation, 319–320
Loans, 43

Medical research organizations, as
    public charities, 98–99
Membership, definition of, 69
Miller, Steven T., 281–284, 286
Mission statements, 58, 278–279

National Association of Attorneys
    General, 83
National Association of State Charity
    Officials, 83, 86
Noncash contributions, 131,
    141–148
Noncharitable organizations,
    fundraising by, 231–233
Nonexempt charitable trusts, 94–95

Operational test:
    in general, 35–36
    for supporting organizations,
        112–113
Organization effectiveness, 270–271
Organization, form of, 34–35

Organizational tests:
    in general, 35
    for supporting organizations, 112

Panel on the Nonprofit Sector, 57,
    60–64, 261, 271, 272–273,
    274–275, 277, 278–281
Partial interest gifts, 169
Personal benefit contracts, 54–55
Planned giving:
    charitable gift annuity, 176–177
    charitable lead trust, 175–176
    charitable remainder trust,
        172–174
    income interests, 171
    introduction to, 170–172
    pooled income fund, 174–175
    remainder interests, 171
    split-interest trust, 171
Point of solicitation disclosure, 9–10
Police power, states', 237–238
Policies, governance:
    and annual information return,
        55–56
    annual information return review,
        62
    code of ethics, 63
    conflict-of-interest, 59–60
    conservation easements, 58
    document retention and
        destruction, 61
    executive compensation, 61–62
    fundraising, 56–57
    gift acceptance, 58, 147
    international grantmaking, 62
    investment, 62–63
    meetings documentation, 62
    mission statement, 58
    others, 63–64
    whistleblower, 60–61
Political campaign activities rules,
    52–54
Pooled income funds, 174–175
Primary purpose rule, 36
Private benefit, doctrine of:

and governance, 286–287
    in general, 20–21, 44–46, 229
Private foundation:
    definition of, 92–93
    rules governing, 95
Private inurement, doctrine of:
    and fundraising, 20, 229, 341–344
    in general, 39–44
Private operating foundation, 93–94
Professional fundraiser, definition
    of, 70–71, 325–326
Professional solicitor, definition of,
    71–72, 325–326
Program service accomplishments,
    127
Prohibited tax shelter transactions,
    54
Property:
    airplanes, 166, 226–229
    appreciated, 159
    automobiles, 166, 226–229
    boats, 166, 226–229
    definition of,
    gifts of,
    intellectual property,
        166–168, 225
    valuation of, 160
Public charities:
    concept of, 95–96, 217
    institutions, 96–100
    public safety testing organizations,
        117
    public-private dichotomy, import
        of, 117–118
    publicly supported charities,
        comparative analysis, 110–111
    publicly supported charities,
        donative, 100–106
    publicly supported charities,
        service provider, 107–110
    statistics, 118
    supporting organizations, 111–117
Public college support foundations,
    as public charities, 99
Public policy considerations, 30–32

Publicly supported charities:
  comparative analyses of, 110–111
  donative type, 100–106
  service provider type, 107–110

Qualified appraisal, 218–219
Qualified appraiser, 220–221
Qualified appreciated stock, 163–165
Qualified sponsorship payments,
  199–201
Quid pro quo contribution rules:
  and charity auctions, 338
  in general, 212–214

Reasonableness, standard of, 41
Recognition of tax exemption, 39
Recordkeeping rules:
  cash contributions, 222–223
  noncash contributions, 223–224
Registration fees:
  in general, 250–251
  sliding-scale, 250–251, 339–341
Relief, proposals for, 351–353
Religious organizations, 77, 256–257
Rental arrangements, 43

Sarbanes-Oxley Act of 2002, 260
Services provided:
  as related business, 202–205
  to related organizations, 206–208
  as unrelated business, 205
Shulman, Douglas, 284
Solicitation, definition of, 68–69
Split-interest trust, 169, 170–176
Statement of Position 98-2, 17–18
Step transaction doctrine, 24–29
Substantial compliance, doctrine of,
  218
Supporting organizations:
  control, limitations on, 116–117
  noncharitable organizations and,
    115
  operational test, 112–113
  organizational test, 112
  required relationships, 114–115

specification requirement,
  113–114
supported organizations,
  substitution of, 115–116

Tax exemption:
  recognition of, 39
  retroactive revocation of, 317–318
Tax liability, officers' and
  employees', 287–288
Taxidermy, gifts of, 168–169

Unified registration, 83
Unrelated business rules:
  business, definition of, 181–183
  convenience businesses, 186
  donated items exception, 186, 197
  donor-recognition programs,
    199–201
  entertainment activities, 186–187
  excepted activities, 185–187
  excepted income, 187–188
  exceptions to exceptions, 188–189
  exceptions to exceptions to
    exceptions, 189
  fragmentation rule, 182
  and fundraising, 189–201
  low-cost articles, distribution of,
    187
  mailing lists, exchange of, 187
  merchandise, sale of, 186, 196
  principal–agent relationships,
    196–197
  and private benefit, 193–194
  and program activities, 194–196
  regularly carried on rule, 183–184,
    191–192
  related businesses, 184–185
  research exception, 188
  royalty exception, 188, 197
  services, provision of, 202–208
  specific deduction, 188
  statutory framework, 180–181
  tax-exempt organizations
    involved, 181

Unrelated business (*Continued*)
  trade show activities, 187
  travel and tour activities, 197–198
  unrelated business taxable
    income, 185
  unrelated businesses, 184–185,
    189–191
  volunteers exception, 185–186,
    197
Unusual grants, 103–104
U. S. Constitution:
  due process rights, 253–254
  equal protection rights, 254
  free speech rights, 236–253
  legislative authority, delegation of,
    255–256
  and religious organizations,
    256–257

Vehicles, gifts of, 166, 226–229

Watchdog agencies and fundraising,
    261–263
Watchdog agencies, standards of:

American Institute of
    Philanthropy, 18, 270, 274
BBB Wise Giving Alliance, 59,
    261, 265–266, 270–271, 276,
    279
Committee for Purchase From
    People Who Are Blind or
    Severely Disabled, 272,
    276
Department of the Treasury
    best practices, 272, 276–277,
    278
Evangelical Council for Financial
    Accountability, 56, 59, 61, 62,
    63, 261, 266–267, 271, 274, 276,
    278, 279
Philanthropic Advisory Service,
    260, 263–265, 273–274,
    275–276, 279
Standards for Excellence Institute,
    56–57, 58, 59–60, 261, 267–269,
    271–272, 276, 278, 279
Widely available exception,
    215–216